Values-Based Leadership

by Maria Gamb

Values-Based Leadership For Dummies®

Published by: **John Wiley & Sons, Inc.**, 111 River Street, Hoboken, NJ 07030-5774, www.wiley.com

Copyright © 2018 by John Wiley & Sons, Inc., Hoboken, New Jersey

Published simultaneously in Canada

No part of this publication may be reproduced, stored in a retrieval system or transmitted in any form or by any means, electronic, mechanical, photocopying, recording, scanning or otherwise, except as permitted under Sections 107 or 108 of the 1976 United States Copyright Act, without the prior written permission of the Publisher. Requests to the Publisher for permission should be addressed to the Permissions Department, John Wiley & Sons, Inc., 111 River Street, Hoboken, NJ 07030, (201) 748-6011, fax (201) 748-6008, or online at http://www.wiley.com/go/permissions.

Trademarks: Wiley, For Dummies, the Dummies Man logo, Dummies.com, Making Everything Easier, and related trade dress are trademarks or registered trademarks of John Wiley & Sons, Inc., and may not be used without written permission. All other trademarks are the property of their respective owners. John Wiley & Sons, Inc., is not associated with any product or vendor mentioned in this book.

> LIMIT OF LIABILITY/DISCLAIMER OF WARRANTY: WHILE THE PUBLISHER AND AUTHOR HAVE USED THEIR BEST EFFORTS IN PREPARING THIS BOOK, THEY MAKE NO REPRESENTATIONS OR WARRANTIES WITH RESPECT TO THE ACCURACY OR COMPLETENESS OF THE CONTENTS OF THIS BOOK AND SPECIFICALLY DISCLAIM ANY IMPLIED WARRANTIES OF MERCHANTABILITY OR FITNESS FOR A PARTICULAR PURPOSE. NO WARRANTY MAY BE CREATED OR EXTENDED BY SALES REPRESENTATIVES OR WRITTEN SALES MATERIALS. THE ADVISE AND STRATEGIES CONTAINED HEREIN MAY NOT BE SUITABLE FOR YOUR SITUATION. YOU SHOULD CONSULT WITH A PROFESSIONAL WHERE APPROPRIATE. NEITHER THE PUBLISHER NOR THE AUTHOR SHALL BE LIABLE FOR DAMAGES ARISING HEREFROM.

For general information on our other products and services, please contact our Customer Care Department within the U.S. at 877-762-2974, outside the U.S. at 317-572-3993, or fax 317-572-4002. For technical support, please visit https://hub.wiley.com/community/support/dummies.

Wiley publishes in a variety of print and electronic formats and by print-on-demand. Some material included with standard print versions of this book may not be included in e-books or in print-on-demand. If this book refers to media such as a CD or DVD that is not included in the version you purchased, you may download this material at http://booksupport.wiley.com. For more information about Wiley products, visit www.wiley.com.

Library of Congress Control Number: 2018937411

ISBN 978-1-119-45344-4 (pbk); ISBN 978-1-119-45431-1 (ebk); ISBN 978-1-119-45432-8 (ebk)

Manufactured in the United States of America

10 9 8 7 6 5 4 3 2 1

Contents at a Glance

Introduction 1

Part 1: Getting Started with Values-Based Leadership 7
CHAPTER 1: Welcome to the World of Values-Based Leadership. 9
CHAPTER 2: Understanding the Evolving Workforce You Serve 21
CHAPTER 3: Shifting Your Consciousness beyond the Self 35
CHAPTER 4: Reframing Your Perception of Business 49

Part 2: Becoming a Values-Based Leader 59
CHAPTER 5: Before You Get There: Knowing Where You Are as a Leader 61
CHAPTER 6: Nurturing the Four Attributes of a Values-Based Leader 77
CHAPTER 7: Activating the Grounding Principles 99
CHAPTER 8: Defining Defiant Workplaces 119

Part 3: Charting the Course and Crafting Your Values 141
CHAPTER 9: Lighting the Pathway to Establishing Trust 143
CHAPTER 10: Facing the Truth about Who You Are 159
CHAPTER 11: Identifying Values and Creating a Values Statement 173
CHAPTER 12: Going It Alone When Your CEO Isn't Interested in Values-Based Leadership 191
CHAPTER 13: Cementing a Career Starlight for the Long Haul 211

Part 4: Supercharging Your Team and the Workplace with Values 225
CHAPTER 14: Hiring and Retaining Great Talent 227
CHAPTER 15: Maintaining Engagement and Job Satisfaction 249
CHAPTER 16: Motivating the Masses 265
CHAPTER 17: Slicing the Pie: Creating a Culture of Leadership. 283
CHAPTER 18: Fostering an Environment of Innovation 295
CHAPTER 19: Being Willing to Let People Go 307

Part 5: The Part of Tens 315
CHAPTER 20: Ten Practices to Stay on Track as a Values-Based Leader 317
CHAPTER 21: Ten Tips for Staying Connected with Your Team 325
CHAPTER 22: Ten Facts about the Millennial Market, Its Values, and Its Influence 333
CHAPTER 23: Ten Workplace Myths 339

Index 347

Table of Contents

INTRODUCTION 1
    About This Book 1
    Foolish Assumptions 3
    Icons Used in This Book 4
    Beyond the Book 4
    Where to Go from Here 5

PART 1: GETTING STARTED WITH VALUES-BASED LEADERSHIP 7

CHAPTER 1: Welcome to the World of Values-Based Leadership 9
    Walking through the Evolution of Company Culture 10
    Understanding the Escalator Effect of Values-Based Leadership 11
    Avoiding a Flatline to Extinction: When You Know Change Is Needed 13
    Building Winning Organizations: Culture Eats Strategy for Lunch 16
        Shaping the company culture with values 17
        Influencing the company culture with your character 18

CHAPTER 2: Understanding the Evolving Workforce You Serve 21
    Pinpointing the Quad Workforce 22
        Picking out postwar, workaholic Boomers 24
        Understanding latchkey, self-reliant GenXers 25
        Meeting digitally savvy, tenacious Millennials 26
        Considering the bumper generations 27
    Leading the Quad with Insight and Understanding 29
        Converting diversity into inclusion 29
        Pivoting work ethic into work ethos 30
        Recalibrating the concept of work-life balance 31
        Creating meaning and a reason to go to work 32
        Wondering whether the Quad cares about your leadership 33

CHAPTER 3: Shifting Your Consciousness beyond the Self 35
    Looking at the Four Be's of Values-Based Leadership 36
        Defining the four Be's 37
        Deploying the four Be's with clarity 37
        Seeing kindness in the four Be's 38

Fitting Values-Based Leadership into the Big Picture..............42
    Thinking of your company as a living thing....................42
    Snapping the puzzle pieces together........................43
Assessing Your Command and Control Temperament.............45
Following the Path Cut by Other Leadership Influencers..........47

CHAPTER 4: Reframing Your Perception of Business...............49

Unraveling the Bad Reputation of Business......................50
    De-villainizing mega-corporations..........................51
    Peeking into a government-affiliated business................52
    Creating opportunity as a business practice..................54
Changing Lives in the Shared Values Economy....................55
    Evolving corporate social responsibility initiatives..............55
    Reinventing new profit centers to meet human needs..........56

PART 2: BECOMING A VALUES-BASED LEADER..............59

CHAPTER 5: Before You Get There: Knowing Where You Are as a Leader..61

Planning Your Adventure into Different Levels of Leadership.......62
    Introducing the leadership trajectory.........................63
    Exploring the four levels of leadership.......................64
    Overstating the importance of charisma in a leader............69
Determining Where You Are on the Journey......................71
    Assessing your current level of leadership....................72
    Rating your willingness to change............................74

CHAPTER 6: Nurturing the Four Attributes of a Values-Based Leader..77

Seeing a Snapshot of the Four Attributes........................78
Embracing Self-Reflection.....................................79
    Honesty: Uncovering the cornerstone attribute................80
    Authenticity: Saying and doing what you mean................82
    Integrity: Doing what's right when it's not convenient, comfortable, or popular.....................................84
Showing Actionable Grace.....................................88
    Humility: Embracing quiet confidence.......................88
    Social distance: Bridging the power gap.....................89
Expanding Agility..91
    Defining the five components of agility.......................91
    Getting real: Unpacking your strengths and weaknesses........92
    Failure: Ensuring success...................................93
Influencing Responsibly.......................................95
    Emulating values: Being a powerful example..................96
    Creating good: Taking the medical pledge to do no harm.......96

CHAPTER 7: Activating the Grounding Principles 99
  Introducing the Ten Values-Based Leadership Principles 100
    Using cause and effect to shift the organization 102
    Changing the value equation 103
    Seeing that evolving, thriving attitudes are a result of the principles 104
    Summarizing the mindset of a thriving team 106
    Knowing that course correction is a values stand 107
    Recognizing that resistance is part of life and evolution 108
  Making It Easy for Your Team to Buy into the Leader (Yes, You) ... 109
    Providing predictable consistency 110
    Providing effective communication 112
  Assembling Your Framework for Deploying the Principles 115
    Meeting your employees where they are 115
    Adding it up: Creating momentum 116
    One size doesn't fit all: Creating your own principle plan ... 117

CHAPTER 8: Defining Defiant Workplaces 119
  Facing the Effects of the FARCE Syndrome 120
    Deploying fear to get what they want 122
    Developing attachment to the outcome 123
    Using resistance or retaliation to control 126
    Engaging in unhealthy competition 127
    Displaying entitlement 129
    Putting the FARCE together: The resulting halted environment 130
  Evolving the Mindsets of People and Organizations 131
    Traversing the seasons of change 132
    Handling cycle disruptions 137
  Becoming Part of the Solution — Or Exiting Stage Right 138
    Giving staff a choice 138
    Taking extreme ownership of the situation 139
    Uncovering if it's you or them 140

PART 3: CHARTING THE COURSE AND CRAFTING YOUR VALUES 141

CHAPTER 9: Lighting the Pathway to Establishing Trust 143
  Surveying Ideas for Building Trust in Business 144
  Defining Trust and Needs in the Workplace 145
    Using Maslow's hierarchy of needs to determine baseline trust 147
    Shifting from Halt to happiness 148
  Getting Others to Trust in Your Leadership 149
    Engendering loyalty 150
    Reducing social distance gaps 150

Setting Standards for Others by Example........................151
    Operating with self-awareness............................151
    Avoiding exceptions yet remaining flexible..................152
    Sidestepping rumor mills and gossip hounds................153
    Encouraging others as a sign of trust......................154
    Mastering the thank-you................................154
Harnessing People Power......................................155
    Following five engaging principles for the team.............155
    Unifying behind a common belief.........................156
    Circumventing passive-aggressive personalities............156

CHAPTER 10: Facing the Truth about Who You Are 159

Understanding How Others View Your Company 159
    Differentiating identity, culture, and reputation..............160
    Assessing your company's reputation in different categories...161
    Surveying groups to see whether a correction is necessary.....163
    Recognizing that your online reputation is a big influencer.....164
    Personalizing your reputation plan with FiRMS..............165
Making Everyone a Trustee of the Company 168
    Sharing is caring, and caring is an investment
    and commitment to excellence..........................168
    Establish online guidelines..............................169
    Embezzling isn't the only unaligned action 171

CHAPTER 11: Identifying Values and Creating a Values Statement..173

Using the Self-Reflective Method for a Public Values Statement....174
    Deciding whether to involve anyone else 175
    Understanding and selecting values.......................176
    Formulating and assembling your statement................181
Rolling Out Your Values Statement to Your Company.............182
    Animating your core values.............................183
    Infusing personality into your statement...................183
    Creating clarity and direction across the board 185
    For solopreneurs: Self-leadership and identifying clients.......189

CHAPTER 12: Going It Alone When Your CEO Isn't Interested in Values-Based Leadership 191

Accepting That the Top Brass Isn't Interested in Values-Based
Leadership 192
Guiding Your Crew When You're Just an Officer, Not the Captain...193
    Giving yourself permission to take the reins.................194
    Curtailing the mutiny and getting everyone back on track......194
    Diagnosing the team's hurdles 195

    Courageously making your own values stand................197
    Minding the gap: The space between you and the team........198
    For entrepreneurs: Considering an alternate point of entry....199
  Creating Your Leadership Starlight for the Team.................200
    Unpacking your toolkit: Using what you have to
    move forward..201
    Assembling your starlight...................................203
  Bolstering Your Commitment to Values-Based Leadership
  with Other Features...206
    Scaling down the four features of values-based leadership.....207
    Leveling with your team...................................208
    Holding your team accountable even if others don't..........209
    Leading when you're gone..................................210

CHAPTER 13: Cementing a Career Starlight for the Long Haul 211

  Building Your Career Starlight from the Ground Up..............212
    Digging into your strengths and weaknesses
    (with a little help)...212
    Breaking down the parts of your career starlight formula......213
    Defining your leadership engagement qualities...............215
    Putting your career starlight into a cohesive form............216
  Translating Your Career Starlight into a Good Fit
  with a Company...217
    Evaluating job offers with your career starlight...............218
    Discerning your leader-to-leader fit.........................219
    Pulling back the mask of a narcissist........................220
  Seeing the Effects of Being Known as a Values-Based Leader......220
    Adding financial value to a company because of your
    reputation..222
    Reinforcing what you stand for to add marketability..........222

PART 4: SUPERCHARGING YOUR TEAM AND THE WORKPLACE WITH VALUES 225

CHAPTER 14: Hiring and Retaining Great Talent 227

  Recognizing Why People Leave One Company to
  Join Another (Like Yours)....................................228
  Distinguishing Yourself from the Competition..................229
    Selling who you are to potential employees.................230
    Uncorking your reputational capital........................232
  Benefiting Everyone with Nontraditional Perks..................234
    Instituting time to volunteer...............................235
    Offering voluntary solutions...............................236
    Providing financial education..............................236
    Demanding balance and flexibility.........................237

Craving the Opportunity to Learn............................238
    Establishing cross-generational coaching...................239
    Rotating jobs and experiences............................240
    Offering skills retraining.................................241
Working toward Compatibility Triumphs.......................241
    Managing personalities versus maintaining company culture...242
    Ensuring a good job fit based on talents....................243
    Showing respect and value to candidates...................245
    Answering the question of why someone should work for your company................................246

CHAPTER 15: Maintaining Engagement and Job Satisfaction....249

Grasping the Importance of Engagement and Job Satisfaction.....249
Staying Active and Happy: Engagement.......................250
    Understanding that revolving doors cost a pretty penny.......251
    Creating an environment of engagement from day one........252
    Avoiding the disengagement of current staff.................253
Keeping the Wisdom Pool Full: Job Satisfaction..................255
    Rethinking the annual performance review..................255
    Assessing job satisfaction with a customizable survey.........257
    Compatibility: Piecing together employees, skills, and managers..259
    Voting on job satisfaction five ways.........................260
    Correlating job satisfaction with morale, learning, and growth...263

CHAPTER 16: Motivating the Masses....265

Peeking into the Human Motivation Theory.....................266
    Looking, listening, and categorizing........................267
    Understanding that fear motivates more than anything else...271
    Deciphering the money motivation myth....................272
Helping People Find Their Meaning and Purpose Again..........274
    Chunking it down: Bite-sizing purpose and meaning..........274
    Helping a team find its footing............................276
Practicing and Reinforcing Motivation.........................277
    Creating an environment where people can fail but learn from it..278
    Playing with pickup sticks: You can always find a solution......278
    Pulling it all together...................................279

CHAPTER 17: Slicing the Pie: Creating a Culture of Leadership....283

Recognizing That Leadership Is a Job for All Staff Members........283
    Setting high expectations................................284
    Overcoming elitism with input and inclusion.................284
    Developing a culture of leadership for sustained impact.......285
    Following leadership demographic trends...................286

Identifying the Leaders in the Field Who Can Help Your Organization..287
    Breaking down three tiers of leaders........................288
    Tapping into a winning formula 291
    Empowering potential leaders to assess their own values......291

CHAPTER 18: Fostering an Environment of Innovation............295
Beginning with a Few Basics on Innovation........................296
    Revealing unconscious and conscious intellects 297
    Comparing traditional and innovative business mindsets......298
    Deploying "shades of gray" thinking........................299
    Exercising your unconscious intellect......................301
    Dovetailing the basics into an HR strategy 302
Igniting Innovation with a Few Principles and Pointers............302
    Setting ground rules with five agreements to foster innovation...303
    Reducing control, increasing trust 304
    Keeping it fresh by rotating contributors...................305
    Challenging your team members to look beyond themselves...305
    Recognizing that people won't necessarily embrace change or growth 306

CHAPTER 19: Being Willing to Let People Go 307
Asking Questions and Showing Acceptance When People Leave ...308
    Playing the "what if" game of possibilities..................308
    Conducting a more detailed kind of exit auditing 309
    Practicing forgiveness and acceptance 310
Staying True to Your Values......................................311
    Rebalancing your efforts 311
    Locating your fellow travelers 312

PART 5: THE PART OF TENS..315

CHAPTER 20: Ten Practices to Stay on Track as a Values-Based Leader...317
Setting a Daily Audit Practice....................................318
Embracing Meditation 318
Finding Your Own Spiritual Practice..............................319
Disengaging Your Ego..320
Forgiving Your Shortfalls 320
Eliminating the Things That Cause Brain Fog 321
Raising Endorphins to Gain Clarity and Reduce Stress 322
Using Technology to Prompt Excellence 322
Establishing a Trusted Feedback Group...........................322
Engaging a Mentor 323

CHAPTER 21: Ten Tips for Staying Connected with Your Team ...325
- Making Time to Get to Know Everyone ...326
- Acknowledging Life Accomplishments ...326
- Keeping an Open Dialogue ...327
- Communicating Expectations with Clarity ...327
- Saying "Thank You" Often ...328
- Maintaining Promises, Inside and Out ...328
- Keeping Your Door Open ...329
- Surveying the Vendor and Resource Base Often ...329
- Showing Transparency ...330
- Modeling Best Practices ...331

CHAPTER 22: Ten Facts about the Millennial Market, Its Values, and Its Influence ...333
- Millennials Are Powering Different Aspects of the Economy ...334
- Emerging Leaders Have Heart ...334
- Coaching Takes Center Stage ...335
- Work Cultures Are Collaborative and Connected ...335
- Flexibility Takes on Heightened Importance ...336
- Making a Difference Matters ...336
- Old-School Values Make a Comeback ...336
- Buyers Vote at the Checkout Counter ...337
- Millennials Resist Mass Media Traps ...337
- A Career Should Have Multiple Experiences ...338

CHAPTER 23: Ten Workplace Myths ...339
- Women Primarily Leave Their Jobs to Have Families ...339
- Men Aren't as Interested in Work-Life Balance ...340
- Flexibility Means Shorter Hours ...341
- Everyone Knows How to Advance Their Careers ...341
- Decision-Makers Know the Key Talent ...342
- Conflict-Resolution Training Is Passé ...342
- Technology Takes Care of Communication ...343
- You Have to Build a Fortress to Stake Your Claim ...343
- Managers Don't Need to Coach Their Teams ...344
- Understanding Motives Isn't Necessary ...345

INDEX ...347

Introduction

Welcome to *Values-Based Leadership For Dummies!* There's always something in life that sets us on a trajectory toward a goal. We seek, consciously or unconsciously, to fulfill that goal our entire lives. For me, it's always been to be a really good leader who does the right thing by my people. I always knew that if you treated people well, they would go to the ends of the earth for you. Treat them badly, and you've got a whole other problem on your hands. I could chalk it up to being one of four children in a boisterous house where my mother taught me to always look out for my brothers and sister — and everyone else. Maybe you're the same. It's just programmed in there. No matter what, it's unshakable. You too?

So, here we are together, about to embark on this journey called values-based leadership (VBL). I've ventured to share whatever I've learned over these many years in business, personally and through my mentors and clients. It's not perfect — after all, I'm not perfect. Even the title "expert" makes me cringe. This book is just one woman's take on the topic of leadership. It may not suit everyone. But it's completely customizable, so you can take what you like and leave the rest behind.

On this journey, there will be good days. There will be bad days. And then there will be those days when you think you just simply can't bear it anymore. But I assure you, you will bear it. You won't abandon your team. I know that because you're here with me. Sure, you may move on, but leaving for other opportunities isn't abandonment. *Abandonment* means not caring about them and saying, "See ya later." You won't do that. I know that with every fiber of my being, because it's not just your average human being who will pick up a book titled *Values-Based Leadership For Dummies*. You're seeking to make the business workplace whole again with an eye on the bottom line. And man, am I happy you're here! The world needs you. The people you lead, or will lead, need you.

About This Book

First and foremost, I want to assure you that this book is for current and would-be leaders, managers, entrepreneurs, solopreneurs, and every other person who exchanges in the art of commerce. I've done my best to include a few key entry points for those who aren't in "traditional" business setups. And just about everything in this book can be used for more than one purpose. Don't shy away from a chapter just because it doesn't seem to pertain to you at first glance. You may be very surprised by what you learn about yourself. Self-reflection plays a central role throughout this process. Without it, you'll be flying blind. Seeing ourselves, our true motives, and how the decisions we make affect many lives requires such introspection.

Values-Based Leadership For Dummies isn't meant to be read as a step-by-step manual. However, you'll need to embrace some foundational principles and attitudes in order to make use of many of the other tools. If you're reading something that isn't quite making sense to you, I suggest you go to Parts 1 and 2 to find the core principle and meaning of why certain tools are important in the process.

Be warned: I'm going to offer you a different way of viewing leadership and business as a whole. Understanding that commerce is a vehicle for something good, even noble, will forever change how you lead other people. It will also change how you look at your role in this grand play. Your role is to create businesses and teams that serve one another and the community around you, and corporate social responsibility (CSR) is the way to achieve this. This all may sound grandiose, but I assure you that it's no longer an option — it's the way things are now, and it's become the normal expectation of employees. Preparing for that will assure survival of your leadership.

The principles of VBL establish a platform to create a great company culture where people are focused on living the values set forth by the leader and the organization. This creates a ripple effect into every nook and cranny of the organization: your business model, investing in your team, building strong partnerships, cultivating future leaders, improving communication, and making sure people are the right fit for the organization. Collaboration is the environment where people win. And this is all built on the foundation you set using trust as the key ingredient.

I'm a pretty straightforward person. I'm not very good at hinting around without telling you what's really going on. In this book you find real steps and concrete activities to help you move through situations. You find real stories of real experiences. Don't you just hate when people skirt around the issue and never get to the meat? Me too! Or they tell you they did something amazing but won't share how they made it happen. Ugh. It's so annoying. That won't happen here.

Some of the stories appear in shaded boxes called sidebars. They're skippable, though when you get the chance you may enjoy reading them. My clients and some of my own personal experiences are pretty amusing. I've also provided some juicy info marked with the Technical Stuff icon to appeal to analytical types who want to know the what, how, and why. Figures and lists are sprinkled throughout for maximum saturation of concepts, facts, and processes.

One more thing: You may notice that some web addresses break across two lines of text. If you're reading this book in print and want to visit one of these web pages, simply key in the web address exactly as it's noted in the text, pretending as though the line break doesn't exist. If you're reading this as an e-book, you've got it easy — just click the web address to be taken directly to the web page.

Foolish Assumptions

Assumptions can sometimes get us into trouble. However, it's really important that we're all on the same page together. So, for the moment forget what they say about making assumptions and have a look at the following laundry list. I assume that you

- Are a leader or manager or aspire to be such.
- Find your current workplace landscape mildly or severely out of step with who you are and what you stand for.
- Want to improve your leadership skills.
- Think your workplace needs to evolve but aren't sure how to go about it.
- Are ready to take the reins and make things better for everyone.

Additional assumptions about you, on a more personal level, are that

- You're seeking some joy, fun, and energy in your leadership.
- You've had enough of stodgy, old-school leadership and know it needs some lightening up.
- You've got a healthy sense of humor and an adventurous spirit.
- You've got a big heart and want to balance profits with your desire to do good in this world.

Icons Used in This Book

Throughout your exploration of this book, you'll notice some markers along the way. I've set these in place to call out certain elements on your journey. The little images in the margins of this book, called icons, are signs to pay attention to. Here's what they look like and how to use them:

This icon alerts you to a tip or action that will help you implement what you're learning.

If you take anything away from this book, it should be information marked with this icon. It's a good place to pause and absorb.

This icon serves as a flashing light to alert you to potential missteps, mishaps, or landmines.

This icon highlights statistics and other more technical things that support the material. This is for those who want to know the stats and results from various studies. If that's not you, feel free to skip this stuff.

Beyond the Book

If you're more of a get-to-the-point, read-it-on-my-phone-during-my-commute, quick-reference kind of person, I've got something to suit your style. To view this book's Cheat Sheet, simply go to www.dummies.com and search for "Values-Based Leadership For Dummies Cheat Sheet" to find a handy reference guide that answers common questions about VBL.

More bonus materials can be found on www.VBLeader.com and www.MariaGamb.com. There you'll find a very cool infographic pathway to VBL that will keep you focused and on track. You can also subscribe to my newsletter while you're there to receive tips and reminders that are short, sweet, and to the point. Best of all, all of that is completely free.

Should you decide you'd like to learn more about VBL training, communication skills, or signature Values 2 Vision Retreats, you can find it on the website or drop me a line at info@mariagamb.com. I customize all training and coaching programs to the needs of the users and the company.

Where to Go from Here

I'm not sure anything in life is completely linear. We can plan, but plans are often trampled by life. Journeys take unexpected detours. But ultimately, we end up exactly where we need to be. You may, of course, skip around this book at your leisure. One element or another may catch your eye, and that could be your starting point. That's fine.

However, I suggest that you consider beginning with Part 1. Business is a bit different today. You may find that the reframing process around how we view businesses and leadership has evolved. I believe that many of these concepts will help you recognize that VBL is exactly what you've been looking for, though you may not have been able to put into words. It's a world where business and leaders serve many — without the fluffy stuff and talking sticks.

Feel free to use the table of contents and index to skip around after that to see what's most appealing to you. If you've got a challenge with motivating people, for example, head to Chapter 16. Perhaps there's a serious lack of trust where you currently work? Jump to Chapter 9. However, all roads eventually lead back the grounding principles and tools to becoming a values-based leader that I discuss in Part 2. Parts 3 and 4 talk about setting your own values standards right here and now — and how to further roll out the influence of your leadership within an organization. Values without actions are meaningless.

All roads also go back to the leader, to how they engage with and lead all who follow them. That would be you. At times, you may wonder whether all of this can actually be done. I respect that. Leadership is a skill that you'll learn to sharpen through experiences. The more you seek knowledge and apply what you've learned, the faster the process will unfold. So, although I certainly want you to get to it, I also advise you to take your time.

Whatever you do, don't treat this book with intimidated reverence. Take it with you on vacation. Mark it up. Sticky-note the daylights out of it. Most of my favorite books are full of highlighting, dog-ears, and penciled-in notes. I'm hoping you find enough value and wisdom in these pages to do the same to this book. If there's a coffee cup ring on the cover, even better!

You're exactly where you need to be to start this journey. Don't tarry. Just jump in.

1
Getting Started with Values-Based Leadership

IN THIS PART . . .

Explore the basic concepts and application of values-based leadership.

Decipher the workforce Quad: who they are, what they want, and how they're reshaping leadership today.

Understand why values-based leadership requires a different type of leader who can focus on *we* rather than just *me.* Narcissism is an outdated strategy.

Unravel what it really means to create a shared values economy and see how it can help boost your organization's effectiveness to make a difference.

IN THIS CHAPTER

» Understanding the progression of company culture

» Recognizing the steps of values-based leadership

» Knowing when change is necessary in a company

» Creating a winning company with values and character

Chapter 1
Welcome to the World of Values-Based Leadership

I wonder why you're here, reading this book. Are you experiencing a problem in your own leadership? Or have you perhaps recognized that you want to move your organization in a more constructive, socially aware, and purposeful direction? Maybe you've begun the practice of values-based leadership (VBL), but something isn't firing on all cylinders yet. You may be looking to find the missing pieces. You may be a Millennial who knows you're going to lead massive teams, and you just want to get a leg up on how this leadership may look outside of the models you've seen already.

All these reasons are valid, but the common thread is the desire for change. People don't always come to change easily. At times, it's consciously accepted, but sometimes change is forced on them. You may be thinking, *I know something has to change, but I'm not sure what to do now.* Knowing there's a need for change is the first step in VBL.

The second step is understanding that *change begins with you.* Then everyone else will follow. In this chapter (and this book), you go through a journey that requires deep introspection, deciding what you stand for, and the courage to carry out a plan. Read on.

Walking through the Evolution of Company Culture

Company culture wasn't always a catchphrase. It was more like a fraternity. The hit show *Mad Men* dramatized the clublike mentality of the American workplace and showed a culture that was mostly male. Women had little power. Business was conducted with copious amounts of alcohol. There was little respect for clients and customers. Leaders, in general, had weak moral fiber. It's true the show was a dramatization, but it was an insightful one.

Some of the 1960s mentality carried through time; fast-forward to the 1990s, and still not many people considered business to be a vehicle to help others or give back to communities. That's what charities were for. Twenty-five years ago, we were far less global, not yet connected to one another through the Internet, and less aware of the world around us.

However, groups like Conscious Capitalism, formed in 2010 and spearheaded by Whole Foods CEO John Mackey, began bringing social and community needs to light and suggested a way of doing business differently. What was once considered *earthy* or *crunchy* consciousness in how we do business has gone mainstream. (See the nearby sidebar "The rise of awareness" for more on Conscious Capitalism.)

The world has changed. Diversity has improved. Immigration is a constant. Women are more prevalent in the workforce than at any other time in our history. Our interconnected lives via social media are bringing us closer in some ways, but also propelling us to need more time to disconnect and have our own life experiences.

American culture has changed as generation after generation seeks better way of living, working, and experiencing new and more interesting opportunities. But now the tsunami is here: the Millennial generation. They are the largest cohort in the history of the planet. They will take all of us over the top to a new way of thinking about business and being corporate citizens.

REMEMBER

The goalposts have moved. Profits are great, but they need to be achieved in conjunction with a purpose or mission, and a company culture that behaves responsibly to its employees, the communities it does business in, and the broader world. (To find out more about how Millennials will influence every aspect of life, head to Chapter 2.)

THE RISE OF AWARENESS

According to ConsiousCapitalism.org (www.consciouscapitalism.org/about/history), a steady flow of influence has been propping up the need for awareness in the business community. Its initiatives have been a big part of this shift:

1984: *Strategic Management: A Stakeholder Approach* by R. Edward Freeman is published.

1995: Economist, banker, and microlending pioneer Muhammad Yunus uses the term *socially conscious capitalist enterprise* in a major publication.

2005: *Megatrends 2010: The Rise of Conscious Capitalism* by Patricia Aburdene is published.

2007 (February): *Firms of Endearment* by Raj Sisodia and David Wolfe is published.

2007 (August): A white paper titled "Conscious Capitalism: Creating a New Paradigm for Business" is released.

2008: The first Catalyzing Conscious Capitalism Conference is held with 120 individuals in attendance (this would later be renamed the CEO Summit).

2009: *Be The Solution: How Entrepreneurs and Conscious Capitalists Can Solve All the World's Problems* by John Mackey and Michael Strong is published.

2010: Conscious Capitalism, Inc., is formed by the merger of FLOW, Conscious Capitalism Alliance, and Conscious Capitalism Institute.

2012: *Conscious Capitalism: Liberating the Heroic Spirit of Business* is published by John Mackey and Raj Sisodia.

2016: Alexander McCobin becomes co-CEO, and Conscious Capitalism, Inc. opens its office in San Francisco.

Understanding the Escalator Effect of Values-Based Leadership

VBL continues the evolution of how we choose to engage in business. It's the next step in the integration of one of the initial Conscious Capitalism principles: Business is good, noble, and heroic because it provides ethical opportunities for everyone.

VBL expands on Conscious Capitalism using a specific, yet customizable, set of values as the platform for norms of doing business with others and internally. Each step in this leadership model (see Figure 1-1) leads to an organization that performs at maximum capacity.

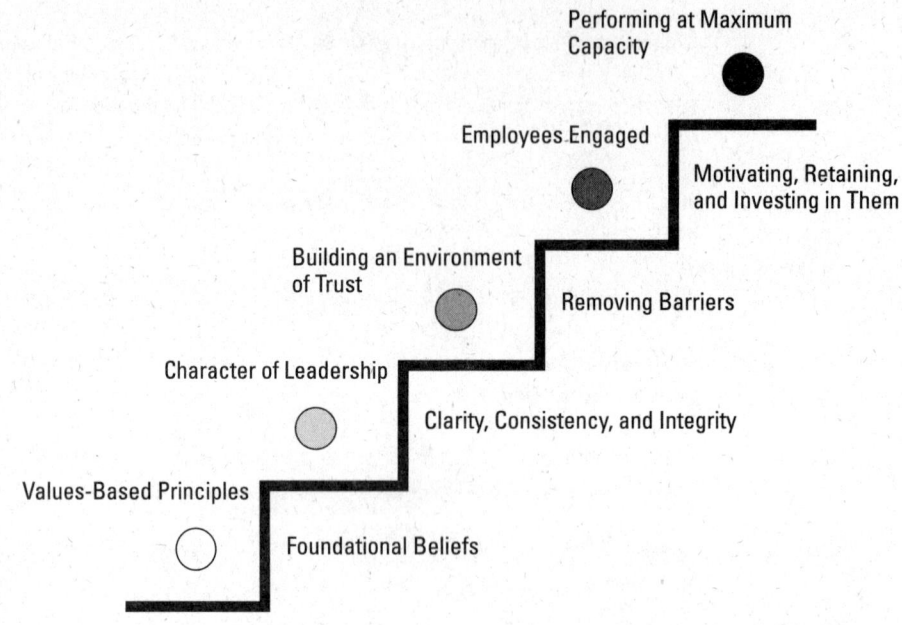

FIGURE 1-1: Leadership escalator.

© John Wiley & Sons, Inc.

REMEMBER

Within each of the five sectors in Figure 1-1, specific tasks, actions, and behaviors need to be instituted. This is the starting point of your journey — the awareness of what I will unfold in this book. Here is an overview of what each sector means:

>> **Values-Based Principles:** There is a difference between what's implied and what's expected. Clarity on which principles are selected by each leader for themselves and their organizations is the foundation for the process.

>> **Character of Leadership:** You'll hear me say many times that character can't be faked. It can be evolved and directed in more constructive ways, but it's not something you can fake, not for long. It is who you are. On our journey, I'll show you how, where, and why you need to expand on who you are to become the leader others really need and want right now. Flip to Part 2 for more information.

>> **Building an Environment of Trust:** This is the part of your company culture that's crucial — without it, you'll fail. Trust in the leadership, one another, and the path you're all on together will determine how productive your teams will

be. Simply put, if they don't trust you, they most certainly won't follow you, at least not wholeheartedly. Part 3 (especially Chapter 9) has more information.

» **Employees Engaged:** Either they're part of the process and the organization's success, or they aren't. Your willingness to invest in them will speak volumes to them. That investment comes in a variety of applications, such as training, development, benefits, perks, and simply making them part of the process. Check out Part 4 (particularly Chapter 15) for guidance.

» **Performing at Maximum Capacity:** The first four elements bring us to this point. Let's reverse the thought process. Engaged employees who are actively involved in the company's success are working from a place of trust. They are all in. This was achieved because the leader has led by example with clarity, consistency, and empathy. People love working with people who they truly believe have their best interests at heart, and not just the bottom line.

So, are you in? Your reaction to the top-level view will tell you a lot about your own capacity to evolve, change, grow, and adapt. What's your willingness level at this point? Rank it from one to five. One means "I'm really not interested at all." (I highly doubt these individuals are reading this book.) Three means, "You've got my attention but I'm not sure," and five means, "I'm all in."

If you're at a three, teetering in either direction, read on. Fours and fives, you're definitely in the right place.

Avoiding a Flatline to Extinction: When You Know Change Is Needed

There's a concept in nature called bifurcation. *Bifurcation* is a process that nature takes to renew itself. Usually it involves a disruption or inflammation that precipitates a split, a morphing into two. For example, deep forests are prone to fires. Within the forest are types of trees, spores, and other flora that require excessive heat for them to reproduce. With fire, they grow and multiply. Without it, they rot and die. One branch of possibility becomes life-affirming as a result of the disruption, and the other (without the disruption) could lead to the species becoming extinct.

When we apply bifurcation to business, we see that normal disruptions happen, and as a result — for example, the market crash in 2008 or massive corruption scandals — the system is forced to make a choice: review, reflect, and enact change, or do nothing at all (see Figure 1-2). Doing the latter often results in the company petering out into extinction. Many companies and their leadership have taken this route. Sure, sometimes staying the course and holding steady are great. But at some point, we all must upgrade our systems, thinking, and ways of being to continue to be viable.

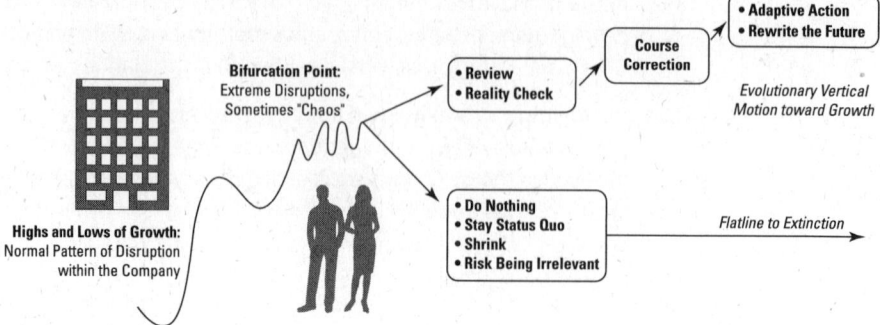

FIGURE 1-2: Bifurcation decision point.

© John Wiley & Sons, Inc.

Not all disruptions or course corrections are a result of such large issues as I've described. Consider the following as potential signs that a change is needed in the leadership approach:

- » **Excessive competition:** While competition will occur, overly aggressive and destructive or disruptive behavior will crumble teams. The attributes and principles of values-based leadership become the remedy (see Chapters 6 and 7).

- » **Exclusions and exceptions:** Creating an environment where only some people need to follow the rules disrupts the level playing field of fairness where everyone has access to opportunities. You can read more about this topic in Chapters 9 and 17.

- » **Excessive gossip and rumors:** These are key indicators that there is a lack of communication and lack of trust seeping into the organization. See Chapter 7.

- » **Team failure:** Teams fail to work together to reach their goals. This topic is covered throughout this book, but a great place to start is Chapter 9.

- » **Us versus them:** When teams, managers, and leaders are pitted against one another, progress is inhibited. The antithesis of these behavior is detailed in Chapter 4.

- » **Employee turnover:** High levels of turnover create gaps in wisdom and continuity in the organization. Find out more about the cost of high turnover rates in Chapter 15.

- » **The decline of trust and motivation:** These elements create the foundation where people work together for the greater good of all involved. See Chapters 9 and 10 for more information.

- » **Lack of ownership:** Leaders and employees who aren't tapped into the vision, mission, or purpose for the organization's work create apathy. Chapters 3 and 4 cover various aspects of building purpose into the workplace.

- » **Stagnation:** Lack of innovation in processes, problem solving, products, services, production, sourcing, and technology causes a great deal of frustration for employees. Innovation, in general, is covered in Chapter 18, but you'll notice the breadcrumb trail of each of these issues addressed throughout this book.

The preceding bullets cover just some of the many issues you can list as reasons to consider making a change. If I missed your particular reason, feel free to write it on a sticky note and place it in this chapter as a reminder of why you're here with me now. Either way, Figure 1-2 illustrates the crossroads.

Once the decision is made that something must change, which is where I think you may be in this moment, the next step is to conduct a review to determine how to course correct and then roll out adaptive action and rewrite the future. You may be on a course that's not sustainable. People may begin walking away from the company (see Chapter 19), or apathy may continue to weigh down progress. I've seen both happen. In your heart, you're probably thinking, *I just need to give this one more shot before I walk away.* Or: *This place has massive potential, but things have to change.*

What's scary is when leaders either refuse to see they have a problem or don't care enough to make any changes. That, inevitably, leads to extinction — dismissal of leadership and potentially the failure of the company.

However, you don't need to wait for your most senior leadership to embrace the principles and attributes laid out in this book. You can get started wherever you are in your organization. Chapter 12 shows you how to do this; there are prompts for those of you who may be on a solo journey inside an organization or who are entrepreneurs.

You make the choice to grow, change, and adapt and create a brighter future — or not. To make this choice, you need to be a leader who is open-minded, ruthlessly self-aware, and willing to look at the truth of your results. You also need to be savvy enough to understand that the world of business is changing. Will you keep up or be left behind?

Although remnants of the old, establishment way of operating linger on, this Millennial wave is becoming tremendously influential and will continue to lead us into a more progressive view of business. Already leaders of today are required to deploy a more comprehensive set of tools that go well beyond a technical skill set and a lofty education. Empathy and awareness are being added to leaders' skill set. So-called "soft skills" are no longer considered intangibles. They're a big component of why people will want to work for you and with you, and why they'll aspire to follow the leadership image you provide for them.

Throughout this book I provide you with several different situational applications of these and other soft tools. The most important is the use of self-reflection to gain insight into yourself and your motivations. You must consider what it will mean for you to operate in a "we" rather than "me" environment (see Chapter 3). Reframing how to view business differently sets the foundation for your journey. You'll encounter the following questions again and again in subsequent chapters because this is always going to be your check-in point:

- » Is what I'm doing about me — or about them?
- » Who is this serving — me or them?
- » Am I setting up a culture that evolves around me — or around us?

You have to assess the selflessness of your leadership. You'll need to make decisions that affect the whole. Knowing which course to take may become murky, but be sure that you're thinking of the whole — the *we* — of the organization. When it gets into *me* territory, you're in trouble. Everyone has a survival mechanism that's designed to look out for number one — to protect yourself. But when it comes to your leadership role, *we* must always be part of the equation.

Building Winning Organizations: Culture Eats Strategy for Lunch

Management expert Peter Drucker once said, "Culture eats strategy for lunch." This is one of those statements that should be posted in your workspace. Your company culture will make or break your success because your culture is a reflection of you and how you've set up the engagement for the entire organization. Although there are some outside factors that you may not be able to control 100 percent of the time, such as rogue leaders or managers, the overall tone of the organization rests on the ground rules you establish (the values) for engagement that establish the working conditions both internally and externally. (See Part 2 for full details.)

Creating that environment of trust and a culture of engagement means people are, literally, engaged and felt taken care of. Employees will stay with a leader they know has their best interests at heart longer than they'll stay with one who doesn't know their name or care about them. This isn't a kumbaya situation I'm talking about. It's about treating others with dignity and respect. This culture wins out every time when coupled with clear direction, goals, and support to exceed expectations. Playing loose won't get you past the goalpost — structure and clarity are what channel talent and enthusiasm toward a productive end. (Check out Part 3 for more information.)

On the flip side, an organization full of apathetic, downtrodden, low-energy employees is usually not operating under focused leadership. It's nearly impossible unless one of the field-level leaders corrals them and applies VBL at that point of interaction. And if that happens, it still means only one team is productive. Guess what? That will lead to resentment. Although there will always be a portion of the workforce who is happy to just come in, do nothing, and collect a paycheck, fortunately that's not everyone.

Being aware of who is willing and hungry for direction is the way to start to mobilize a potentially demoralized group of people. People will follow those who offer hope. Through VBL, you'll be able to extend that feeling to harness the amazing talent in your organization. In the following sections, I introduce the two vital components of building a winning organization: values and character.

Managers and leaders in the field can create their own private nirvanas using VBL principles, as you find out in Chapter 12. This version addresses how you can fill in the gap between your employees and potentially leaders above you who are either too busy or uninterested in VBL as a solution. It's not always easy, but it can be done successfully.

Shaping the company culture with values

What exactly do I mean by *values*? To start, let's get on the same page with regard to terminology here:

» **Values:** Fundamental beliefs that make you who you are or make your organization what it is. There are several categories of values — this book focuses on core values only (flip to Chapter 11 for details).

» **Values-based leaders:** Based on core values, setting the foundation of how everyone will engage creates an expectation that the leader always operates for the greater good of all. The expectation is that the leader has a well-developed character that establishes an environment of mutual respect, at a minimum. (Part 2 focuses on becoming a values-based leader.)

» **Values-based organizations:** A business isn't just the building that contains the staff that works with and for you. VBL extends beyond and reverberates into everything the organization stands for. Based on the values selected, values-based organizations determine ground rules for how we do business, how we invest in others, how we serve the community, and how we create sustainability (see Chapter 3 for more information).

When the leader sets the organization on a clear track and models from the front rather than lecturing others, the team will follow suit. This creates a fair, level working environment imbued with the values and clear expectations that employees use when they work with vendors, suppliers, and overseas partners without exception. Core values are woven into every aspect of the company's being and presence. They're the commitment and promise made as to who you will be and how you will operate every day — not just on good days, but always.

This process not only creates a consistent company culture, but it also provides the framework to build your *reputational capital* — capital that doesn't necessarily have a price tag but that will affect your bottom line (see Chapter 10). Investors, creditors, and stockholders want to know you're consistent. Staff, vendors, and suppliers want to know you're trustworthy. Cultivate a positive reputation, and people will flock to work with you and for you. Get a poor reputation, and you may never get the best talent or the funding to expand your situation. It's as simple as that.

Influencing the company culture with your character

Character is the means between two extremes. It is the balanced point between a deficiency and an excess of a trait. It's nearly impossible to always take the middle road; humans tend to lean to one side or another of the characteristic embodied. This is also called the *near-mean*, or the one *favored*. The favored isn't always the darker or more extreme side of the spectrum.

REMEMBER

In this book, you traverse a number of the traits that make up a values-based leader, but the singular trait all leaders require is *courage.* On a continuum, courage ranges from timidity and caution to boldness and rashness. Sitting somewhere between caution and boldness is what would be required of any leader in just about any demonstration. That's because the fundamentals of leadership require not just insight and perception but also efficacy — getting things done.

People can't have the greater good in mind or the desire to fulfill a purpose as part of their leadership without embodying a balance of courage to persevere in various states of challenge.

REMEMBER

Additionally, how you behave is an example to everyone around you. The saying "When someone tells you who they are, believe them" rings true. You tell people who you are by the way you speak to others, by the level of care, respect, and discretion you show. You tell them who you are by the depth of honesty that you embody while balancing truth. Each of these characteristics will either build or damage trust (see Chapter 9).

Trust promotes faith in your leadership. It also establishes a playing field where people can express creativity and innovation without feeling judged or confined to the four walls around the existing process or product. Trust promotes growth, which is essential to the organization's life.

Wherever there is backstabbing, gossip, and judgment in your leadership, replace it with kindness, temperance, patience, and acceptance. This would be a way to demonstrate the action you want others to emulate as well. You can't manage other people until you manage yourself — that includes your own emotions and possible blind spots.

IN THIS CHAPTER

» **Dissecting different generations in the workforce**

» **Leading employees of all ages**

Chapter **2**
Understanding the Evolving Workforce You Serve

Lumping people into one category creates tension. Lack of inquiry into knowing who your people are causes frustration. When you know who they are and what matters most to them, you're deeply connected to your audience. Business creates *audiences* — the focus is usually on the customer or end user, but for this conversation, the audience that will consume your leadership is made up of the staff, stakeholders, team, tribe, or however you describe the group of people powering the company and your ideas. They're your best resource because they're the ones who run the show every day.

Knowing them and their hearts is one way of tapping into the power of your audience. Famous orators and leaders such as John F. Kennedy, Martin Luther King Jr., and Nelson Mandela knew their audiences and knew how to speak directly to them in order to mobilize their ideas. But to do so with your employees, you'll need to know the influences that fuel their wants and desires.

Having insight into your audience's wants and desires will help you comprehend the factors that lead to their perceptions of authority, leadership, values, virtues, and work ethics. These are mobilizing factors. In this chapter, I show you how to gain that insight by breaking down the workforce into the beautiful *Quad* — the four generations currently operating in the workforce today.

Here's what I'll be looking at:

- Who makes up the workforce today?
- What do they want?
- What inspires, encourages, and motivates them?
- What do they want from you, their leader — or do they want to lead?

Pinpointing the Quad Workforce

During adolescence, people make determinations about what is cool, healthy, natural, and worth their time; sexuality emerges, and passion and ambition start to pique their interest. Opinions based on outside influences create the framework to ultimately determine what they want. The formative years also play a large part in determining how people will view the world. Their perceptions and reactions to different stimuli, such as how their parents raised them, current events, music, politics, and so on, create opportunities to draw conclusions on safety, security, money, career, government, and so on. These outside factors create their mindset and way of being in the world. Although no two people will react the same, general conclusions about generations can be derived.

REMEMBER

Listen with an open mind. Don't judge. Be aware of what may be your own preconceived notions of who and what each generation in the Quad represents.

Generational cohorts are defined by a period of development within a certain span of time. To some extent these boundaries are arbitrary, and defining and labeling generations can vary from sociologist to sociologist, though for the most part they vary by only a few years. I'll be using the research of noted sociologists William Strauss and Neil Howe to bracket the generational periods. Feel free to adjust the years I use based on your understanding if needed.

In Figure 2-1, you may be surprised to be classified not as a Baby Boomer, but on the outer edge of Generation X. Or you may be more Millennial than you knew.

There are three main generations that make up the current workforce: Baby Boomers, Generation X, and Millennials. On the outskirts are the almost completely retired Silent generation and the emerging Homeland generation. Together, they make up the "bumper" generations of the current workforce and are classified as the fourth part of the Quad.

The Current Quad Workforce

SILENT GENERATION			
1925–1942			

While most Silents have already retired, others remain working until 75–80 years old.

BABY BOOMERS 1943–1960 — Boomers are delaying retirement. — *Not so much since Covid*

GENERATION X 1961–1981

MILLENNIALS 1982–2004

HOMELAND 2005–Present

Homeland enters the workforce by 2023.

© John Wiley & Sons, Inc.

FIGURE 2-1: The current workforce Quad.

GENERATIONAL DEMOGRAPHICS

Understanding the pitfalls around values-based leadership and its many initiatives is relevant to creating success. The workforce continually evolves; generations come in, make their mark, and then hand the baton to the next generation. One generation hopefully learns from the more experienced generation and influences the next.

The effects of the global financial crisis of 2008 have altered American workers' perceptions about everything from security to money, authority, and work. For example:

- Boomers plan to work "forever" and potentially have a second career. Money is a status symbol.

- GenXers aren't as worried about money and security; they prefer to change careers and/or take a sabbatical to have different experiences. Money is just a means to an end.

- Millennials put a high premium on living for today; they hope to change the world and do meaningful work. Money is a payoff for today.

GenXers and Millennials currently make up the bulk of the workforce. Millennials represent the largest generation in history: They number some 75 million in the United States and 2.5 billion globally. By 2020 they will make up 46 percent of the workforce. This generation will change the norms of business and politics. (For more information, check out the Pew Research Center's 2016 paper on the topic at www.pewresearch.org/fact-tank/2016/04/25/millennials-overtake-baby-boomers.)

The generation after the Millennials, called the Homeland generation, is coming of age quickly and will begin to enter the workforce in 2023 when the first ones turn 18. Some may enter earlier, depending on their track.

Picking out postwar, workaholic Boomers

The parents of the Baby Boomers (born 1943–1960) were traditionalists. The Boomers grew up in a postwar era of growth fueled by patriotism. They watched their parents work hard and the American dream unfold. The United States entered a period of great prosperity while Boomers were in their formative years. As they became young adults, human rights movements dominated the headlines, and the sexual revolution unfolded. During this time, they learned that hard work equals success; what could have been perceived as a material approach to the world around them began to shift into wanting to do something good in the world.

Here is a snapshot of the events and people who influenced Boomers:

- **Events shaping their world:** Civil rights, women's rights, and gay rights movements, the moon landing, the Vietnam War, the OPEC oil embargo, the sexual revolution, the advent of birth control, and the second highest divorce rate in history, as well as the assassinations of John F. Kennedy, Martin Luther King Jr., and Robert Kennedy.
- **Famous figures:** Martin Luther King Jr., John F. Kennedy, Gloria Steinem, Rosa Parks, The Beatles.
- **Emerging technology:** The microwave oven.
- **What they learned to value:** Hard work, patriotism, authority, equal rights, equal opportunities, optimism, personal growth, wanting to make a difference in the world, resisting authority but then conforming.
- **Prevailing attributes:** Challenge authority, live to work, optimism, political correctness (PC), willingness to take responsibility, competitiveness, ambition, consumerism, capitalism, diplomatic communications.
- **Work motto:** "Live to work." Work is their life.

TECHNICAL STUFF

Late Baby Boomers will retire around 2025 or later if they choose to work beyond age 65. All Baby Boomers will retire, of course, but situations such as the need to finish paying off mortgages and student loans keep them working. (Did you know that if you still have a student loan debt at the time you begin to collect Social Security, if you're still working, your earnings will be garnished for what's owed?) In addition, rising medical costs make employee benefits such as health insurance a very enticing reason to stay. Other Boomers just love the challenge of work and keeping their brains engaged and learning. This phenomenon isn't restricted to the United States. In 2011, the U.K. abolished the default retirement age of 65, thereby preventing employers from automatically retiring workers. Due to many factors, the Organization for Economic Co-operation and Development (OECD) reports that workers over 65 account for a noteworthy percentage of the population, as you can see in Figure 2-2.

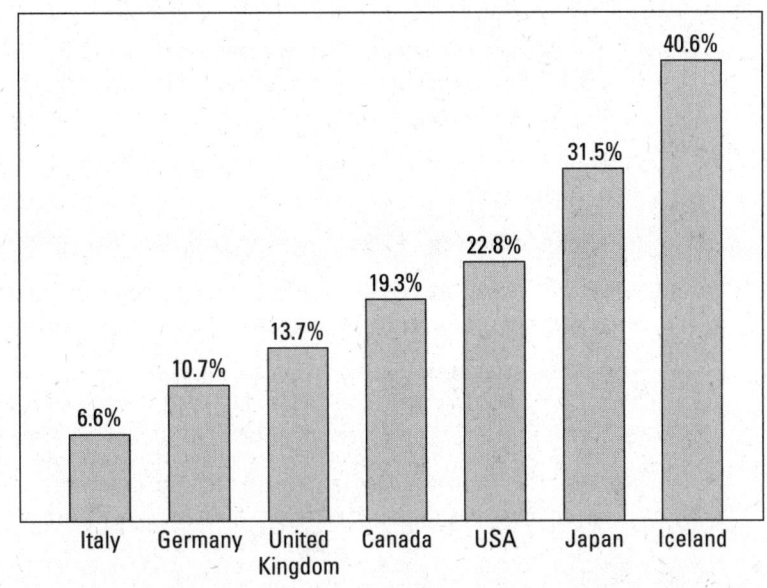

FIGURE 2-2: Population working beyond age 65.

Country	%
Italy	6.6%
Germany	10.7%
United Kingdom	13.7%
Canada	19.3%
USA	22.8%
Japan	31.5%
Iceland	40.6%

© John Wiley & Sons, Inc.

Although the data in Figure 2-2 doesn't state the specifics within each country contributing to the rise in late retirement, the global financial crisis of 2008 put a dent in many individuals' plans. The immigration population worldwide also continues to circulate more Baby Boomers in the workforce. The European Union has fluid borders allowing citizens to work more easily in any nation within the EU. Technology is another big factor — the next evolution in telecommuting from India to Chicago isn't far away. National borders can't stop the globalization of the talent pool.

Understanding latchkey, self-reliant GenXers

Generation X (born 1961–1981) is the first generation to experience working mothers as routine, not the exception. *Latchkey* kids had both parents still at work when they got home from school, and they had to amuse themselves until their parents returned home. They were self-reliant and self-directed, doing homework and chores without after-school supervision Monday through Friday. Daycare was created. Divorce rates remained high, spurring GenXers' desire for family and a fierce commitment to work-life balance. Early GenXers lived through the Watergate scandal in 1972, while later Xers saw the Clinton-Lewinsky scandal in the 1990s and formed the belief that politicians and authority cannot be trusted.

Here's a snapshot of the events and people who influenced Generation X:

» **Events shaping their world:** The end of the Cold War, Watergate, Title IX, the assassination attempt of President Ronald Reagan, the fall of the Berlin Wall, the Space Shuttle *Challenger* disaster, grunge and hip-hop, the AIDS epidemic outbreak changes dating and marriage perceptions, and the rise of dual-income families and single-income families led by women.

- **Famous figures:** Madonna, Mikhail Gorbachev, Grandmaster Flash, Nirvana, Stone Temple Pilots.
- **Emerging technology:** Personal computers, cell phones, PDAs.
- **What they learned to value:** Diversity, entrepreneurship, education, independence, self-reliance, skepticism and cynicism, pragmatism.
- **Prevailing attributes:** Focus on results, ignore leadership, mistrust government, pampered by parents, unimpressed with authority, confident, competent, ethical, willing to take on responsibility, will put in extra time to get it done.
- **Work motto:** "Work to live." GenXers sacrifice balance occasionally but prefer to work to fund the life they desire.

Meeting digitally savvy, tenacious Millennials

Growing up during the era of mass school shootings and terrorist attacks, Millennials (born 1982–2004) learned that they should enjoy today because who knows what will happen? Early Millennials left adolescence and college before the Great Recession hit, but the later part of the generation found their college tuitions and family finances compromised. This generation has experienced economic highs and lows unlike any other generation since the Great Depression. Despite this, they look toward the future and want to contribute and find meaning in just about everything they do. In their own way, they are truth seekers, trying to understand the why and how of everything. Digitally connected and technologically savvy, they have access to the world like no generation before them.

Here's a snapshot of the events and people who influenced Millennials:

- **Events shaping their world:** Columbine, 9/11, ISIS, terror attacks, the first black president, the Great Recession, and race riots.
- **Famous figures:** Barack Obama, Mark Zuckerberg, Miley Cyrus, Prince William, Justin Bieber.
- **Emerging technology:** Facebook, Twitter, Napster, Snapchat, Tinder, smartphones, a fully integrated digital existence.
- **What they learned to value:** Transparency, efficiency over long hours, skepticism of leaders, pragmatism, independence, entrepreneurship, fun, diversity.

» **Prevailing attributes:** Self-sufficient, results driven, unimpressed with authority, willing to take on responsibility, loyal to manager, an antiestablishment mentality.

» **Work motto:** "Work to live." Like the GenXers, Millennials prefer to work to create a lifestyle. If they're given the choice of a work promotion or maintaining a desired lifestyle, lifestyle usually wins.

Considering the bumper generations

The bumper generations are those that are either on the cusp of leaving the workplace or preparing to enter the workforce. Both are worth taking a look at because they add something to the mix.

Recognizing the Silent generation

Although some in the Silent generation (born 1925–1942) may still be working, the percentage is very small. They are mentioned here because of their influence as a generation of hard workers with respect for authority, government, and conformity. They raised the Baby Boomers and GenXers. They're grandparents to Millennials and some Homelanders. The Silent generation grew up during the Great Depression and World War II. Patriotism is a hallmark of this cohort. Their influence continues.

Anticipating the Homelanders

This cohort has been cast and recast several times. First called Generation Edge or Generation Z, being born 1996–2010, the term *Homeland* is becoming the established moniker for those born in 2005 and later, having been coined not long after 9/11. They will begin entering their formative (teen) years starting in 2018, developing into adulthood around the age of 21. During that time, influencers will help them form their perceptions, values, and virtues. They're so young that we know little about them at this point (although you can check out the nearby sidebar "Projecting through the saeculum" for some informed speculation).

Homelanders will be part of your workforce beginning in 2023 when they start to turn 18. Some may join even earlier. I include them in the current Quad because anticipating their arrival as the Silent generation leaves the workforce is important.

The Homeland generation was raised by GenXers who experienced the last years of prosperity as we knew it, prior to the global financial meltdown. In that light, GenXers may be less willing to allow these children to take big risks. They are growing up in a culture that emphasizes homeland security and surveillance. Those in this generation will spend more time at home as digital advancements continue to allow them to do so. They're more isolated and may need help with socialization in the workplace.

Here's a snapshot of the events and people who are influencing Homelanders (in many cases, we don't know enough about this generation yet to fill in most of the list):

> » **Current events shaping their world:** North Korea nuclear threat, the Donald Trump administration, climate change, and prolonged war in the Middle East.
>
> » **Famous figures:** The Kardashians, Prince Harry.
>
> » **Emerging technology:** AI advancements, TBA.
>
> » **What they learned to value:** TBA.
>
> » **Prevailing attributes:** TBA.
>
> » **Work motto:** TBA.

What we do know is that the jobs they will have in their lifetime have not yet been created. Technology continues to evolve and expand rapidly. So, stay tuned! It will be fascinating to watch this generation unfold.

PROJECTING THROUGH THE SAECULUM

According to one interesting line of thought, there is a cycle of generations that signals what the challenges and the values may be for a new generation even before they arrive. Each generation is made up of a roughly 20-year span and assigned a designation: artist, prophet, nomad, or hero. Within each cycle are four generations that comprise a *saeculum* — the normal lifetime of a person or period that renews the human population, which would be roughly 80 years. Sociologists William Strauss and Neil Howe's work on these cycles, in their book *The Fourth Turning,* provides a fascinating look into this theory dating back to ancient Etruscans.

If there's something to this idea, Homelanders will mirror the Silent generation, bringing a return to old-fashioned values, hard work, family-centric activities, a unified patriotism, a strong work ethic, and faith in authority and government. Unfortunately, to closely mirror the Silent generation, Homelanders would likely also experience some major confrontation, such as war. But remember, after World War II hard work brought expansion and prosperity in the later part of the generation and well into the next.

Of course, because it's unknown what these children will experience, it's also unknown how they would digest the events and change the workplace. Considering what Homelanders may experience can lead to speculation about how this will form their values and attributes. Homelanders will be entering your workplace soon — observe and draw your own conclusions!

Leading the Quad with Insight and Understanding

Every cohort in the Quad brings something unique to the overall culture. Each has strengths and weaknesses. Finding common ground can help pull a single thread through uniting the group. The effectiveness of your leadership will be determined by how well you communicate and reach these groups; this section provides pointers.

WARNING: Don't be one of those wonderful, talented, insightful leaders who speak to their staff in terms that they just don't *get*. When a group knows the leader doesn't get them, they remain skeptical and cautious.

Converting diversity into inclusion

Human and civil rights are part of the fabric of American society, touching all in the Quad in one way or another. Boomers grew up when segregation was still practiced in various parts of the country. They watched Martin Luther King Jr. peacefully demonstrate and then they added women's rights to their activism. GenXers watched their mothers fight for equal pay, and throughout both GenXers' adult years and Millennials' midlife years, race riots, police brutality, and immigration discrimination have permeated the news. In the Millennial and Homeland generations, LGBT rights have come to the forefront of equality movements. Each generation has raised awareness around diversity and inclusion in society.

The tide of diversity is no longer an ideal — it's a necessity. Each generation mentioned has participated in breaking down discriminatory boundaries. Diversity is set to become a seamless part of society rather than something we must direct. Inclusion will be the name of the game as immigrants continue to become a bigger part of the population. The blending of people of color will become less defined and more integrated. There will be those who may hold out on these issues, but the momentum of change continues toward the path to seamlessness.

TECHNICAL STUFF: The Center for American Progress (www.scribd.com/document/99937416/The-State-of-Diversity-in-Today-s-Workforce) has found the following:

- People of color make up 36 percent of the workforce.
- Women make up 47 percent of the workforce. Sixty-seven percent of them are non-Hispanic white, and 33 percent are women of color.
- Gay and transgender workers make up 6.28 percent of the workforce.

> » Between 2020 and 2050, 83 percent of the workforce population will be made up of immigrants and their children.
>
> » By 2050, census data projects that there will be no single majority race.

TIP

Here are a few tips to pave the way toward inclusion:

> » Do accept and embrace the seamlessness of the workforce. This is an unstoppable global force.
>
> » Do include diversity programs with the goal of being able to phase out "diversity" labels, most likely starting 2030 and into 2050.
>
> » Do pay attention to the growing female demographic in the workplace. Women will be taking more and more leadership roles.
>
> » Don't permit racial, gender, and sexuality exclusions in the workplace. Raise awareness where needed.

Pivoting work ethic into work ethos

Boomers like taking risks; they're driven and want to make a difference. Their work ethic is almost that of a workaholic, and many are obsessed with success. GenXers prefer efficiencies and results. They're entrepreneurial by nature and self-directed, preferring to focus on tasks and results. Structure and direction are welcome, but standard 9–5 working conditions aren't. They prefer to work smarter rather than harder. Get it done and move on. Millennials are seamless multitaskers of life and work. There is no beginning or end — it's all happening at once. Check their Instagram accounts to see it. Also entrepreneurial, they are tenacious and ambitious. Millennials are globally focused and are natural networkers.

The commonality is that each group in the Quad is willing to work hard, but they do it differently according to their *work ethos*. You need to acknowledge the different work ethos. No one is "special" — they're just different. Boomers will work until midnight, but perhaps not by working smarter, just working harder. Xers have a heads-down hyperfocused approach, but they will rarely work a ten-hour day. They broke that cycle. Millennials are always working because they consider work and life to be one seamless activity. However, they won't allow work to disrupt their lifestyle.

So, the notion that any cohort is lazy is pure stereotype. They all work hard — they just do it differently and utilize different *equalizing triggers*. The two main triggers that propel work ethos are *work-life balance* and *meaning*.

TIP

Here are a few ways to address differing work ethos and still get the job done:

» Do allow the team to work in the style that makes them most comfortable.

» Do set deadlines so that no matter how they choose to work, the work gets done on time, every time.

» Do provide the structure to support the team and the direction to get it done.

» Do remind everyone that they all complement one another.

» Don't allow it to become a free-for-all. Circle back to "provide structure."

Recalibrating the concept of work-life balance

Work-life balance means different things across the span of the Quad. Asking for a couple of days off as a reward for a job well done is commonplace for Xers. They may seek to spend time with their loved ones or hang glide off a cliff. Experience is everything to them. They crave it in their workplace, but they also want a life full of memories that may not always involve work. Balance is also important to Millennials, who seek to not upset their lifestyles, even at the risk of losing a promotion. There's no reason to think Homelanders won't follow suit. And, well, Baby Boomers have learned the hard way that perhaps they need a little more balance in their lives. Even though they're becoming the elder statesmen and stateswomen, it's still hard for them to slow their drive. They're learning from the rest of the Quad to enjoy life more and stress less.

I once overheard a Millennial manager speaking to a Boomer vice president: "Don't you have a family, dog, cat, or hobby to go home to?" It wasn't said with malice or sarcasm, but with genuine concern for the VP's out-of-whack, late-night work habits. Remember, Millennials are ambitious too. They'll take flexibility in their work schedule to accommodate the balance they seek — all they ask is to not be judged for it. They can't understand anyone who doesn't make balance a priority.

The aforementioned OECD (www.OECDbetterlifeindex.org) has determined the indicators for *balance* as time devoted to leisure and personal care compared to the number of hours employees work (see Figure 2-3). The OECD further ranks the overall quality of work-life balance amongst the workforce; with 1 percent being the lowest ranking and 10 percent being the highest, the United States achieved a 6.2 percent ranking for work-life balance. The U.K. scored 6.6 percent, Canada got 7.2 percent, Germany came in at 8.8 percent, and the Netherlands provided the best work-life balance opportunity with a whopping 9.4 rating. Each nation has work to do in creating better balance in the workforce.

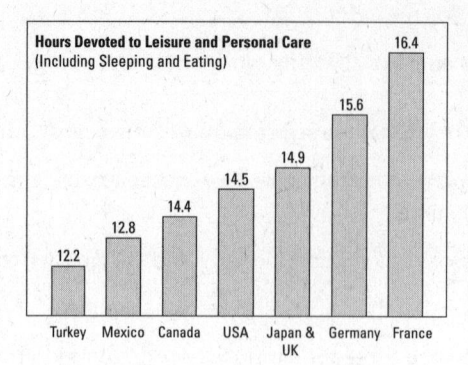

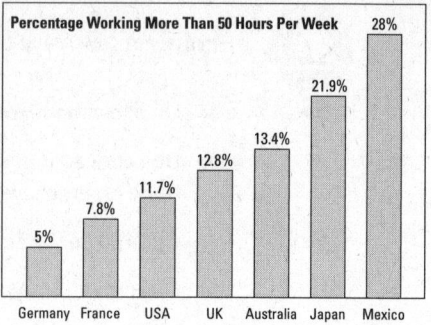

FIGURE 2-3: Indicators of work-life balance.

Hours Devoted to Leisure and Personal Care (Including Sleeping and Eating): Turkey 12.2, Mexico 12.8, Canada 14.4, USA 14.5, Japan & UK 14.9, Germany 15.6, France 16.4

Percentage Working More Than 50 Hours Per Week: Germany 5%, France 7.8%, USA 11.7%, UK 12.8%, Australia 13.4%, Japan 21.9%, Mexico 28%

© John Wiley & Sons, Inc.

TECHNICAL STUFF: One final statistic to further emphasize the need for work-life balance to be taken seriously: 95 percent of all human resource leaders believe that the biggest sabotage to retention in the workplace is burnout. (For more on this, check out www.kronos.com/about-us/newsroom/employee-burnout-crisis-study-reveals-big-workplace-challenge-2017.)

TIP: Some generations don't crave work-life balance, but for others, it's a mandatory component in their equation for happiness. To help everyone find their balance and set your own expectations at a realistic level, consider the following options, making them available to everyone in your organization. Start with what you think can realistically be implemented into your organization:

» Do permit flexible work hours — you'll get more out of your staff's talents.

» Do encourage volunteerism and, if possible, offer volunteer time off (VTO).

» Do set mandatory personal time off (PTO) requirements.

» Do abolish inefficient, time-sucking meetings. Reduce the number of meetings on a whole so people can get their work done without having to burn the midnight oil.

» Don't expect everyone to work ten-plus hours every day.

Creating meaning and a reason to go to work

"Sue" looks up from her desk covered with reports, meeting notes, and an enormous coffee from yesterday still sitting on her tablet. She asks a colleague, "Remind me: Why are we doing this?" They both laugh in exasperation. You may be surprised to learn that, for the most part, *money* is no longer the main motivation for most of the Quad. People want happiness and they want meaning.

Happiness and meaning are not the same. In studies, researchers found that participants associated happiness with *taking*, whereas meaning was associated with *giving* — the suspension of one's own needs and desires in favor of someone else's.

Easily the biggest common denominator among the cohorts is the deep desire to make a difference, though each generation expresses it in a slightly different way. Boomers want to *make a difference,* Xers want to *do good and create impact,* and Millennials desire *impact for the greater good* (with global reach) and desire work they feel *connected to.* Don't be surprised if Homelanders' desire for having global impact circles back to old-fashioned values and the concept of "helping your neighbor" literally.

REMEMBER Values-based leadership is a pathway to creating meaning for everyone in the company.

Here are some common questions your staff members are asking themselves. Consider how the concepts you discover in this book will help them answer these questions positively:

- Does we do change the lives of anyone? How?
- Do I feel connected to the company's values, mission, and purpose?
- If we weren't doing this work, would it really be missed?
- If I don't feel that this work is meaningful, will I stay?

Wondering whether the Quad cares about your leadership

Isn't it interesting that you, the leader, have barely been mentioned in this chapter? Just so you know, the Quad has mixed feelings about you and what you can or can't do. They wonder about your ethics, trustworthiness, and commitment. Are you surprised? You may chalk it up as normal, and it is. But you should know why they may mistrust you. Emotional intelligence, sensitivity, and reflective moments will be a staple on our journey together.

Everyone has life experiences that help create perceptions of how things should or will be. Each cohort has reason to be skeptical and critical of leaders in general. In the outlining of the Quad earlier in this chapter, you can see the thread of events and experiences that may have caused them to mistrust authority and leadership. These events fostered the seeds of mistrust.

Workers of all ages have become exasperated by leaders who lack authenticity, compassion, and transparency. Will their leaders do what they say they'll do when they say they'll do it? Tell them the truth and take responsibility. For example, in 2015 Japan's Takata Corporation recalled their airbags and set out to repairs tens of millions of products placed in Honda motor vehicles. However, it wasn't without pressure from U.S. regulators that set this remedy in motion. Takata leadership took responsibility for the issue and ultimately made it right.

REMEMBER

The Quad is a reflection of our society — fatigued by empty promises, unaligned values, and the inability to trust authority. They want more. The good news is that they are willing to give more. You can't change history or their life experiences, but there are some things you *can* do to change their experience right now. That starts with you, not them. Welcome to values-based leadership.

> **IN THIS CHAPTER**
>
> » Defining and using the four Be's of values-based leadership
>
> » Incorporating all of your values into your leadership
>
> » Determining your stance on command and control
>
> » Following the evolutionary pathway being cut toward values-based leadership

Chapter 3
Shifting Your Consciousness beyond the Self

"When we quit thinking primarily about ourselves and our own self-preservation, we undergo a truly heroic transformation of consciousness," said author Joseph Campbell. And so the journey begins. Values-based leadership (VBL) is, indeed, a shift of consciousness beyond ourselves. In past decades even broaching the subject of consciousness was tantamount to fluffy stuff. This is no longer a fluffy concept. It's part of who we are and how we decide to show up in the world. As a leader, the impact on those around you is amplified simply because of the scope of influence you command, knowingly or unknowingly.

Over the years, I've met many accidental leaders. They never wanted the responsibility because they were afraid of it. However, fate had other plans for them. Others have always wanted to be leaders and made very conscious steps toward these roles in their lives. However you have arrived or plan to arrive at the destination of leadership doesn't matter. What does matter is the level of awareness you have about your impact.

Values-based leadership is all about maximizing your impact for the greater good of all — not just you, the leader. This shift in consciousness becomes a foundational component. When your thinking is correct, the rest of the attributes you're asked to embody and actions you will be asked to take will be easier for you to grasp. You can start to make the shift beyond yourself with the help of this chapter.

Looking at the Four Be's of Values-Based Leadership

Unfortunately, every generation has had an exposure to corrupt leaders, politicians, or people in powerful positions. Often the common thread is that they were more concerned about themselves than others. In many instances, their own personal greed became their demise. Referencing history, we can look back at companies like Enron as an example. In 2001, the company acknowledges that they had overstated earnings by approximately $600 million since 1997. They filed for Chapter 11 bankruptcy on December 2, 2001. Three months prior to the admission, the CEO raised capital by encouraging stakeholders to buy Enron stock. In the bankruptcy, many employees lost everything while the leadership had pocketed millions in the biggest corporate bankruptcy in U.S. history at that time.

In values-based leadership, the leader is asked to consider the well-being of all the lives the company touches. This may seem to be a very logical principle to some but completely far-fetched to others, which is why the clarification of this concept and mindset is important to detail. Even those who believe they are generous may not fully be expressing it through business. Philanthropy is one expression of generosity. But generosity also means helping people reach their highest potential. Consider asking yourself the following questions:

- Is my leadership about me gaining exposure or the company's greater good?
- Am I operating from a place where everyone wins?
- Do I care about the health and well-being of my stakeholders, vendors, and customers?
- Am I fair and ethical in my business practices?

Values-based leaders are selfless rather than selfish and consider the whole rather than themselves. Don't misunderstand. This is not a matter of becoming a doormat or giving until you have nothing left — becoming an exhausted giver. It also doesn't mean that the leadership doesn't profit from sound business strategies, hard work, investments, and so on. Shifting your consciousness is the animation of the mindset of selflessness. The term *servant leadership* became popular in 1970, when Robert K. Greenleaf launched his essay "The Servant as Leader." We are expanding that concept into the practical application in the workplace for you and your leadership team. The four Be's discussed in the following sections offer a means to help you compartmentalize and contextualize the VBL mindset.

Defining the four Be's

You may not be responsible for others in your company, literally. You can't control others. You're responsible for yourself and your own actions. You can guide others down a pathway, but the choice will always be theirs. However, as a leader you have responsibility to your stakeholders, shareholders, and business associates to operate from a higher level of consciousness.

The following four Be's provide a good framework for the agreement you make with each stakeholder to operate with a higher consciousness and establish an alignment of cooperation, caring, and selflessness:

» **Be of service.** Serve and facilitate the business by providing the stakeholders tools that create jobs, profits, and opportunities for all.

» **Be a guardian.** Safeguard against actions motivated by ego. Be willing to keep others' egos in check too, so the group's results are in alignment with the values you've set forth.

» **Be generous.** Be willing to give to others. Nurture the highest good in all members of your team so they can reach their highest potential. Share your wisdom. Be supportive and encouraging.

» **Be diligent.** Do whatever you can to ensure that the rights of others aren't violated due to your business practices.

Deploying the four Be's with clarity

When the agreement between the leaders and the stakeholders is based on the four Be's in the preceding section, the translation is as follows:

I, the leader, will always do my best to give you the tools you need to do your job. If I can offer any wisdom or advice to shortcut the process for you, I will happily do so. I will do my very best to be ego-neutral and ask you to do the same. And I promise not to turn the workplace into a fight club where only one survives. This means no unhealthy competition or discrimination.

I'm not suggesting that there is a literal statement to be issued to every new employee. But all leaders and managers within the organization should be aware of your expectations of behavior. This is one aspect of creating a safe, healthy workplace for them. When you do — when you deploy the Be's and ask the leaders and managers on your hierarchy tree to be in alignment with them — you may need to provide an example.

REMEMBER: Clarity is king. Never leave them guessing.

At times, I'll be asked to work with teams within an organization. They may be slightly off the mark in some way. Leadership realizes that they need some help, but they may not be quite sure what the issue is that's affecting morale and/or productivity. In the case of company ABC, after interviewing several team members, including the team leader (I'll call him Chuck), it became clear that Chuck had been withholding tools from his team. In fact, he was having them compete for the tools they needed to do their job. Whoever was in his good graces received the necessary tool(s): connections, leads, contacts, or other resources such as required data. Those who weren't often stayed late and struggled to meet their deadlines. Morale on the team was terrible. Productivity and effectiveness were very low.

One team member told me, "It's not that I don't like my teammates, but every day it's a competition. It's exhausting. Just give me the tools I need and I'll do my job well. But without it, I feel like I can't win." Another told me, "I'm set up to fail. Some days I just don't want to be bothered." It was clear no one felt like they could win. Everyone was in survival mode.

In case you're wondering, Chuck was presented with the findings from my survey. He was very surprised. Chuck didn't realize the damage that he had inflicted on the team. Unfortunately, this was the model that Chuck knew — this is how his previous company had operated. So it was completely normal for him. He was taught that this would be motivational for all involved. As the expectations were explained, he became annoyed and defensive. However, given 48 hours to think about it, he returned to the conversation, acknowledged his bad behavior, and gave his word to work more in alignment with the company's values. Three years later, Chuck is still thriving at that very same company. Even he's admitted, "You know, even I'm happier working this way, although it's not always easy."

REMEMBER: People may not always realize that what they're doing is hurtful or destructive. Be gracious enough to give them the benefit of the doubt and the opportunity to shift their own consciousness.

Seeing kindness in the four Be's

As many have observed, we are spiritual beings having a human experience every day. As we continue to evolve on our human journey, the call to integrate our spirituality into everything we do is a gentle wave that permeates our culture. This is the integration of heart and soul. Several aspects of spirituality can be expressed in business, but the foundational concept for this discussion about values-based leadership is to couple selflessness with one of kindness.

Kindness is a concept that has been taught in most major religions and philosophies in the world today (see the nearby sidebar for more information). Be kind. In that kindness, be generous and care for others. There are different specific applications based on any given situation, but the four Be's represent kindness in a leadership position:

>> **Be of service.** Transparency is a great example of service to others. To be kind is to be forthcoming with information to get a project done on time, well, and thoroughly. Leaders who play shell games with their teams are being manipulative or passive-aggressive. However, taking the time to provide what's needed imparts the team members with the capacity to win.

   A good leader, a kind leader, helps remove obstacles so a team member can do their job to the best of their ability. Coaching sometimes comes after the issue has been resolved. For example, Joan can't submit project plans for a new hotel without a complete survey and a budget. The survey has been provided, but the budget seems to be taking a long time. When it reaches her desk, she sees information missing. No matter how diplomatic Joan is, she can't get the complete report from the finance team. Joan's leader, Tim, steps in and helps her get what she needs without chastising her. After the project is complete, Tim coaches Joan on how to handle the situation the next time.

>> **Be a guardian.** Egos can run rampant within a team. Socially, even within the most aware organizations, a belief of "us versus them" betterment may be in place. When a win is more about one person or a small group of people needing to be right, it's a red flag that the shadow side of ego is in play.

   Consider this example: Dan was a field leader with an enormously talented team. He allowed them to run projects and sites without interruption, which should have made his team feel empowered. However, Dan liked to ride in like a knight on a white horse and offer the perfect solution in front of senior leadership and wipe away anything the team has done. The light shone solely on Dan, and the team knew he was an egomaniac. Ultimately, the senior leader needed to remind Dan that while he was in charge, making the solutions all about him and not working with the team through the process made him look self-serving and diminished his talented team. Unfortunately, Dan never could allow himself to be part of the process and a guardian of the team. It was always all about him. Ultimately, Dan parted ways with the organization because he could never fully embrace the kindness he was asked to display. In fact, it baffled him.

> **Be generous.** Allowing others to grow and shine is one interpretation of this concept. As in the preceding example, Dan just couldn't handle anyone growing or shining except himself. Another example of generosity is extending yourself to those around you in order to make others feel nurtured. I know this principle sounds fluffy, but here's the thing: If you know what someone needs (like encouragement or to be included or given a shred of hope), isn't it the kind thing to do? It costs you absolutely nothing but a bit of your time. Ask your peers and staff what they need and how you can support them. I don't mean that you should do everything for them, but give them what they need to excel.

> **Be diligent.** Preserving the rights of others in your pursuit of personal and professional accomplishment isn't often discussed, but nonetheless it's part of the code of a values-based leader. Violating the rights of others comes down to a few basic questions: Are you violating their freedom, environment, ability to make a living, or safety? Basically, many of these issues are part of most companies' human resources guidelines in their most basic interpretation. A leader is required to consider the ramifications of their decisions and actions on others. Kindness and common sense are the tools.
>
> Here are some examples: During a blizzard, staff shouldn't be required to risk their safety to get into the office. Avoid placing the production of products in areas that allow toxic dumping that pollutes homes, either in the United States or abroad. Those examples are pretty obvious. Additionally, you may have seen a leader who holds production or orders over a vendor's head to bend the vendor to their will; that's a violation of dignity and the right to make a living. Engaging with resources that use child labor is also a violation of law and consciousness. Instead, the kind and diligent path is to find resources that negotiate fairly, treat their own teams in accordance with the law, and allow all parties to profit from their work together.

We can roll out our yoga mats. Spend hours in meditation. Pray. Take a silent retreat. Fast. These are all worthy practices that are very personal and fulfilling. It's time to take that goodness into business to create an environment that will allow capitalism to flourish, being ethical and fair to all. In selflessness and kindness, we find a platform that will spur mutual respect and commitment to follow the leader.

Many years ago, I worked for an amazing leader. He was without a doubt one of the best living, breathing examples of kindness I'd ever witnessed in big business. He operated under the belief that everyone has the capacity to exceed his expectations and that every team member should win in the process, and he made sure wages and hiring practices were fair. Milestones, accomplishments, and successes were celebrated. He milled around the cubicles getting to know each person in this triple-digit-million-dollar organization and was always willing to offer encouragement or a joke.

KINDNESS AROUND THE WORLD

Specific spiritual belief systems aren't necessary to impart kindness into your leadership; however, it's a principle expressed in nearly every faith:

- In **Judaism,** *chesed* is a word that implies kindness. *Chesed* is established as part of the four human behaviors to be expressed through good deeds, hospitality, generosity, and service to others.
- **Christianity** describes kindness as the core of living. It means to do good to others in thought, word, and deed. Kindness is universal, comprehensive, and spiritual in nature.
- The **Muslim** faith teaches that in the end there is only kindness and that there is always a reward for kindness to every living thing.
- From the Four Immeasurables of **Buddhism,** kindness is the practice of wanting all beings to well, happy, and cared for, as well as teaching them something so they may be able to care for themselves. *Metta* is the term used for kindness.

Note: Please don't feel like you must have a spiritual practice to express kindness to others. Kindness is simply an expression of respect and compassion for other human beings. Each person can express kindness in their own way.

This man was so loved by his team that it was inspirational. He made all of us want to be better leaders — leaders like him — not only because he was so kind to everyone but also because he was able to make tough decisions when necessary. With his genuine expressions of kindness and business sense, he was able to pull a division out of the depths of failure, restoring it to a thriving entity again. His ceaseless generosity inspired others to work harder and stay on the course he laid out, even through dark, ugly times. During any shift, things can indeed get messy, but even during those tough times, he never wavered in his commitment to kindness. *It is under the greatest adversity that there exists the greatest potential for doing good both for one's self and others* is a sage insight from the Dalai Lama.

WARNING: The integration of kindness should be seamless, graceful, and without fanfare. When it's not, you'll be at risk of looking as if you're seeking attention for yourself. Just embody kindness without the desire for acknowledgment.

Fitting Values-Based Leadership into the Big Picture

To embrace all the attributes and components of values-based leadership, you need to complete the establishment of a certain mindset: clarifying how and where the concepts of kindness and selflessness reside within your organization will be helpful. Think of them as resource centers that fit together like puzzle pieces. Each is an integral part of the organization. They all must operate in conjunction with one another seamlessly. When a team is aligned under a mandate of values with a complementary mission, you have harnessed something very powerful.

If you can see the big picture first, it will be easier for you to embrace our journey together. It will also make it easier for you to jump from section to section more easily. This section is your map of how to weave VBL into everything you do.

REMEMBER The concept of VBL isn't stagnant. It's a fully integrated model for you to act on once established. Saying one of your highest values is "innovation" without installing the value throughout the organization is a rose dying on the vine. Also, you'll have some pretty unhappy stakeholders. Today's workforce is savvy. If they think you're being hypocritical, they will be more than happy to tell you, anyone you're trying to recruit, and probably your customers, too. Follow this motto: Be clear. Be seamless. Be authentic. In other words, say what you believe, do what you believe.

Thinking of your company as a living thing

Your organization is a living and breathing organism. It requires four essential components to survive: a healthy environment, nurturing/development, sustainability, and cooperation/serving. How will you feed that organism so it continues to thrive? How do you keep it alive? Do you fertilize only one part of the pot? Do you suppress the fruit it would like to expose to the world or encourage it? Would you leave the plant in the pot long after it's grown too big or replant it into a larger garden?

Most people who have a minimum of gardening experience would tell you that the way to grow healthy plants is to do the following:

- » Plant in good soil (environment)
- » Fertilize equally (nurturing/development)
- » Provide sunlight and water (sustainability)
- » Transplant into a larger area/garden as needed (cooperation/serving)

REMEMBER: Ultimately, the plant thrives in its new space. That plant generates even more fruit that can be shared. Therefore, the plant serves more people. Business isn't all that different. Creating a positive environment, nurturing and sustaining your people and resources, and investing in those people make a business work.

Snapping the puzzle pieces together

You may well be a feeling, emotional human being, but I also would like you to see VBL as a business proposition — the animation of what you believe is important, which also creates profitability. Figure 3-1 shows you the puzzle pieces that, when snapped together, can create an organization that can be reflective of your values fully. It provides the overview of the four areas that can be permeated with values.

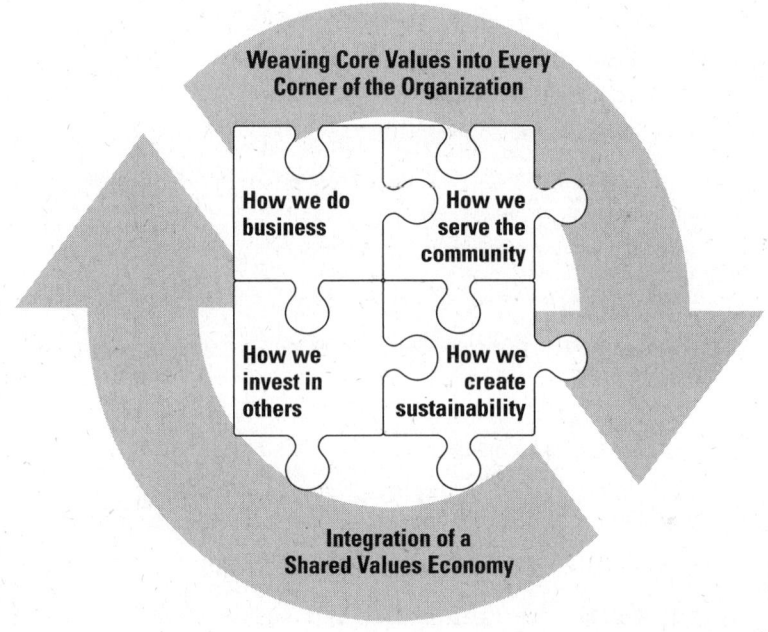

FIGURE 3-1: Weaving core values into every part of your organization.

Weaving Core Values into Every Corner of the Organization

- How we do business
- How we serve the community
- How we invest in others
- How we create sustainability

Integration of a Shared Values Economy

© John Wiley & Sons, Inc.

The following are some examples of the animation within each area. They are by no means the only applications.

Relating these puzzle pieces to the analogy of a living organism in the preceding section:

>> How we do business is the capacity the healthy environment built on mutual respect (see Chapters 7 and 9).

- » How we serve and impact the community (locally and globally) is a representation of cooperation and serving (see Chapter 4).
- » How we invest in others illustrates both nurturing and sustainability (see Chapters 6 and 7).
- » How we become sustainable in business creation depends on elements and outcomes of the prior three areas.

How we do business:

- » Establishing the rules of engagement — values statement (see Chapters 11 and 12)
- » Creating an authentic company culture (see Chapters 6, 7, and 9)
- » Creating a healthy workplace (see Chapter 9)
- » Developing relationships with vendors and resources (see Chapter 4)

How we serve the community:

- » Philanthropic corporate social responsibility (CSR; see Chapter 4)
- » Economic corporate social responsibility (see Chapter 4)
- » Defining the meaning in the everyday minutia (see Chapters 4, 11, 12, and 16)
- » Supporting our own stakeholders' families with fair wages (see Chapters 14 and 15)

How we invest in others:

- » Recruiting and retaining the best talent (see Chapters 14 and 17)
- » Establishing a culture of learning (see Chapters 14 and 15)
- » Creating values partnerships with vendors and resources (see Chapter 10)
- » Offering human resource programs and initiatives (see Chapters 14 and 15)

How we create sustainability:

- » Encouraging creative problem solving (see Chapters 4, 11, 12, and 18)
- » Reinventing processes and business models (see Chapters 4 and 18)
- » Addressing global human needs (see Chapters 4 and 18)
- » Circling back around to investment, serving, and how we do business

Each of these areas represents a mindset shift opportunity for you. Consider the whole, the individuals you work with, and the lives you can affect beyond your own physical space. These are your direct impact opportunities as a values-based leader.

> **TIP:** On a sticky note write down three or four of these bullet points that are of most interest to you. Perhaps you've got some of these down pat — others, not so much. This list will serve as a priority list for your own education and development. Feel free to scan the table of contents to find those areas in this book that dive more deeply into those possibilities.

Assessing Your Command and Control Temperament

Contrary to everything so far in this chapter is the command and control mindset that has existed in leadership for decades. Businesses ran with a command and control form of leadership, which meant that whatever the top dog(s) said, went. There was little or no discussion. To put it simply, you just did what you were told and didn't make waves.

The entry of GenXers and Millennials into the workplace caused a major disruption to this methodology, as detailed in Chapter 2. Doing what they're told is usually not part of these demographics' makeup. They're free-thinkers and creatives and want to take responsibility for what they're doing. A misconception is that they will blame others or deflect responsibility, but this is untrue. The drive to take responsibility is just one piece that helped propel values-based leadership into play. They seek meaning and impact in their work.

Part of the challenges with many command and control forms of leadership is that they're based on egotistical practices. The leaders are the end-all, be-all experts on every subject. Everyone looks to them to get everyone marching in one direction, without questioning anything or allowing contribution to the process. Failure is not an option, ever. Results are the only objective, and usually leadership is built on individuals who would exercise policies and implement plans. Command and control is very limiting to the growth of business. As we continue to ride through the age of technology and information, it's nearly impossible to stay so cloistered yet be competitive in the market.

Command and control absolutely has an important leadership role within society. Our military and law enforcement are based on a command and control model. Let's face it: We certainly don't want military personnel coloring outside the lines of literal life-and-death commands. It is *control* of something extremely dangerous. Rightfully, command and control leadership in these cases ensures safety and order.

But in business there needs to be a careful balance within the leadership of enforcing policy but allowing for creativity and following compliance requirements that keep stakeholders safe without reducing them to mindless robots moving on conveyor belts from task to task.

We all possess some level of desire for control — one needs to when leading a group of people anywhere. *Control enthusiasts* may take things a bit too far, though. Too much of a good thing can turn bad, fast. Do you lean toward command and control? Find out with these questions:

- Do you need to be the center of attention in your organization at all times?
- Would you prefer people to simply say yes rather than challenge you?
- Do you consciously or unconsciously shut people down when they disagree?
- Would you prefer to make all the decisions yourself?
- Do you find yourself wondering why you have to include anyone at all in decisions?

TACTICAL PEARLS OF WISDOM

Growing up as a daughter of a New York City detective, I was highly trained in command and control. My sister, my two brothers, and I often operated like a SWAT team when something had to get done. My parents would give us a task such as cleaning the house. The plan would be laid out, and everyone would be assigned a specific set of chores. No questions. No amendments. And certainly no whining. Then it was go time. We'd clean that house from top to bottom in a matter of hours, often imitating an actual SWAT team in our motions for our amusement. The success of our mission was tied into how well we all did our jobs. If one fell short, we all fell short. When we did well, we all did well. The reward: ice cream or a movie.

To this day, I still "plan a mission" every time I have a task to accomplish or project to break down, complete with diagrams — much to others' dismay. I do ask for input. Command and control may be limiting, but it offers some extremely useful tools and lessons: When running a team, being able to break down massive projects into bite-sized pieces is an art form. This helps people feel safe if you don't suffocate them with detail. Instilling in your team that you all win together promotes collaboration. Understand that each contribution contributes to the whole. One part can't exist without the others. These lessons are worth taking with you on your journey. There's always something good to be learned in any situation.

If you answered yes to all of these questions, then yes, you're a command and control leader. If you answered yes to two or three, you're at risk of being a command and control leader. If you've answered yes to one or two, it's time to consider whether you may be limiting the expansion of your organization. Armed with your results, turn to Part 2 to help you reconsider your approach to leadership.

Following the Path Cut by Other Leadership Influencers

Several different influencing methodologies and philosophies have led up to the shift in our consciousness in business and, in fact, in the world in general. We didn't just wake up one day and think: I'm going to be loving and compassionate in everything I do. The light didn't shine down from on high illuminating a pathway. The change of perception and the application of new beliefs take time to evolve within people's exchanges. Each has contributed to our ability to reframe who we are as humans working in a business environment with others. New contributing factors always come into play, acting as disruptors to what we believe is true and changing our perceptions. Here I illuminate one widely known influencing theory, Emotional Intelligence, and perhaps a less mainstream thought process, Global Leadership Theory:

» **Emotional Intelligence (EQ):** We can look toward the Emotional Intelligence (EQ) work by Daniel Goleman as a strong rudder that has brought us down this path. EQ taught us how to consider our emotional responses to stress and examine the effect they have on those around us. Goleman's research suggested that those who register a higher EQ have consistently been more successful than those who don't. In effect, it has been a way to evaluate one's leadership effect on creating happiness, empathy, resilience, and mindfulness — or not. Goleman's work helps individuals identify the strengths and weakness of how they engage with others. That awareness, in my opinion, has been a large contributor of the demise of the command and control form of leadership described earlier.

» **Global Leadership Theory (GTL):** GTL is a leadership framework developed to navigate many cultures and create a collaborative community despite cultural value differences. The research of Geert Hofstede narrows down more than 40 attributes that create any culture. Each culture prioritizes different attributes slightly differently. This illustrates how disconnects can happen within a global workforce. But the fundamental belief is that everyone, from every culture, has something to contribute and can create an

> innovative problem-solving environment despite these potentially differing priorities. Globalization of the workforce amplifies the need to find solutions and work together seamlessly.
>
> Wise leaders know that this cultural common ground is a *necessity* — not something that would just be a nice thing to establish. Despite fringe political movements of nationalism around the globe, we simply won't be able to stop the globalization of the workforce. The digital era of connectivity has forever changed the workforce. Immigration restrictions and limitations will have a hard time keeping up the integration of international and remote stakeholder workplaces.

When we honestly appraise ourselves, bossing people around is obviously counterproductive to improving productivity. When I consulted with companies a few years ago, they often argued that productivity is what's important because it generates the income to pay everyone. And I completely get that. But it took time for leaders to understand that constructing a healthy work environment and mindset toward the work at hand actually improves productivity. It was worth it for them to work on their EQ and see what would happen. The result? As people were given the tools to improve communication with others, production increased, and happiness — yes, happiness — increased tremendously. Happy people are productive people. Period. As Eleanor Roosevelt said, "Happiness isn't a goal. It's a by-product of a life well lived."

WARNING Scowl and pooh-pooh this concept at your own peril. People who are happy have been shown to be more productive than unhappy people, and happy leaders are more likely to create happiness in their organizations.

IN THIS CHAPTER

» Understanding how perception drives your outlook on business

» Evolving corporate social responsibility initiative practices

» Integrating the resolution of social problems into a new business model

Chapter 4
Reframing Your Perception of Business

Perception is a very powerful force. What we believe to be true is, in fact, true to us in our lives. It may not be truth to others, but to us, we'd stake our lives on it, depending on the depth of emotion evoked by the subject. Perception is a filter — the pair of glasses we view the world through. It colors meaning and context and triggers an emotional response.

The limbic system of the brain governs emotions. Emotions are a very primal part of who we are. We distill context and meaning through past emotional experiences, and when we accept them as truth, they're subconsciously imprinted on our reactions and behaviors. It's visceral. It just happens. Sometimes it's outwardly apparent, but sometimes it's not. It's internal.

It's important to know two things:

» People can have varied responses to the same stimuli, so don't be surprised.

» Your own emotional responses are dictated by a prior experience or framing.

For example, when I teach people about emotional responses within the limbic system, I often project an image of a large green snake on the presentation screen. Immediately a response happens in the room. Several people physically draw back in their seats. Others gasp. Some are neutral. Others smile as if they were looking at a cute little kitten. The response is predetermined by the memory of an experience, interaction, or belief that has been stored within the limbic system. Not all people digest and store information the same way.

Those who gasp or draw back in their chair may have had a bad experience personally or learned that snakes were dangerous. The message was *Run!* They don't have to think about it; they immediately react with a negative emotion. Our neutral friends may have had similar or the same exposure but didn't internalize it — they just saw it as more information that's good to know and may save their lives someday. The cuddly kitten people — well, they may have grown up handling snakes. The emotions ingrained in their limbic systems could be that snakes are freaking awesome and fascinating, and make great pets. Yes, such a varied response.

We have the option to reframe our perceptions at any time through awareness, education, reframing the context, and having a different experience. Knowing that an emotional response is built into the primitive side of your brain helps explain why, at times, it can become a powerful visceral force in your attitudes.

REMEMBER

The questions to ask yourself are *why* and *what. Why* are you reacting to certain situations with an almost knee-jerk reaction? *What* is the story that you've accepted as truth that would create this response? Think about those questions in response to how you or your team may be feeling about business today.

In this chapter, I describe the two main parts of reframing your perception of business:

>> Discovering what you may have internalized without knowing it: a potentially negative reputation for big businesses, corporations, and/or major institutions

>> Shifting to a view of the shared values economy (SVE), in which business changes lives for the better

Unraveling the Bad Reputation of Business

Unfortunately, *business* has gotten a very bad reputation. This isn't new. Still, it saddens me when I read or watch media coverage espousing that businesses are greedy, dirty, or unethical, or when some activist rallies against "the man" by refusing to purchase from corporations. Sometimes the complaints even come from those employed by corporations, who enjoy paychecks generated by decent companies doing their best to operate fairly. It never ceases to amaze me that there is such a vast misunderstanding of the value business brings not only to its customers but also to the communities where it operates. Clearly there have been influencers who have informed this belief about corporations. However, I, the eternal optimist, believe that business is and can continue to be a positive force in this world.

Additionally, some individuals contend that corporate businesses are bent on destroying small businesses and taking advantage of workers. It is unfortunate that media coverage of some corrupt business practices has tainted much of the rest of the business community. Those who are doing well and operating ethically are nevertheless often maligned. Negative emotions around the perception of business have become deeply embedded in the limbic systems of many people.

We can choose to understand the true purpose of commerce in society, or we can throw it away. I'm opting to help people reframe their perception of the business community, and by that I mean *all* businesses. Big. Small. Medium. Mega-sized. Understanding that business can enrich many people and their communities is important, as the following sections show. The world needs leadership that will embrace business and scale it to new heights.

REMEMBER

In the current demographic makeup of our workforce, stakeholders seek meaning. Those who will become values-based leaders seek to understand how to mobilize this meaning productively.

De-villainizing mega-corporations

Business is the only structure that can not only materialize but also scale capitalism. The role of commerce and business in society is to create opportunities for others — plain and simple.

Recently a Starbucks opened in my bucolic Brooklyn neighborhood. For years, the central business initiative (CBI) refused to allow any retail chains on the main shopping drag, but slowly they began to appear. It took many years, but a Dunkin Donuts finally opened, followed by a Subway a few blocks down. The community tolerated it, even if many weren't happy to see big-name franchise stores moving in. Old-timers muttered that the area was going to rack and ruin with these big-name stores.

The tipping point was the new Starbucks that moved in above the train stop. For the first couple of months, I'd noticed only a handful of brave souls venturing in daily — usually to the jeers of locals telling them they were horrible people for supporting a mega-corporation. The protests were never organized, but the insults and jeers became steady. One day a man stood at the bus stop alongside the Starbucks with a sign that said, "You should be ashamed. Support small business, not corporate greed." One woman — one of my more colorful, vocal neighbors — shouted, "Hey, these kids working here have jobs so they can pay for their college educations. Most of the small businesses can't support enough staff for them to fulfill their dreams. So shut up!"

I smiled. Not so much that the exchange got inflamed, but that this woman, in her own way, was able to express the real role of business in society. Mind you, I don't mean to say that small businesses don't contribute to employment, but their capacity can be limited until they become established. They still make very valid contributions in measure as they scale. It takes time.

Starbucks is also a very interesting target for some of the hatred being tossed at them. The company has a robust corporate social responsibility (CSR) platform that includes 99 percent ethically sourced coffee, the creation of a global network of farm support centers, green footprints for store build-outs, and the contribution of millions of hours of volunteerism to community services. Additionally, through a partnership with Arizona State University, Starbucks provides tuition reimbursement toward a bachelor's degree for all full- and part-time employees. They continue to add to their social responsibility footprint by addressing the environmental impact of their cups, using renewable energy, and establishing a food rescue program. (See `https://globalassets.starbucks.com/assets/9265e80751db48398b88bdf09821cc56.pdf` for more information.)

I personally want to support such a business because of these attributes. Of course, I also support my local Italian *officine alimentari* where I can still get a shot of espresso that reminds me of my grandmother's house. There's a place for both. And both businesses, within their own ability to scale big or small, create jobs. Jobs create opportunities for people's lives. That's why scalability is important to our conversation. The more a company can scale, the more jobs and opportunities it creates. This is perhaps a reframing of the way you may have considered expansion and growth in your prior organization.

Peeking into a government-affiliated business

Government-sponsored endeavors often rely on taxes, tariffs, or other ways of procuring working capital, but they may be subject to regulations and restrictions that often have them operating at a loss. I don't mean that government agencies can't create opportunities for people through job creation. They can participate in the cycle of commerce, but their ability to scale is limited.

The United States Postal Services (USPS) illustrates the challenges of many government-run agencies. Although it has an enormous national reach by providing nationwide mailing and shipping services, it's also subject to restrictions on those services. For example, it can't increase service fees at a faster pace than the Consumer Price Index-All Urban Customer (CPI-U), a measure of consumer price inflation published by the Bureau of Labor Statistics. This restriction creates a pricing ceiling for the USPS that can't be breached, even if its costs increase faster than the CPI. Such restrictions represent a cap on roughly 90 percent of USPS revenue sources (which are the fees paid by customers). The USPS, unfortunately, is an example of the restrictions placed on government-run agencies that, conceptually, have the potential to scale but in practice can't because of their government-related nature. As a result, the USPS lost money in six out of the ten years from 2001 through 2010.

Although the USPS may be limited in its ability to scale, it is clear about its participation in commerce. The 2009 United States Postal Services Future Business Model (available at `https://about.usps.com/future-business-model/mccannslentz.pdf`) includes the following impact statement. I applaud the ability of USPS to be fully aware of its impact in the marketplace:

1. Direct Impact of the Postal Service

   The Postal Service has a direct financial impact in two fundamental ways. First, this year it will generate nearly $70 billion in revenue and $75 billion in expenditures. This translates into about $55 billion in salary and benefits, and $20 billion in other costs. That money will be paid to employees, contractors and vendors who will spend it in their home communities, creating more income for other businesses and jobs for other workers. Second, the Postal Service directly impacts the economy through the delivery of bills, packages and advertising that facilitates commerce, creating sales, income for businesses, and wages for employees. One measure of impact: One out of every 200 workers in the U.S. is a postal employee.

   Source: Department of Labor (2009) at `www.dol.gov`. 140 million workers in the U.S. and 656,000 postal employees.

REMEMBER

Government entities can play a part in the cycle of commerce and can create opportunities for others, but because of their limitations, they're not scalable in the way commercial businesses are; they can scale to increase their capital reach. It's therefore in our best interest to encourage business growth as much as possible. As a leader, you play a large role in this process. This is a critical concept for you to grasp. It's one of the most important concepts of values-based leadership (VBL). When you can fully embrace that business is a vehicle for good — for the enrichment of others and for those who work in business — you'll never rally against another business again, not even subconsciously. You'll also never look at how you run your own organization again without considering the impact of what you do every single day.

TIP: I implore you to impress what I'm about to share with you on all your stakeholders. Pull out a sticky note and write simple reminder of the role of commerce in society: *to create opportunities for others.* Place it in your work notebook or as a screensaver on your work device. Never, ever forget it. This is the ultimate mission for all businesses.

Creating opportunity as a business practice

Businesses provide goods and services to consumers. Sometimes these are essential items such as food, clothing, and fuel. Other times these are goods and services that make someone's life easier or more enjoyable: takeout delivery food, dry cleaning, electronic devices, or apps that identify star constellations to your child as you look up at the night sky together. The sky's the limit on what a business can provide, but the core is still the same: creating opportunities for others. Consider the far-reaching effect that one salary can create, shown in Table 4-1.

TABLE 4-1 Opportunity Ripple Illustration

Business Exchange	Immediate Opportunity Application	Ripple Opportunity Application	Far-Reaching Opportunity
Mary works for a company, ABC Corporation, from which she receives a paycheck.	Mary can provide a home for her family.	Mary spends money on housing, which supports the builders and other craftspeople to sustain their families.	The builder scales his business and creates more jobs.
	Mary can purchase high-quality foods.	Mary supports her local CSA (community service agriculture).	The CSA expands and is able to serve more people.
	Mary can provide healthcare for her family.	Dr. Glick is Mary's children's pediatrician. Her payments allow Dr. Glick to pay off her student loans.	Dr. Glick is able to move to a rural community and serve those individuals without a debt weighing her down.
	Mary can educate and/or train her children.	Mary's three children make their way in the world. Sarah buys a pig farm and creates a new artisan, compassionately raised pork product for the market. Joe becomes an architect who creates new homes. Justine is a dental hygienist who helps people maintain their oral health.	Sarah creates jobs and supports sustainable product production. Joe provides a safe place to raise families. Justine helps people stay healthy and reduce health costs.

REMEMBER

As you can see in Table 4-1, the chain of opportunity ripple is nearly endless in its generation of opportunities that come from a simple exchange that takes place in a commerce relationship. Mary's single paycheck has an everlasting effect beyond providing for Mary's immediate needs. Often, we don't consider the far-reaching impact a job has on our community. What you do everyday matters in the lives of those who work for you and those whom *they* engage with through commerce for everything they want or need in their lives. Remind yourself and your team of this — often. I bet you'll never look at your own paycheck, and where you're spending it, in the same way ever again.

Changing Lives in the Shared Values Economy

The *shared values economy* (SVE) is the principle that the opportunity created by a business transaction extends further down the economic chain. It is, in fact, a business model, one that moves beyond giving time, energy, ideas, and capital to creating a sustainable environment. *Sustainability* is one of those words that's become an overused marketing term — it gets batted around until it's at risk of losing its impact. But sustainability is part of a business model that allows opportunities within your organization to create a profit center in an underserved level of the market. It's the remarkable ability to harness capitalism to resolve a social issue. It's another expression of kindness and compassion in action.

In the following sections, I discuss the evolution of corporate social responsibility into the shared values economy.

Evolving corporate social responsibility initiatives

Corporate social responsibility (CSR) is an approach based on the belief that people in a position of authority have a duty, if you will, to give back, motivate, assist, or help others around them. It's not limited just to authority figures but also extends to members of the corporations, associations, and many other types of organizations who also share the belief in that the same societal rule. CSR initiatives have been deployed to fight human sex trafficking, prevent polluted water, curtail causes of cancer, address problems in education, and on and on. These initiatives are usually funded by freebies, donations, or the discounting of products by businesses. Unfortunately, CSR initiatives often only make a dent in solving many social issues. They often run out of money before the problem has been eradicated. However, according to the 2016 PwC Global CEO Survey (https://www.pwc.com/gx/en/ceo-survey/2016/landing-page/pwc-19th-annual-global-ceo-survey.pdf), 64 percent of all CEOs are planning on continuing to invest in CSR because it is key to building trust with their customers and staff.

From a marketing perspective, CSR initiatives help create loyal customers. People have a deep desire to be part of a movement. Shoppers will be loyal to a brand if it supports a cause they believe in, even if the product or service costs a little more. The sacrifice is worth it to them. They will recommend brands to friends because of a company's CSR. Consumers have learned that their dollar has impact far beyond the purchase of a product.

WARNING Attaching meaning to your brand or product can produce amazing results when it's done authentically. When it's clearly a marketing ploy, though, customers and watchdogs will sniff that out in a heartbeat.

CSR has a direct correlation to how an organization impacts the community, which can be local or global. The CSR movement created a philanthropic platform as well as a means for companies to address social and environmental issues and to give back to the communities that have supported them. However, many companies struggle with consistency: Initiatives are run by different leaders across the organization, and sometimes the diffusion of various initiatives dilutes the overall set purpose and mission. Results are fractured.

REMEMBER CSR can play a very important role for a company when it's structured, maintained, and developed within a coherent portfolio of initiatives aligned with the overall mission. The CSR model is evolving into a fully integrated model where what we do can dovetail with impacting other communities. The giving is no longer just philanthropic — it's the integration of business and the fulfillment of human needs for those at the base of the economic ladder.

The concept of *philanthropy* is and always will be essential to our society. And building a business that allows people to sustain their own lives plus have a social impact is what's driving the triple bottom line: social, financial, and environmental.

Let's now look beyond Mary's paycheck and the USPS to the development of a shared values economy.

Reinventing new profit centers to meet human needs

The basic premise of SVE is to use the resources of a company to create new profit centers. These profit centers then create an economic opportunity for workers that help meet their human needs. Michael E. Porter and Mark R. Kramer of Harvard Business School, experts on SVE, argue that work and social impact no longer operate in separate arenas. They need to be integrated to be sustainable. The SVE marries the triple bottom line (social, financial, and environmental). SVE promotes this integration in order to have a positive impact — and, by the way, make a profit so it's sustainable. That means the SVE doesn't rely on donations or volunteerism.

Porter and Kramer point to three areas to consider when attempting to build this aspect of your larger business model:

- **Reconceiving products and marketplaces:** Finding opportunities at the bottom of the markets to expand upon
- **Redefining productivity:** Improving yields or streamlining processes
- **Building clusters:** Enhancing relationships with vendors, suppliers, and so on all located in a single location or supporting a specific product

These three avenues are not new to business growth, but their application is a bit different when the outcome isn't just for profits but also to help resolve social and environmental issues. For example, Nestlé sought to improve the yield of coffee from its farmers. To do so, the company reverse-engineered its thought process. The farmers were trapped in a cycle of low productivity due to environmental impacts. Nestlé deployed experts to help educate the farmers on how to improve the quality of their product without compromising the environment. The farmers developed a sustainable income that broke the poverty cycle. Nestlé had a quality product it could sell and compete with in the marketplace and satisfied its triple bottom line objective. By resolving Nestlé's issue and including the farmers in the solution, all parties have increased opportunities. All parties won.

Refer to Table 4-1 and think about Nestlé's scenario. That same reach is now providing to the farmers, their families, and their community. It's a beautiful, eloquent way to address social issues. Although SVE isn't necessarily the easiest route, it fulfills a company's desire to be a positive influence in the world — and a community's desire for a better future.

The SVE isn't about ingraining values, per se. It's more of a mindset and attitude of sharing within the business model rather than outside of the literal business model. Whereas CSR is an added program, SVE is an integration that becomes an overarching desire to create a ceaseless cycle of opportunity for each person involved in the process. As such, it's a further demonstration of the principle of kindness that informs values-based leadership. Porter and Kramer believe that SVE is a strategy that will be part of many companies' business plans within the next five to ten years. SVE is being viewed as a tool to foster creative thinking, innovation, and new business ideas. It's possible. Feel free to do the research on both thought processes and choose for yourself.

For much more on the SVE concept, check out Porter and Kramer's works on the Shared Value Initiative's website at www.sharedvalue.org.

2
Becoming a Values-Based Leader

IN THIS PART . . .

Orient yourself to become a values-based leader. Establish the groundwork with essential principles (like the four levels of leadership) and attributes to chart your journey.

Understand the nuances in how you will evolve as a values-based leader. Nurture the four attributes of a VBL leader: self-reflection, grace, agility, and responsible influence.

Accept that the shift in creating a values-based environment must first come from you before anyone else can follow. Get to know the correlation between building trust and your ability to be trusted by those who work for and with you.

Avoid the pitfalls, minefields, and difficulties involved in bringing your team along on the shift.

IN THIS CHAPTER

» Uncovering the four levels of leadership

» Assessing your current leadership level and how to proceed

Chapter 5
Before You Get There: Knowing Where You Are as a Leader

Sometimes people will jump into a process with both feet as quickly as they can. I equate this to getting your first bike. It was both exciting and scary. Still, you probably jumped on, tried to pedal, and then tipped over and hit the ground with a loud thump. It wasn't the best introduction to the concept of adventuring out on your bike. You may have even been a little wary of trying again. But with encouragement and a helper's hand on the seat, you steadied yourself enough until you could ride, enjoying a sense of freedom you hadn't felt before. Exhilarating, thrilling, and the entry point for fun throughout the years.

Learning how to get up on the bike properly to propel it forward is one step. But knowing where you're going is another. When we were young, it really didn't matter. We just pedaled away until dusk when we were called in for dinner. As an adult, it's quite a different story.

In this chapter, I roll out a map for you to see what your options for leadership development can be. At any point, you can change course and alter your goals. In fact, I think that will probably be an option to seriously consider. Before you arrived here, in this place within this book, you may have had only an inkling of your level of leadership. Or perhaps you weren't familiar with the terms I'm about to discuss. This is your opportunity to quickly place yourself into a map, assess your resources and needs, and follow the general planning for your adventure into values-based leadership (VBL).

Planning Your Adventure into Different Levels of Leadership

Two people are about to go on a trip to Paris. They can't wait to see the Eiffel Tower, stroll through the Musee d'Orsay on the Seine River, and buy French tea at Mariage Freres in the Marais. They will avoid the tourist scene at the Louvre and Sacre-Coeur this time around. They want to live like Parisians during this trip. Therefore, a stop at the world-famous Poilane bakery on Rue de Cherche Midi is a must. There they will enjoy those little *punitions* or little butter cookies they call "punishments" (the punishment is having to wait for them to cool before eating them). For many months the destination has been researched. Lists have been made for the great trip that will be taken and the memories that will be created. Our travelers, Maggie and Marcel, can't wait to leave.

Maggie is leaving from New York. Marcel is in Provence. Their maps to Paris will be different. Maggie maps out her journey: taxi to JFK airport, flight to Charles de Gaulle, and another taxi to the hotel where she will meet Marcel. He will walk to the train station in his town, take an express train to Paris, and cab it to the hotel.

The destination itself is an amazing goal, but the map for getting to that goal is even more important. Different "travelers" will leave from different spots to arrive at the goal. If you don't know where you're standing, how can you get where you want to go? It isn't enough to say, "Well, I'll just wing it." In the example of Maggie, I highly doubt winging it would get her across the ocean and into central Paris. Marcel, who is geographically closer to the destination, may have more success more quickly, but to plan any adventure, in travel or business, you have to know where you're standing before you start. You can assess your assets, resources, and time tables before moving forward. Armed with that information, it's much easier to map out the ways and means to get where you want to go.

So where do you want to go? What kind of leader do you want to be? Ultimately, what is it that you want to achieve through the vehicle of business? In the following sections, I show you the leadership trajectory, delve into the four levels of leadership, and explain whether charisma is critical for leadership.

Introducing the leadership trajectory

There is a direct correlation between the level of leadership a person achieves and the impact they can have on the world. This is your opportunity to gauge the effect you'd like to have through your work. We all have impact in some way or another — sometimes positive, sometimes negative. In each level of leadership there are positive attributes as well as blind spots. That's the principle of *polarity:* the state of having two contradictory, oppositional attributes. Which one becomes the dominant marker on your leadership is entirely up to you.

Figure 5-1 illustrates the four levels of leadership (Spark, Inspire, Elevate, and Enrich, all covered in detail later in this chapter) and their corresponding level of impact (short-term, middle-term, or long-term):

» A short-term impact is felt immediately, no matter which level of leadership you embody. It affects the team in the moment. When you inspire people to do a better job by creating a path for them to complete a project, they are happy and motivated. However, without building on that immediate euphoria and fulfillment, the momentum can sputter and stall out.

» The middle term, or interim legacy, is when your reputation as a leader is built based on the performance of your team and your ability to create a resilient organization. Elevating and enriching others is the path to achieving longevity.

» The long-term effect creates impact across multiple generations. The organization is a living, thriving organism. The leadership creates ways and means to impact the lives of others by shattering the norm to create resiliency and social impact on a grand scale.

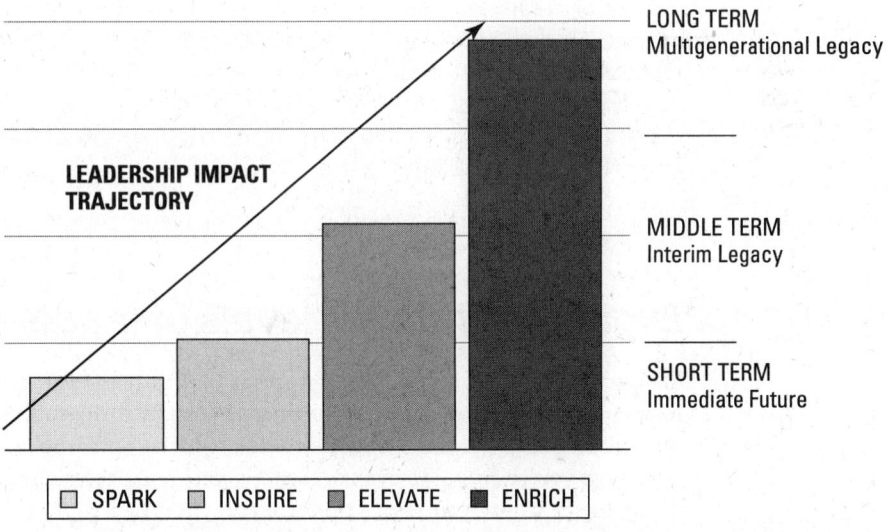

FIGURE 5-1: Leadership trajectory.

© *John Wiley & Sons, Inc.*

The potential impact of each level of leadership becomes clearer as you move through this chapter. Consider where you may be residing now. Where and how are you impacting the team and the organization currently? Are you in the immediate punch of creating an impact but haven't yet incorporated some components into your repertoire? Perhaps you already know how to inspire others but lack the ability or the desire to move to the next level. Or maybe a high-level impact scares the heck out of you and you can't see yourself there, ever. Perfection isn't the goal; clarity is.

TIP

In this section, I'd like you to simply reflect and see where you may be now, then pinpoint where you'd like to be on your trajectory. Decide how much of an impact you want to make, and write it down — for example, use one brightly colored sticky note that says, "Impact level now: short-term; Impact level goal: mid-term, create a career legacy." Leave that note on Figure 5-1.

REMEMBER

You don't have to do all of this alone. The beauty of being a leader is that you can assemble talent to address and bolster each level of leadership required to create a strong, resilient organization.

POLARITY IN EVERYTHING

We are human, and that means we are imperfect beings. We all have blind spots and the capacity to allow our level of leadership to slip into a negative manifestation of itself almost at any time. Polarity exists in everything and everyone. In any given state, both our dark and light sides can exist simultaneously. They may not necessarily operate simultaneously — they may cross over, or go back and forth at times.

The level of leadership you express may be focused within your blind spots rather than a lighter, more constructive part of you. It's where we choose to focus that determines the outward expression of any given quality. Within the four levels of leadership this polarity can also exist, and the impact depth would still be the same. It's fascinating that even leaders who lean more on their blind spots can still create an immediate future, an interim legacy, or a lifetime legacy impact on an organization, community, or even a nation.

Exploring the four levels of leadership

Clearly, some leaders are more effective than others. Sometimes effectiveness happens via dictatorship or force. Other times it's through innovation. In Chapter 6, I discuss in detail the attributes that make up a values-based leader, but right now you're trying to evaluate where you are on the leadership ladder. You're trying to see where you're starting from on your map.

TIP Make sure you identify where you are now and what kind of impact you want to have; see the preceding section for help before getting into the more detailed conversation in this section. Sticky note it!

REMEMBER I want to make it abundantly clear that we're not discussing titles within your organization. We're discussing impact, temperament, actions, and deeds. We're also pinpointing the intersection where values-based leadership integrates within the different levels on the ladder. However, this is not, I repeat, not about positions.

Leaders manifest in roles beyond the CEO. Many leadership schools of thought pin a lot, if not all, on the role of the leader within the organization, plus maybe a small group of captains sprinkled throughout. I believe that this philosophy on the distribution of power is collapsing. The org chart is flattening; power is being distributed across the silos of business. The C-suite may be steering the ship, but other leaders are also necessary. As you see in the command and control model of leadership discussed in Chapter 3, it's nearly impossible for any CEO to be the be-all and end-all in an organization.

The following sections walk you through the four levels of leadership on the trajectory introduced earlier in this chapter:

» Spark

» Inspire

» Elevate

» Enrich

You also find out how each level relates to values-based leadership. Keep an open mind: You are a leader or desire to become one. Making distinctions, understanding where you are in your development, and adjusting are all part of the journey.

Level 1: Spark

Level 1 is characterized by *spark*. These individuals have a lot of great ideas. They are the pioneers who break new ground and lead the way for others. Think of them as the spark that lights a flame that spreads to others. You can find level 1 leaders at every level of business. You see it in entrepreneurs who are creating new businesses and business leaders who are evolving new way of doing business. Sparks love to rush in with new ideas, big or small. Being first is very important to them. They can resolve an immediate issue with their creativity. With their rush of energy, they can enlist many people with their excitement and flash of ingenuity.

Mark Zuckerberg, the founder of Facebook, is just one example of a very successful and highly influential Spark. Fortunately, Zuckerberg surrounded himself with platoons of strong leaders and a variety of skilled staff to make his social media creation a worldwide opportunity for people to connect with one another.

WARNING

The blind spots for Sparks are that they may not take the actions required to bring their ideas into the world, and they may not be able to collaborate with others to make their ideas real. They become frustrated as the flame dies. Disillusioned, they may recruit others into their developing belief that things aren't working out. Or they may simply decide that they prefer not to be a leader at all, that they're happy allowing others to make decisions for them. In worst-case scenarios, they may come to embrace a victim mentality. Their work can feel like drudgery.

The best case would be that Sparks move to the next level of leadership, turning their short-term spark into an actionable plan. Unfortunately, values-based leadership will most likely not even be a consideration for those who remain in this first level. They're moving too fast and ping-ponging too much from one idea to another to implement anything yet. VBL may be one idea they have to better their effectiveness, but it's usually not the priority.

Level 2: Inspire

Level 2 leaders love to inspire others to do, be, and have more than they currently do. They can excite, exhilarate, and tap into the emotions of others to move ideas forward. They're natural encouragers and motivators. When they are in their groove, you will find them championing many initiatives throughout their organizations, providing positive, measured movement to remove hurdles. Level 2 leaders marry ideas and inspiration together with a plan. They create forward movement, excel at execution, and deliver on promises. Staff members often feel hopeful that the future being painted can become reality.

There's something so powerful about a change agent who is brought into an organization to, well, change the direction of the group or launch a new initiative. When they operate from level 2, they inspire everyone around them to believe in the process and the change. They even make everyone understand that the process may get bumpy and a bit ugly and that they may feel like giving up — but that they shouldn't. I have known many leaders who operate masterfully from this level. They inspire, plan, and execute with great precision without being household names or having their own Wikipedia pages. They are just leaders in the trenches facilitating change.

A visible Spark, Muhammad Yunus, crossed into level 2 leadership with the creation of Grameen Bank, pioneering the microloan business model. Yunus put structure and planning around his idea to alleviate poverty by offering microloans to women in Bangladesh. Today Grameen Bank lends to people globally, including 11 cities in the United States. Yunus inspired other microloan opportunities such as Kiva.

WARNING: Talk about a blind spot, though: The level 2 leader can also be a dictator. Dictators have ways to inspire others too — including fear, retribution, creating roadblocks, and holding back important information or resources. They can manipulate others, either directly or by being passive-aggressive, and cause frustration and infighting. One of the key markers of this blind spot is divisive behavior that pits groups, teams, and individuals against one another to cause confusion. In that confusion the level 2 leader becomes the answer or the enforcer who ultimately makes the final decision, elevating them to an even more powerful position within the staff and suppliers' minds. Politics is a place where you see this play out in dramatic fashion. Pick any dictator, autocrat, or kleptocrat — that's who I'm talking about. Yes, these examples are extreme, but they serve as a template for you to consider places you've worked and who these individuals may be in your own work history. These leaders created an interim legacy for themselves — albeit negative to most of the outside world.

Whether positive or negative, the effect on the organization can create an interim legacy. The leader creates a company culture that is lasting. Their impact may span the lifetime of their tenure or beyond, depending on how those around them have been nurtured.

Hopefully, you're not a dictator but rather are someone who's inspirational, skilled, and effective. If so, you're in the realm of leadership that can embrace VBL. You may be using some VBL components but not others, or you may be unsure how to do so. That's fine. Continue to ascend. There are other levels to strive for.

Level 3: Elevate

Level 3 leaders elevate their staff, team, and vendors. They believe everyone can excel and exceed their expectations. This isn't bright-eyed thinking — it's the ability to place trust in individuals to do the right thing, according to the plan and values set forth by the leader. Level 3 leaders prefer working one-on-one with people, sometimes in a coaching role. The personal connection is most important to them, although the focus is always on the entire team winning. These leaders don't get involved with the minutia of growing teams within the company; instead, others are mandated to do so with the full blessing of the leader.

Level 3 leaders embrace VBL principles throughout the organization and can create a larger imprint by doing so. Consider both Mark Zuckerberg and Muhammad Yunus as examples of those who elevate others. In order to scale, they know they need other people to share wisdom and effect change and expansion on a microlevel. For example, Yunus installed the "16 Decisions" not only as an expression of Grameen Bank's mission in the world but also as a variation of the values they wish to express in their work. Have a look at www.grameen.com/16-decisions/.

WARNING

The blind spot for level 3 leaders is that their praise can sometimes be perceived as inauthentic or calculated, and this can breed mistrust regarding their true intentions. Additionally, this leader may foster a culture of competition that becomes destructive and interferes with the growth of the individuals, teams, and potentially the entire organization. Rather than focusing on the whole, some level 3 leaders go within, selfishly sustaining themselves only. They may turn on those closest to them, and in the worse-case scenario, their fans may consider this leader a turncoat who would throw them under the bus at any moment.

Level 4: Enrich

Level 4 leaders are quite unconventional. Sometimes they're characterized as oddballs, misfits, dreamers, or upstarts. They may not be the most polished individuals. Some stumble into the enrichment level of leadership without even knowing it. They're visionaries who may not really know the far-reaching legacy they set in motion. They create enormous impact that shifts or changes a generation, culture, or paradigm. These leaders create cultures or institutions. They may not be recognized in their day as being so influential. Level 4 leaders shy away from celebrity, fanfare, and recognition. Titles and awards aren't very important to them. The classical Chinese philosophy text *Tao Te Ching* refers to this level as *selfless leaders* who show resiliency and unrelenting passion toward the enrichment of people and advancement of a mission as their priority.

Who are these Level 4 leaders? Consider a couple of famous examples:

» Abraham Lincoln, 16th president of the United States, led his country through the Civil War, keeping the nation intact and abolishing slavery — only two examples of his vast influence on American democracy that has lasted until the present day.

» Bill Gates, founder of Microsoft, is also the founder of the world's largest private charitable organization: the Bill & Melinda Gates Foundation, which focuses on domestic issues, health, and education. Gates not only impacted our way of using computers but also the greater community within the United States and the poor all over the world. "Money has no utility to me beyond a certain point," he once said. "Its utility is entirely in building an organization and getting resources out to the poorest in the world."

Lincoln was thought to have Marfan syndrome, which made him an odd-looking fellow with long spindly legs and an unusual gait. Gates, with his bookish, geeky style and low-key demeanor, shuns the limelight. Neither would be considered typically powerful type men of stature. However, what they both share is the ascension of leadership through all four levels:

- » They start with a spark, idea, or dream.
- » They inspire others to share the dream, placing hope in their hearts to come along on the journey with them.
- » They elevate not just those who have been on the journey but those all around them to succeed.
- » Finally, they land on the fourth level of leadership, where they've shifted a culture, paradigm, or community in a way that will have long-lasting effects for generations.

WARNING There is, of course, a blind spot for level 4 leaders. Utilizing polarity as our looking glass, the opposite of the entire ascension through all four levels, in summary, would be selfishness, corruption, and deception. History warns us of leaders such as Adolf Hitler. Modern examples can be found in Eastern European autocratic political structures, where the leaders raid the coffers of their countries (or companies) and make sure the gains are for them and them alone.

Overstating the importance of charisma in a leader

Although many believe that charisma should be part of the equation for leadership, I believe that charismatic leaders are often the marketing arm of a company, but they aren't always the leaders who get things done. I'm sure you can think of a charismatic leader who arrived on the scene but, despite passionate enthusiasm for hyperbolic plans, fell short. (Check out the nearby sidebar "Smiling Joe" for an example.)

Being a skilled orator who can move people and engender devotion is a powerful tool — one that's often necessary to bring people together in times of crisis. Their skillful communication is the element that helps glue people together around an important cause or a specific goal.

Charisma is often associated with a well-put-together, shiny veneer, but that shiny veneer is the cautionary element of charisma. A charismatic leader creates "celebrity" around who they are. Although they may have a plan for success, it's often overshadowed by their desire for personal celebrity status. The celebrity CEO trend reminds us that the Hollywood-ization of business serves to feed individual egos instead of the whole.

The workforce is far savvier than in the past. Politics has tainted us, making us wary. Many are moved by the passionate hope conveyed by a charismatic leader. However, as the Millennial generation rolls toward more positions of power, they're focused more on the "we" than the "me." An egocentric focus feels inauthentic, false, and often selfish to them. Therefore, the information contained in Part 1 is so important. Values-based leadership and the shared value economy are the antitheses of ego-focused businesses. The philosophy and mindset of business are changing. Charismatic celebrity CEOs are now like your grandfather's old pocket watch — nice to have but outdated.

REMEMBER

The ability to move a room full of people in the direction you want them to go is a special skill. Moving from level 1 to level 4 requires that you dispense the critical ingredient of hope to many rooms full of people. You can do that by authentically speaking from the heart and having a firm plan. Do your best not to complicate it. And always check your ego: Is this about me? Or is it about us as a whole?

SMILING JOE

"Joe Smith" (not his real name) was a persuasive man who adeptly wooed a CEO and a board with his flowery speech and charismatic mannerisms. Clearly a man of great education and upbringing, Joe arrived at a major financial firm in 2011. The young, charismatic leader was the hope of the organization to move forward into new growth markets. His arrival was greeted with great pomp and many press releases.

To his credit, Joe rolled up his sleeves right away and began meeting with each manager and department head to learn about the business firsthand. Then he moved on to smaller team meetings. He could engage most of the people in the organization with his rousing references to Shakespeare's *Henry V* "Eve of St. Crispin" speech, rallying the troops to fight the good fight in the trenches of war much as Henry did against the French. But many looked left and then right and realized Joe had no idea what he was talking about. His inexperience not only in business but in the realm of military credibility was transparent to the more experienced team members. There was no real plan, just fanfare and gloss.

Through it all Joe just smiled and dismissed many questions as accusations from the ranks. Offenders were dismissed or quietly fired. Smiling Joe, as he became known, dismantled the main arm of the organization that provided 40 percent of company profits. He hired his friends, granting them senior vice president titles to create an insular protective barrier between him and the staff. Leadership and management became extremely top-heavy while the "worker bees" dwindled and became stretched thin. Eventually the shine came off — Joe was fired. Unfortunately, it was too late to prevent major damage to the firm's bottom line and the company culture.

Moral of the story: If it's all about you, it isn't values-based leadership. The wins will be short-term only.

> **TIP:** There are passionate leaders in the world who are here to do good, but charisma isn't an essential part of being a leader. It's only a tool. So heed your good judgment. Look beyond what's flashy, shiny, and supposedly impeccable to see who those charismatic leaders truly are in their hearts and minds.

Determining Where You Are on the Journey

Leadership is an ascension process, moving from one set of skills to the next, using each as a building block. Maturity, seasoning, and life experience move the individual with the desire to lead along this journey. The journey is very personal, and no two journeys are the same. Some people may struggle in the first level of leadership until they have the confidence to move to the second level. Another person may move through levels 1 and 2 easily but find the perceived loss of control in the third level very difficult to accept. Few may be able to even conceive the fourth level of leadership.

It's important to see where you are on this journey in this very moment. Before you evaluate yourself, consider Figure 5-2. The ability to integrate VBL will affect your overall impact in the world. There's a correlation between each level of leadership and the number of VBL concepts and practices that are woven throughout the organization. This aspect of leadership becomes the mechanism to generate specific, positive results.

It's not always easy to see how impact and VBL integration line up. Figure 5-2 illustrates how each level of leadership corresponds to the depth of VBL deployed and the impact it has on the organization. For example, to reach a high or very high impact, you need to integrate a number of VBL initiatives into the organization (see Part 4 for details). Education serves as an excellent example; when you educate people, you create an empowered group of individuals because they no longer feel confined by what they don't know or what limits them. Education is also a retention tool.

> **TIP:** As you look at Figure 5-2, consider that sticky note you left earlier in this chapter that noted your current impact and what you want it to be. If that impact goal is mid-term or long-term, you can see the corresponding level of leadership required, as well as the depth of VBL you need to deploy to achieve it. If you're still unclear, continue to the assessment in this section. It can be your checkpoint to determine your level of leadership — is what you think you are really the truth?

VBL INTEGRATION WITHIN THE ORGANIZATION

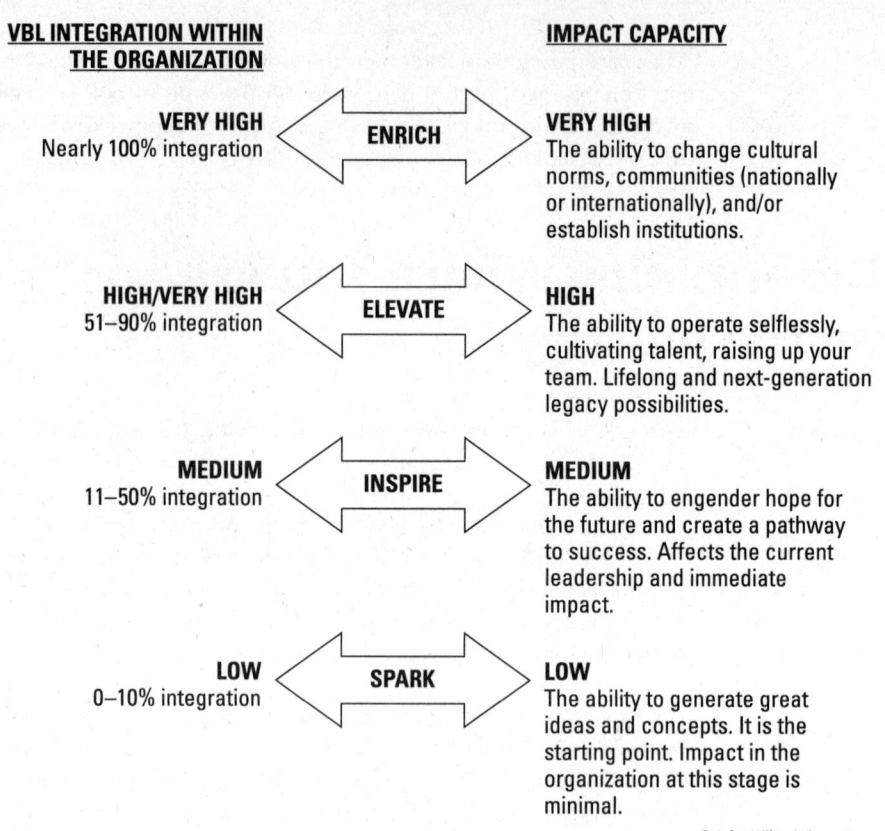

IMPACT CAPACITY

VERY HIGH — Nearly 100% integration ⟷ **ENRICH** ⟷ **VERY HIGH** — The ability to change cultural norms, communities (nationally or internationally), and/or establish institutions.

HIGH/VERY HIGH — 51–90% integration ⟷ **ELEVATE** ⟷ **HIGH** — The ability to operate selflessly, cultivating talent, raising up your team. Lifelong and next-generation legacy possibilities.

MEDIUM — 11–50% integration ⟷ **INSPIRE** ⟷ **MEDIUM** — The ability to engender hope for the future and create a pathway to success. Affects the current leadership and immediate impact.

LOW — 0–10% integration ⟷ **SPARK** ⟷ **LOW** — The ability to generate great ideas and concepts. It is the starting point. Impact in the organization at this stage is minimal.

FIGURE 5-2: VBL correlation to leadership levels and impact.

© John Wiley & Sons, Inc.

REMEMBER Keep in mind that you can ascend to the next level and the next integration at any time. If you're able to commit only to a partial integration, that's a fine place to start. The point is that you've begun. Your awareness has been raised. You will be in a self-reflective process each step of the way, which will help you identify what you'll need to do to reach the third and fourth levels of leadership, if you so choose.

The journey begins with you. The following sections help you assess your level of leadership right now and figure how willing you are to change it.

Assessing your current level of leadership

Every human being has capacities far beyond what they may know at any given moment. Over the span of a lifetime, more capacities are revealed and embraced. Some are disposed of, for good reason. In the early part of your career, you may have been more willing to take the back seat, allowing others to make the important decision even though your desire was to jump in with both feet, guns blazing. Later you may have become more focused on the lifetime legacy you would leave to the world. Each step requires development and, as I've mentioned, life experience, which helps us learn what works and what doesn't.

The following assessment is for you to get a snapshot of where you may have evolved and where you reside right now in your leadership. Being able to see your own growth path is as important as knowing where you are right now. Both help create a way forward.

Responding to assessing and reflecting statements

Read each of the following statements and determine which resonates most with you. Use a scale of 1 to 5 to mark your progress on the line provided:

1 — I don't embrace this philosophy or ethic.
2 — Sometimes I do this, but not very often.
3 — I would consider this to be me half the time.
4 — I tend to lean in this direction most of the time.
5 — This is me 100 percent of the time.

A1. I'd prefer not to be in the leadership role. I'm fine making everyday decisions, but I'm more comfortable with others making the bigger decisions. ___

A2. People tend to notice my emotional highs as well as my emotional lows more easily than they notice others' highs and lows. ___

A3. I have plenty of ideas, but they don't always move forward. ___

B1. I'm happy to set my own goals and work independently when necessary. I like the autonomy. ___

B2. I enjoy inspiring people and championing new ideas and initiatives. ___

B3. I expect that others will live up to the goals and processes set in place without my handholding. ___

C1. I like to take the initiative. It's hard for me not to do so. ___

C2. Developing and empowering my people gives me a great deal of joy. I get a kick out of watching others soar. ___

C3. Building, scaling, and growing a great organization is important to me, but I set the mandate and allow my team to handle the minutia. ___

D1. Coaching is a normal part of how I engage others. ___

D2. I consider and affect how we can contribute something of value and importance to the world daily. ___

D3. I'm committed to creating a healthy, dynamic, evolving company culture that lasts for generations to come. ___

Scoring your assessment

Each group of three statements relates to one of the levels of leadership. Add up your scores to determine which group(s) had the highest scores. If the B questions produced your highest score, then you reside within the level 2 of leadership (Inspire), for example:

A. Spark

B. Inspire

C. Elevate

D. Enrich

REMEMBER

You may be a combination of two levels — or a smattering of all. Any of that is fine. Throughout this book you're given more tools and clarification on the leadership attributes and skills required to provide the depth of impact you're seeking. How far you want to go is up to you.

Rating your willingness to change

Change isn't something many people are willing to embrace comfortably. Human beings crave stability, consistency, and predictability. We like patterns. Often, we default to past patterns when in crisis or during times of uncertainty. Using those patterns in a positive manner helps ease the transitional shock to the system. This is an example of working to your strengths rather than continually trying to build from thin air.

Whenever crisis strikes, for example, as it often does in business cycles, I know I become hyper focused and super organized and to have the team operate like a tactical team. This has been my default setting from childhood, growing up as a daughter of an NYPD detective. It was my training, and it's served me really well in my life. In crisis, my team has always remarked that even though I don't literally walk around with a clipboard full of tasks, assignments, and directives, they know my head is organizing in that way. After a crisis passes, I'm happy to let them tease me about it. One team member mimicked my hand signals directing them, bellowing, "Operate as a unit, in unison, like a well-oiled machine. Together. Stay together." Yes, that's my father's voice coming through me. Even without me literally uttering those words, the team felt it. We all roared with laughter.

Laughter can sometimes help us understand how others see us in action and offer insight into how we may need to temper our behavior. I asked them if I was too militant. Sincere smiles gave way, and they acknowledged the depth of the structure as necessary during a difficult time, but also remarked that it wasn't harsh or controlling. They knew I trusted them to handle the minutia. Whew! Crisis on a team-morale level averted! Appropriate, constructive leadership preserved!

TIP: As you're moving through the assessment in the preceding section, can you hear your own default patterns in your head? Chances are they're ingrained so deeply within you that you can't help but see or feel them. Don't let them go. Use them. Temper what you have with knowledge and willingness to expand and grow into the next level. Everything in your life is an experience worth using when applied in a constructive manner — that's why you were given it.

Now, on a scale of 1 to 5, rate your willingness to change, grow, and evolve in your leadership, with 1 meaning, "No way, I'm staying put," and 5 meaning, "I'm all in!"

TIP: Pull out another sticky note (if you haven't yet noticed from other chapters, sticky notes are one of my favorite tools). Write your number on it with a big, fat marker. Circle it. Adhere it to your notebook or make a photo of it the screensaver on your favorite digital work item. This number represents your commitment to yourself and your team, every single day. In those difficult moments, seeing the number 4 or 5 flash before you will remind you to stay steady. And as you and the team win more and more, seeing that same number will remind you that through your commitment they all got there. Reinforcement at any age or developmental level is a strong tool.

> **IN THIS CHAPTER**
>
> » Uncovering your character-building journey
>
> » Starting with self-reflection
>
> » Displaying grace and agility
>
> » Taking action to influence responsibly

Chapter 6
Nurturing the Four Attributes of a Values-Based Leader

Character isn't something that can be faked, bought, or disguised for long. Character isn't found in the clothing you wear, the car you drive, or even in an endorsement of your favorite charitable organization. Character is the amalgamation of your personality traits — how you amplify yourself in the world based on your morals and values. Character is something you develop.

There is a very common pattern available in the world you may be familiar with: *the Hero's Journey*, coined by Professor Joseph Campbell. The Hero's Journey charts the stages and development of an individual or a culture using a mythological story line: starting from the ordinary world, venturing through tests, ordeals, rewards, and the development of the hero's character to where he/she uses everything learned to triumphantly save the day. You see this pattern often echoed in many movies.

The Hero's Journey is simply a metaphor for growth and development of character that allows the hero or heroine to triumph regardless of what has come before. Every step backward is a lesson, every mistake is a teaching moment, and all of it is used in creating an ultimate triumphant moment. But most of all, courage to continue the journey is emphasized as one of the most important virtues.

Courage isn't for the faint-hearted. It requires us to go beyond what is comfortable or superficial to achieve goals. Much of the courage residing within values-based leadership (VBL) is the willingness to let go of many character flaws provided to us in the seven capitol vices, more commonly known as the seven deadly sins: pride, greed, lust, envy, gluttony, wrath, and sloth. The polarity of these vices consists of the seven virtues: humility, charity, chastity, gratitude, temperance, patience, and diligence. The seven virtues are echoed in the four traits of a values-based leader utilizing a compact, modern vernacular with direct application:

- » Self-reflection
- » Grace
- » Agility
- » Responsible influence

These traits are the main topics of this chapter.

Seeing a Snapshot of the Four Attributes

Character can be built upon. It can be contracted or expanded. Context can be reframed at any time to shift your perceptions or awareness. I briefly touch on reframing in Chapters 3 and 4 in regards to how people view business. You can now do the same reframing by understanding the importance of character. A leader doesn't necessarily have to be a brilliant, clever scholar or a Renaissance man/woman. Wise leaders can hire experts to support their mission, vision, and goals.

The by-product of a strong character is that you become predictable. I know this probably sounds terribly beige in a world that prizes colorful self-expression. However, human beings like certainty. They want to know that when they turn on their devices in the morning that their favorite publication pops up with the news of the days, promptly. They want to know that they can purchase their favorite brand of dog food at the local market every time they need it. And they want to know that the person leading them is consistent in their behaviors. When they can't rely on or trust the source of their news, dog food, or their leader, the apple cart is disrupted. Repeated, consistent behaviors — ways of be-ing — build trust.

In Chapter 7, I get into activating VBL principles with your teams. Here in this chapter, you venture into your own character development. As entrepreneur and author Jim Rohn once said, "The challenge of leadership is to be strong, but not rude; be kind, but not weak; be bold, but not bully; be thoughtful, but not lazy; be humble, but not timid; be proud, but not arrogant; have humor, but without folly."

Figure 6-1 depicts each attribute's highlighted effect and the actions that illuminate it. Each takes a degree of courage to embody, and all of them combined build trust in an organization between the leader and the group. The figure is an overview of a strong, trusted character.

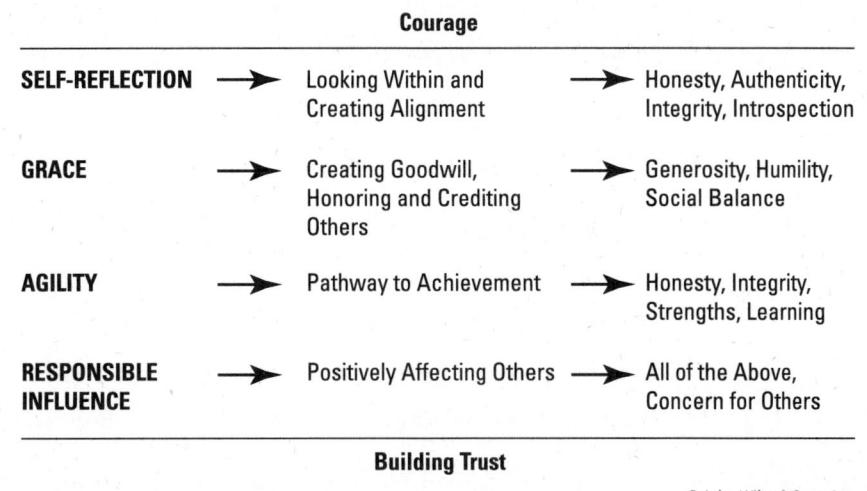

FIGURE 6-1: A snapshot of the four attributes.

	Courage	
SELF-REFLECTION →	Looking Within and Creating Alignment →	Honesty, Authenticity, Integrity, Introspection
GRACE →	Creating Goodwill, Honoring and Crediting Others →	Generosity, Humility, Social Balance
AGILITY →	Pathway to Achievement →	Honesty, Integrity, Strengths, Learning
RESPONSIBLE INFLUENCE →	Positively Affecting Others →	All of the Above, Concern for Others
	Building Trust	

© John Wiley & Sons, Inc.

Embracing Self-Reflection

Self-reflection is a checkpoint for your character and an examination of your mind. It's an opportunity to check in with yourself throughout your day. You'll notice as you progress through this book (and through your development as a values-based leader) that self-reflection is used in every chapter, in multiple sections. It's primarily there to build toward a conscious awareness of yourself, your motives, and your reactions in many different scenarios.

TIP Some seek a meditative or prayerful practice. Colleagues of mine will take a walk to clear their heads; they say the quiet and emptiness help them avoid distraction from the everyday noise in their heads. Sometimes there's simply too much clutter in our minds to be able to gain perspective on any given predicament. No matter what vehicle you choose, do what works best for you.

If you aren't used to hitting the pause button to evaluate yourself in a formal manner, I suggest that you end every day with ten questions. That's it. Ten simple questions. After a few days, you may find yourself doing this without thinking.

Here are five self-directed self-reflection questions:

1. How am I living my values every day?
2. Have I been honest with myself today or am I self-deceiving?
3. Have I fully used my talents today?
4. Did I hold fast to my priorities today?
5. Am I committed to expanding my knowledge?

Here are five others-directed self-reflection questions:

1. Have I done good today?
2. Am I an example of the behaviors I want my employees to model?
3. Have I harmed anyone in the process of day-to-day work?
4. Am I living up to my commitment of providing opportunities for others?
5. Where do I need others' expert help to overcome an obstacle?

The following sections dig deeper into some important traits for you to reflect on: honesty, authenticity, and integrity (especially when making difficult decisions).

Honesty: Uncovering the cornerstone attribute

As I mention earlier, exercises on self-reflection are dispersed throughout this book. At each step, I ask you to check in with yourself. If egotistical behaviors are the basis for what have caused detours in businesses, it's essential that you always ask yourself questions that require an honest self-assessment.

I believe that most of us strive to exhibit the character of honesty. But we often can fall short. There are many ways to be dishonest besides embezzlement and tax fraud. When dishonesty, even in small ways, becomes a habit, there can be critical consequences. Gossip, innuendo, and little white lies are easy to justify as being okay in the moment, but once that premise is set, it can become a way of being. If it's okay to lie a little here or there because no one finds out, then the allure of lying or being deceptive when bigger issues arise becomes easier to internally justify.

Empirically, it's easy to see the pattern when reflecting on an individual in your life with a reputation for deception. When someone exhibits a pattern of lying, you're far less likely to believe anything they say because, well, they lie all the time. What would be different about this time? It's most likely not going to be different because deception is a default behavior for them.

I've always found it interesting that one little lie often leads to another, and then to another, all in the name of preventing the initial lie from being discovered. The guilt or embarrassment of being found out spurs a series of cover-up lies. And then things get just plain crazy. Something that started out so small becomes an avalanche of deception.

When deceiving others, we practice denials and rationalizations of why we did or said X or Y. Therefore, in practical application, self-reflection is required of any leader on a regular basis. Sometimes the question is simply, "Am I kidding myself about what has occurred?" We often need to ask ourselves whether we're being honest not only in our dealings in general but also in our perception of different situations. Often the skewed perceptions have more to do with ego. Therefore, I often ask, "Is this about you or them?" and "Is this about personal gain or ego?"

When you reinforce honesty in small ways, every day, including self-reflection, you're building a reflex so that in difficult times the default response is to be honest. You don't even need to think about it — it just becomes a knee-jerk reaction every time. You're not covering your butt or justifying bad behavior in yourself or others. Rather, you're building trust with others and reinforcing the behavior you want to see among the team.

Even if you're regularly checking in with yourself on these issues, you're still living a busy, fast-paced life. In the name of speed and deadlines, the culture around you may hit some hiccups you hadn't initially recognized; people are grumbling, they look unhappy, you may feel a little bitterness or resentment in the air, or your numbers may begin to lower. All are subtle signs that something has disrupted the ecosystem. Take a step back and ask yourself:

>> Where may I have practiced self-denial or self-rationalization at work?

>> Thinking about the last difficult situation I encountered, did I make this decision based on my gain or what was best for others?

>> What negative behavior have I brought into the office that's now being emulated by others?

REMEMBER
The discovery within these questions will help you right the ship. Turning a blind eye will only cause bigger issues down the road. Be honest and courageous enough to fix whatever happened promptly.

REMEMBER
Take the practice of self-reflection and honesty to heart. You'll learn more about yourself in this practice and accelerate your growth exponentially. Everything else covered in this book cascades from honesty in your reflection.

> **WARNING:** Dishonesty perpetuates an environment of laziness — taking the easiest way out. Of course, every person has the capacity to be lax at times. But be diligent within yourself, and expect the same level of excellence in others.

Authenticity: Saying and doing what you mean

"A man or woman without deeds speaks hollow words" is a piece of wisdom given to me many years ago. Or more simply: Actions speak louder than words. Equally important is that words are a point of impression and therefore creation in your world. *Authenticity,* or the truth in actions and deeds, is a powerful creation source within your organization. If you don't care about certain aspects of the business, you can fake it only for so long. That which you're passionate about will be very tangible to others.

The ability to be authentic is a direct expression of that which is true for you. Authenticity is simple — don't complicate it. It's truth. If you're not sure what truth is for you, check in with yourself to find that passionate response. If you still don't know what that is, I bet your team, family, and friends can easily tell you what's truly important to you in your life and what you're reverently passionate about.

> **REMEMBER:** As a leader, you'll be watched more than you know, listened to more than you realize, and felt more than you think anyone could feel you. Specifically, your words make an impression on others that creates a reality, consciously or unconsciously. Words lead to action, behavior, and ultimately momentum. Whatever your values are, they should be reflected in what you say and do. If they don't feel authentic — if others perceive them as not being authentic — your team won't respect you. But when they know you're being truthful in your authenticity, they'll follow suit. They'll know that you are what you project.

Take a moment to reflect:

- Are you consistent with your words, actions, and behaviors?
- What are you projecting as important to your team right now?
- Where are you not being entirely authentic in your work?

> **TIP:** If you're not sure about the answers to any of these questions, ask your friends and family how they see you.

LIVING BY LOYALTY

"Steve" was a big-talking, aggressive New York type who had been around the block way too many times. His growl was formidable, as was his ability to intimidate people with his sharp words and enormous, powerful presence. Yet at the end of his stream of barking, he would end the conversation with a gentle handshake and warm thank-you. Others often asked how I could bear this man. I smiled. Although he is a character, I would say he also has character. It's all a smoke screen — watch. I admit it took a few barkings for me to see it myself.

The dance went on for months. Over that time, Steve softened. The aggressiveness slowed, and before me appeared a very principled man. One day he said, "Loyalty is a big deal to me." He explained that he had a vendor who was performing poorly; many of his clients complained about the vendor's customer service. But he was stuck between a rock and a hard place. That vendor had also become a friend. He had no intention of damaging her income. Still, the complaints were real. On the other hand, Steve had another vendor vying for his business who was rated very highly for just that — customer service. Steve was visibly torn.

"What's stopping you from telling your friend to step it up or lose the business?" I asked.

He replied, "Loyalty. Even beyond the money, if you're not loyal, you're nothing to me. I extend the same to them as I expect them to extend to me."

"Okay," I said. "But how will you reconcile the declining business from your friend with needing to support your own business?"

He paced like a panther.

Several days later he laid out a very simple and eloquent plan. New business will be given to the new vendor. Old business that wants to remain with the friend-vendor may do so. Any client seeking a change will be introduced to the new vendor. Period.

For a principled person with a high moral character who holds loyalty as his highest value, that wasn't an easy decision to make. Some would say all the business should have been pulled from the friend-vendor and moved to the new vendor. Such a decision always depends on your character and your values. There isn't one right answer for every person. For Steve, he's consistently loyal to his clients and vendors — almost, at times, to a fault. Everyone knows Steve's character is trustworthy. Why? He's consistent in his behavior. He's authentic.

Integrity: Doing what's right when it's not convenient, comfortable, or popular

Your decisions won't always be popular. They may not even be comfortable for *you* to make. Still, you have to make decisions based on personal values, morals, and professional ethics. There is a clear-cut difference between situations of fairness and ethics. Discerning which situation you're encountering may have similar character-building opportunities. One, clearly, has higher stakes attached, but both require an honest assessment of the situation:

» **Fairness decisions:** The situation you encounter may or may not make you feel comfortable. But it doesn't breach any legal or professional ethics or violate any laws. The decision at hand is about making decisions that will be fair and equitable to all parties involved and in the best interest of the organization. Sometimes these decisions may be encountered in cross-team conflicts or amid general disagreements on issues or authority.

» **Ethical dilemmas:** A situation may put you in a position of feeling uneasy. Your decision may have professional, legal, or ethical repercussions based on the code being violated or potentially violated. These are often personnel human resource or compliance issues — either of which could have legal ramifications if not handled correctly.

In either circumstance, you may not be making a choice that everyone is going to agree with. Welcome to leadership. If you try to make everyone happy, you'll lose. If you try to make only one person happy, you'll lose. How you win is to make the best decision for the longevity of the business based on morals, personal values, professional values, and law or policy where applicable. It's Character Building 101: choosing what's best for the whole group rather than what's popular. It's easier said than done.

The following sections discuss reflection processes you can use in the event you need them. Alter them as you see fit. Use them as often as possible so it becomes a reflex to think this way. In either a fairness or ethical situation, you may already be asking some of these questions — but perhaps not all. Integrate the missing pieces to enhance your comfort level with your decision-making process. If you can back it up, you'll most likely be less likely to waiver or doubt your choice.

The following assessment sequence is an excellent coaching tool for you to use with other leaders or managers in your organization. It can provide insight into how you think. Additionally, you're giving them a behavioral directive as well as a character-building opportunity. Defusing emotion is key to clear thinking and decision making.

Assessing a fairness decision

To ease discomfort and create a clear process for you, try using the following line of questioning to assess a fairness decision:

1. **Detail the problem in a few sentences.**

   What is the conflict? Is it ego or logistics driven?

2. **Deep dive into the facts.**

   Look at the contributing factors to the disruption.

3. **Create a "What is fair?" list.**

   Ask yourself several questions, prefacing them with the words "What if?" For example, "What if I made X decision rather than Y decision?" Then ask, "Is this fair to both parties?"

4. **Try a sink or swim test.**

   You could consider several responses in any given situation:

   - **Empowerment test:** Will this compromise either person's capability or credibility?
   - **Shoes test:** If I were in the other person's or entity's shoes, would I still think this was the best outcome?
   - **Organization test:** Is your decision in the best interest of the team and/or the organization or the individuals involved?
   - **Social media test:** If this decision became part of the organization's reputation, would that enhance or hinder your ability to build a healthy company culture?

5. **Make the best choice based on the preceding steps — then pause.**

6. **Engage in reflection before action.**

   You want to avoid this issue coming up again in the future. Before taking any further action, there will be questions. Consider these four and know the answers before you act:

   - Where have you made mistakes during this process?
   - What would be the best actions to be more supportive if this arises again?
   - What clarification or edification might be needed in terms of roles, responsibilities, or decision-making authority?
   - How can you or another person in the organization coach the individuals should they need it?

Assessing an ethical decision

Try using the following line of questioning to assess an ethical decision and get a clearer picture:

1. **Detail the problem in a few sentences.**

    Start with what it is that makes you uncomfortable or uneasy about the situation or decision at hand.

2. **Deep dive into the facts.**

    Look at all the contributing facts to determine whether this is really a problem or not.

3. **Refer to points of guidance.**

    Are there company guidelines or policies that touch on the situation? Do specific laws apply? Are there other applicable codes of ethics or conduct you can refer to? Who within the organization or your colleagues may have experience handing this type of issue?

4. **Create a "What if?" list.**

    Ask yourself several questions, prefacing them with the words "What if?" For example, "What if I made X decision rather than Y decision? What would the repercussions be?"

5. **Try a sink or swim test.**

    You could consider several responses in any given situation:

    - **Harm test:** Will this be harmful than another route?
    - **Social media test:** Would I be comfortable having my response posted all over social media?
    - **Peer test:** Could I defend my decision to my peers?
    - **Legal test:** Is there anything here that would constitute legal jeopardy?
    - **Shoes test:** If I were in the other person's or entity's shoes, would I still think this was the best outcome?
    - **Organization test:** Would our legal counsel, ethics, or compliance offices feel comfortable with this decision? (By the way, you should ask them.)

6. **Make the best choice based on the preceding steps — then pause.**

7. Engage in reflection before action.

You want to avoid this issue coming up again in the future. Before taking any further action, there will be questions. Consider these four and know the answers before you act:

- Where have you made mistakes during this process?
- What would be the best actions to be more supportive if this arises again?
- What clarification or explanation is needed in your employee handbook?
- Is there any legal or compliance training required for management or staff?

REMEMBER: Ethical dilemmas may require help from your legal or compliance teams. Get them involved earlier rather than later. They can be very helpful in navigating a precarious situation.

THE BYSTANDER EFFECT

The *bystander effect* is a phenomenon in which the more bystanders there are as witnesses to a victim in distress, the less likely any one of them is to offer help. It's thought that diffusion of responsibility is responsible for the effect — each bystander assumes one of the others will respond. It was also termed *Genovese syndrome* by *The New York Times,* based on the circumstances surrounding the murder of a young woman, Kitty Genovese, in Queens in 1964. Though the actual number of witnesses has been disputed over the years, initial reports claimed 38 individuals either saw her murdered or heard her cries for help and did little or nothing about it. Sadly, ten years later another woman was murdered nearby the scene of Kitty's murder. Once again, neighbors said they heard the woman's cries, but no one helped.

Nowadays we have cell phone voyeurism — phone video footage of crimes and other disturbing events in progress, often posted online. Rather than call police, people take video of the incident while the victim continues to suffer.

In business, a leader may turn a blind eye to an indiscretion by a manager because "it's really not hurting anyone" or because the leader prefers not to have to face the issue — that is, until the story comes out. Then a fair sum is spent on lawyers to resolve the issue.

Each is an example of people behaving as bystanders who are aware of an issue but unwilling to do anything about it. The degree of impact varies depends on the severity of the situation. In life, as in business, it's not always necessary to fight with others. However, doing the right thing should be the norm.

Showing Actionable Grace

Grace is not a word you often hear about when it comes to the character of a leader or a workplace. Images of ballerinas or ice skaters may come to mind, but not a leader or a workplace. Long, elegant movements, precise timing, and the ability to evoke emotion don't often fit into the world of work. However, in the context of values-based leadership, the elegance of grace is an attribute of kindness and generosity along with the ability to extend goodwill to others in any given situation. Grace helps create a stable environment of mutual respect.

The following sections discuss two aspects of grace more fully: showing humility and bridging social distance.

Humility: Embracing quiet confidence

Projecting *quiet confidence* is the antithesis of the loud, boisterous, in-your-face, know-it-all demeanor of what I call the "jock-leader" or old school "masters of the universe" hedge fund types depicted in films like *Wall Street* and *Boiler Room*. Yelling, screaming, shaming, and demeaning and bullying tactics are displays of character often associated with an inflated ego and insecurity.

Grace is about humility — accepting that you may *not* know something. Grace expresses an earnest curiosity. It means bringing your power and presence into a room by establishing trust through open engagement. It means refusing to exert energy on what you can't control and instead focusing on your own attitude and effort. Understand that the best way to avoid dispersed focus is to set priorities and boundaries and, yes, to put blinders on at times. Finally, grace is about honoring and crediting others for their work rather than focusing on what *you* have done.

The state of grace isn't about questions. It is about certain actions or, sometimes, inaction:

- » Being still and listening
- » Being curious and asking questions
- » Recognizing what you can't control and focusing on what you can control
- » Maintaining focus

REMEMBER It may seem counterintuitive, but what we all do in our quiet times — for the betterment of others, without accolades or fanfare — is what will have the greatest effect on the company culture. Those quiet times can be in the middle of a busy day, during a meeting, or in a one-on-one with someone. It's a practice that's not exclusive to introverts. A balanced and well-measured leader can always benefit from mindfully practicing quiet confidence daily. It is the gap between thoughts and actions, and between words and deeds. Grace integrates just about every attribute, virtue, and character trait discussed in this chapter.

The posture of someone who possesses quiet confidence is chest up, shoulders back. This body language conveys confidence to others and that you are open to communication. Most people tend to slouch — a lot. Be mindful of your body language. Notice when you may be feeling less confident. Are you slouching? If so, prop yourself up and take a deep breath. Remember, it's always about practicing and reinforcing a habit until it becomes your default.

Social distance: Bridging the power gap

Social distancing can occur up and down, leader to team, or side to side, across similar levels within a team. Sometimes it's also called *status distance*. As I continue to unpack the attributes of a values-based leader, I focus here on the up-and-down social distance issue.

Social distancing creates a gap between the leader and others. It's a direct reaction to power. Some are intimidated and often defer to a person they perceive to possess power. Others aren't affected at all — they go along their merry way without disruption. The gap disrupts productivity, innovation, and growth. Think of it as the perception of division between who you are and who they are, with one being better or more important than the other. This division can be polarizing. Perception, as previously discussed, is very powerful to its beholder. Although a certain degree of social distance is necessary to establish decision-making authority, if it's not monitored and tempered, it can create a very counterproductive environment.

It can be difficult to even be aware that a distancing is occurring. But the solution to social or status distancing is simple: Create an environment of equality (see Chapter 9 for more information):

>> **Be approachable:** Embody an everyman/everywoman posture.

>> **Be empathetic:** Allow people to share their stories and experiences.

>> **Drive balance:** Encourage people to communicate with you and others in the roles of teacher, student, and mentor.

Take a moment to reflect:

>> Do you unknowingly or knowingly create social distance within your organization?

» Name five people in your office whom you may not necessarily work with daily. What do you know about them?

» Are you willing to allow others to share their stories, even if they're just about how they make espresso? (See the nearby sidebar "A tale of two leaders" to find out what I mean.)

» Does your team feel safe flowing between the roles of teacher, student, and mentor at work?

A TALE OF TWO LEADERS

Two leaders within the same organization, "Tom" and "Nate," hold the exact same position in two different regions of the country. They have similar backgrounds, education, tenure at the company, and depth of experience. Both possess great passion and drive for success. If you met either one of these men socially, you'd instantly like him and sense that he was a good person. However, one leader's team is growing exponentially; the other's team is not.

Nate and his team work out an office in a bucolic storybook town out west. Every week he has a meeting with his leadership team to detail the goals for the week. They engage in healthy conversation to determine resources and strategies necessary. Nate listens intently as others offer suggestions or alternate plans. They agree on a direction, and then the group disperses and engages the rest of the team, where appropriate, to fine-tune the plan for the week. Although Nate is in meetings intermittently, he makes an effort to stroll through the office. Sometimes he'll sit with one of his leadership team, recounting points from the meeting. Other times he'll pop into a team member's cube to ask how things are going or what they thought of the new rollout. He visits pockets of staff members throughout the week. Today, a spirited debate with a team member about the best way to brew espresso turns into a brief story about her family coming to the United States from Croatia. Throughout the week, collaboration is openly occurring, goals are being achieved, and momentum is building.

Our other leader, Tom, has a lovely office outside Denver. The growth potential for his team is tremendous. He also has leadership meetings weekly. Healthy conversation is had. However, most alternate opinions are met with a lukewarm reception. Subsequent team meetings occur with staff members who are eager to move forward. The team slows or maintains status quo until directed otherwise by Tom. The leadership team does its best to stay positive and provide direction. Tom's door is closed all day. In fact, it's closed every day he's in the office. Occasionally, he'll high-five or chat with some team member, but there is no real connection between him and them. By the end of the week, most ideas considered in the initial weekly team meeting have been shot down or forgotten.

> Guess which leader is more successful? That's right. Nate makes himself approachable by engaging with his immediate and overall team regularly — beyond formal meetings. Communication is open, fluid, and welcome. He's confident and secure enough within himself to allow collaboration. Nate also takes the time to know his team. Empathy isn't just about sharing your challenges in doing a job or navigating a life-changing experience. Empathy can also involve simply knowing who your people are and what's important to them. That's grace in action by consciously narrowing the gap of social distancing.

Expanding Agility

Whenever I hear the words *agile leader*, I think of someone running through an obstacle course, knees pumping up and down as they navigate the tires. They're nimble, resourceful, and willing to look beyond what they know. They just go for it. There's a real sense of courage about this type of individual. Sometimes it can feel a little reckless, but somehow there's a sublime focus to what they're doing. We all may feel this way on occasion. You're not out of control. You are very much in control and fully focused.

Technically, *agility* is about the willingness to answer (not ask) this question: How can we come to completion? This isn't specific to one particular issue. It's the broad question about how the group can achieve goals. It's the equivalent of the "royal we" — all-encompassing. Fundamentally, the broad answer will require the values-based leader to embody a circular mindset and teams who can follow suit.

The following sections define the main components of agility, show you how to evaluate your strengths and weaknesses, and talk about the importance of failure (yes, you read that right).

Defining the five components of agility

Agility can be broken down into the following five components:

- **Optimism:** Believing that what isn't apparent now can be, will be, or is already in existence.
- **Commitment to success as a whole:** The entire team wins, not just the leader.
- **Commitment to learning and exploration:** An ability to learn and explore new skills.

- **Commitment to focus:** Learning what and where the problems may be, rather than providing a knee-jerk or emotional response.
- **Utilization of failure as a teaching moment:** Every failure provides feedback about what needs to be changed or shifted either practically, technically, or in our character.

These concepts are probably familiar to you. They're incorporated into many of the philosophies, attributes, and overall framework I'm unpacking in this book. However, you are about to uncover a personal area that takes enormous courage: learning. Self-reflection is done privately to obtain a view of ourselves — that's an internal mechanism for evaluation, but it's not necessarily *learning* in the formal sense.

Before embarking on new learning, take the time to assess your current skill set (see the next section). Finding out where your strengths and weaknesses lie can make you feel very much like the emperor without clothes on — maybe just a little *too* transparent. Nonetheless, it's essential. There are options to allow you to assess privately or in a more public forum.

Getting real: Unpacking your strengths and weaknesses

You must start with yourself because it's where you're in firmest control of the outcome. You can't control others; you can only control yourself. For decades, a school of thought has prevailed that says one has to improve their shortfalls to create strengths. Many people have spent more time trying to reduce that gap rather than investing their efforts in what they excel at doing. Education is an essential part of willingness to shift, change, and grow. But if you're spending more time trying to excel at something you don't naturally grasp (or care to grasp), you're wasting a lot of precious time.

REMEMBER Work to your strengths. Expand upon them. Sure, be aware of your weaknesses. Educate yourself enough so that you're knowledgeable about the things you don't do well — but hire others to be the experts in those areas. Agility allows you to tap into others' expertise to create the best possible solutions. If you don't know what you need, how can you fill the gaps?

TIP What are your strengths? If you're not sure, here are two ways to learn more about yourself and your abilities:

>> **Gallup Strength Finder:** You can try a well-known assessment such as Strength Finder from Gallup. More than 17 million people have taken this survey to better understand where their brilliance may lie. You may be surprised at what you find out about yourself. Check it out at www.gallupstrengthscenter.com.

>> **360 Review:** This is another opportunity for you to gain a bit more insight into what you're doing well and what needs improvement. A 360 Review is a far more vulnerable process, but it's worthwhile because it provides honest feedback on your leadership and what skills may need enhancement. Often a 360 can be overwhelming to coordinate or navigate. Try using Survey Gizmo's system to make it easy for all parties. Survey Gizmo offers tips and other useful information on setting up a 360 for yourself or others. Try it out at www.surveygizmo.com/survey-blog/guide-to-360-reviews-what-is-a-360-how-do-you-administer-360-feedback/.

Failure: Ensuring success

I've met very few people who can view failure as a measure for success. Upon entering any company, I meet leaders, managers, and team members who regard failure as a mortal sin. Most will admit their shortfalls, conveying the experience with a measure of shame. Others are unapologetic and defensive. My experience is that about 5–10 percent are okay with failure and simply move on. Much of this depends on how failure is viewed by their family of origin, their belief system, and the ways in which leaders and managers around them react to failure.

Making mistakes, missing out on a crucial detail, having a project unequivocally crash and burn — they're all part of life. Mind you, I'm in no way condoning laziness, incompetence, or poor judgment. But things happen. When honesty is part of your character, you admit your errors. If you have a leader who can help you see the teaching moment *without* shame, it takes the sting out. It will also increase your ability to bounce back more quickly should another error occur. (Unfortunately, they usually do.)

REMEMBER

Emotional reactions cause unnecessary drama. When someone makes a mistake, 90–95 percent of the time they're upset about it. An emotional fireball builds inside them, even though their exterior may be the picture of calm. Responding emotionally to them at such a moment will, without a doubt, damage the trust between you. Take three deep breaths before you respond. Control your breathing. Everything is reparable. Resolve the issue — *then* use it as a teaching moment for both of you. The lessons learned could be character-building items: agility, integrity, and transparency. Additionally, some process or procedure recommendation will come from it.

Have a moment of reflection on your last foible:

> What caused the issue?

> What did you learn from that near catastrophe?

> What will you do better next time?

Isn't character building fun?

THE COLLAR SPREAD CRISIS

"Casey" had been leading a team launching a new brand within a large apparel company. Every detail was handled with the utmost care. The small team allowed everyone to be involved with every nuance. In a very formal meeting, the senior vice president said, peering over his glasses, "No matter what, I don't want to see spread collars on any of these shirts." Casey said, "Yes, I agree." The designer working on the project scribbled her notes accordingly.

Fast-forward two months later when all the samples arrived. You guessed it: A third of the assortment had spread collars. After a little digging through her notebook, the designer acknowledged her mistake to Casey. Casey knew this could potentially be a powder keg, and so did the designer. This piece of the business represented about $2 million.

As the leader, Casey took the responsibility off the designer's hands and addressed it with the vice president. Casey could understand the concern about the monetary impact on this blossoming expansion, and both Casey and the designer wondered if they'd be fired. To their surprise, that's not what happened. The VP laughed and said not to worry about it: "Fix it for production, and the buyers will just have to use their imaginations." He smiled and continued to his next meeting. No shame. No scolding. He said, "You're not the only one who's ever made a mistake. Everything is reparable, if you learn from it. Do that, okay?"

Upon regrouping, Casey and the designer put in place a checkpoint to avoid a similar mistake in the future. The issue was over. Both were relieved. The mess-up came with an important lesson that facilitated a process improvement. Lesson learned. Financial fumble recovered.

Influencing Responsibly

Power is an enormous responsibility. Let that sink in for a moment.

Not everyone is comfortable being a leader, nor are they necessarily comfortable with the perceived responsibility they may feel. Yet there are only two avenues of responsibility:

» **Responsible to others:** Develop your own character first. If you haven't found your own way, you can't teach someone else what you don't know. You should

- Know who you are.
- Know what's important to you.
- Know your priorities and values.
- Keep your lessons top of mind.
- Keep working at it for a lifetime.

That doesn't mean you can't help others, but you can take them only as far as you've gone yourself. Personally, I would never take leadership advice from anyone who hasn't held a leadership position. Would you? There's no way they could fully understand the highs and lows of this type of service in the world — because it *is* a service position. They couldn't possibly understand what it's like to navigate cross-cultural teams locally and overseas simultaneously, for example. It's a path you must walk first in order to share powerfully about the experience.

» **Responsible for others:** You take your knowledge, experience, and consciousness and apply them to the environment. All your values-based leadership tools and real-life experience help nurture and grow others. Just remember, your responsibility to them is to help them grow, not to do it for them. The culmination of the Hero's Journey is when the hero brings his hard-earned knowledge or "elixir" back home to nourish everyone. Not all will accept it, nor even respect it, but that's okay. Painful mistakes or missteps may be needed before they do. You never know — you may unwittingly become one of their mentors along their own Hero's Journey. But in the meantime you'll be required to use your wisdom and experience to help others succeed.

The following sections explain two ways to influence responsibly: emulating your values and creating good.

Emulating values: Being a powerful example

REMEMBER

Every day, in everything you do, embody your personal values and the values of values-based leadership. Your example of what you do and how you do it is more influential than words could ever be. Although there are several different learning styles to consider, many people learn visually better than any other way. Children mimic their parents. Kittens mirror their parenting animal, which is not always their biological mother. As you influence and teach those around you how to behave based on what we do, they'll follow the template you set. "Because, hey, if it's okay for the leader to grease the books, then I can too. Why not? On the other hand, if the leader is generous with their time and helps the team grow, then I can do that too. I may not do it perfectly, but I'll do my best."

As Albert Schweitzer, Nobel Prize winner, humanitarian, philosopher, and writer, once said, "Example is not the main thing in influencing others. It is the only thing."

Here you have a self-reflection opportunity:

- What behavior are your staff members mirroring back to you?
- Is that behavior productive or counterproductive to establishing a VBL position?
- Is there something here you need to correct or change?

Creating good: Taking the medical pledge to do no harm

"The thinking man must oppose all cruel customs, no matter how deeply rooted in tradition and surrounded by a halo. When we have a choice, we must avoid bringing torment and injury into the life of another, even the lowliest creature." That's another profound quote from Albert Schweitzer. Simply put, don't exert your dominance of others in an exploitive, abusive manner. This abuse can be as subtle as a subversive form of discrimination based on socioeconomics, as in paying someone less because of their low socioeconomic status. And of course, too often it's an all-out assault on someone being profiled and discriminated against due to race, ethnicity, or sexual orientation. Both kinds of abuse are harmful.

My coaching client "Trisha" told me recently about another peer leader in her organization who was using her power as leverage to get what she wanted. Leverage isn't always a sinister tool, unless it's being used to intimidate others. And that, unfortunately, is what was happening. To break the tension, I asked her this question: "What would it look like if this leader used her power for good rather than evil?"

She laughed. "You make her sound like a supervillain."

I said, "Well, she could be if she persists." Trisha agreed.

REMEMBER: The power of leadership is not a license to become a supervillain, as Trisha observed. It's the ability to enrich and nurture those around you. Never forget, as I've said before: The primary use of commerce in this world is to provide opportunity for others — to do good by providing jobs with a fair wage paid out of the profits made.

Time for self-reflection again.

>> Are you maintaining a pledge to do no harm?

>> Where are you, consciously or unconsciously, inflicting harm?

>> Do you have a supervillain alias? If so, what is it?

Knowing yourself is critical to making corrections along the way. Blind people can never see daylight — catch my drift?

REMEMBER: At times even the best leader can stray into supervillain mode (that includes myself). The important part is recognizing your behavior and righting it, *tout de suite!*

> **IN THIS CHAPTER**
> » Aligning principles with the character of a values-based leader
> » Helping your team buy into your leadership
> » Customizing a principle plan to build momentum

Chapter 7
Activating the Grounding Principles

The effectiveness of a values-based leader is based on the ability to integrate the four essential attributes of the leader's character (covered in Chapter 6) into the organization. These attributes are as follows:

> » The ability to self-reflect often to maintain focus on both fiscal goals and values
>
> » The capacity to show actionable grace with humility and quiet confidence
>
> » The agility to find the path to achievement
>
> » The ability to use their influence responsibly

In this chapter, I roll out ten principles to help with that integration. When deployed, these principles amplify the leader's character, reflect values-based leadership (VBL), and create an organization operating in unison: effectively, efficiently, creatively, compassionately, and productively.

VBL establishes an environment in which the individual and the organization can thrive. The principles offered create that environment where individuals feel that they're seen, heard, and recognized for who they are, what they do, and how they can contribute. An organization without a mindset focused on possibilities and encouraged to operate at full capacity cannot thrive. Simply put, if the environment is a black cloud of despair and discouragement, individuals won't operate at their peak. They can't.

REMEMBER

Think of your organization as a field of beautiful flowers. With sunshine, water, and nourishment, they flourish and provide you with delight. If that field were covered with a tarp, left unwatered, and never fed, they would wither away. There's nothing delightful about wilted flowers.

This chapter discusses the ingredients that create a positive environment, and it starts with mindset. A domino effect is created when the principles are put into action, fostering a positive company culture and long-term, sustainable results that have momentum.

Introducing the Ten Values-Based Leadership Principles

For years, as I've worked with leaders of many small, medium, and large businesses, we've used what has lovingly become "The Big Ten Manifesto of VBL" as a snapshot reminder of their commitment. The ten values-based principles are coupled with actions to foster a healthy environment, illustrated in Figure 7-1.

At times, this model has been subject to debate over which comes first: the chicken or the egg. Rather than debate whether mindset, action, or result comes first, consider the model as a series of interweaving actions and results with mindset as the connector points. These connector points are the starting place, sometimes consciously, sometimes subconsciously. What you believe is an important part of the sequence of accepting a change of behavior and therefore a change of results.

REMEMBER

As Mahatma Gandhi said, "Keep your thoughts positive because your thoughts become your words. Keep your words positive because your words become your behavior. Keep your behavior positive because your behavior becomes your habits. Keep your habits positive because your habits become your values. Keep your values positive because your values become your destiny."

REMEMBER

I've placed the ten principles into four categories that also reflect the four puzzle pieces discussed in Chapter 3. The titles may not be exactly the same, but the purpose is.

ATTITUDES/ MINDSET	ACTIONS	RESULTS
Hope Trust Courage Optimism	**Basic human level:** • Treating others with respect • Practicing acceptance • Practicing tolerance • Forgiveness • Compassion • Equality and fairness **Engagement level:** • Cooperation and collaboration • Questioning from a place of curiosity • Allowing others to do their part • Contributing constructively • Operating within the values structure (theirs and the company's) **Long-term focus:** • Envisioning the long-term health and goals of the organization • Creating an impact socially, globally, or locally • Creating a win-win scenario	**Company culture:** • High morale • Increased productivity and effectiveness • Teamwork • Creative critical thinking • Creative expansion • Desirable company to work for • Ethical, fair, inclusive, and creative organization • Impactability: satisfying human needs and the need to help others **Long-term result:** • Advancing products and services • Cutting edge • Emergence of new industries • Creation of more efficient processes • Job creation • Expansion • Profitability • Positively impacting the world around them

FIGURE 7-1: Values-based leadership model.

© John Wiley & Sons, Inc.

I. Sets direction:
   1. **Creates** a values statement to serve as a guiding force for all
   2. **Provides** meaning and purpose to the company and its stakeholders
   3. **Reflects** the company's values in everything they do, everywhere they do it

II. Creates proactive company culture:
   4. **Increases** value in the lives of stakeholders and the community
   5. **Utilizes** their influence responsibly to achieve goals
   6. **Creates** an environment of mutual respect

III. Betterment of individuals:

    7. Invests in the education and development of the stakeholders

    8. Empowers others by developing other leaders

    9. Commits to correct job fits to foster job satisfaction and improve effectiveness

IV. Expands business opportunities:

    10. Inspires collaboration and innovation by creating a shared value community

You don't have to execute all the principles all at once. It takes time to plan and create support for each. But each is a call to action for you to consider.

As you find out in this section, each action you take introduces a cause-and-effect pattern. Our lives are made up of small actions, words, circumstances, and reactions to the stimuli around us. Later in this chapter, I illustrate this concept further when it comes to how you, as a leader, affect others.

Using cause and effect to shift the organization

A values-based direction creates an organization that operates with the leader's specified and expressed definition of a value. There are also three overriding characteristics in operation — kindness, compassion, and acceptance — that create a healthy mindset where people feel safe. People become hopeful, optimistic, courageous, and willing to trust (refer to Figure 7-1). Deploying the principles sets the stage for a positive cause-and-effect sequence:

» What you believe to be true in any given circumstance is your mindset, attitude, and thought process.

» What you believe to be truth dictates the actions you may or may not be willing to take.

» Those actions create a result.

When individuals are treated with respect, they give respect. The result is a group of people who operate with the belief that everyone has something to contribute, and that circumvents negative attributes, such as competitiveness. It stands to reason that if you respect a person's input, you won't cut them down to get your way. Right?

The principles set up the cause-and-effect dynamic. Treat others the way you want to be treated — create a domino effect by starting with your own actions. That's the power of the principles. You'll have the opportunity to be verbose later — articulate to the group what your values and expectations are right now. Know that you can transmit those expectations by utilizing the principles. You create the momentum and sow the seeds for possibilities — whatever those goals and aspirations for the group may be. This is the framework.

Changing the value equation

The ten principles in practice also provide value to the staff in a way that you may not have considered. This isn't about product value, value proposition, or added value items. (Thank you to the marketing community for all that positioning!) In this case, changing the value equation is about utilizing the principles to help others grow and allow them to flourish. In other words, value is about changing the course of their lives for the better. Never underestimate the impact that encouragement, kindness, and empathy have on others. Multiply that by providing skills to advance others — in the long term that allows them to thrive and contribute on a greater scale. As a values-based leader, you give to others by providing them with the skills and opportunities to feel safe and secure and grow.

Each principle highlights the verb — the action word in each statement. This is purposeful, indicating to the leader that there is action to be taken to ignite each principle. In doing so, real value is added to changing the trajectory of the team and the organization. Here are seven action words and actions that positively ignite a group:

- Inspires
- Creates
- Provides
- Increases
- Invests
- Empowers
- Commits

Sitting stagnant on the sidelines sipping coffee doesn't add value for anyone. Leadership is about taking action. The principles illustrate how a values-based leader mobilizes people and resources: by bringing them together in concert with one another. Clear accountability is given to the leader. If you want the desired results in Figure 7-1, then this is what you need to do when it comes to engaging your people. These are the principles that will help you create that result.

Refrain from lofty leadership speak. Take a look at the principles and verb lists. Use them as a starting point for consideration. Ask yourself the following questions:

» How am I creating value for my team today?

» What value do I bring to my team?

TIP Should you choose to post the principles in your office or cubicle, leave the verbs in bold font. Each verb pops out and immediately registers as a call to action, and subconsciously you will take the cue to begin moving forward.

Seeing that evolving, thriving attitudes are a result of the principles

Each of the ten principles is life-affirming, expansive, and inclusive. They are all put in place to create consistency in your leadership. They also foster an environment of hope, trust, courage, and optimism. One feeds into the next, as if it were one season passing to another, creating a team that thrives.

We all change, grow, and adapt, and hopefully in doing so, for the better, we thrive. The evolution process closely mirrors the five-step change-management model:

» Request for a change

» Do impact analysis

» Approve/deny

» Implement change

» Review/report

Here I look at the progression of attitude or mindset shift of those within the organization.

In the model shown in Figure 7-2, the evolution of the organization can be seen in the process of looking at results (reveal), evaluating the steps to move forward (evaluate), pausing to course correct or take a value stand, forming and beginning implementing plans (adapt), and building and adding momentum (expand).

FIGURE 7-2: Evolving mindset of a thriving organization.

REVELATION — Mindset: Hope
EVALUATION — Mindset: Courage
EXPANSION — Mindset: Trust
ADAPTATION — Mindset: Optimism

Evolutionary stages of a THRIVING organization

RESISTANCE Yes/No
COURSE CORRECTION Yes/No

© John Wiley & Sons, Inc.

Notice that seasonal elements are associated with each phase of the process. These icons are in place to help you associate a season with certain activities, and the progression of the seasons with the evolution of an organization. For example, consider winter (the snowflake icon) as a time of hibernation when people slow down and evaluate occurrences in their lives, often around the time of the new year. This seasonal icon serves as a prompt; you can't move from the revelation period (fall) to the adaptive period (spring) without the evaluation period (winter) of the equation. (Well, you could try, but chances are that the process would fail.)

This figure depicts a common way of viewing how we all change and evolve as human beings. It also happens to be the pathway to a business's evolution. When it comes to the numbers side of business, these stages will make complete sense to you. Ideally, business returns are audited, reviewed, and improved each quarter. It's expected that most healthy businesses will tweak what they're doing to improve performance or expand a product they sell through more cost-effective means, distribution, and so on. Businesses lean forward into expanding fiscally or in their vision for the future.

The parallel occurs for those within the group as well. Individuals within the organization take similar steps. In their process, it's the mindset and attitude that grow, change, and adapt. These affect whether the workplace thrives or halts. Individuals also traverse this cycle not just once in a lifetime, but throughout their lives. It's a necessary part of shifting from one plane of awareness to another. (If you don't have the ideal environment, you may want to skip to Chapter 8, which shows you how to use the evolution process to transform a potentially resistant team into a thriving one. You can see the possibility of resistance in Figure 7-2.)

Summarizing the mindset of a thriving team

Ideally, the leader is creating a platform with the principles, and as they positively affect the work of the team, their mindset and attitudes continue to evolve and grow simultaneously. The reward becomes a team and vendors who lean more toward the positive, light aspects of their character, creating the best returns.

Within each season, a person grows and expands, though not all individuals will evolve at the same rate. It takes time for the group to change over. Not everyone will grow equally and be at the same point at all times. Nonetheless, the process creates four phases where the individual or group chooses how they will react within the cycle (refer to Figure 7-2):

- **Hopeful individuals** have the capacity to believe that the future will be bigger, better, brighter, and so on. Their hope allows them to view the current results and consider leaving behind what's no longer useful or constructive in the process.

- **Courageous individuals** are willing to take a leap of faith to move forward. The risks are usually calculated. When they're following a leader they trust, they're willing to bypass what may be a natural propensity to avoid putting themselves out on a limb with new ideas, processes, or business opportunities.

- **Optimistic individuals** focus on what's possible in order to be adaptive. Humor is also a key component of optimism. Fun becomes a staple for the group as they adapt to the upcoming changes.

- **Trusting individuals** rely on others, including the leader, to do their parts. Investing in critical thinking brings expansion. Flexibility is a natural part of how they operate because they're secure in themselves.

The environment creates the safety to make course corrections without fear of retribution or shaming. Transparency permits any needed changes, tweaks, or course corrections to be considered out in the open, even if they're uncomfortable.

REMEMBER: Reactions will vary. Some people may exhibit more trust than courage. Others will have hope and optimism but need a bit more time and experience in the process to trust. It's not necessary that they all be at the same point.

TIP: Allow different mindsets to positively influence each other. It's an ebb and flow. Let's face it: Even the most optimistic person has a few bad days.

Knowing that course correction is a values stand

A *values stand* is the capacity to understand what it is that you value most in your life and work, and then take the required action to maintain your alignment. In our scenario, the values-based leader is considering their fiscal and social responsibilities to the shareholders, the board of directors, and the team itself. To maintain a thriving environment, the leader makes the best decision without allowing an ego-driven solution to dilute the situation. The solution is focused on *we* rather than *me*.

Values stands happen in a variety of different ways. In the following list, I illustrate a few ethical and moral examples, personal and/or professional:

- » **Example 1:** You're asked to use a specific vendor because their pricing is more competitive, but you know they're using child labor to get that price. You're encouraged by your peers to overlook this violation of your morals. A values stand here would be to say no, to explain your position, and then to find the solution that satisfies the target — or get as close to it as you can. You've taken a stand for yourself and others. The awareness of the potential ethical and moral violation is out in the open. That makes it harder for others to cross the line. Additionally, you've come to the table with a solution — if you don't have one, offer to work with others to create one. Saying no without an alternative creates the opportunity for you to be overridden.

- » **Example 2:** You witness something that could be perceived as bullying or borderline harassment among team members. You would like to let the instance slide, but you know it's something that could get out of hand. As a human being, you can't allow it to continue. It's a violation of the trusting environment of the workplace. You take a stand against it, identify the issue, and find the resolution to correct it.

- » **Example 3:** You're working for a leader or an organization whose way of working feels slimy and underhanded. Do you stay or go? This is your own personal values stand. You may need the money, and yes, sometimes you must do what you need to do to support your family. But at what point do you take a values stand for yourself and your way of being in this world? Caveat: If you decide you must stay, how will you create a safe environment for you and your team? If this is your predicament, fast-forward to Chapter 12.

These are examples of different ways a values stand and course correction (shown in Figure 7-2) may occur. Every time you make a decision based on what you value, you reinforce your character traits. Consistently doing so is an example to those around you, reminding them who you are as a leader and that you live by your values. People trust you and will model themselves after you.

Recognizing that resistance is part of life and evolution

We all resist in some way at times. It's normal. Resistance is where doubt and skepticism intersect with a fear of some kind — as if something could be lost. When focused on a positive result (as in Figure 7-2), resistance can open up the communication channels to honest, inquiring questions. People want to understand before accepting the shifts to the organization and/or means of engagement. When doubt overrides the ability to move forward with the objectives set by the leader, then it can become negative response.

Resistance is defined as defiant, oppositional fighting and the refusal to accept something or someone. Depending on the issue and where you're sitting, you may view the resistance of others as positive or negative. It could go either way. Our focus is on the positive, constructive aspects of resistance.

Questioning can sometimes be perceived as resistance. Too much questioning could become resistance, but questioning in earnest is a fact-finding mission. A person who questions needs more information before coming onboard with whatever idea or plan is on offer.

When you or I resist any form of change, we may argue our point passionately, but we're also willing to listen. Engaging in a healthy debate, conversation, or line of questioning until your fears are satisfied can be constructive. Some people can shift more quickly than others. Patience is required, as are listening skills. Even if people don't agree with you, you've done your level best to win their trust and respect by hearing them out.

You have the principles and you also now have a basic understanding of the evolutionary process. Where should you go from here? Here are some ideas:

» Consider what you may already be deploying and be aware of what you may want to add to your way of leading.

» If you're resisting, ask yourself why. Are you being curious — or defiant? As you've seen, they're different.

» Remove the judgment. Accept that you're just on a fact-finding mission.

Your passionate, feisty champions of others are a powerful resource. These people serve as ground-level influencers over the group. Take the time to get them onboard. They will move the rest of the group more easily than the leader can at times. Here's how to get them onboard with the mission or task at hand:

- » Identify the ringleader, the person who is a ground-level influencer.

- » Recognize the influencer as an individual who really cares about the outcome: "Sue, I can tell that you really care about what's happening here; otherwise, you wouldn't be so worked up (or withdrawing from the situation)."

- » Invite the influencer into the process by saying something like this: "I'd be happy to have your help, but I need you to work with me toward a solution." Often I've had to add this bit: "Because either we're working toward a solution or we're just complaining. What would you like to do?" Trust me: Given the opportunity, they will help unless there is a values disconnection for them.

WARNING Be mindful not to shut down those who question. Although at times it can be annoying, questioning plays an important role in the process. Those who question will help you to see flaws or areas where more clarity is needed. Always look for the benefit in these exchanges. But create boundaries so it doesn't become a runaway exchange.

Recently I worked with a team member who had a question, an answer, and a rebuttal prepared for just about everything I said to her. I knew it wasn't personal; her negativity and pessimism affected everyone around her, and this was her normal engagement with others. Although I truly didn't believe she was intentionally annoying, a boundary needed to be created to curb her negativity but still allow her the ability to contribute. I said to her, "You are entitled to ask questions and inquire, but I will not go down the rabbit hole with you into your negativity. I ask that you stay focused on the task, avoid taking detours into things you need not be involved with [well outside her purview], and maintain a positive attitude." It took a great deal of reinforcement — she slipped up every now and then — but placing the boundary, or setting the expectation for how to engage with others, dramatically reduced the negative impact.

REMEMBER Boundaries aren't always easy to set or comfortable to reinforce. However, they are necessary. People who like to take you down that rabbit hole will distract you from executing your priorities and objectives.

Making It Easy for Your Team to Buy into the Leader (Yes, You)

After several economic challenges over the past two decades, the misuse of power has been prevalent. There is a general mistrust of those in power by the Gen Xers (born 1961–1981) and Millennials (born 1982–2004). They probably have good reason to mistrust those who inflicted the wounds — the Silent Generation (born

1925–1942) and Baby Boomers (born 1943–1960). Therefore, the conversation about power and the appropriate use of power is a major point of concern.

Traversing the VBL attributes, character, and guiding principles still brings us back to the question "Can they trust you?" People need to buy into the leader — to trust them to be, do, and say exactly what they say they will do, be, and say. Then and only then will people buy into the vision, mission, and purpose being set forth. It doesn't matter how epic a vision you have or how lofty your social intention for good may be. People must *believe* that you can lead them to where they want to go, and that's a question of character.

Additionally, applying appreciation in the process helps retain great people. The place to start is with your everyday engagement with your team and your vendors.

Providing predictable consistency

Author Maya Angelou once said, "When people show you who they are, believe them." That's a profound statement that can be applied to many different situations. Leaders show people who they are through their consistent and almost predictable actions and reactions.

Colleagues can sometimes be heard saying, "Oh, if you tell Mike about that, he's going to flip out." Or: "Don't worry, Mike is a very understanding person — just be up front with him and he won't chastise you." They know their leader, Mike, and they know what kind of reaction Mike will have in certain scenarios. They know this because they've observed him. They recognize his patterns, and for the most part, they understand his expectations.

Think back to when you wanted to borrow the keys to the family car. You knew which parent to ask and when they'd be most receptive. And you knew how to come up with the best reason you should be allowed to borrow the car. How? Because you knew your parents' expectations of you. They had provided a consistent stream of reactions, which you recognized as a consistent pattern.

REMEMBER

Set up your behaviors to be consistent in key areas. Your employees will know who you are and will believe that you'll consistently be that same person every day. When an off day occurs, they'll be much more tolerant.

Keep your promises

When you promise that something will be done, does it happen? Or are you a bearer of false promises? The team and your vendors need to know that you will honor your promises and keep your word. Before you speak, think about the ramifications of what you commit to or promise others. If needed, pause for a minimum of five minutes before you make a promise.

Avoid exploitation of others

To know whether you may be exploiting others, consider basic human rights and the tenets of respecting other people. Have you in any way violated those rights or tenets? Avoid doing so at all costs. In fact, consider doing more to uplift and enrich others' lives in whatever way feels most comfortable. Refer to the ten principles earlier in this chapter as a starting point.

Give others the benefit of the doubt (BOD)

Chief compassion officer Rena DeLevie calls this this *BOD baby.* As in, "have you considered *BOD*, baby?" Don't pounce — give others the opportunity to express what may have occurred or clarify what may be perceived as conflicting points. Pause. Breathe. Asking for clarification may save an uncomfortable exchange that could impair your relationship with the other person. Avoid being labeled as an overly emotional leader who reprimands without knowing the facts.

Maintain an even temperament

Having a hair-trigger temper is one emotional reaction you should consider not utilizing daily. Other reactions to avoid include impatience, judgment, ridicule, and accusation. That said, I assure you that you're not perfect — nor will you ever be. That's one of the most humbling aspects of being a human being. Developing a constant in your reactions and interactions is what's key. Maintaining your equilibrium is achieved by continuing to evaluate and self-assess your motives behind your reactions to varying issues, people, and challenges.

TIP If you *do* snap, know why you did it, and apologize if necessary. If you need to speak firmly, still be kind. And if you're about to lose your marbles due to an extreme situation, take a walk or close your office door for a few minutes so you can collect your thoughts.

Share your wisdom constructively and in a timely manner

Bear in mind that your job is to add value to the lives of others. Constructive feedback provides others with the opportunity to learn and grow. Be gentle, but where necessary it's okay to apply firmness. Just be careful not to chastise others. Provide feedback in a timely manner so adjustments can be made in real time. Don't helicopter around your team.

Simple expressions bring big rewards when done consistently

Thank you is such an underused expression. I don't want to sound like a grandma here, but simple expressions of appreciation do go a long way in helping others to feel appreciated. But let's back up a little. To *be appreciated* means meeting someone's basic human need of being seen or heard by you. You can recognize them with a "Thank you, Joe" or "Great job, Jacinta. I appreciate your diligence in getting this done. Thanks!" Simple expressions like these show the imprints of inclusion.

REMEMBER: A leader without followers is just someone talking to themselves. A leader leads people.

TECHNICAL STUFF: In a 2013, Glassdoor surveyed 2,044 adults over the age of 18 about motivation and the workplace (to read the full survey, check out www.glassdoor.com/press/employees-stay-longer-company-bosses-showed-appreciation-glassdoor-survey/). Here are some of the findings:

» Eighty percent of employees were motivated to work harder when they felt appreciated.

» Forty percent of employees were motivated when their boss was either demanding or they feared losing their job.

» Employees who valued being appreciated also said they'd stay at the company longer if their boss expressly appreciated their efforts.

Providing effective communication

Communicating well with the other leaders in the organization and with the staff is a key component to bringing everyone along on the journey. Silence may be golden, but clarity is king. Employees want more and better communications from their leadership teams. Creating engagement to form relationships creates an inclusive culture.

In the following sections, I offer several aspects of communication to consider. Communication is as much about nuance, technique, and context as the content of your words. Oh, and, don't forget that feedback is also a part of the give-and-take of an exchange.

WHAT EMPLOYEES WANT FROM THEIR BOSSES

Comparably surveyed 20,000 employees at tech companies of various sizes between March 2016 and June 2017. When asked what the number one thing employees say they'd like their boss to improve, the respondents gave the following answers:

- Communications: 50 percent
- Accountability: 20 percent
- Positivity: 14 percent
- Honesty: 9 percent
- Work ethic: 7 percent

Here are a couple of results based on demographics:

- Male and female responses were almost identical.
- Workers aged 56–60 (59 percent) were more likely to choose "communications" than workers age 18–25 (44 percent).

For more on this survey, visit www.comparably.com/blog/study-bosses/.

Pay attention to the basic content

Knowledge of the concept or process you're discussing is essential. At a bare minimum, have a working knowledge so that discussions can be fruitful. When you don't know something, tell your people that you need them to fill you in. This should be occasional, though — not the norm. Expectations that you already know everything are unrealistic, but don't fake it.

Crisp, up-to-date content delivered to the group or in an individual format shows you care about the quality of the exchange and take it seriously.

Be clear and concise

Deliver your message clearly and concisely. Avoid rambling stories, overt references to random facts, and so on. State your purpose and deliver the facts or action points cleanly and concisely. People respond to the efficient use of words. Those who want more color around any given point will ask for it.

WARNING: Always be clear on your directions. One of the most common stumbling points for leaders is to find out after the fact that they hadn't made sure the tasks were understood, and people didn't understand how the tasks would be managed and achieved. Avoid being that leader who sends out the orders and doesn't take the time to work out the who, what, where, and how to get to the goal post. Details provide clarity.

Be real, be authentic, and connect

In a world flooded by virtual socialization, emerging artificial intelligence, and the like, people want real, genuinely authentic connections with other human beings. This takes only moments to achieve. When a person speaks to you, intently listen, react, and ask questions. If you express interest, be sincere. Share something about yourself that relates to what they're sharing, but don't eclipse the conversation with your own stories. The focus and the connection should be with them and for them.

TIP: Individual focus comes first, group focus second. This point is particularly about speaking in public to a large group. First, address the individuals. Forget you're on a stage or in front of a large room; just talk to the room as if there is only one person there. You're having a conversation with that person one-on-one. Connect and make everyone feel like you're talking to them — to their hearts, minds, and concerns. They want to know that you know them. Then speak to the room in terms of "we are," "we will," "we know," and so on as you discuss the solution. This shift in framing is very powerful.

WARNING: Avoid referencing that you and whomever went out for dinner or golfed together.

Pause, listen, then speak

Wait for the person speaking to finish what they're saying before you speak. Experts deem this *active listening*. I call it basic manners. It's not easy to live by. If you're like me — always excited by intelligent, insightful conversations — you may have to be extremely deliberate in monitoring your response time or your tendency to talk over others. If the conversation turns humorous, I usually bite the inside of my lip to stop myself from laughing. (I know it's because I'm totally engaged in whatever the conversation may be, but I suppose it could also be perceived as rude or even obnoxious.)

WARNING: People's perception becomes their reality, which in turn becomes their truth. If they perceive you to be a rude person, then that is the truth in their realm of existence. So be mindful.

Request feedback

Ask for feedback from your peers and from the team. How are we doing? What do you think we can do better or different? Do you feel clear on the direction I've set for us? These questions are an opportunity to have the team members let you know how your decisions are affecting them. It may not always be the most comfortable exchange to have at times. But it maintains the commitment not only to excellence but to transparency and humility, too. You're willing to listen to the good, the bad, and the ugly if necessary to bring about positive changes. What you may perceive to be a great solution may not translate to the practical application for the front line. Be humble enough to consider what is offered.

Assembling Your Framework for Deploying the Principles

Several essential components are available for use in assembling your framework for putting the principles into action in your organization. There is a lot of information to dig into. I don't mean to overwhelm you; I just want to provide choices so you can customize the information shared. I have a formula for you to use that will bring together all the various components in this chapter.

REMEMBER: Before beginning to structure your own plan, consider one additional aspect: Know who you're talking to before you say a word.

Meeting your employees where they are

Knowing who your leaders and team members are and what's important to them matters. Speak and engage with them in a way that makes sense for them. Much can be said for the way we approach people with our words and our actions. Consider how they may become more willing to hear you, literally and figuratively.

Other schools of thought advise speaking to people in terms of where you want them to be rather than where they currently are. I'm not suggesting you talk down to people, but you also don't want to talk over their heads. Walk the line carefully.

I recall a story a client told me recently. He's an insurance representative working on installing a large 401(k) retirement plan for a dairy plant. Prior to the day he was to present to the employees, he asked the HR team what dress was appropriate for the group. Being accustomed to a suit and tie, he wasn't 100 percent sure what was appropriate. The HR rep suggested jeans and a polo. He obliged. He chose to meet the employees where they were in a manner that was most comfortable to them. Being approachable put the group at ease. If he had shown up in a suit and tie, the group may not have felt as comfortable with him. His shift helped him achieve great results that day.

REMEMBER: Meet others where they are. Avoid talking at them — engage them instead. Make people feel comfortable while helping them aspire to be, do, and have more in their own lives. That may be material or it may not. Don't assume. Know what's important to whom you're speaking with.

Adding it up: Creating momentum

Great amounts of time and energy are poured into building your leadership. Positioning your principles to create a values platform is something truly amazing. A business or corporation that moves together in unison to the goals positively permeates the community around them. Although there are additional components, the momentum equation can be summed up in Figure 7-3. It's a two-part equation.

PART 1: $(P) \times (A) = (EM)$

Principles × Action = Evolved mindset and environment

PART 2: $(CN) + (CM) \times (EM) = (SM)$

Consistency + Communications × Evolved mindset and environment = Sustained momentum

FIGURE 7-3: Momentum equation.

© John Wiley & Sons, Inc.

The first part is the combination of the ten principles amplified by action, which creates a healthy mindset and workplace environment. Then use consistency and communication skills, which are further amplified by your evolved mindset, to create momentum. Each piece of this equation has been detailed as tools earlier in this chapter. Additionally, you find a more expansive rationale behind the equation in the next section.

Momentum carries the group beyond their challenges by assuring them there's always another opportunity to do better and be better. It makes navigating the highs and lows easier — particularly the lows. The leader and the team are consistent, communicate, and are walking on the same path toward the goal.

A proven formula for success is one that leaves an indelible mark on those involved in the process. I can think back to two teams I've led that I've never forgotten. We were part of something very special. It wasn't always perfect, but we rode the momentum through the highs and lows. To this day, I receive emails on LinkedIn from past members of my team thanking me for being the leader I was. They were paying attention and had begun to incorporate some of the skills I'm sharing with you here. Success is duplicable. Show them the way so they can then bless others too.

One size doesn't fit all: Creating your own principle plan

The ten principles from earlier in this chapter are a starting point for you to determine what more you'd like to add to your organization. As the business world continues to evolve, they may need to be tweaked. The language may not be a fit for your group, or you may want to tweak the verbs. Please feel free to alter as necessary — meet them where they are in a way that they can not only hear you but also feel a connection to you.

Starting with what's possible

Ten principles may feel overwhelming to deploy all at once. Rolling them out could be handled in a variety of ways:

- Consider the four sections as a phased implementation. Quarters one and two will be Phase 1: Set Direction. The second half of the year could be Phase 2: Create a Proactive Company Culture. And so on. Adjust the timing as needed.
- Roll out the two or three principles that could provide the biggest impact sooner rather than later.
- Start with principles one and two then select another few to begin with.
- Set the direction in principles one, two, and three. Live with that for a year or more to make sure they work before doing more.

This fulfills the principles (P) × actions (A) part of the equation from Figure 7-3. Even in small measures, that will start the (EM) evolution of mindset and environment.

Overlaying reinforcement strategies

Consistency and communication strategies (described earlier in this chapter) reinforce the values-based environment being built. Connection is created not solely to you as a leader but also as an example of how behavior toward others is expected within the team. Integrate as much of these skills and tools into your principles to accelerate your momentum. As shown in Figure 7-3, consistency

(CN) + communication (CM) × an evolved mindset (EM) creates a powerful, sustained momentum (SM) for the group.

REMEMBER: You don't need to roll everything out all at once. Review and reflect on your principles plan often. Tweak as needed.

REMEMBER: Sustainable momentum is created for the team, but never forget that your ability to create this result makes you a valuable leader out in the workforce. Your reputation for results goes with you throughout your career.

CHRISTINE'S MAGNETIC LUXURY PROBLEM

My client "Christine" works for a major financial firm leading a multinational team. When we started working together, she felt overwhelmed by all the detail in values-based leadership. Still, she persisted. She took some serious feedback to heart, not only from her own manager but also from her staff. She needed to correct the perception that she was only in it for herself. If you met Christine socially, you'd know that here was a woman with an enormous heart who really wanted her team to succeed. They were a motivated and effective group, but the uncertainty of Christine's motives caused uncertainty and led to a lack of transparency about what they were doing.

Over the months we worked together, she reframed her approach with everyone she engaged with, focusing on the *we* rather than the *me*. Her communication became clearer, more effective, and motivational. It wasn't that Christine didn't care — she just needed some adjustment in her engagement with others.

Fast-forward a few years, and Christine is thriving. She's become a leader that others want to work with and for — a consistent, clear, openly communicative leader who puts her team first. She operates with conviction with regard to the values that she and the organization hold dear. Over lunch one day, she told me it astounded her that she's become a magnet for great talent. "Why is that?" I asked. "I don't think I'm any better than any other leader in the organization," she said. "I've just tried to live and exercise the expectations of the company's direction authentically. I do my best to integrate as much as you've taught us into what I do and how I do it." She paused. "Maybe it's because the team knows I am their champion."

Learning to refine a skill, such as communicating more effectively, increases your effectiveness exponentially. It's totally worth taking the time to upgrade your approach. People will be more inclined to be naturally attracted to you as a leader.

> **IN THIS CHAPTER**
>
> » Uncovering the five mindsets that create a Halt environment
>
> » Helping your team convert a negative workplace into a thriving organization
>
> » Discovering your role in shifting the hearts and minds of others

Chapter 8
Defining Defiant Workplaces

Road trip! GPS ready to go. Friends in the back seat. BFF in the passenger seat. You're rolling out of the driveway headed for your big adventure. The group starts out singing a happy tune. Everyone is smiles — except Eve, who went back to sleep and has no desire to wake up until you arrive at the destination. She's made that clear by wearing an eye mask and headphones. The rest are all happy travelers ready for adventure.

An hour or so into the drive, people are getting fidgety. The rest stop is coming up, so everyone except Eve takes the opportunity to stretch their legs, get snacks, and then pile back into the car. A couple of hours later, Harry offers the group sandwiches he's packed. Everything is going great. Then the integrity of your GPS is called into question. Everyone has a different app they'd like you to use. And the debate for the best app becomes a struggle for control of doing it "their way." The travelers become irritated with one another after a few detours get them lost. Rodrigo is nervous that you'll never find the way. Ultimately, there's an outburst, maybe a little shouting — huffing and general annoyance with one another, for sure. The happy group has turned into a car full of brooding adults.

Eventually you arrive at your destination. Everyone is tired but fortunately had cooled off about 50 miles ago. Eve wakes up and begins to ask why the trip took so long, is the hotel ready, didn't you order dinner, are there snacks? She yawns and stretches her arms, blissfully unaware, to the sky. "Could someone bring my bag up?" The simultaneous eye roll is in motion as she walks away. Everyone in the group would like Eve to go back to sleep. She missed the whole trip and now she's demanding that her every need be fulfilled.

This car trip may sound a lot like what happens in the workplace. Your joyful, motivated, happy employees can turn into a mob of angry, annoyed individuals. Let's face it: Every day is not going to be full of rainbows, unicorns, and gold star moments. There will be challenges. People will have normal reactions. Feathers will be ruffled at times. But a sustained state where individuals are uncooperative and unhappy is something that can erode team morale and effectiveness.

It's always the attitudes and mindset residing under the surface that are troubling. Seeing them isn't always easy, but the defiance, resistance, and general malaise are most certainly there. Course correction is necessary. However, applying the inappropriate correction can be more inflammatory than not doing anything at all.

Before I discuss how to start moving the needle, I would like to show you what a defiant and possibly dysfunctional environment — what I call a *Halt environment* — could look like, as well as the root cause that needs to be addressed. As a values-based leader, it's your responsibility to guide your employees out of potential pitfalls. Your job is to show them the way — not to do it for them.

REMEMBER A team operating within a business is one part of the mechanism churning to create opportunities for everyone, including themselves. When this mechanism fails, often its nature and purpose haven't been made clear to the group. Rewind. Go back. Start over.

Facing the Effects of the FARCE Syndrome

Several years ago, when I first started teaching values-based leadership (VBL), my coaching and corporate clients would ask me how to fix what they perceived as a broken team. If we're administering values, how does that change a dysfunctional team? Can a dysfunctional team be shifted? I recall one gentleman who raised his eyebrow and said, "This is all well and good, but if I tell them to be transparent when they're fighting among themselves or with other teams, it won't happen. They may pause, nod their heads in my direction, and then turn around and keep fighting."

This gentleman is not wrong. In fact, he's 100 percent correct. Telling a team to be transparent when the core issues haven't been dealt with won't garner positive results. He added, "Respectfully, don't tell me kindness triumphs over all." That's also correct. To defuse whatever is causing the disruption, the leader needs to apply an appropriate measure to change the course of the group. (By the way, I absolutely love when my clients are direct about their issues and concerns. It shows me how much they care.)

The easiest way to identify the issue is to look at the FARCE Syndrome. If the profile of a values-based leader's effect on the team is about optimism, trust, courage, and hope (as detailed in Chapter 7), the antithesis of VBL would be the effects of the FARCE Syndrome: fear, attachment, resistance, competition, and entitlement. FARCE creates a negative environment (see Figure 8-1). The good news is that by reverse-engineering the process, you'll be able to see where the wheels started to fall off the bus.

MINDSET	What they say and do
FEAR	• "This is the way we've always done things; why change now?" • Old-school way of doing business, set in their ways • Do what I say, not what I do • Lack of transparency
ATTACHMENT	• "I know what's best" • Self-preservation and advancement focused • Takes the outcome personally • Prefers to control the outcome with an iron fist
RESISTANCE/ RETALIATION	• "I'm not doing that/this" • Rules are for other people, not me • Deflects deficit attention away from themselves • Someone will pay
COMPETITION	• "Winner takes all" • Viciously fighting until the end/Take no prisoners • Unwilling to cooperate or collaborate well with others • Modeled after movies such as *Wall Street* and *Boiler Room*
ENTITLEMENT	• "It's all about me and what I get" • Me first, me only, you're not my problem • No personal responsibility to the organization, team, clients, or customers

FIGURE 8-1: FARCE Syndrome overview.

© John Wiley & Sons, Inc.

Teams may embody any or all of the beliefs in the following sections and may act out accordingly. Letting that continue is a sure way to have your company culture crumble and your vision die on the vine.

REMEMBER: This assessment of mindset is as much for you as a leader as it is for your organization. Mirror, mirror, on the wall, guess who's reflecting your own fear, insecurity, and doubt back at you? They are!

Deploying fear to get what they want

Fear is a very powerful motivating tool. It's said that people are more motivated by they want to get away from than by what they want to move toward. Chapter 16 covers this in more depth. Here, in the process of uncovering what causes dysfunction or defiance, fear is *an expression of concern about losing control.* Fear sits at the top of the FARCE acronym because it permeates all the other behaviors. Individuals may feel secure enough in themselves not to be competitive, for example, but they may fear that something could be taken from them, so their fear shows up in attachments and/or resistance.

WARNING: Fear can manifest in a familiar way: heels dug in, "I'm not going to change, and no one can tell me any different," coupled with a threatening tone, body language, or even passive-aggressive behavior. This particular form of fear comes from the unwillingness to evolve, grow, and change. Some just won't do it and feel threatened by those who do. However, fear can also be deployed in conjunction with a dearly held value. Values, or the belief in values, can be used to manipulate others with fear. Fear either keeps people in bondage or repels them. It has a polarizing effect.

Assess the fear mechanism in your organization with these questions:

- **Does someone feel threatened when left out of a conversation or plan?** If the person should be involved, be sure to include them. If they should not be involved, clarify parameters of involvement through a discussion of roles and responsibilities.

- **Is someone more concerned with people doing what they say, rather than what they do?** Clarify that in a values-based organization, the expectation is to lead from the front by being a positive example.

- **Does someone feel like they must hide information or contacts from others?** Reinforce that the organization is about everyone winning. In order for that to happen, cooperation and transparency are necessary. Ask them to choose to be part of the solution.

- **Would you or anyone else deploy fear as a mechanism for motivation in a threatening manner?** If this is occurring, it means that there is a culture of permission to do so. Each remedy in this list also applies here; a discussion of roles and responsibilities, clarification, and the addition of coaching them to positively affect others instead of resorting to fear and intimidation tactics.

> ## USING FEAR TO MANIPULATE VALUES
>
> "Samantha" requested a transfer from her current manager to a new team. In her view, the current manager, "Will," wasn't training her or helping her grow. She sensed a deep negativity and laziness about him. Samantha was passionate and committed to her work and wanted to politely distance herself from the negativity. Will told her that HQ wouldn't look favorably on her request for transfer because, in his words, "it's a matter of loyalty."
>
> Her mouth gaped open. "Are you threatening me?"
>
> "No, I'm just telling you that you may be asked to leave the company if you persist in asking for a transfer. They don't like disloyal people." Needless to say, that didn't sit well with Samantha, who was sharp enough to know that wasn't company policy. She knew it was Will's own fear of losing control surfacing.
>
> Ultimately, Samantha did get her transfer. Will was reprimanded for the nature of his misleading comments and, shortly after, dismissed from the company for continued inappropriate behavior.

The prescriptive remedies in the preceding list help everyone get on and stay on the same page. Always refer to the principles of VBL for yourself and the organization (see Chapters 6 and 7) to create clarity on the expectations of conduct and engagement with others.

Developing attachment to the outcome

Those who are attached to an outcome are invested in the process personally — or may want to be. Outcomes feel as if they will in some way affect them personally, professionally, fiscally, or in matters of prestige or reputation. No matter what level a person is operating at in your organization, when things get tough, you may hear them say, "This is going to kill my reputation if I continue to work here" or "I put so much time into this, and now they're going to change it — why bother?" This person is attached to an outcome in an almost unhealthy way. In most cases, it's a survival mechanism being triggered, where they've lost hope for a better outcome, and trust doesn't permeate their existence.

Control enthusiasts are unwilling to let go, period. They simply don't trust others to do a job well. Leaders, managers, and team members alike may clutch work or projects so tightly that they can block progress. Letting go and allowing others to handle the work is very difficult for them.

Part of our psychological development is to learn to recognize what no longer serves us and let it go. Attachment stifles development. This is a fear of the unknown and becoming attached to what is safe and familiar. A person who's become attached believes they know what's best. If you'd just follow them, everything would be perfect.

Those who form attachments may not always mean to do harm, but their outward behavior breeds mistrust and pessimism, as illustrated in the story of the control enthusiast in the nearby sidebar "Using fear to manipulate values."

WARNING Suffocating your team, or your team members suffocating one another, will only cause complacency, boredom, resignation, and general annoyance.

An interesting caveat to the attachment issue is that those who try to control the outcome often, but not always, think they're trying to keep themselves and others safe. In a workshop I gave at a chapter of the National Association of Women MBAs, one of the participants used a bus as a metaphor for a broken process: "If I can get everyone on and off the bus without disruption, then I know what's what." She further explained that she indeed knew what to do, so don't change her methodology and system because they weren't broken. When I inquired further, she told me that she just wanted to make sure everyone was "safe." She could control the pitfalls because she knew them well. The words are very telling. People who are attached and controlling are sometimes that way to ensure a safe ride from point A to point B in the process.

This is a cue to you as a values-based leader to consider whether the transition you want to make is "safe." Assess the attachment mechanism in your company with these questions:

» **Are you or others hyper attached to a specific process or outcome that may be perceived as a bit obsessive?** (Ask your friends and spouse to weigh in on your own attachment mechanism if necessary.) If it's you with the attachment, consider why you're attached to it. What does it mean to have a process kept in place or removed? Does it trigger your ego? If so, you need to reframe and consider whether the process is about you or the greater good of others.

If you have a hyper attached employee, simply ask them why they seem so attached to the solution or outcome. What does it mean to them? I'm willing to bet you that no one has ever been brave enough to gently ask them that question. When you do, it will jolt them a bit. You're giving them a chance to consider their own motives without making it too confrontational.

» **Have you or anyone else ever been called a control freak/enthusiast?** Control enthusiasts are my favorite people — seriously. They just want everyone to be safe, focused, and on track. Recognize this, but understand that you're stifling everyone around you. Let . . . it . . . go! (This is an observational step when it comes to others. No need to ask them this direct question.)

- **Is someone often being told to "just let it go"?** Just what I did in the preceding bullet point! If you really can't let something go, you need to gain some perspective on your attachment. In whatever way, it's important to reflect as to why you cannot let go. What is the motivation? Knowing that will help you reframe your attachment to something healthier and more productive. When engaging with others to move them past the attachment, ask them why they are having such a hard time seeing another point of view.

- **Who are you or they trying to protect?** Protecting others is a noble rationale. Perhaps trying a different path to achieve that same protective quality would garner a better result. It's something to consider, which is a step in letting go.

   This is the question you ask if you haven't been able to crack the shell of an attached employee. Perhaps rephrase it a little: Who stands to win or lose in this scenario? That's a less confrontational way of asking the question.

Gently and patiently guide an employee through variations of the questions as you see fit. I suggest not asking them if their ego is involved; that will most likely close them down and have them run from you. I think you get the general idea here. Sometimes just asking the direct question will get to the bottom line. Then ask them to reconsider their perception of the situation.

LOVING YOUR TEAM TOO MUCH

"Miss Evelyn," as she's affectionately known, can never let go of the process. She is a control enthusiast. She loves her team, truly. If you ask her about their capabilities, she'll rave about each of them. When a job is done well, she's the first to congratulate the team on the other side of the finish line.

However, Miss Evelyn also can't allow any piece of the process to happen without her oversight, commentary, or input. So, although she loves her team, she also drives them insane. They feel that nothing they ever do is good enough. Her enthusiastic tendencies sometimes feel like micromanagement. She takes the reputation of her leadership to heart and is always afraid she may be perceived as incompetent herself. Her strong work ethic overrides the capacity of others on a regular basis.

Her team reacts to this behavior in two ways: The members of one group stay, understanding her excess need to control, but often leave after a year or two. The members of the second group leave more quickly. Either way, her team's turnover occurs on a more regular basis than other leaders' team turnover.

There is a theme here: Let go. Find a compromise and be willing to look at alternate options to achieve your desired result. Honestly, I recognize that this is easier said than done. For most people, this is a process and an exercise in honestly evaluating motives. It's deeply personal.

Using resistance or retaliation to control

The *R* in FARCE could stand for *resistance* or *retaliation*. What's the difference?

- **Resistance** is the inability to participate, accept, or even acknowledge something. It's also the refusal to take action to prevent something from occurring. There are positive and even constructive aspects of resistance. However, in a *Halt environment* — where people aren't thriving and expansion isn't occurring — resistance impedes direction and processes. Heels dug in, arms crossed, head slowly moving from side to side telling you no, and a clenched jaw are some of the physical cues. But there is also quiet resistance that smiles, takes notes, and says yes but then deploys passive-aggressive behavior as the preferred resistance method.

- **Retaliation** is another form of resistance. There's a price to pay if you don't do XYZ. It's a threat to ensure compliance with the intent to cause harm as a repercussion. Sometimes retaliation is subtly deployed; resources a coworker may need to complete a project may be held back to damage that coworker's effectiveness. More overt retaliation might include sabotaging someone so that they are ultimately fired. Retaliation can be ugly and harmful.

    Additionally, it's important to make the distinction between retaliation and consequences. Consequences are a domino effect based on an action — sometimes known, other times unknown. Retaliation is calculated.

WARNING: There can sometimes be a fine line with people who resist; some are making their own values stand because they care and are passionately attached to the outcome. Some have no intention of participating in a manner different than what they believe is appropriate.

Resistance and retaliation can erode effectiveness and trust. Here are a few questions to help you assess a resistant or retaliatory environment:

- **How are people who don't agree handled?** Acknowledge their position but explain why you've made a different choice. Often, it's more important to those people to have the acknowledgment of their solution or grievance. They want to be seen, heard, and recognized, even in their resistance.

- **Where have you or they dug heels in just because?** It's time to take a look inside. Is it just because you like drama (some people do), you're addicted to conflict (some people love it), or you just have to be right (too many people fall into this category)? You can adjust your perspective.

Others who exhibit this type of behavior need to have their behavior pointed out to them. In my humble opinion, most of the time they don't realize they're being, well, jerks. "Sally, do you realize that you've dug your heels in so deeply that there's just no pulling you out?" Again, this is a polite and sometimes humorous way of jolting them a bit so they can take stock of their own behavior (dispense humor only to those who also have a sense of humor). Awareness works wonders.

» **Does anyone fear retaliation in the workplace in any way?** Retaliation is a form of bullying. This becomes an HR issue. Direct anyone in this situation to this group of trained professionals for next steps.

REMEMBER

Remedies should be deployed quickly. Left too long, bad habits and patterns develop, which will take longer to correct if they're reinforced.

Engaging in unhealthy competition

Competition is a natural part of the world. You sell widgets. Another person sells widgets. And there's probably more than just the two of you selling similar products. Each of you will set out to sell a unique product in one way or another to edge out your competitors, perhaps through pricing or quality.

Where competition goes off the rails and becomes negative is when unsavory tactics or unnecessary aggressive moves are used — for example, through marketing techniques or creating disruptions to others' businesses by discrediting them or maligning their leader or team. Ugly competitiveness takes many forms: Play hardball. Trounce or annihilate your competition. Make them bleed and beg for mercy. These are some of the extreme ways of viewing competition. In the world of mergers, acquisitions, and capitalizing on stumbles or diminishing earnings, companies sometimes use these situations to eclipse their competitors.

I'm not disputing that you need to be aware of your competition and make moves to improve your products and services. Playing extreme hardball in the short term can be productive, but in the long run it creates a winner-takes-all dynamic in the workplace.

Perhaps a softer, less supervillain-like but still harmful version of competition you may see involves staff members undercutting one another. Compromising or undermining another team member by disempowering who they are, what they do, and how they contribute, with the goal of moving them to another team or out of the company, is another form of competitiveness. It's a way to take the focus and attention away from someone so it may shine on the aggressor as champion. Most of the time, this is done in a very subtle manner.

REMEMBER: Critics of my stance on this argue that competition is healthy when respect is integrated into the process. Competition raises the bar of expectations and elevates the group. It creates better efficiencies, and ultimately improves quality and passes lower costs back to the customer. Nothing needs to become cutthroat to achieve these results other than the commitment to use competition as the catalyst to do a better job, and that's done only through the ability to cooperate and trust others in the process.

Assessing a competitive nature in your company involves the following questions:

- Consider how you or your team engaged with your last competitor — was it a cage fight until only one was left standing?
- Where have you or your team potentially engaged in undercutting the work of another to get ahead?
- Do you encourage level competition among the team and other companies?

The story in the nearby sidebar "Learning from giants" serves as an important lesson about curtailing negative competition. Healthy competition, rather than negative competition, serves as a catalyst for two giants to continue to motivate and propel one another forward. One company's advancement pushes the other to do even better. Express that this is the *constructive* way to compete to those who violate fairness; it makes clear that such behavior isn't necessary.

LEARNING FROM GIANTS

In 1997 Microsoft invested $150 million in Apple to help the struggling competitor. Microsoft promised to support Microsoft Office for the Mac for five years while Apple agreed to make Internet Explorer the default web browser on the Mac as part of the agreement. Everyone got what they needed and continued to grow.

Microsoft could have let Apple collapse and then took over their market share — but it didn't. Instead, Microsoft founder Bill Gates understood that both companies could benefit by not allowing that to happen. By 2003, Microsoft had sold off its stake in Apple.

The moral of the story: Both competitors continue to thrive and push one another to be better. There is room for both in the marketplace.

Displaying entitlement

Inherently believing that one deserves special privilege is the mindset of entitlement. Entitlement can be expressed in a healthy manner — for example, the belief that human beings have the right to take care of themselves and their families and to be treated with dignity and respect. The unhealthy form of entitlement would be the inability to comprehend that others are also deserving of certain rights. The development process from childhood into adulthood, through experience and guidance, teaches us to respect others. A balance between what you need and what others need can be found through mutual respect. Sometimes the understanding of mutual respect isn't fully developed, which leads to the negative projection of entitlement into the workplace.

The person who feels entitled believes their needs, wants, and desires are more important than those of others. The focus borders on narcissism; oblivious to others, they spend more time on self-satisfaction, disregarding the needs of the team as a whole. The words *special treatment* may not be used, but the feeling that they consider themselves, in some way, to be special and therefore exempt permeates the team. They believe they are deserving of perks without the work. At times, entitlement can show itself in statements such as "I've been here a long time, so therefore I am entitled to" whatever it is. That could be anything from not needing to work, to enjoying a free ride, to not needing to comply with new expectations. Displays of selfishness may also be demonstrations of entitlement: "I've got what I need" (such as recognition, status, or employment) "and the rest of you can figure it out for yourselves." Entitlement is therefore perceived as selfishness.

Here are some questions to help you assess entitlement in your organization:

- **Have you or anyone ever been selfish or stingy in reaching a goal?** This signals the belief that it's all about the individual and not the group's win, together. Spend time reinforcing that reaching the goal is a team effort. Have a discussion with the individual, detailing how one person's willingness to focus only on themselves and not the group creates a negative impact on everyone.

- **Where has someone skipped to the end and demanded to be heard, catered to, or had their needs met before others?** Reinforce that no one person is more special than another. Special treatment and exceptions are not applicable.

- **Does someone believe they deserve special treatment because of who they are and what they do?** Again, reinforce that no one person is more special than another.

> **Are you and your team respectful of others' needs and wants, or is it all about you?** Checking in with yourself and with others on the team is a way to circumvent this ever happening. However, if it does happen, peer intervention to shed light on the perception of behavior usually suffices as a correction point.

REMEMBER: There actually are exceptions within all the preceding remedies. Those with health issues or special circumstances (like those in cancer treatment or someone who may have a personal emergency) do require legitimate exceptions to some criteria. Grant them the flexibility they need. What I'm detailing in this section has more to do with people believing they are above the criteria and expectations of everyone else.

Putting the FARCE together: The resulting halted environment

The result of FARCE is the creation of a Halt organization, stuck in its tracks and unable to move forward (see Figure 8-2). Human capital moves businesses forward. Technology helps and accelerates this forward movement, but human capital — your beautiful team — is what determines progress.

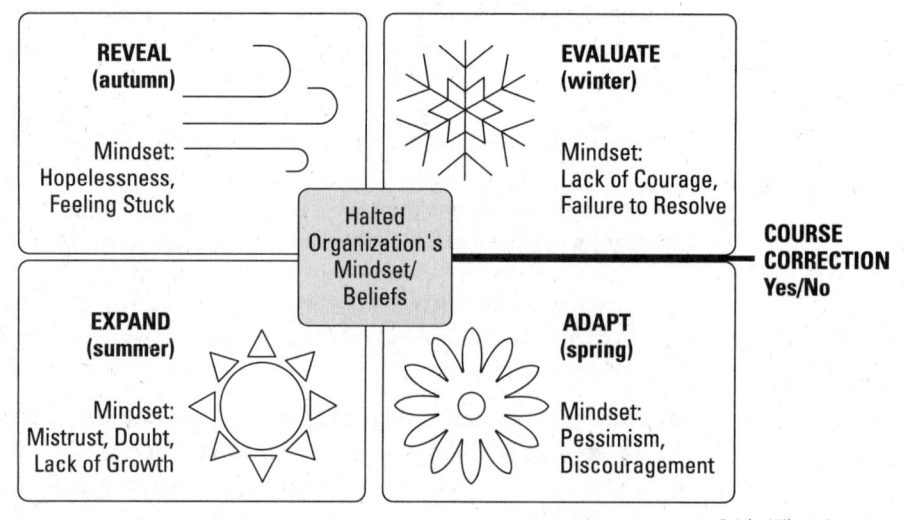

FIGURE 8-2: Model of a halted organization.

- **REVEAL (autumn)** — Mindset: Hopelessness, Feeling Stuck
- **EVALUATE (winter)** — Mindset: Lack of Courage, Failure to Resolve
- **EXPAND (summer)** — Mindset: Mistrust, Doubt, Lack of Growth
- **ADAPT (spring)** — Mindset: Pessimism, Discouragement

Center: Halted Organization's Mindset/Beliefs

COURSE CORRECTION Yes/No

© John Wiley & Sons, Inc.

The mindset model of a thriving organization in Chapter 7 has been translated into Figure 8-2, which illustrates the mindset of a halted organization. Seasonal symbols are used again to flag an association with what is occurring seasonally and within the organization during that period. For example, during the reveal period (autumn), the bright leaves of a tree, bursting with energy, turn golden then brown and fall to the ground. Winds blow in, the air turns cold, and people go inside. This is often a period of review (as in "the summer was great, but now I've gained a few pounds").

In business, the reveal period is when the results of efforts are shown — for example, recounting sales, productivity, or a specific project's effectiveness. Halted organizations with negative mindsets may experience feeling stuck or hopeless even if their results were good.

Each season or period of time within a halted organization is detailed later in this chapter. As you find out, these seasons are counter to those of an organization that is thriving, evolving, making adjustments, and learning from their mistakes. It's important for you to be aware of these nuances because you'll then be able to diagnose where you and your team stand.

WARNING Self-doubt, insecurity, and fear, even at low levels, create an unhealthy work environment where people are afraid to take a step in the wrong direction. Or they may feel that whatever they do won't matter. A Halt environment is more focused on *lack* than anything else. FARCE is effective because it plays on the fears that there will never be enough to go around — not enough skills, resources, opportunities, direction . . . the list goes on. Some figuratively collapse inside themselves as protection and deflect as much as possible to survive. Others walk away, which becomes another problem.

TIP Should the nitty-gritty detail become overwhelming, ask yourself one simple question to find your starting point: What does the team feel they lack to cause such a stagnant environment? The answer always springs from what they feel they're missing.

Evolving the Mindsets of People and Organizations

Have you ever noticed that patterns appear in just about every aspect of your life? It could be that you seem to date the same kinds of people. Perhaps you're stopped at the same point in your progress, whether it be dieting or getting to the next level in your career. Potentially, you've noticed that before you have a breakthrough, certain steps seem to be part of that process that ultimately prepares you for that breakthrough. You've learned from challenges and have taken the next appropriate action to get where you want to go. Those steps aren't a figment of your imagination.

Growth, transition, transformation, and evolution follow similar patterns. Usually they encompass central themes and choices. I mention Joseph Campbell's Hero's Journey concept of personal development throughout this book. Each stage brings a new lesson or way of being in the world.

In the following sections, I walk you through the process of getting your employees' mindset out of the FARCE Syndrome. Over the years, I've had leaders tell me over and over again, "If I just knew where I was in this process, it would be so much easier to handle." Welcome to the road map — to being able to bridge the gap between where you or your team may be and where you need to be.

Traversing the seasons of change

Chapter 7 introduced the concept of the evolution of a thriving, values-based organization that fosters trust, courage, hope, and optimism. In this chapter I'm unraveling the mindset, attitudes, and beliefs that create a defiant workplace perpetuated by the FARCE Syndrome.

Once this is understood, the group can be shifted away from FARCE. My intent here is to help you identify where you or your brilliant team may be in their process. That will help you find the best solutions to encourage them to the goal post. Earlier in this chapter, I had you identify which aspects of FARCE Syndrome may be alive and well in your organization.

At any point, individuals can self-correct, or it may require the mentor, leader, or colleague to help them see the alternatives. It depends on the depth of the problem within the organization. There is the assessment of self, as I've asked you to engage in as we journey to VBL together, but there are also external influences to course correct. Both views are offered.

REMEMBER

You are the example to the group. As we explore shifting the team, you too must do your best to sincerely participate in the process and exhibit the same behaviors you're asking of them. Leadership is a templating process: Do what you ask them to do, say what you're asking them to say, engage, perceive, and react in alignment with who you are as a values-based leader.

The following sections provide a deeper understanding of each season or period in the process.

The reveal period (autumn)

During this period, individuals look at the results of their efforts. Consider sitting in your office on any given day and having a flash overview of your job satisfaction, personal satisfaction, relationships, fulfillment, environment, flexibility, impact, the direction of the company, and your effectiveness as a leader. With FARCE as the current state, some combination of feelings of hopelessness, guilt, regret, resignation, and sadness are the predominant emotions.

Individuals make decisions about what they want to keep and what they want to get rid of. It could be their current bad attitude, resistance, processes, and/or ideas that no longer work. At the highest level, it may be their understanding that they are limiting themselves.

Hope becomes the way and means of shifting resignation and self-doubt. Basically, the living breathing organism that is your company is looking for something to hold onto. Employees are seeking *permission* of sorts to let go of the prior results and mistakes, and to replace them with an agreement to move forward. There is nothing more powerful than celebrating accomplishments like reaching the organization's annual goal. Leaders either say, "Job well done, but we can do more" or "We can do better; let's show them." We turn the page and move forward, not backward. This creates a foundation from which hope can spring forth. In essence, a sort of forgiveness is provided so the group can let go of the past and focus on the future (see Figure 8-3).

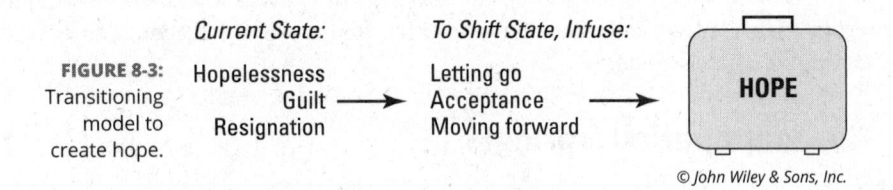

FIGURE 8-3: Transitioning model to create hope.

Current State: Hopelessness, Guilt, Resignation → To Shift State, Infuse: Letting go, Acceptance, Moving forward → HOPE

© John Wiley & Sons, Inc.

Letting go other behaviors or business practices that no longer serve the individual or the group can also be part of this season. This period of time becomes a very important self-assessment period for an individual who may be wrestling with happiness, fulfillment, balance, and the ability to make a difference.

The evaluate period (winter)

The results have been revealed. In the winter phase, the results are analyzed, evaluated, and calculated, and perceptions have been quantified. Either the person will have the courage to move forward to shift the results, or they will sink into self-criticism and possibly shame: "How could I have made so many mistakes? How is it possible I've fallen so far short on my goals? How did this get so out of hand, and how did I not see it?" At the worst, the individual may feel duped by the leader and company.

I don't believe any person is immune to self-doubt. Encouragement and assurance are essential to allaying those fears, as you see in Figure 8-4. It makes it incredibly difficult to take courageous steps forward when feeling this kind of doubt. And it's increasingly more difficult when the focus becomes more on the shortfall — skills and strengths aren't recognized. Staff may want to hide or perhaps lash out in frustration.

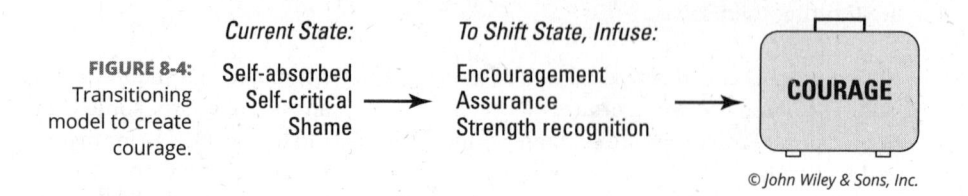

FIGURE 8-4: Transitioning model to create courage.

Current State: Self-absorbed, Self-critical, Shame → *To Shift State, Infuse:* Encouragement, Assurance, Strength recognition → COURAGE

© John Wiley & Sons, Inc.

TIP Although there are VBL principles in place to foster courage, let's not forget the everyday bolstering of the confidence of the team by celebrating small successes and milestones; every step forward moves toward the completion of a goal (see Chapter 16), nurturing their skills (see Chapter 14), and trusting them to do their job (see Chapter 10). The ground-level leaders, managers, and coworkers are required to have the empathy and compassion to help those who are struggling to regain their confidence by forgiving mistakes and making corrections to ensure they don't happen again.

The adapt period (spring)

Spring represents a fresh start, a new page turning or the winds of change coming into the cycle. This is the intention, but those that are still stuck in a negative pattern may experience the season of adaptation to new possibilities in a very different way. They may not be experiencing any newness — instead they feel stagnant and bored to tears by what they are doing.

This is where people are often stopped. The cycle of nature is constantly in motion. It doesn't stop. Fall and winter naturally progress into the spring, and then spring into summer. Just because the individual chose not to participate in the phase of adaptation doesn't mean competitors and other colleagues also chose not to. The world around them continues to move through the phases. Because they don't participate doesn't mean the cycle isn't continuing around them. If they stay stuck too long, they get left behind.

Encouraging individuals to move beyond their boredom, stagnation, and malaise often means injecting some fun, play, humor, and creativity into the process (see Figure 8-5). Even the most hardened individual will respond to one or more of these stimuli. It cracks them open, and even the smallest crack allows light and possibility to seep into their psyche. As the momentum around them builds, they may outwardly still scoff — but bits of optimism come in until they embrace it.

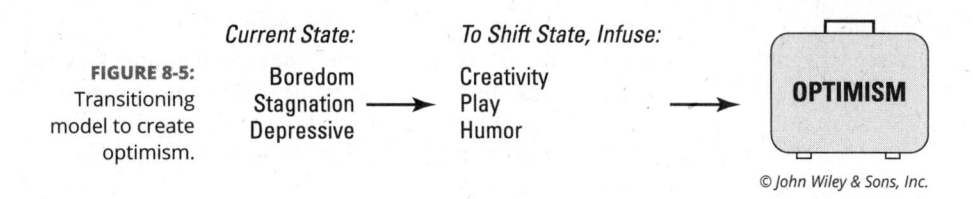

FIGURE 8-5: Transitioning model to create optimism.

Current State: Boredom, Stagnation, Depressive → To Shift State, Infuse: Creativity, Play, Humor → OPTIMISM

© John Wiley & Sons, Inc.

Many years ago, I was working in Melbourne, Australia. My team was small but mighty. When they would hit this phase of feeling bored, depleted, or stuck in repetition, I'd move our staff meetings to St. Kilda Beach, where we could find café tables to work at. The fresh air and sunshine and breaking the routine allowed everyone to relax, joke, and gain a new perspective. We'd still accomplish a lot, but somehow it just felt lighter. The group would return to the offices with smiles and new positive energy to move forward.

Additionally, engaging the group in play allows their brains to disengage from a pattern of negativity. It's as if you've hit the pause button on doubt. There's an insightful reason that games such as Ping-Pong are being installed in offices and sales teams run zany themed competitions. The distraction allows the brain to shift gears and be open to other possibilities. It's like clearing brain gridlock.

TIP

Humor is also a great neutralizer. Dispense liberally.

The expand period (summer)

The demonstration of this phase may surprise you a little. Consider that everyone has been moving toward the expansion phase. They've overcome the feeling that the process is hopeless, boredom is replaced by enthusiasm, and they've stopped or limited their judgment of others. Everyone is adapting, changing, and growing for the most part; you've hit the season where everything starts to come together. Creativity is flowing, critical thinking is just a part of every day, and innovation is making business thrive. Everyone is thriving. The positive aspects of this season are just that — people trust one another to do their job and do it well. They trust the leader, the direction, and the mission. It's one big happy family, right?

Not always. When success and progress are all around them, people can sometimes slip into the habit of hiding concerns so they don't upset the apple cart. Success and the drive toward success become so great that people may not be completely transparent. Compromise and shortcuts come into play — not out of laziness but because the desire for fulfillment is so great.

The ability to establish and maintain a trusting environment is one, above all others, that erects the framework for the entire organization and its inhabitants. Leadership and stakeholders have a partnership agreement, sometimes expressed literally, sometimes implied. Those that may not be engaging in the agreement of trust will need to be reminded that flexibility doesn't mean defeat and that all problem solving is a step in the right direction. Regular open dialogue is essential to maintaining transparency of concerns to avoid breaking trust. Trust is such a big issue that Chapter 9 is devoted to it. (Also consider reading Chapter 10 on motivations; they go hand in hand.)

In Figure 8-6, transitioning from a group's current state to one of trust is created by the suspension of disbelief. In that moment of suspension, they are trusting the leader to pull them through to the other side. Enthusiasm, a belief in possibilities, and the potential for achievement or impact are the vehicle to get them from where they are to where they want to be. This can be based on facts, stories, expression of vision, and motivational language. It all depends on who your audience is (the staff) and what they relate to most. Watch what happens when a leader puts up revenue projections on a screen alongside a full plan; half of the room starts buzzing. Coupled with encouraging or motivational language, the side of the room not driven by stats reacts positively as well.

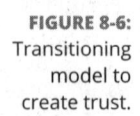

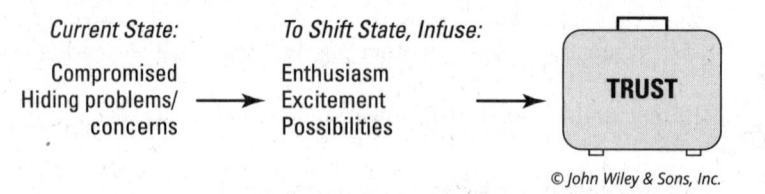

FIGURE 8-6: Transitioning model to create trust.

Current State: Compromised Hiding problems/concerns → To Shift State, Infuse: Enthusiasm Excitement Possibilities → TRUST

© John Wiley & Sons, Inc.

TIP Always consider that half of your team will probably be made up of left-brain thinkers (creatives tapped into their emotional centers) and the other half will be right-brain thinkers (linear thinkers tapped into their logical centers). Speaking to both types of audiences simultaneously will produce a greater effect on what you're proposing.

Clarity working in tandem with enthusiasm, excitement, and possibilities creates hope. Provide that clarity of direction by sharing with them what the future plans for the team or organization may be. Show them how the impact of their work contributes to those goals (see Chapter 16), and they will shift.

TECHNICAL STUFF In one survey conducted by the Society for Human Resource Management, 61 percent of employees said trust between them and their senior management was important to job satisfaction. Thirty-three percent were very satisfied with the level of trust in their organization. For more information, visit www.shrm.org/hr-today/trends-and-forecasting/research-and-surveys/Documents/2017-Employee-Job-Satisfaction-and-Engagement-Executive-Summary.pdf.

Handling cycle disruptions

I've provided a snapshot of the cycle, uninterrupted, and how to shift people and the organization from being defiant and dysfunctional, avoiding car crashes along the way. However, disruptions to the cycle can occur. You are the guardian of your people. This is one of the four Be's of leadership (introduced in Chapter 3) — it's your responsibility to keep your ego (and theirs) in check so the organization can move forward without stumbling.

People are imperfect and can fall off the tracks at times. Your star leader may lose their enthusiasm, for example. If that's the case, at least now you know that there may be a trust issue lurking behind that change of demeanor. If you've got a team that's exhibiting signs of boredom and stagnation, what do you do? You take them out to play or find something humorous to insert into their daily existence to help them snap out of it.

REMEMBER

You now have a road map to handle these situations before they turn the team and/or the organization into a halted environment. Some people will come along; others won't. Freewill can't be overridden. All I ask is that you give it your best. People respond to those who care enough to, well, care. Here is a brief synopsis to remind you why it's important to consider these opportunities for change:

>> **Resistance — defiantly standing still:** As you know, nothing in life is simple or picture perfect. At any time, participants can stop and stay in place. Yet, as I've mentioned, evolution never stops. The clock keeps ticking, the sun sets, and the moon rises. So it is with the cycle of development. Standing still only allows others to move forward faster. That's not to say that taking a pause to digest, formulate, consider, or otherwise assess isn't part of the process. Consider that, generally, each season is about three months. Phases in the cycle take time. For most people, making any shift won't happen overnight.

>> **Values stands and course corrections:** Leaders and stakeholders can, at any time, make a course correction that may be confused as a values stand (see Chapter 12). Making an adjustment to a plan or correcting flaws in the direction you've provided are course corrections — they're not values stands. A *values stand* is specifically related to that which you value or have set as a values standard for the organization. In the case of a negative environment, drawing a line in the sand for the betterment of the organization constitutes a values stand, which becomes a course correction for the group.

>> **Purposeful remedy applications:** Within each phase or season, I've provided the remedy for a negative environment, either with individuals or with the entire team. Use them often. Reinforcement creates results.

Becoming Part of the Solution — Or Exiting Stage Right

As you begin to shift your organization, there will be people who are ready to embrace your vision and run forward toward the solution before you can get the sentence out of your mouth. They *want* change. They embrace it. And they can't wait one minute longer for it.

Then there is the majority. They too want change. They're open to the possibility that change can occur. But they need more information to know whether it's possible or whether they can trust you to do it. Potentially, they need to understand you better and buy into your leadership before fully committing. Wouldn't you agree that these concerns and requirements are completely reasonable?

Then there will be the group of naysayers and negative Nellies. Some of them will come on board, but some won't make the journey with you. Invest your time and energy in those who want to move forward. In the following sections, I provide pointers on how to become part of the solution as you shift your employees out of the FARCE Syndrome.

Giving staff a choice

Freewill permits people to decide for themselves as to what they want to do. In this case, will they come onboard and participate constructively — or resist, obstruct, or perpetuate the current pessimism? They can choose either, but choose they will. Shifting a group or changing the environment is something that will draw on the basic character of a values-based leader: emotionally intelligent awareness of others, compassion, and inclusion. The leader establishes the direction, but the rollout can't be done alone. It requires buy-in and engagement (see Chapter 7).

Here are several factors to consider when making a change:

- Do they believe in the direction of the change?
- Do they believe in your strength as a leader to pull the group through the process?
- How will they be supported and included in the process?

REMEMBER: Not everyone processes information at the same rate. Not all individuals may feel safe without moving cautiously and questioning throughout the process. Be aware that these people may not be resisting you. Instead, they are "processing." Each current contribution needs to be weighed alongside their potential contribution. The long and short of it is this: Giving them a choice engenders deeper commitment.

CHOOSING TO BE PART OF THE SOLUTION

During a particularly tough time with a major corporation, senior leadership was replaced and a new agenda was being deployed. It was a scary time for everyone. I was nervous hearing about this while I was on vacation, and upon my return I was summoned to the new leader's office. He quickly gave me an overview of the plan moving forward. I nodded all the way through. Then he asked me point blank, "We'd like you to be part of the solution." My heart pounded. "I'm hoping you'll agree to stay onboard and help us; will you?" I smiled and nodded yes. "That's good because we want people to be part of the solution, not the problem." This was a respectful, thoughtful conversation that in all my years I've never forgotten.

It was empowering to be asked to participate instead of assuming my participation was a given. This imparted a greater sense of responsibility in the changes that were going to occur. In turn, I delivered a somewhat similar question to my own team. We were all in. And in the times when change and/or transition were tough, this conversation and our commitment to the process sustained us.

In my experience, when people are given a choice, they will rise to the occasion and often exceed expectations. Choice is a powerful tool.

The process being discussed is as much about trust (see Chapter 9) and investment in the organization (see Chapter 10) as it is about being included in the process as well as making the employee a guardian of the organization.

Taking extreme ownership of the situation

Navy SEALs Jocko Willink and Leif Babin call their level of commitment to leadership *extreme ownership*. These leaders of SEAL teams take on the ownership of the mission, returning everyone home. It's a heroic and selfless way of operating. It ensures that no one is left behind, no one is compromised, and everyone is kept safe during the execution of a mission.

REMEMBER: Move this kind of leadership into your world by considering the concept of selflessness. Take ownership of the evolutionary process outlined earlier in this chapter and ask others to do the same. Make everyone a partner in moving the group forward. Peers, colleagues, and formal mentors and leaders all play a part in the overall success of the organization, one team and one person at a time. Avoid making excuses, blaming other people, or avoiding resolving problems that arise. This is what true *extreme ownership* means in leadership. It takes practice. And even on our best days, being perfect isn't possible. Do your very best every day.

Uncovering if it's you or them

You must by now have an inkling of where the problems may be regarding the forward movement and momentum of your organization. Values-based leaders ask themselves, "Is it me or is it them?" Self-reflection points and assessment opportunities are sprinkled along the path to help you ascertain where the problems may be.

REMEMBER

Having led and observed teams for many years, I've seen that ownership of the issues is 50/50. The leader takes half the responsibility because they're assigned the guardianship of the organization. The employees take the other half of the responsibility because they're the ground-level team doing (or not doing) the job. While there may be equal liability, the leader is ultimately responsible. Somewhere, the partnership agreement isn't working between the two entities. Locate the problem and use the solutions provided to shift the team.

3
Charting the Course and Crafting Your Values

IN THIS PART . . .

Discover the framework for trust to create powerful relationships and partnerships and establish an environment everyone can be proud of.

Develop awareness of and maintain your company's reputational capital as you create attraction for key partners in the market.

Embrace values as a part of the company culture. Define and detail a values statement for yourself as a leader and for your organization.

Find and encourage adoption of the values-based statement for both entrepreneurs and middle managers who seek to create their own powerful presence.

Be deliberate and measured in creating a career that reflects values you can use to leverage yourself to bigger opportunities. Make yourself marketable as a leader people want to work with, work for, and strive to emulate.

IN THIS CHAPTER

» Getting a handle on ideas for building trust

» Defining trust and uncovering needs

» Earning loyalty and reducing social distance

» Leading by example

» Encouraging trust among the staff

Chapter **9**

Lighting the Pathway to Establishing Trust

The key factor in a leader's ability to influence a group is *trust*. In this chapter, I dive into the basic human needs fulfillment as outlined in Abraham Maslow's hierarchy of needs theory, explore the defining factors we deploy subconsciously when assessing others, and look at what a leader can do to bolster trust within an organization. Additionally, I take a snapshot of the actions a team can take to create a trusting environment.

REMEMBER

Trust is a two-way street. Trust given is trust returned. It's a full circle of intention and way of being in the world. People follow those whom they trust. Keep this adage in mind: "People don't quit jobs — they quit leadership."

Surveying Ideas for Building Trust in Business

REMEMBER

Let me say it again: The key factor in effective leadership and the ability to influence and move a group forward is trust. Trust *is* power. Tapping into this wellspring provides access to great talent, resources, and the ability to amplify productivity. A trusted company is rewarded by customer/client dollars, vendors who want to work with you, and a motivated team who will move mountains to accomplish tasks.

Trust is a rapport built on genuine connection with others and is the foundation from which everything flows. Therefore, establishing trust as a leader should be one of your main goals. Unfortunately, only 37 percent of the population believes CEOs are "extremely/very credible," which is similar to the 39 percent rate for government leaders. Ouch! Businesses were distrusted by 48 percent of those surveyed in the 2017 Edelman Trust Barometer report. Clearly, there's work to be done.

Repairing and reinforcing trust should be a priority for every company and its leadership. When looking at the major contributors that erode trust, you can look at core needs not being fulfilled. When people question the credibility of institutions, it erodes confidence in belief systems, and that makes them prone to economic and social uncertainty. When people don't feel they're being taken care of or looked out for by the institution, government, or business, they question the ability of authority to be aware of and meet basic needs.

Table 9-1 shows the percentages of those who say each attribute is important to building trust in a company.

We need to look at a leader's ability to bring about a marked increase in trustworthiness in an organization. Values-based leadership (VBL) is a big part of moving from a *Halt* environment (described in Chapter 8 and later in this chapter) to one of growth and sustainability. In Table 9-1 you may recognize many of the values-based attributes covered elsewhere in this book. That's not coincidental. VBL is the remedy for that which ails business on a deep, personal, connected, core level.

TABLE 9-1   Ways for Businesses to Build Trust

Attributes	% of Those Who Feel the System Is Failing	% of General Population
Treating employees well	72	62
Offering high-quality products and services	68	59
Listening to customers	67	58
Paying their share of taxes	66	56
Engaging in ethical business practices	65	56
Transparent and open in their business practices	65	55
Placing customers above profits	65	55
Taking responsible action to address issues	64	55
Communicating frequently and honestly	60	52
Protecting and improving the environment	60	52
Creating many new jobs	55	47
Profits remain in the country	56	46
Programs with positive impact locally	53	46
Addressing social needs in everyday business activity	53	46

Source: 2017 Edelman Trust Barometer — see www.scribd.com/document/336621519/2017-Edelman-Trust-Barometer-Executive-Summary-fullscreen&from_embed

Defining Trust and Needs in the Workplace

So what is trust, exactly? Is it telling the truth? Perhaps the words *ethical behavior* come to mind, or *transparency*. Those sound right. To better understand what defines trust in the workplace, though, consider Dr. Duane C. Tway Jr.'s three perceptions to contextualize trust:

» **Capacity for trust:** The ability to trust others based on your experiences, interaction, and life wisdom

» **Perception of competence:** The evaluation of yours or others' skills and the ability to do the job effectively

» **Perception of intention:** The effect of words, actions, and deeds as positively or negatively impacting others

This framework provides a compact assessment when it comes to trust. On a mostly subconscious level, we utilize these categories to determine the trustworthiness of those we date, hire, and follow, seamlessly. Wait — did I say date?

TECHNICAL STUFF

Consider this example: When you're dating someone, you first wonder whether you can trust them. Past experiences will dictate the depth of your abilities to trust — if someone once cheated on you, chances are your trust threshold will be lower. Next, you assess your dating partner: Is this person suitable to be in a relationship with me (or anyone else)? Do they possess the capacity to fulfill my needs? Then, based on going out a few times, comes the assessment of everything from table manners, to how they speak to their mother, to how they treat coworkers and friends and engage others on social media, and so on. Your assessments create a perception of the other person's intention in the world to be positive or negative, stable or volatile, violent or gentle — and all factor into figuring out whether you should trust them. Your assessment may happen consciously or unconsciously.

A similar process takes place in a business environment:

» The staff will make their own determination on how much they can trust you (or anyone in a position of authority).

» From there, they will decide whether you have the skills and experience to do your job and therefore effectively lead the organization. You may be surprised just how much research they may do on you through networking and Internet searching.

» Then they will watch you, listen to you, and assess your every move to determine the authenticity of your intention as "real" or not. They will interpret your body language and evaluate your engagements with different team members to decide whether you're fair or whether you show favoritism.

The list of assessments can seem endless. Assessing others' level of trustworthiness is a survival mechanism deeply ingrained within each of us. It's very real.

The baseline needs of a human being come into play when establishing trust, as this section is meant to show. Everything you do to embrace the attributes and principles detailed in prior chapters leads up to establishing and reinforcing trust. Trust is also the precursor to motivating people (see Chapter 16). Snap one puzzle piece into the next to continue cement a powerful leadership position.

TIP

Building a foundation based on trust creates the power needed to move your organization forward. It's worth the time and attention because you'll reap massive benefits down the road.

Using Maslow's hierarchy of needs to determine baseline trust

The most widely known needs theory is Maslow's hierarchy of needs, developed in 1943. Abraham Maslow's concept of needs has been applied to such areas as politics, social impact of events, and workplace attitudes for good reason — it makes perfect sense. The theory was updated in the 1960s and 1970s, but still intact are Maslow's three levels of needs each human being experiences:

- **Deficiencies:** Basic needs including fundamental physiological human needs such as food, water, health, shelter, and sex, but also, interestingly, employment, safety, and sociability.
- **Growth:** Feelings of accomplishment, achievement, respect for others and self, esteem, prestige, connection, meaningfulness, and belonging are some examples.
- **Self-achieving:** Self-awareness needs, achieving one's full potential, giving back, and helping others achieve self-actualization and transcendence.

REMEMBER

Chapters 3 and 4 invite you to reframe consciousness and awareness around your leadership and the role of business in the world. As I explain there, the primary purpose of commerce in the world is to create opportunity for others. As a values-based leader, you have responsibilities *to* your people: to be a guardian, to be of service to those you lead, to be generous, and to diligently safeguard their rights. Those may sound like lofty ideals. However, consider that your organization is the one that will fill an employee's basic deficiencies by providing gainful employment with fair wages, permitting them to pay their rent, buy food, and create a warm, safe, and dry environment for themselves and their families. That's reality — not a lofty ideal. Additionally, providing a safe, growth-oriented company culture fulfills the growth needs of feeling accomplished, prestige, connection, and so on.

The survival mechanism within each of us drives us to fulfill these levels of needs, partially, through our work. The depth of trust an individual feels depends on how well those needs are filled. Tway's framing of the three contexts (listed earlier in this chapter) provides the sequence toward establishing trust. As employees view you, their leader, and the organization as ones that treat everyone fairly, with esteem, affording them the dignity to create a life for themselves and their families, the sequence is satisfied.

Employees can and do assess and reassess trustworthiness at any time. Consistency in keeping their trust builds loyalty and forgiveness. When you stumble, they will forgive you and keep working because, after all, everyone makes mistakes. On the flip side, if you're consistently careless, they won't give you the benefit of the doubt if there are missteps — ever.

REMEMBER: As a leader/employer, you hold these needs in your hands; they are each individual's social and economic requirements to feel safe and secure. Although not every person can be hired, and not every person will be retained indefinitely, understanding the impact you have on their lives will, hopefully, provide the motivation for you to stay the VBL course.

Shifting from Halt to happiness

A *Halt* environment is one where trust is in limited supply. A continued state of distrust creates tension. People feel defensive and are always "on guard." Staffers look over their shoulders to see who or what may be lurking behind a comment. They wait for the other shoe to drop, anticipating the thump as it hits the floor. It's a terrible company culture. The team burns out, and creativity atrophies. *Cultural entropy* engulfs the group with unproductive and often unnecessarily extra work, fostering resentment and discontent. This isn't a fun or inspiring place to work.

WARNING: Note that although sometimes distrust *may* create an immediate, short-term gain or growth spurt for a company as staff compete internally for recognition and success, it is short-lived. VBL is very much against the idea of sowing mistrust to foster internal competition.

Sifting through theory, practical and applied, of how to build connectivity and trust comes down to a few basic components. People want those basic needs in the preceding section met, but they also want to be seen, heard, and recognized, and they want to do meaningful work, with the goal of giving back to others. This is similar to the shared values economy (SVE) circle discussed in Chapter 4, though on a smaller, day-to day level. Figure 9-1 shows the conversion of the original needs that Maslow defines into three categories of workplace needs.

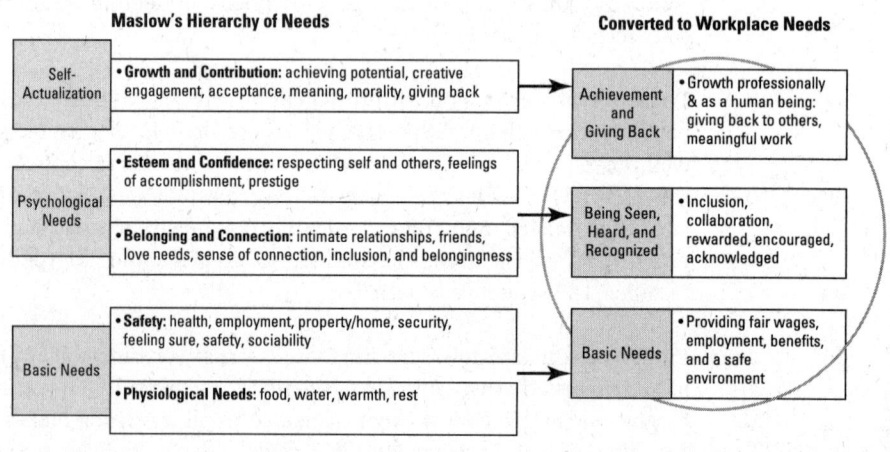

FIGURE 9-1: Needs conversion to the workplace.

Maslow's Hierarchy of Needs		Converted to Workplace Needs	
Self-Actualization	**Growth and Contribution:** achieving potential, creative engagement, acceptance, meaning, morality, giving back	Achievement and Giving Back	Growth professionally & as a human being: giving back to others, meaningful work
Psychological Needs	**Esteem and Confidence:** respecting self and others, feelings of accomplishment, prestige	Being Seen, Heard, and Recognized	Inclusion, collaboration, rewarded, encouraged, acknowledged
	Belonging and Connection: intimate relationships, friends, love needs, sense of connection, inclusion, and belongingness		
Basic Needs	**Safety:** health, employment, property/home, security, feeling sure, safety, sociability	Basic Needs	Providing fair wages, employment, benefits, and a safe environment
	Physiological Needs: food, water, warmth, rest		

© *John Wiley & Sons, Inc.*

TIP: When working with someone, ask yourself: Has this person been seen, heard, and recognized? I frame this as regular team maintenance. It's not about breaking out trophies. The things that are often most meaningful and motivating to others are simple and cost very little. Providing a team member or colleague the opportunity to be an effective member/contributor to the team, to listen to what they say, and to recognize, verbally or through actions, that you've heard and seen them takes very little time.

Individuals aren't all the same; how they like to be recognized may vary. They may want to be allowed to

- Share their ideas (see Chapters 15 and 18)
- Support others through formal or informal mentorship (see Chapter 14)
- Have their small successes celebrated on the road to larger achievements (see Chapter 7)
- Be involved with problem solving (see Chapter 18)
- Train for current and future roles (see Chapters 14 and 15)

Getting Others to Trust in Your Leadership

Balance is *power* — this is a concept all leaders should seriously consider. Being a balanced individual of sound mind, competence, and behavior is necessary. Those who exhibit erratic, unpredictable behaviors aren't considered trustworthy. Humans are built with an internal survival mechanism. If you spook them, they're not going to trust you. It's as if Halloween is happening every day when you have an unbalanced or overly emotional leader in the driver's seat. You just never know when they're going to jump out from behind a door and say boo. This type of behavior keeps everyone on pins and needles.

Exemplifying a balanced, even-keeled presence, with the help of the following sections, will provide the consistency necessary for trust to be established. Trust is the absence of doubt. When the team, vendors, and investors know that you'll consistently engage with them today and tomorrow in the same way you did yesterday, you're giving them that certainty.

REMEMBER: Be clear and be consistent in everything you do and how you do it.

Engendering loyalty

Trust is a partnership. It requires that all parties operate with the same intentions and by the same guidelines. It builds loyalty and commitment in the group. Throughout the years, I've seen countless teams stick together, even through some particularly difficult times, because they trusted their leader and one another. Commitment to one another and the process was the yield resulting from a bond of trust. Motivational speaker Brian Tracy sums it up well: The glue that holds all relationships together — including the relationship between the leader and the led — is trust, and trust is based on integrity.

What binds leaders and employees is a commitment to excellence and the knowledge that they can rely on each other. This connection takes time, experience, and continued repetition to cement in place.

"Stella" is a top-level leader of a large multinational pharmaceutical company. Her reputation for toughness has produced a highly productive group of managers and teams. I asked her how she manages to balance her expectations and mobilize the teams to operate at such a high level. To be honest, I was wondering if it was "brute force." She smiled and told me that the only way people work at this level is because they trust her and they trust each other: "Trust is the default engagement tool for us. Without trust, there is nothing else."

Reducing social distance gaps

Social distance is the belief in the difference between "us" and "them." To be sure, at times it's valid to make those distinctions when it's about context, not judgment. Social distance in the workplace, particularly now as the workplace is becoming more global, is the perception of power, distance, value, and belonging — who is "in" and who isn't.

In the case of leadership, social distance may be about which piece of real estate home office sits on. When there are multiple offices, there can be a territorial aspect to the perception of power — that where the leader works gains favor and priority. For example, if the leaders are in Baltimore, those working in the other offices located in Dallas, Dubai, Dublin, and Des Moines are prone to the isolating belief that they are secondary citizens and are less of a priority to the company. "Out of sight, out of mind" is the lament. It's easy to feel a sense of uneasiness or mistrust of those you don't see on a daily basis, or to create a sense of "them" being an enemy. The unknown isn't always something people can feel at ease with or trust. Therefore, it's important to address any social distance issues immediately.

TIP: Social distance in this case can be resolved through inclusion and communication:

- **Unify:** Continually steer the focus back toward common goals, challenges, and opportunities, including the values statement described in Chapter 11.
- **Puzzle pieces:** Illustrate, often, that each team in each office makes an important contribution to the total goal. Highlight these interlocking pieces to the leaders on the ground and the staff regularly.
- **Consistently communicate with clarity:** Communication is a key attribute of a values-based leader. Communicate goals, missions, plans, and contributions regularly.
- **Who, me?** Seek to find ways to include leaders and managers from other offices in your plans. Doing so amplifies your emphasis on inclusion and promotes a feeling among everyone that they are making contributions.

By using these skills, you'll be able to debunk the myth that there is only one central source of power and influence.

Setting Standards for Others by Example

I was standing in the back of the room at an annual meeting for a mid-sized company. The leadership team was rolling out initiatives and sharing the plan for their bright future. There was a lot of energy and applause throughout the morning. When we took a break, I observed the attitude in the room. The ground-level leaders were happily engaging in conversation with team members, and the general feeling was one of optimism about the future. When I asked why, the answer was that the leadership team would do what they said they were going to do. Although the fine details were still unclear at that moment, the teams weren't worried about the execution. They trusted the leadership because the leaders had been consistent in their behavior so far.

One of the highest awards a leader can receive is the trust of their people. When you do what you say you're going to do and do it consistently, your platform is a sure one. As this section explains, leading from the front, by example, motivates everyone around you to do their part.

Operating with self-awareness

Understanding your own motives for what you do — uncovering and keeping in check your trigger points to avoid projecting your *stuff* on others — is all part of being a self-aware leader. So is observing how you affect others. Much of this point goes back to the opening statements about being a steady, stable leader, but it's also about being emotionally intelligent and able to adapt and act in an appropriate manner.

Have you ever given a presentation and then looked around the room only to see mouths wide open or, even worse, everyone sitting with their arms folded and looking agitated? You look down at your notes and wonder what happened. Something triggered the response; your delivery, your tone, or the examples you gave may have caused a silent mutiny. The point is that you affected people negatively; this isn't about being a poor presenter.

A more common example is your attitude being projected onto a group. Perhaps there is an initiative you don't want to be part of or you don't believe in, but if that eye roll or quick negative quip slips out, you convey to those around you that you don't believe in it, you don't care, and it's nothing more than a nuisance. The team may respond with annoyance toward you if they believe in the initiative, or they may follow suit with your defiance. Either way, your example signals to them that public displays of defiance are acceptable. They may judge you for not being a team player.

Self-awareness is about understanding that you impact others, both knowingly and unknowingly. Keeping yourself in check to ensure that you don't negatively impact others takes self-awareness and discipline. Let's face it; everyone has bad days, is asked to do things they don't always agree with, or has to deliver bad news. As a leader, you're the lightning rod that influences these reactions.

REMEMBER

Set the standard: Equanimity always.

Avoiding exceptions yet remaining flexible

Making exceptions becomes a very fine line to walk at times. Compassionately engaging with the team means understanding that there may be circumstances beyond one's control to be addressed. This would fall under the category of flexibility, not exception — for example, allowing a parent to take an additional day off to care for a sick child even if their personal days have been used up. I've led teams where this has been the case. Another teammate stepped up to fill this parent's workplace duties on that day, and even offered one of their own sick days to prevent the teammate from losing a salaried day off.

That's very different from an exception within the organization that favors one employee over another — for example, granting high performers exceptions to attend certain mandatory trainings, even though they need the required training. Delaying a required activity is one thing if they meet the requirement set for everyone else. When high performers show up and do what they're required to do, it's a powerful example to others in the organization that no one is better or more important than anyone else here.

If you're unsure whether you're playing favorites or making exceptions, all you have to do is listen to the complaining or resentful comments made by the surrounding staff.

REMEMBER: Set the standard: We are equals, without exception.

Sidestepping rumor mills and gossip hounds

The best way to circumvent the rumor mills, gossip, and conspiracy theories is to be transparent. Although it may not be appropriate to divulge sensitive information, it is important to dispense information such as financial results and plans for future correction and growth to the team and stockholders. When the information is out there in the daylight, it slows rumors. And do it in a timely fashion. Delay only creates a sense of fear and uncertainty. Conveying certainty and transparency is key to gaining trust.

TIP: Water cooler moments will happen. It's inevitable. Humans will be humans. Put three people in a room together, and they will have three differing opinions and interpretations of a common event. Perception is a powerful lens through which we view the world, but everyone wears different glasses, and so opinions are formed that differ, sometimes mildly, sometimes wildly. It's just a fact. However, there are things you, as the leader, can do to help prevent rumor mills and gossiping in the workplace:

- » **Accept the elephant in the room.** Okay, so there's something going on. Everyone knows it. This is the action of *acceptance*. Recognize that it's happening and you're probably not going to be able to stop it. You can, however, slow the process down from becoming a canker sore.

- » **Gather the group.** Level with them: Yes, XYZ is happening. Let's wait before everyone jumps to conclusions. In the case of personal or interdepartmental rumors, be direct: "How about giving everyone in this situation the benefit of the doubt?" You ask them to reach into the compassionate side of themselves before creating a negative situation.

- » **Draw a line.** Plain and simple: "We don't gossip or spread rumors on this team. Although I can't stop you from speaking to one another, I do ask that you treat each other with dignity and respect, because this is what we stand for. If you must speculate, take it outside. Within these four walls, I ask that you refrain from this behavior."

Blowing off steam to defuse one's own fear, anxiety, or concern for security is normal and very human, but too much of it can erode trust by casting doubt into the minds of those around. Allow employees to have their process, but don't permit it to spread like wildfire and engulf the entire group.

REMEMBER: Set the standard: This workplace is a no-drama zone.

Encouraging others as a sign of trust

Trust given is trust returned. Encouraging others to do their job and to do it well is a form of encouragement. There may be a period of training before an individual can fly solo within their position, so train them well, encourage them to do it, and allow them to go for it.

REMEMBER: Set the standard: Encouragement is generosity amplified. You can find out more about generosity in Chapter 3.

Mastering the thank-you

Old school? Yes. Good basic manners? Yes. Necessary to build rapport and trust with your team? Abso-freaking-lutely! Keep in mind that people want to be seen, heard, and recognized (refer to Figure 9-1). When a job is well done, an extra effort is made, or a new level is achieved, recognize your folks. Those famous two words go a long way. Dispense generously and often.

TECHNICAL STUFF: Have a look at the following stats (according to an article at Employee Benefit News: www.benefitnews.com/news/employee-personalization-drives-pre-and-post-hiring-technologies). Clearly employees appreciate even the smallest expression of appreciation for what they do, but leaders don't see the need for it:

» Twenty-two percent of senior decision-makers don't think that regular recognition and thanking employees at work have a big influence on staff retention.

» Seventy percent of employees say that motivation and morale would improve "massively" with managers saying "thank you" more.

REMEMBER: Set the standard: Gratitude is our way of being.

Harnessing People Power

Your organization is made up of many parts, but the common thread is its people. When you harness the energy, talent, and skills of a group, amazing things can unfold.

Being an example sets the tone for the team — give them reason to trust you, and they will follow. You will be challenged or questioned at times. Just remember, a leader who gives trust receives trust. Allow your example to trickle down through the organization.

Following five engaging principles for the team

Building on your example, add the following simple ways of acting as a healthy team to the checklist, bearing in mind that trust still needs to be nurtured within all layers and levels of the organization:

- » **Be honest but not mean.** Be honest with your engagements. Always tell the truth — even little white lies can cause damage. Share and provide all relevant information, even if it puts you at a disadvantage.

- » **Dispense good judgment.** Use your best judgment when sharing information with others, but first ask yourself some questions: Is this necessary? Will it compromise someone else? And is it kind or judgmental? Treat others as you want to be treated and treat confidential information with confidence — not because it's compliant, but because it's the right thing to do.

- » **Be reliable and dependable.** People refer business to, share information with, and want to collaborate with those they know to be reliable and dependable. I've never heard anyone say, "I want to work with Joe because he's a lazy dude who never shows up on time." That's never going to happen. Show up for your team, on time, every time.

- » **Look one another in the eye.** When someone looks you in the eye, it's a sign of honesty and sincerity. It's a small, simple act of body language, a cue others pick up on immediately. When you feel as if someone is untrustworthy, often it's because they don't look you in the eye. Additionally, studies have shown that eye contact of 30 percent or more of the time increases retention of the information shared — that's not even 20 seconds out of a minute.

- » **Embody the "fireman carry" attitude.** The seated fireman carry is a symbol of four hands interlocking. In 1964, a more stylized version of this image became the logo of financial giant Oppenheimer Funds to symbolize "Greater strength and support than any one individual can provide alone." This is the essence of the fireman carry attitude.

Unifying behind a common belief

Human beings enjoy being bonded together by a common goal or mission. Major religious organizations are founded based on belief systems. Civil servants such as firefighters, police, and military are also united by common missions. Companies have long done the same. Belonging is a big part of the human need. Being bound by goals, beliefs, or a common mission helps create a desire to achieve/win together.

Advertisers have long used slogans and catchphrases to create memorable brands, share key benefits, differentiate products from one another, and impart a positive feeling toward brands. Here are a few examples:

- **Think Differently:** Apple
- **Got Milk?** California Milk Processors Board
- **Imagination at Work:** General Electric
- **Every Little Helps:** Tesco
- **There are some things money can't buy. For everything else, there's MasterCard:** MasterCard

As you've read this list, you may have smiled as you thought about your favorite catchphrase or slogan. We all have them. They create unity and a way of experiencing a brand, which also makes it feel like an exclusive experience. Either you're part of something, a club, group, brand, and so on — or you're not. So, why wouldn't you want to engender this same uniting, positive feeling under your brand of leadership? Does that sound complicated? Yes, it does. It sounds like it could be perceived as a massive marketing endeavor. But it really doesn't need to be complicated.

TIP Here's the one uniting phrase used over again with great success: *We are all in this together!* You can't all be in it together unless you trust one another. This is a simple, useful slogan to rally people around you. It's all-encompassing. Dispense daily, when the team is up or when it's down. Share it at annual meetings, cross-divisional meetings, and everywhere the employees gather to gain focus. It's a reminder to them that they are to and can rely upon each other. Set the expectation that they meet or even exceed your expectations — they will, as long as you continue to operate under the principles of VBL.

Circumventing passive-aggressive personalities

One passive-aggressive apple can spoil the entire team.

Among the narcissistic personality types, the most common may be the passive-aggressive. You know the type: It's all about *them*. That, of course, runs counter to everything VBL advocates. Passive-aggressive behaviors are not only maddening, but they're also subversive in nature. I'm talking about the process of avoiding a confrontation (passive) but using *behind your back* conversations with others to tear down another person (aggressive).

WARNING

It's imperative that passive-aggressive behaviors be addressed. They can easily derail your efforts to establish trust and cast doubt and shame throughout.

Bypassing a passive-aggressive personality takes enormous patience and is an exercise in "compassion management." Individuals exhibiting passive-aggressive behavior usually do so because they have at some point in their lives experienced harsh criticism or they may feel their voices haven't been heard. There's no need to find the specific root of their behavior — just be aware enough to realize that the behavior stems from such influences in their lives. This awareness provides a glimpse into who they are and will lead you to approach the situation with compassion, circumventing a potentially explosive confrontation.

Passive-aggressive behavior creates an environment where people don't feel safe. For example, someone isn't sure if what someone else is saying to them is the truth or if the truth is only being told to others. Other examples would be the dreaded "cold look-through stare" in the hallway, or having a hello ignored, or a teammate agreeing to take on a task and then not doing it — even though everything else has been completed. It can be signaled by patronizing statements such as "Bless your heart." Backhanded compliments and a deep desire to be right are also part of this narcissistic profile.

TIP

As a leader, it's not always your place to address these situations. Although it could happen on a leadership level, depending on the ratio of staff to leadership, many issues will remain at the staff level. If you do need to address it, here are some tools to help you and your ground-level leaders and managers defuse these individuals:

>> **Keep your cool.** Avoid overreacting or permitting an attack on a personal level. Don't take the bait.

>> **Keep it at a distance.** You can't win nor please them, nor should you think you can. Simply agree to disagree but convey that the work still needs to get done — on time.

>> **Reflect.** You can't change them or their behavior. This is an opportunity to self-reflect: "Do I do this too?" or "Why am I trying so hard to make them happy or comfortable?"

- **Adopt Mother Superior positioning.** Exemplify your best composure, sitting high and quietly without arguing. Think of that famous nun in a black habit, sitting, listening, and nodding. Behind that habit was a calm, cool, collected, and powerful presence who hardly had to say a word. It's very effective positioning.

- **Utilize humor.** Laughter releases tension and forces people to breathe, which helps defuse anger naturally.

- **Mind your language to prevent victim mode.** When in direct conversation, avoid using words like *you* or *your* directed at the individual. Rather, replace them with *I, we,* and *our.* Doing this can circumvent their perception that they're being attacked.

- **Defuse resistance.** Offering a form of consequence for their lack of cooperation will often break down resistance to taking on or completing actions: "When this isn't done, the result is that there may be negative fallout around your capabilities." Or: "When this situation isn't resolved, the unfortunate fallout is that you may not be considered a team player, which will only have negative long-term career repercussions." The consequence doesn't need to be punitive, but the potential chain of events should be illuminated.

> **IN THIS CHAPTER**
> » Realizing the impact of your company's reputation
> » Making the employees trustees of the company's reputation

Chapter **10**

Facing the Truth about Who You Are

Many times in this book, I say that trust is the foundation from which everything flows. When embraced, trust (the topic of Chapter 9) becomes the reality of an organization, and all conflicts will come back to a simple question: Did we break trust with X or Y? Marketers today believe that trust is the critical ingredient in marketing their efforts in everything they do, including reputation. In this chapter, the deep dive will be into how the public, prospects, and investors may be viewing the organization with regard to their trustworthiness and consistency on both a personal level and through social media.

Here, I make distinctions among company culture, identity, and reputation. Your reputation is the capital that either attracts people to or repels them from your organization. I provide an opportunity for you to assess the situation formally or informally in order to determine your reputation imprint.

Understanding How Others View Your Company

Knowing how you're viewed is the foundation for correcting and/or honing your ability to not only attract great talent (see Chapter 14) but also create more deliberate interaction with others. The relationships you're building are structured around a common interest, mission, or goal. Those inside and outside the organization look at how your connections to others affect them. They form a perception about the entity's reputation. This judgment leads to a number of questions:

- Would they buy from you again?
- Would they invest in your business?
- Do they have faith in your leadership?
- Do they care about what you care about?
- Do they want to work with you or for you?

This perception cascades down even further to influence potential candidates interested in working at the company. The same goes for vendors: Based on what they know, are you a risk worth taking? Do you pay your invoices and negotiate fairly? Vendors, investors, and lenders are usually more willing to negotiate and provide flexibility to those entities they know will perform and engage with them responsibly.

> **TIP:** I'm speaking, in general, about the reputation of the company, but please consider all concepts in this chapter as a parallel road map to self-reflection about your own specific leadership reputation. Removing rose-colored glasses is key in understanding how you're being viewed. In both situations, gaining a clearer picture is the first step to making lasting change. Many companies believe they have a positive reputation, which may not be how they are actually perceived by the general public.

Differentiating identity, culture, and reputation

> **REMEMBER:** Many terms describing companies are batted around and used interchangeably. The following list breaks them down so we're all on the same page regarding the terminology here:
>
> - **Corporate identity:** This includes branding markers such as a company's colors, logo, typeface, and other branding matter. Corporate identities are so important that companies take infringement seriously. For example, the simple yet elegant duck egg blue box with a crisp white ribbon is unique to Tiffany and Co. Neither that exact color nor its name "Tiffany Blue" can be used anywhere other than on Tiffany merchandise, period — just ask its legal team. The Twitter bird, the Prudential rock icon, and the Starbucks mermaid are all examples of corporate identities that evoke a recognition or connection to a promise, but they're not part of the companies' reputations or cultures.

- **Corporate culture:** Corporate culture is organically developed based on the personalities of the group and how they engage with one another internally and externally. These behaviors are based on shared values, beliefs, convictions, and ways of being together. That includes the leadership. It is contingent on group beliefs.

- **Corporate reputation:** This is the collective judgment of the organization's engagement and results — financially, socially, and environmentally, including its quality of management, products, and services. Reputation is created by how integrated, interwoven, and engaged the company is in its relationships with people and communities.

Reputation and culture are connected to one another. Corporate reputation becomes a result of competencies that are engrained in the company culture. For example, if your leadership is flaky and inconsistent, the company culture often reflects that character. Investors and/or job seekers may well view certain aspects of the company to also be flaky and inconsistent, resulting in high turnovers and investors not being very interested in working with you.

Now flip it. If your reputational capital is high — the company is perceived as one that invests in people, cares for them, and treats vendors and partners well — then you'll have lots of talented people wanting to work with and for you. You'll have your pick of the best of the best. And those who are already within will stay longer because they don't want to risk working for a company that doesn't care as much about them or won't treat them as well. Investors and vendors know they have a sweet deal because this company isn't going to cause them headaches in cash flow and lack of consistency.

Reputation is your intangible capital that affects your bottom line.

Assessing your company's reputation in different categories

How you're viewed in the eyes of others can be narrowed down to the following categories:

- **Fiscal responsiveness:** Are management and the organization fiscally responsive? Being *responsive* is about the ability to be flexible when the need arises — to shift gears when necessary. It's also about earning profits, repaying loans, and negotiating fairly. However, what's new in this equation is the awareness of the impact on others — economic, social, and/or environmental. The question to ask is this: Are you a good corporate citizen in these areas?

- **Management confidence:** Competent, capable, consistent leadership builds confidence in the team at the helm. Does the management team make sound decisions and take calculated risks, or are they a wrecking ball? One additional layer to consider is the reputation of the down-line managers. I address this part in greater detail later in this chapter.

- **Social awareness:** Corporate social responsibility (CSR) initiatives represent the philanthropic side of corporate culture. According to the PricewaterhouseCoopers CEO 2016 Survey (www.pwc.com/gx/en/ceo-survey/2016/landing-page/pwc-19th-annual-global-ceo-survey.pdf), 64 percent of CEOs consider CSR initiatives to be core to their business rather than something done on the side. CSR helps build trust with employees, governments, and partners.

   An extension of CSR is social imprint — how the company impacts others. Is the company committed to the health and well-being of the people in the local areas where it operates? Does it create jobs, pay fair wages, and protect the environment? Refer to Chapter 4 to better understand CSR.

- **Resource connectivity:** A synergy occurs when people collaborate and everything just works. Resources are very much part of that type of easy, graceful dance, even if a few toes get stepped on at first. Resources may include raw and hard material vendors, manufacturing facilities, outsourced marketing, graphics, coding, and more. How you work with these people also affects how you're viewed. The best resources want to partner with reliable, consistent companies. They also want to feel as if they are actually partners in your success.

- **Relationships and affiliations:** You are who you associate yourself with and the company you keep. They will be a reflection of who you currently are or aspire to be. This can be positive or negative, depending on the situation. Working with or being mentored by a well-respected person in your industry is an example of associating with others who have reputational capital; by association, you are given some of that capital too. However, suppose your association is with someone who doesn't have a great reputation; then the common thinking is that you're of a like mind.

- **Local engagement:** Is the company engaged in outreach to the local community? This engagement may include volunteerism, community activism, "giving back" programs such as planting trees, or contributing to school or libraries. Does the company work with local or national vendors? This is where local becomes a point of national pride and commitment.

- **General public/promises:** Does the company keep its promises? Everything listed earlier leads back to this one statement. Promises reflect the integrity of not only the leader but the organization itself.

Surveying groups to see whether a correction is necessary

Surveying both your leadership team and the staff to find out where you stand in terms of reputation is a perfect place to start. Depending on the size of your organization, you may also survey investors, board members, and other partners, including your customers. Each represents a *community group* of people that you're engaging with or would like to engage with. Each community has an experience with you and the company in general.

Surveying different community groups will provide feedback to you about your reputation in the market. It's important that you also include leadership teams as part of the survey, plus at least one other community group. None of us can truly see or perceive ourselves as others do. Figure 10-1 shows sample data from a survey taken by a company's leadership team and employees.

Competency	Ratings
	1: Nonexistent 2: Needs improvement 3: Doing okay 4: Increasing 5: Excellent

Competency	1	2	3	4	5
Fiscal Responsiveness				X	E
Management Confidence			E	X	
Social Awareness	E X				
Resource Connectivity			E	X	
Relationships and Affiliations		E			X
Local Engagement			X E		
General Public				X E	
Promises		E	X		

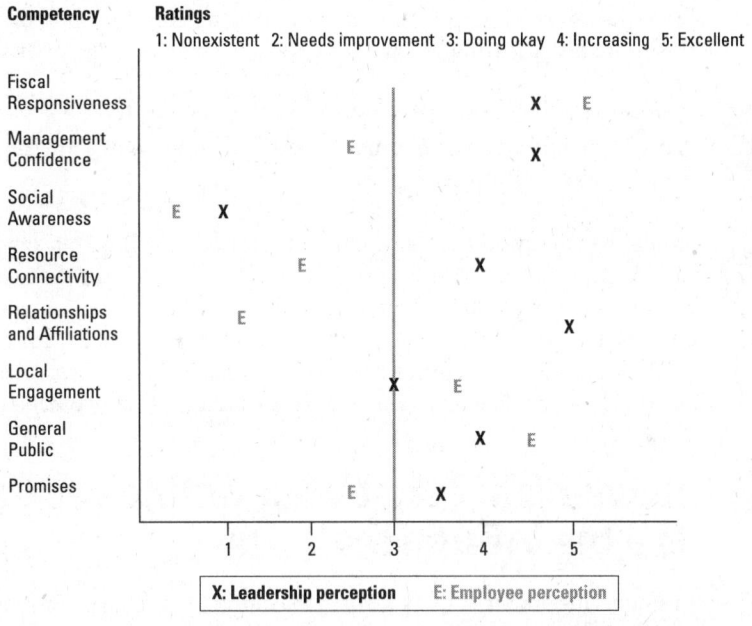

X: Leadership perception   E: Employee perception

FIGURE 10-1: Assessing where you stand.

© John Wiley & Sons, Inc.

In Figure 10-1, you can see the areas where the employees and the leadership team mostly agree, such as fiscal responsiveness and social awareness. You can also see where the perceptions are miles apart — for example, management confidence. The employees rate it as somewhere between *needs improvement* and *doing okay*. Leadership members rate themselves as increasing their effectiveness. Leadership may be making substantial moves to boost confidence in this area, but employees are saying they don't see or feel it. And they don't fully trust the leaders. This is the gap between what two groups perceive to be true. It's also an indicator that there is a correction to be made to your approach to this facet of your business and reputation.

Management confidence draws the largest amount of scrutiny, in my opinion. Had the survey been done with leadership, investor, and board member communities, the result may have been similar, but the reasoning would differ from the employee community. Each community group perceives things differently because their engagement with leadership is often in different contexts.

You can sometimes drill down into surveys to find out why competencies are rated as they are. Be mindful of leadership's relationship to the community group and ask questions accordingly. You have to know what is broken before it can be fixed. One of the biggest mistakes I see is that leadership thinks they know what the problem is, but there's no data to support it. I'm all for following a hunch or intuition, but sometimes a little more data can shed light into the nooks and crannies of an issue so that the resolution isn't just cosmetic but directed properly to facilitate deep, lasting changes.

> **TIP:** Bad news stings more than good news causes euphoria. Take both in measure. This is merely an instrument to improve your results in the marketplace and within your community groups.

> **TIP:** A number of resources can help you with conducting this type of survey. First, decide what you're surveying. Is it your online reputation? If so, www.business.com has a number of resources that can help. If you're seeing insight into your culture and the company as a whole, try https://getworkify.com/ for template questions and methodologies. Culture Amp (www.cultureamp.com) can also be helpful. Each site has its own take on how to quantify reputation, so you need to be a bit flexible.

Recognizing that your online reputation is a big influencer

A staggering statistic: 58 percent of executives believe that online reputation management should be addressed, but only 15 percent actually do anything about it (according to www.vendasta.com/blog/online-reputation-management-stats). Anything you want to know about a company can be found through social media and reviewing sites. More people than ever are checking out companies, potential bosses, and coworkers online. Online articles and blog posts make it easy to learn about companies, their products and services, their reputations, and general feelings toward them. Therefore, safeguarding and nurturing a positive online reputation is an essential component of brand building.

In short, there's literally no place to hide a reputation.

TECHNICAL STUFF

Here are some more interesting stats about online reputation (see www.vendasta.com/blog/online-reputation-management-stats for more information):

» More and more large companies are hiring full-time online reputation managers.

» Seventy percent of customers prefer getting to know a company via articles rather than advertisements.

» More than 80 percent of reputation damage comes from a mismatch between the buzz and the reality.

» According to a study by the World Economic Forum, on average, more than 25 percent of a company's market value is directly attributable to its reputation.

» Among U.S. recruiters and HR professionals surveyed, 85 percent say that positive online reputation influences their hiring decisions to some extent. Nearly half say that a strong online reputation influences their decisions to a great extent.

» Twenty-six percent of working Americans would consider a company's environmental record a major factor when considering taking a job with that company, according to Gallup.

» Forty-five percent say they've found something in an online search that made them decide not to do business with someone.

» Eight of ten U.S. Internet users say that negative information read online has made them change their mind about a purchasing decision.

» Fifty-six percent have found something that solidified their decision to do business with someone.

TIP

Consider investing in an online reputation and marketing manager. It can save you a lot of heartache later and provides a much better, more realistic idea of how others view the organization, including current and past employees who may have never voiced their opinions. Make anonymous internal surveys for exiting employees an option so you can hear the truth.

Personalizing your reputation plan with FiRMS

It can be hard to know where to begin when it comes to building and improving your reputation. Allow me to show you a path in the right direction. It begins with you — who you are and how you engage in the world on various levels. Not to sound too crunchy, but it's the energy you put out into the world that other people pick up on subconsciously. The energy needs to be supported by intentional actions that show others they can trust you with their money. They want to trust you to do the right thing — to be ethical in your dealings and associations. *FiRMS* is an acronym for working on your personal fiscal responsiveness, relationships, management skills, and social awareness. These cornerstone competencies are a good starting place.

> **REMEMBER**
> This is a shift from short-term to long-term thinking. Be prepared to play the long game.

> **TIP**
> For entrepreneurs or managers, this section may seem overwhelming. I can hear you saying, "Okay, Maria, that's great; I'll take care of this later." Um, later is right now. If you're reading this book, either you're in a leadership position or you aspire to be in one. Start your practice of consciously building your own reputation by prioritizing the items in FiRMS first. You're right. You don't need to do all of this immediately, but integration and establishing good personal habits are certainly worth the effort.

Fiscal responsiveness

When you're new to the game or steadily scaling toward leadership, understanding fiscal responsiveness is a critical skill. First, tackle it in your personal life. (I can feel your eyes rolling. I know, I know. Hear me out.) When you establish a pattern of personal financial literacy, which means being responsible with your finances, it makes it easier to make tough decisions in a professional setting. MBAs and finance degrees are amazing, but anyone can pay bills in a timely manner, repay loans, save money, and establish a retirement plan. In the latter three examples, establishing the practice is more important than the actual amount. When it comes time for you to handle a budget, and the team needs more than you can finance, it will be far easier for you to express priorities and limitations when they're part of your everyday life. You've practiced prioritizing and handling money when it's emotionally charged — we've all wanted something but couldn't afford it. You can either blow out your credit cards or put off the purchase and establish a plan to afford it in a few weeks or months.

> **REMEMBER**
> Figuring out how to deal with the emotion of money is as important as the dollars and cents of a spreadsheet. Make handling your own money a priority because it will bring up all the feelings your staff will ultimately have when there are corporate and departmental budgets to adhere to. Life is the training ground.

If you're an entrepreneur, at some point you may seek funding or investors, which will make your financial track record even more important. Banks and investors want to know that you can handle money responsibility before they'll give any to you.

Relationships and affiliations

Be mindful of those you partner with and do business with. People may say they don't judge you based on your relationships and affiliations, but they'd be lying to you. We live in an interconnected world. There's a reason why social media is so popular — we all like to know what others are doing, even in their private lives.

Candidate prescreening today often involves looking up a candidate's Facebook or Instagram page. Those who interview to be on your team may also be doing the same to you. We live in a culture of everyday voyeurism through these platforms.

Those you associate with in your professional life leave an impression on others. The people you associate with in the office or in a professional setting don't go unnoticed. Associating with a known gossip, even if you're not one yourself, can cast doubt on your trustworthiness. The same can be said for people who are openly hostile or pessimistic, or who do things just a little on the shady side. Be mindful, as you're gearing yourself to be a values-based leader within this or another organization, that all of this becomes part of your reputation.

Values-based leaders, managers, and entrepreneurs all seek to be surrounded by others who are positive, transformational, optimistic, clearheaded, mature (read: not petty), and supremely talented in their specific area of brilliance. Why? Because we all want to change the world in our own way. When you stay focused on that, there's no room for Debbie Downers and Pessimistic Petes.

Management skills

Be the best manager you can possibly be. Read, learn, and be sure to have not just a coach in the workplace but also a mentor who may be outside your current company. Seek out those who are accomplished and a bit ahead of you on the success curve. These individuals have been where you are and can help you move on a straighter line to success. Read books such as this one and others on the management topics that interest you the most. Leadership may be inherent, but honing the skills to be effective takes time to perfect.

You'll never stop learning to be a better leader. It's a lifelong journey of understanding yourself and others.

Social awareness

Think locally first. Ask yourself where you can make an impact and what your why may be. When you're starting out, you can't change the entire world. Try out your wings locally before you fly long-distance.

For one person, social awareness may mean going to Africa to teach literacy. For another, it's to be part of Habitat for Humanity home builds once a year. Setting out on a social mission can start small and build from there. If your heart tells you that you must do something now, this is how you can start.

Making Everyone a Trustee of the Company

Is the leader of the organization totally responsible for the reputation of the company, or is that just implied unconsciously? It's an interesting question. Without a doubt, the leader bears responsibility for setting standards that create the company reputation and attraction qualities. But it's not just this one individual's responsibility. It's the entire leadership team's responsibility. It's the managers' responsibility. And it's the employees' responsibility.

In Chapter 9, I mention that one of the most binding and important ways to motivate a team is to embody the rallying cry "We're all in this together!" Because, well, you are. Everyone is a trustee of the company. Their behavior reflects the company culture. If you espouse fairness and inclusion as a values-based organization, trespasses to the contrary tarnish the reputation of the entire group.

I've addressed various levels of hierarchy in a company and asked them this single question: If this were your company, how would you want to be perceived? Not what you would change. What perception would you would want to project? The answers come from the heart. People want to be proud of where they work, for many reasons discussed in this book. They want to proud to say they work for your company. Do you know any professional who says they want to work for the worst company with the most questionable reputation? Exactly! They don't. Neither do you.

The only way to foster this type of pride is to extend ownership to every employee, with the help of the following sections. Today, you are a trustee of this company. Think of it as your own. Love it. Own it. Protect it. Imbue this feeling to everyone on your team.

Sharing is caring, and caring is an investment and commitment to excellence

When individuals take deep ownership of the organization, it facilitates the ability for the community of employees to support one another. For example, Sally in cubicle

427 on the 15th floor isn't going to allow Joan on her same floor, 15 cubicles down, to become so discouraged that she takes a compromising shortcut to make her deadline or hit a goal. Instead, Sally will help her. Here's why: Because you're all in it together. Not only will they want their colleague to win, but they will also want the company not to suffer the consequences. They know they are trustees of the organization.

The word *trustee*, as I'm using it, can have the following meanings and connotations:

- Teamwork (see Chapters 14, 15, and 16 for more information)
- Operational excellence (see Chapters 14, 15, and 16)
- Commitment to excellence (see Chapters 11 and 14)
- Extreme ownership (see Chapters 4 and 8)
- Taking responsibility (see Chapters 4, 6, 9, and 12)

Depending on your company culture, you can hear this principle and implied practice being embedded in various ways.

Establish online guidelines

Roughly one quarter of all companies have established rules or guidelines on how employees should represent themselves online. That number is very low considering how influential the Internet has become to decision-making processes, from where to eat dinner to searching for a new job.

This fluid form of communication is an amazing tool, but due to some well-publicized indiscretions shared by workers on social media, such policies were deemed necessary to create boundaries and behavioral expectations for employees. Putting a policy in place creates boundaries around just how far employees can go. It also provides the ability to clarify proper communication channels for the company, set expectations around productivity, and actually encourage employees to shout from the rafters how much they love working for their company. Consider such a policy to be a form of brand continuity protection.

Social media policies

- Define what is considered social media — for example, it should be clear if a company is speaking only about Twitter but not about Facebook, if that's the case.
- Explain what information is considered confidential.
- Designate the company spokesperson for addressing company issues on social media.

- » Provide a guideline for engagement, often in alignment with a combination of common sense and core values.
- » Define what the company considers illegal.
- » Detail the boundaries around personal use of social media during productivity times (in other words, your working hours).
- » Clearly lay out disciplinary consequences of policy violation.

REMEMBER: As always, when setting policy be sure to check with your legal team to make sure everything aligns with the laws of your state.

The company has a trained spokesperson and legal experts, and they are the guardians of the company reputation when it comes to public matters pertaining to the organization. Allow them to do so. Your employees can be advocates for the brand, the culture, and the opportunities they engage in through various programs, but more high-level matters require boundaries and specific rules of engagement.

A SAMPLING OF SOCIAL MEDIA POLICIES

The following are some highlights from corporate social media policies:

Best Buy: The idea of "protect the brand, protect yourself" is the summation to just about everything in the company's policy guidelines. See http://forums.bestbuy.com/t5/Welcome-News/Best-Buy-Social-Media-Policy/td-p/20492.

Hewlett-Packard: These guidelines are directed more specifically to the blogging culture. They're short, sweet, and to the point. See www.hp.com/hpinfo/blogs/codeofconduct.html.

Cisco: The guidelines discouraging contact with media outlets are a big focus. See www.scribd.com/document/33461366/Cisco-Social-Media-Policy-Guidelines-and-FAQs.

Dell: The emphasis on "Be Nice, Have Fun and Connect" is clear. So is the company position on ownership of social media accounts. See www.dell.com/learn/us/en/uscorp1/corp-comm/social-media-policy?c=us&l=en&s=corp.

Coca Cola: This company gets bonus points for including both its core values and integrated value statements into its social media policy. See www.viralblog.com/wp-content/uploads/2010/01/TCCC-Online-Social-Media-Principles-12-2009.pdf.

REMEMBER: Values-based leaders with values-based organizations and cultures can and do experience missteps by well-meaning leaders, employees, and consultants. Set yourself up to preserve your reputation in case of emergency. Think of it as a life insurance policy for the organization.

Embezzling isn't the only unaligned action

I spend a lot of time with professionals in financial firms. Just this week, a client told me there was a call to arms for all employees: Protect the brand, protect the company! I'm all for that, but context is always essential, so my initial reaction was to cringe inside and make a scrunched-up face. *Protect the company* felt weird — off in some way. Almost as if the company was asking employees to do anything to make sure the brand wasn't tarnished. Better to frame it so that people know you're talking about ethical behavior and not a cover-up. (Maybe it's just me being paranoid. But the world is a little weird at the moment.)

Do you remember a time when you were a child that you and your friends may have gotten into some mischief? You looked at one another and swore an oath never to tell anyone what you'd done — pinkie swear. Everyone dispersed, and then within an hour someone cracked as their mom asked them a simple question, tears streaming down their face, and gave a full confession. You were all sunk for the cover-up as much as for the deed. That's somewhat how the *Protect the company* statement landed for me. You're going to be found out anyway — someone always spills the beans.

In Chapter 11, I discuss the concept of *given values* — those that we assume a person will abide by without specific policy. When that person doesn't abide by a given value, it becomes an unaligned action that violates basic trust between the employee and the company. There are many ways leaders, managers, and staff can engage in an unaligned action. Lying or falsifying or fudging facts are some examples. It isn't always about embezzlement or corruption. If someone always knows, eventually you'll be found out. Even if it's subtle cheating — a little bit here, a little bit there. When it happens, the reveal tarnishes everyone around you, including your team, and if it's a bigger infraction, the company as a whole.

REMEMBER: Just do the right thing and you'll never have to worry about this facet. Encourage others to do the same. Peer pressure can be a very useful tool when it comes to making sure everyone, as they say in the finance world, stays compliant. A strong company culture reinforces the expectations for everyone in your workplace.

IN THIS CHAPTER

» Putting together a values statement for the public

» Creating clarity and defining expectations for the company

Chapter 11
Identifying Values and Creating a Values Statement

More than a decade ago, I heard Bob Proctor speak to a crowd of 1,200 people at an entrepreneurial forum. Bob is a leading expert on mental toughness in achieving business success. He said (I'm paraphrasing):

> If you cannot tell me what you do and why you do it with a few sentences on the back of a cocktail napkin, then you've made it too complicated. Furthermore, if you've made it so complicated, no one can hear you. No one can understand you, buy from you, or follow you.

Since then, I've recognized this as a simple litmus test of truth. Many CEOs and leaders can address a few of the necessary components but not all of them: who they are, what they do, their strategy, and their values.

In this chapter, you use the do-it-yourself method of creating various values statements for different end uses, and it won't cost you anything except a little quiet, self-reflection time. How much you collaborate with others is completely up to you.

First I cover a simple four-step process of creating a values statement for the public. Your values statement signals to shareholders, customers, and stakeholders who you are and what you stand for in a simple, clear, concise manner. You *will* be able to write it on the back of a cocktail napkin, just as Bob suggested.

I also show you how to expand your values into clarifying statements for the staff so they understand your expectations of them regarding the core values you've established. We have a saying in my home: "All needs can be met when I know what they are." It's a simple statement of cooperation between my husband and me that extends into all our relationships. It takes the guesswork out of the equation and removes the expectation or assumption that each of us knows what the other really wants or needs. That's exactly what you'll be doing in this portion of the process.

When the staff understands your behavioral expectations of them, it makes it far easier for them to execute. Ambiguity is removed. Clarity brings unity and cooperation within the organization.

Using the Self-Reflective Method for a Public Values Statement

Full disclosure: Although I love the intricacies of many of the more established, structured systems to identify and construct values statements, I am more of a get-it-done kind of gal. Like, right now. I don't like to wait. Patience, unfortunately, isn't my strong suit, especially when it comes to making changes or shifts. During my corporate career, I realized that when all else fails, one just makes a calculated leap forward. There's a pretty good chance you may feel the same way, so I'd like to offer you two ways to create your values statements using a simple process and aligning it with different end uses:

- » **SRM (self-reflective method):** Do it yourself on the back of a cocktail napkin.
- » **SRM+ (self-reflective method + some):** Do it yourself on the back of a cocktail napkin *but also* seek input from key team members before you action anything.

The following sections explain how to decide whether you should involve anyone else in your self-reflective method, how to choose your values, and how to put together an external statement based on those values.

Deciding whether to involve anyone else

Whether you use SRM or SRM+ will be determined by the size of your team and/or organization. Unless you're commanding a massive corporation, more structured assessments may not be as critical to your effectiveness. They may offer amazing insights into your organization, but for the everyday end user of this book, I want to make this a more accessible process.

REMEMBER

Self-reflection is a key component to uncovering values. The key questions are as follows:

- Who am I?
- What do I stand for?
- What does this company stand for?
- How are we going to execute all of this?

There are times when self-reflection is done solo in the quiet of our own minds and hearts. Sometimes the self-reflection results are brought to a group of peers for review and examination. Depending on your company culture, you will need to make this decision about participation. You are the captain of the ship, so ultimately you will land on the values you choose to bring forth into the organization.

If you decide to seek the input of others, here are some simple guidelines you may use to help determine whom to invite into the group participation portion of the process:

- **Small company:** If you only have a handful of people in your company, all of them can be involved in shaping the statement.
- **Small to mid-size company:** For a company with three or more divisional heads or managers, ask them for input.
- **Growing mid-size company:** Utilize your senior vice presidents (SVPs), but also include some of the boots-on-the-ground managers. They know more about the company culture than anyone else.

The larger the company, the further away from the real company culture the leader is. Self-reflection also means being truthful about how in touch you are with the team day to day. If you don't know them or their challenges, they may have difficulty executing your vision and values. Always include some of the boots-on-the-ground managers to ensure that what you're creating isn't just lofty, fluffy stuff but is something they can achieve.

> **MOVING FORWARD EVEN WITHOUT CONSENSUS**
>
> A few years ago, I was contacted by a national nonprofit in New York City. The leadership team was having difficulty creating a direction for the team. When I asked the managing director where she thought the problem lay, she said a few key players didn't want to cooperate. With great exasperation, she listed several examples of initiatives that had been derailed by challenges and disagreements. I asked whether everyone was clear on the mission and purpose of the organization. She responded with a strong yes. I then spent a few days observing leadership meetings and team engagement on various levels, and it became clear to me what the problem was. The managing director was unwilling to move forward with any initiatives without the entire leadership team's consensus, and they were deadlocked on accomplishing even the most minor activities necessary.
>
> *Cooperation* means contribution, but it doesn't always mean reaching a consensus. Ultimately, the derailment of the great work this nonprofit could have been achieving in the community was due to the managing director's belief that everyone had to be on board before projects could move forward. Remember, ultimately, *you* are the leader. That means you can call for input and contribution, but consensus isn't mandatory to move forward. This is your responsibility and duty.

REMEMBER Limit the size of your collaborative group, or nothing will get accomplished. The more people who get involved, the more opinions (and egos) you will have to navigate. As always, keep it as simple as possible.

Understanding and selecting values

Some values are fluid — they're ever-evolving and changing. Some are ingrained in our hearts and minds based on family, friends, and cultural influences. Others are acquired by other associations. However, the key values you'll be working with are *core* values, which can at times be confused with other types of values.

Distinguishing four types of values

You can place common values into four buckets. Understanding the differences will prevent diluting your message to the stakeholders by solely focusing on the core values:

» **Core values (CV):** These are the fundamental beliefs of an individual or group. They become guiding principles — an autopilot mechanism — for behaviors and actions. CVs also help discern right from wrong, serving as litmus tests for whether the group is on a constructive or destructive path to achieving their goals. They are inherent and foundational principles that everything else is built upon.

For example, leaders who believe justice is a CV of their organizations may have this attribute deeply ingrained within their personalities and mindsets. They automatically seek fairness and equality and tend to defend the underdog. You might see this manifested in diversity training, hiring, nonviolent communication resolution standards, and various other implementations.

» **Aspirational values:** These are values an individual or company aspires to project. It might also be called persistence. The desire to retain more accounts and clients, for example, may be the goal. You may seek to make every one of those folks fall in love with you so they never want to leave your services. That would be considered an internal, aspirational goal for the organization, not a core value.

» **Given values:** Values that don't vary from company to company are called *given* values. An example would be asking your employees not to falsely represent themselves and their credentials. Another would be that they would never embezzle from the company. These may be important, but they don't necessarily distinguish one company from another. They're the often unspoken but understood values of operating in the business world.

» **Vogue values:** Looking around your current workplace, you may notice that many on your team are young hipsters with tattoos and piercings. Yes, they're "cool," but to incorporate these elements into corporate values such as being "hip, edgy, and counterculture" wouldn't qualify as a core value. A vogue value is more about appearance — what's here today could be gone tomorrow — but a core value is constant and permanent. Yuppies gave way to hipsters, and nobody knows what the next incarnation of cool will be.

Vogue values often have a negative impact on organizations. They could perpetuate an environment of exclusion. Your 50-year-old neighbor may be a perfect fit for your company, but if they don't fit a vogue value, they'll be bypassed for a job. Be mindful of vogue values seeping into your organization. A culture naturally attracts certain types of people, but it shouldn't exclude others.

Stay in the CV lane when you're creating your values statements. Everything else in the preceding list will only muddy the waters and confuse the stakeholders. Your statement should be clear and never confusing.

Choosing values that speak to you

Take out a piece of paper and a pencil. Let's begin delving into your values. I've provided a list of more than 60 possible core values in Figure 11-1. The list doesn't represent every core value possible, of course, but it's a good start. As an exercise, write down eight or ten of the values in Figure 11-1 that resonate with you and that you would like to see reflected in your organization. Feel free to make notes next to each as to what or why these particular values mean something to you.

Accountability	Equality	Loyalty
Achievement	Excitement	Nature
Advancement	Fairness	Order
Adventure	Faith	Personal Development
Affection	Fame	Pleasure
Artisitic Impression	Family	Power
Authority	Financial Reward	Predictability
Autonomy	Freedom	Recognition
Balance	Friendship	Respect
Caring	Fun	Responsibility
Challenge	Generosity	Risk Taking
Collaboration	Health	Service
Communication	Helping Others	Spirituality
Community	Honesty	Stability
Compassion	Independence	Status/Prestige
Competence	Influence	Structure
Competition	Innovation	Teamwork
Contribution to Society	Integrity	Tradition
Cooperation	Intellectual Challenge	Trust
Creativity	Job Security	Variety
Diversity	Justice	Wealth
Economic Security	Love	Wisdom

FIGURE 11-1: A chart of possible core values.

© John Wiley & Sons, Inc.

REMEMBER: Do your best to avoid self-judgment. This is your quiet space to explore right now. You may choose values that are different from those of your family of origin, for example. That's okay. It's more important that you are honest about what's important to *you*.

Once you have these values written down, put down the list. Make a cup of coffee. Take a walk. Allow the exercise to sink in for several minutes. Don't rush.

After a while, go back to your list. Now, which ones are the most important, essential, or perceived critical values? Circle three. (If you're finding this difficult to do, don't worry — that's perfectly normal.) See whether you can group two of the three values together that may mean almost the same thing. For example, *community* and *service* may have similar meanings to you. They might be defined like this:

» **Community:** Contributing to the community to share the company's success, revenue, and resources

» **Service:** Serving the surrounding community through fundraising, projects, and service such as volunteerism

In this example, you might select *service* as the umbrella core value to represent both intentions; that's one essential core value. Continue working until you have at least three essential core values and a maximum of five.

REMEMBER: Core values are highly personal. They are part of the very fiber of who we are, as well as what our teams are and what our companies embody. We're unconsciously attached to them. When they're challenged, it makes us very uncomfortable. When they're illuminated and ignited, we walk with pride and conviction. They drive our words, behaviors, and deeds every day. Core values are the autopilot program hardwired into your being. When harnessed, they mobilize people toward a common mission or purpose.

TIP: Apply your favorite colored sticky note to this page and write your top three to five values on it. You can move this sticky note from chapter to chapter if you like. It's your traveling cheat sheet while you're working through the content of this book. I suggest putting one on your bathroom mirror, too. Talk about a literal reflection point. (By the way, you're allowed to change them after living with your selection for several days.)

THE DIFFICULTY OF PICKING CORE VALUES

A few years ago, I took a group of business owners and team leaders on my Values to Vision retreat in Utah. On the first day, everyone was seated with the backdrop of the red mountains behind them. I asked them all to tell me about why they came and what was most valuable to them. They waxed poetic: "I am here for my family" or "I want to be a better leader." Okay, but, what do you value, I asked again? They all looked at me blankly. One woman piped up and said, "I value this," stretching her hands out to the horizon. "Nature — I can't get enough." The group listed more, including the love of their spouses, pets, and so on. But no one got to their core values. This is a very common occurrence.

I provided them with the same exercise I am giving you in this chapter. They were instructed to select eight to ten core values from a deck based on the chart in Figure 11-1. There was a lot of mumbling, laughter, and requests for clarification. "Maria, what if I don't pick *trust* as a core value — does that mean I'm dishonest?" One man said, "If I select *communication* as a core value, does that mean everyone gets to talk all at once? I have that problem already!" Another participant poked at him. "Just give them all a talking stick." There was more nervous laughter. Most of the group found it difficult to pick only eight or ten. Then it got even harder.

"Okay, everyone, hand me the values you've filtered out." The laughter stopped. "Next step, narrow it down to only three to five." You would have thought I'd asked them to give away a child. They were flabbergasted. Almost in a split second, this group of mild-mannered professionals turned into a mob of protestors. (Inside, I admit it, I was giggling to myself.)

"If I don't pick *compassion,* I think my church is going to ex-communicate me!" said one woman.

"They're not here, so don't worry about it." I assured her. "I won't tell them, I promise."

A lot of begging, pleading, and negotiating ensued.

"Can I have that one back?"

"Nope."

"Can I combine core values to create a super-value?"

"We're not working with super-values today — only core values, sorry."

I asked that they review the meaning behind each of the values they've selected. "Do any of them have the same or similar meaning to you? If so, combine them. They're not super-values, but one value word could become an umbrella for the intended meaning behind two or three."

"Umbrella, I like that!" one woman said. They nodded and went on refining their lists.

The next day when they arrived at our meeting site, the group was buzzing about their lists. Remarkably, the ones they had left our session with the day before had been changed. They'd discussed the exercise over dinner with one another. Many had called spouses and significant others, and one even called a member of her board of directors to get some feedback. That morning, they all felt they'd made honest and insightful choices that would better themselves and their organizations. This became a very emotional period as each stood and shared their core values and why they meant so much to them. A heartfelt process like this gives us a peek into the humanity of each leader.

Formulating and assembling your statement

The company's purpose and mission are most powerful when combined with the core values. That makes a complete values statement and projects a cohesive, well-thought-out position to shareholders, investors, and customers. In our world of reduced attention spans, brevity is king.

REMEMBER

Four questions are the only ones you'll need to answer:

» Who are you?

» What is your strategy?

» What is your purpose?

» What do you value?

Most businesses declare who they are in their mission statement. For example, Marriott clearly states that it is "committed to being the best lodging and food service company in the world." Home Depot tells its customers that it's "in the home improvement business." Where many leaders fall short is in conveying their strategy and purpose:

» *Strategy* should be broken down into a verb. Strategy is about direction, which requires a definitive action in order to arrive at a certain destination or result. Strategy should always be action-oriented.

» *Purpose* defines how you're benefiting your customers and/or the community around you.

The core values are what make your company different from others. Core values speak for themselves in a corporate values statement, although in other iterations, different details may be necessary. For example, CVS Health does an exceptional job of utilizing this four-question model to convey its reason for being in the market and why anyone would want to work for or buy from CVS. Here's the statement:

> We are: A pharmacy innovation company
>
> Our strategy: Reinventing pharmacy
>
> Our purpose: Helping people on their path to better health
>
> Our values: Innovation, Collaboration, Caring, Integrity, Accountability

It's simple, elegant, and straight to the point. In this example, the strategy verb is *reinventing*, and the purpose verb is *helping*. Best of all, this values statement can be written on the back of a napkin. Bob Proctor would be proud.

Rolling Out Your Values Statement to Your Company

There are different end uses for values statements. Some are external, as in the CVS Health example in the preceding section. External values statements act as beacons to the business community and consumers of one's products and/or services.

Within an organization values become the *rules of engagement*. However, not everyone will always be on the same page. Providing animation of the company core values becomes the guiding force, or starlight, for everyone involved in the execution of the company's strategy. First, you need to define that animation. Second, you need to infuse personality into the statement. Finally, you combine all components to create and deliver a values statement to the internal leadership, stakeholders, and external resources. Everyone moving together in the same direction, with the same intention, agreement of rules of engagement, and conduct, creates a powerful force.

The following sections discuss those steps and provide guidance for entrepreneurs who work solo.

REMEMBER

Here are four good reasons to execute a statement and plan for your team:

- Convey what is important to you, the leader.
- Establish guidelines for engagement and behavior.
- Set the example and follow through so they will follow suit.
- Create unity across the organization.

Animating your core values

Words without action are useless and hollow. The best intentions and purest of motives are fantastic but will remain stagnant without actions. As human beings, we like clear boundaries because they create a central point of focus and reason. When you clearly illustrate your expectations, your team has a picture of how you're asking them to execute the values set forth. It enables everyone to internalize the concepts, create consistency among different areas of the company, and build trust.

Ask five people for their definition of honesty, and you'll get five different answers. Someone may say, "It means you don't cheat." Another may offer, "It means you don't lie." A third may add, "It means you treat your vendors fairly, you pay them their worth, and you're always forthcoming with your staff." People may have a difference of opinion on exactly what a core value may mean. But the third participant described the value *in action* by providing context and practical application.

REMEMBER

A value in action could also be termed a *means value* or *animation of a value* (AV for short). An AV is framed in a manner in which all participants can clearly understand the expectations of the leader and see how it can be achieved. Devoid of that framing, achieving it could become a free-for-all.

Infusing personality into your statement

Every organization has a kind of personality, almost like having celebrity status. Organizations have Instagram accounts, and people follow them on Facebook and Twitter. Some companies *are* celebrity worthy. People love the idea of image, association, and lifestyle. We always have. It's not a new phenomenon. Companies with personalities are the new brand. For example, the personality of Whole Foods is all about community — both internally, among staff, and externally with vendor partners. Whole Foods prides itself on its mission: "Whole foods, whole people, whole planet." People work for the company because they want to be involved with and associate with a company who loves, feeds, and cares for the community. Step into any Whole Foods to see those individuals.

Here's another example: Volkswagen has embraced the *Fun Theory* as part of its company culture and overall mission to generate innovation and ideas. According to the company: "The Fun Theory is based on the idea that something as simple as fun is the easiest way to change people's behavior for the better. We apply this thinking to every environmentally friendly innovation we make. It should never have to be a compromise to help the planet. Moreover, we believe more people will act responsibly, and drive greener, if they have fun on the way." The fun factor is very much part of the personality of this company. VW imbues fun into every marketing campaign and within its own company workplace. Fun is the personality of Volkswagen.

There are several companies that ensure that the values of fun, high energy, and community involvement are part of their personalities. Keep this in mind as you're working toward your values statements. The *last* thing you want is a statement that feels bland or as sensible as a high-fiber cereal.

The list of personality types could be lengthy. Consider the personality of your organization. Are you a high-energy group? Do you value adventure and exploration as part of your process more than anything else? Or are you straight-down-the-line, process-oriented linear thinkers? Either one suggests a personality and tone you can immediately recognize.

TIP As you walk through the doors, what does the entrance say to you about what your company is all about? Does it feel like an old-school institution with lots of structure — or a place where creativity lives? Would it make you feel like you were in trusted hands — or is it a place where adventurous people are thinking outside the box? What's the personality that hits you when you enter that office?

WeWorks is one of the largest co-working companies in the United States. Upon entering a WeWorks office space, you immediately sense that great, creative, energetic, and significant work is being done there by a variety of professionals. It's exciting, full of promise, and energizing — and no one has even spoken to you yet. You can feel that the WeWorks personality is one of an *explorer*. Its personality comes through and supports the mission statement: "To create a world where people work to make a life, not just a living."

TIP Circle one of the following personalities that best suits you and your organization (or add your own personality type to the list):

- Fun
- High-energy
- Change agents
- Adventurers

PART 3 **Charting the Course and Crafting Your Values**

- Explorers
- Pioneers
- Archeologists
- Programmers

Self-reflection comes into play once again. Ask the following questions:

- How is this personality currently being reflected in the workplace?
- How would you like this personality projected into your workplace?
- How does this personality amplify the talents and the values of you and your organization?
- Would it be important to wrap this personality trait into your values statement?
- Is the personality trait necessary or just "nice" for the organization to have?

Based on the information you've compiled, consider how and where you'll implement your personality into the company. The easiest place to start is with the appearance of your office and online presence and the attitude of the talent you have. The earlier examples of Whole Foods, Volkswagen, and WeWorks provide some insight into how to project your values and personality into your workplace.

Creating clarity and direction across the board

Snapping all the components into one picture will create clarity, direction, and rules of engagement for your staff, vendor engagement, and overall responsibility in the marketplace. Writing it out will help you clarify your thoughts. There will be less guesswork by the staff to determine what you really meant by "Trust is our core value." Creating clarity saves time because the directive will be very clear.

REMEMBER: Inconsistency in messaging or behavior sends mixed signals, confuses direction, frustrates staff, and creates an environment of distrust. Using the following simple formula conveys the clarity necessary:

Core values (CV) + Animation of a value (AV) = Desired result

Use Table 11-1 as an example and follow these steps to create clear rules of engagement:

1. **Move your three to five core values that you identified earlier in this chapter into the table.**

   See the earlier section "Choosing values that speak to you" for details.

2. **Decide how you want those core values animated.**

   Consider what the animation would be in the real world. Use specific context and/or engagements.

3. **Consider the result of the CV and AV.**

   What specific outcome would manifest?

TABLE 11-1 Putting Everything Together for Rules of Engagement

Core Value (CV)	Animated Value (AV)	What the Action Achieves
1. Honesty	1. Give it to me straight so the best decisions can be made for everyone involved. 2. I'd rather know than be kept in the dark about our ingredients.	1. Builds a culture of transparency and trust. 2. Allows us to make the best choices for the customer and in turn the customer can make the best decision for their family.
2. Respect	1. Negotiate fairly, not to exploit our vendors, but to form partnerships that are beneficial to all.	1. Creates a culture where vendors are treated as part of our company and not outsiders. 2. Fosters a culture where everyone wins, and not at the expense of others.
3.	1.	1. 2.

TIP If it's easier for you, change the order you fill in the table as follows:

» What desired result are you seeking?
» Which of your core values best associates with that result?
» What actions or engagement would animate that value?

The following sections provide examples of putting together clear rules of engagement for people within an organization.

Example 1

CEO Sally sees teamwork and collaboration as important core values for her organization. She has an incredibly talented group of individuals around her who she knows possess even more talent than is currently being utilized. They need creative solutions and cutting-edge ideas to grow the company. That's the result she's trying to cultivate. She wants to connect the CV with the result need. Sally's statement can look something like this:

> *Teamwork and collaboration are essential components of this organization. Constructively challenging one another to think creatively, we find solutions that change our customers' lives.*

She conveys to the team that challenges to ideas are acceptable when done constructively. Collaboration and working together toward a creative solution are the activities she expects. She's also reminding them of whom they ultimately serve: the customer. This evokes a sense of responsibility beyond themselves, connecting their daily activities directly to the people who purchase the solution they've come up with for them.

Can you find the personality in Sally's statement? It's very subtle. She is very caring. A pioneering personality is also evident here.

Example 2

A company that prides itself on honesty and respect can construct a values statement. Here are two versions for different companies:

> *We believe our clients deserve our honesty about our products' ingredients. We see this as our responsibility to be transparent so they can make the best choices for their families.*

Or:

> *Our staff, vendors, and suppliers are our treasured partners. We hold each of these individuals in the highest regard, treating each with the utmost respect and fairness in all our dealings.*

Either way, the directive and the engagement are made clear to the team. In the first version, the leader is telling the team they're not permitted to hide details from the consumer that may or may not be desirable. Out of respect for the customer, they are providing the information necessary so the customer can make a personal choice for their family.

A VALUES-BASED LEADER: MARTIN LUTHER KING JR.

Dr. Martin Luther King Jr. became the prominent leader of the civil rights movement in the United States during the 1950s and 1960s. He was the leading figure advocating an end to racial discrimination using nonviolent methods for making social change. On August 28, 1963, one of his most powerful and memorable speeches was made in front of the Lincoln Memorial in Washington, D.C. His "I have a dream" oration still evokes the emotion of the possibility of change. It invites listeners to connect with the hopefulness inside themselves that racial equality could become a reality.

One of the most memorable lines was "I have a dream that my four little children will one day live in a nation where they will not be judged by the color of their skin but by the content of their character." Dr. King's speech represented a values-based statement for the movement he galvanized. His main values were fairness and equality. His core means (the verb) was nonviolent methods, which he also made clear. As a gifted orator, he could emotionally connect his dream, his values, and the result he wanted to achieve. It was a very clear and precise message and a call to action for the civil rights community. Dr. King was a tremendous example of a values-based leader, movement maker, and beacon of hope.

Today when the words "I have a dream" are spoken, people perk up. They unconsciously take a breath, listening with every fiber of their being, waiting to hear what that dream of a better tomorrow could be. It is part of a cultural psyche. It's also part of a brilliant marketing opportunity. It conjures up a visceral or visual image in a person's mind.

In the second version, a clear directive is provided about how everyone is to engage with one another in the process — nothing short of dignity and respect by dealing with them fairly. Does that mean they can't negotiate? No, it means that they need to be fair and not pillage a supplier needlessly. You may think that people wouldn't do that anyway. I can assure you from my 20 years of negotiating deals with overseas vendors, on more than one occasion I've watched others bring vendors to their knees just for the sport of it. Setting the expectation of fairness sets a bar. In this example, you never negotiate for sport. You negotiate for what you need and what they can offer.

For solopreneurs: Self-leadership and identifying clients

Values-based leadership can also found in modern-day movement makers and *solopreneurs.* Although such solitary entrepreneurs may not care to use the earlier methods for deriving a values statement, they do need to consider integrating a values statement into their marketing. People want to be moved. They want to be inspired in the same way Dr. Martin Luther King inspired a nation to act (see the nearby sidebar for more about Dr. King as a values-based leader). People want to feel connected to a greater mission and purpose. That solopreneur may be one individual working out of their home office, but it doesn't matter. For movement makers, the community and movement they seek to mobilize need a clear direction and clear rules of engagement.

Solopreneurs become a hybrid of movement makers and small businesses. It's imperative that consumers know what you stand for, what you care about, and sometimes even more importantly, why they should want to be part of *your* growth strategy.

REMEMBER: Values conveyed properly, for a solopreneur, can establish who the core client may be and what kind of engagement they're seeking to work with you. The values become a checklist for fit right off the bat.

This is brilliantly illustrated by solopreneur Carolyn Herfurth, owner of The BizTruth. She flips the rules of engagement around to her customers, basically saying, "Hey, if you want to work with me, this is what I expect of you" — potentially a landmine approach few have navigated with such precision. She teaches female business owners how to master the sales process so they can grow their company. Simple, right? But what makes her stand out from every other person who may be offering the same services is her values statement. It starts with two powerful words: "I believe."

> *I believe it takes courage to start a business — and a bit of crazy to continue. When things get tough it's not time to back down — it's time to step up. Ego & Fear give you excuses to keep you where you are — don't let them win. Everything we do is "on purpose" — even our mistakes. We have the potential to play bigger — if only we'd believe in ourselves more. There's nothing more scary — or as rewarding — than daring to live your truth. Women entrepreneurs can gain financial freedom faster — and do it their way. Freedom takes guts — drop the "shoulds." Self-trust is your greatest asset — claim it!*

Her statement infuses the three important factors discussed earlier in this chapter, but in a slightly different manner:

>> **Statement of belief:** The outcome or desired result

>> **Expressions of core values:** Fun, freedom, and adventure

>> **Animation of core values:** Addressing the fears and offering a path out

If you didn't know it, Carolyn's core values are fun, freedom, and adventure. Her personality is the personality of her company, one of the "joyful risk taker, ardent adventurer, and gregarious business owner." Reading that statement, don't you feel like she's taken you on a journey already? Doesn't it make you want to work with her?

IN THIS CHAPTER

» Recognizing that you can chart your own course solo if need be

» Diagnosing and finding solutions to your team's challenges

» Creating a starlight to be a guiding principle for your team

» Applying larger vales-based principles on a smaller scale

Chapter **12**

Going It Alone When Your CEO Isn't Interested in Values-Based Leadership

As I say many times throughout this book, leaders aren't just CEOs and C-suite executives. As the business community is evolving, the perception of leadership is too. I go into this concept in more depth in Chapter 17, but for now, just remember that you can effect change as a leader of a team or group within your organization.

When you were a child, did you build forts? Indoors you could make them from blankets and furniture, and outdoors you could put them between trees, stumps, and natural cover canopies. Those forts became places of magic. Outside, the world was whatever you experienced in your everyday life. But inside your fort, *you* managed who came and went, what activities you engaged in, what you ate, what you drank, and where you slept. You ruled. It didn't mean that when the authorities (your parents) called you in for dinner that you didn't sit at the table.

It just meant that *in the fort,* you could control several elements. Sometimes as the world became challenging for you — in school, for example — your mind might drift back to your fort. It was a source of pride and an expression of creativity.

Your team is that fort. It doesn't mean that you don't adhere to the rules and plans of the authorities outside the fort. But inside the fort, you determine how to get where you need to go. In this chapter, I show you how to guide your team with values-based leadership (VBL), even when you're not the CEO. *Note:* To be clear, I'm not talking about going rogue or creating anarchy. The opportunity for you here is setting up an environment to spur growth and provide inclusion.

Accepting That the Top Brass Isn't Interested in Values-Based Leadership

In some cases, neither the CEO nor the C-suite leadership may be interested in turning the company into a values-based organization. It may seem just a little too *fluffy* or *out there* for them. They may not believe there would be a benefit to going through the process. "After all," they may argue, "we're an ethical team already — why formalize it?" Or, simply: "We really don't have time for this." If they're a group of knuckleheads, to put it politely, you can pretty much guess why VBL would be of no interest to them.

But let's assume they're completely engrossed in their daily dealings and simply don't have the bandwidth to add VBL to their repertoire. They're operating without any malice and truly want the company and the team to thrive. The idea of a shared values economy may be too complex to consider because there are other pressing priorities at the moment. Got it?

It's important that you do actually get it. Otherwise, you're at risk of feeling frustration and resentment toward these individuals, and that's not a good place to start. Even if your situation is more negative than that, you still need to make a decision to accept who they are and where they are. Becoming emotional does nothing more than create a time and energy vortex. Have your feelings, sure — but don't linger. You may never fully shake off the negative emotions if you give in to them.

One of the main ideas in this book is to embrace that C-suite individuals are not the only leaders in the company, although they certainly are the pinnacle. You can address the issues on your own team, whether they are infighting, aggressiveness in how they compete with others, or a lack of willingness to cooperate with other departments or team members. My feeling is that if you're here with me now, you're trying to resolve an issue and you've decided to take action where you are. This is exactly what any good leader does: taking responsibility for making the environment and culture of their own team. Ultimately, this leads to better performance.

Use the following statements in accepting the choice of the C-suite individuals:

- » These are their behaviors, both pluses and minuses.
- » This is their focus at the moment.
- » They simply are who they are.

Here is an example: *While leadership is lacking in direction and clarity, they actually are very caring people. Their focus right now is addressing other specific issues. This is where we are, and I need to accept who they are.*

Be matter of fact about it, as if reading a car manual: *It simply is. They simply are.* Then move along because you're sitting on the precipice of a choice for your own leadership development. If you stall out here, that's your choice. Chances are you'll be dialing a recruiter soon. You could just sink into hopelessness. A much better idea is to view this situation as a fantastic opportunity. That's what I am hoping you'll do — give it your best shot before you explore other opportunities.

It's not your job to change anyone but yourself. Period.

Even if you decide to walk away from your current situation, remember this: Wherever you go, there you are. At some point, you'll have to deal with the same or similar situation until you change your own approach. In this case, you should decide to be powerful rather than powerless.

Guiding Your Crew When You're Just an Officer, Not the Captain

Not all organizations may be ready for VBL yet. Focus on those individual and group leaders who understand that VBL isn't just a workplace trend, but a way to work that will be infinitely clearer. When people are clear about the expectations set, they can meet them. In a rudderless organization or one with distracted leadership, sometimes the team questions where they're going, how they're going to hit goals, and where the path is to get to there. They may waste a lot of time and energy trying to figure it out. Often, they just need someone to point them in the right, consistent direction but be consistent in that direction. This includes your behavior; actions speak louder than words.

It's not unlike being left in a rowboat in the middle of the ocean. The captain, or perceived leader, hasn't provided the tools or direction to get you to shore. You have two choices: Sit still, allow everyone to flounder, and hope someone else steps up to guide — or *you* step up and guide the group.

Step up and guide your own group with the help of the following sections.

Giving yourself permission to take the reins

You don't need permission to act with integrity. There's no paperwork that needs to be filled out to authorize you to direct your team to play fairly. No one is going to take away your access card to the building if you set reasonable expectations and goals with accountability standards. Overthinking this will cause paralysis.

It is completely within your reach to positively affect your team. Here's a little rationalization to consider when you weigh your options:

» If you're leading a team, you can establish how they work.

» To ensure your operational expectations are met, your managers continually reinforce them.

» Staff members can participate because the expectation will be set by you and then reinforced and clarified by your managers.

» It's within your purview to set up accountabilities for yourself and your team.

REMEMBER

I'm not talking about going off script, going rogue, or declaring your emancipation from the company. I'm offering you the opportunity to change your own mindset and that of your team so they can thrive. Realize that you are more powerful and influential than you may realize.

Curtailing the mutiny and getting everyone back on track

Nothing is more demoralizing than seeing your team become embroiled in conflict or paralyzed with self-doubt. It's heartbreaking. Here you have a group of talented individuals whom you have come to know personally. You know that Sam just got engaged to Jesse. You're aware that Tim, Lourdes, and Larry have become dear friends who are about to go whitewater rafting together. Joan and Antonio have kids in the same grade together. They're real people, with real lives, personalities, and emotions. You have empathy for them. If you didn't, you wouldn't be so profoundly affected by this situation. Empathy is an equalizer. It makes you aware and it makes you care. It facilitates the willingness to step beyond your own defenses and excuses for an unhappy environment or result.

There are times when everything just erupts. Everyone is under so much pressure that it may feel like they're all going to jump ship. I'm going to suspend some of the bigger issues discussed earlier and bring this concept down to the everyday frustrations that are occurring. It could be as simple as people experiencing a lot of conflict interdepartmentally, all the tech systems not working properly (my own personal nemesis), shipments being late, deadlines moving . . . and the list goes on.

What should you do?

>> The first step in curtailing mutiny is to remove your emotional response from what's happening. Step back. It's not always easy to do this with a loud vortex of people and emotion swirling around you. Additionally, it can be very overwhelming if there are financial repercussions manifesting. Be still and think (reflect).

>> Find empathy inside yourself, for yourself. Even if you feel like that's selfish, do it. You need a moment to ease the self-inflicted pressure you may be feeling.

>> Now find empathy for all team members — inside and outside your purview. Even if you're unhappy with some of the people on your team, you can find empathy for them.

>> Suspend judgment of who did (or didn't do) what to whom.

Now go through the rest of the process in the following sections: Diagnose the team, determine where and how you can effect change, and ready yourself to make a values stand.

Diagnosing the team's hurdles

Your diagnostic tool for your group's hurdles is introduced in Chapter 8, which discusses the mindset of the organization in various stages. Here, I overlay those tools onto an individual team.

Practical application in multiple scenarios will help you digest the concepts more fully. First, knowing where everyone's head is will be helpful. You don't want to offer a solution that may not fit the discomfort occurring. If you were to ask people to have faith in your ability to move the needle when that's not the issue, it wouldn't positively affect them. It's better to understand that the real issue is that they're afraid they will be shamed in the current environment, and then offer an appropriate solution for that.

How the discomfort is happening is equally important. Have you ever listened to a leader recite a litany of remedies and sat there thinking, "They have no clue what's really going on"? That's why taking the time to diagnose the situation is so important.

Note: I won't be detailing specific business solutions, only the leading of others. It will be up to you to diagnose and address those issues as well.

REMEMBER

The mindset of your team can be broken down into four clearly defined categories: courage, hope, optimism, and trust. Positive and not-so-positive animations (how they are expressed) can be found within each:

- **Courage:** Willingness to take action. Lack of it means refusal to act out of fear of shame or criticism.
- **Hope:** Excited about the future, as opposed to hopeless and resigned to what is.
- **Optimism:** The ability to see the best. The opposite is being engrossed in negativity and pessimistic thinking.
- **Trust:** Having faith that everything will be okay, as opposed to lying and/or digging into another way of going.

One flows easily into another. You may be having an issue with optimism on the team, but it may not always be coupled with hope — it may be a trust issue. As you go through the following assessment process, always consider whether there's a secondary component to the hurdle.

TIP

I can add more categories, but for the sake of simplicity, do your best to operate with just the preceding four to avoid stumbling into values at this point. Values are beliefs of importance and guidelines for ways of being, while courage, hope, optimism, and trust are about mindset or psychology.

To assess the team's current mindset, follow these steps:

1. **Take out a piece of paper. Write the names of three to five people who reflect the general mood or attitude of the group at this moment. Next to each name write one or two of the mindset headers (courage, hope, optimism, or trust) and then a correlating animation (for example, fear of criticism).**

   If you need more descriptive prompts, refer to Chapter 8.

2. **Review your list. What are the common denominators? Select two and write those words big and bold with a thick black marker.**

   If you have secondary components to add, do so in parentheses. Conflating them is perfectly acceptable.

3. **Determine whether those words and sentiments reflect what you're also feeling.**

Chances are that you and your team are having very similar experiences. You may already know the mindset and the circumstances behind why the team is unhappy. Allowing yourself time to let it sink in may provide an opportunity to ask a team member why they are paralyzed in their actions. You may be very surprised by what you hear. Although you won't be able to address every situation, and you certainly don't want it to become a therapy session, the point of this exercise is to get some clarity apart from your own emotions, as an objective observer.

Hold onto your list. I'm going to come back around to it throughout the rest of this chapter.

Courageously making your own values stand

Courage is the ability to walk into the unknown. It requires great strength. When your self-confidence lags, courage is the attribute that you'll need to lean on. Even the most confident leaders I've ever met, who seem cool and together on the outside, can doubt their abilities and capacity to effect change.

Making a values stand represents a course correction, and often a course correction brings you into a space of the unknown. That's where courage intersects the desire for change and the willingness to do so. In this conversation, a course correction is about injecting values into the equation.

Figure 12-1 illustrates a potential conversation going on inside your head. It may not always be as dramatic as deciding to stay or leave a job, but it is always a decision point that you can be pushed toward. A decision is necessary. Although pauses may be necessary to reflect, ultimately a choice is made.

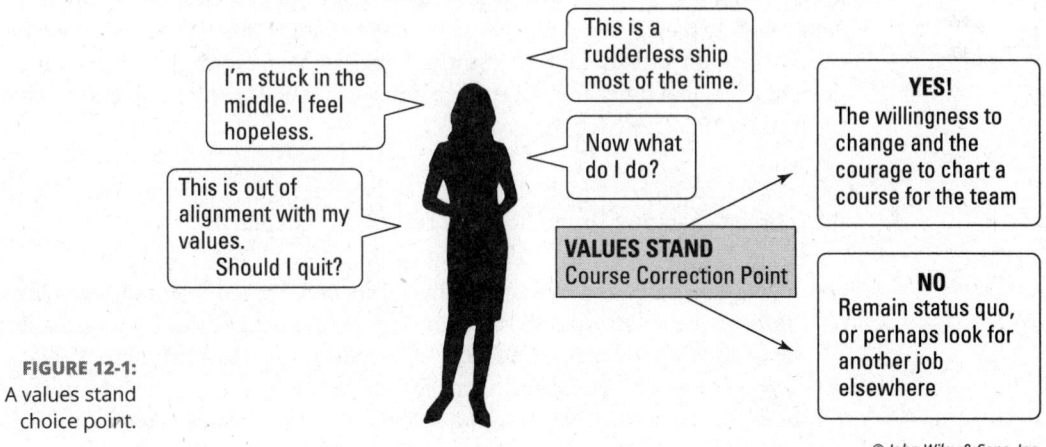

FIGURE 12-1: A values stand choice point.

© John Wiley & Sons, Inc.

You already know, from the exercise in the preceding section, what the problems may be. You've got the reins — what will you do? Will you continue to go along with the status quo, or will you make a course correction for you and your team?

WARNING: Sometimes the status quo is the appropriate choice. You may have obligations that you feel prevent you from taking a risk where you are now. Or you've become so frustrated that the appropriate choice is to find another job somewhere else. There's no judgment implied in these choices. You should make the best choice for your particular situation. However, realize that if you stay, you're at risk of falling into a victim mentality: *I cannot change anything. It is what it is. This is futile. Oh well.*

Minding the gap: The space between you and the team

You are the gap between senior leadership and your people. Whenever I hear leaders complain about what's going on "above" them or "below" them, I ask them: "What are you doing to mind the gap? Are you participating, resisting, or creating a more cogent pathway to the end?"

At Union Square station in New York City, there's a considerable gap between the train and the platform. Just prior to the train rumbling in, the announcer says, "Please mind the gap. Stand clear." Once the train stops, automatic platform extenders slide outward to meet the train's edge. Such is your role as a team leader. You are the gap between the platform and the train. In this space, you reside stagnantly or actively. Either way, what you do in the gap affects the team.

When you're sailing solo into creating a values-based environment, there may come a time where you have to make a values stand. That is, you may be willing to change whether you have the support to do so or not. Establishing your leadership *starlight* (described in more detail later in this chapter) is for you and your team. It means the willingness to make changes for the better so everyone can operate effectively and efficiently. Consider your starlight as not only the guideline for how the team will engage but also a way of expressing and clarifying the mission challenge for the group.

As an example, here's a look at values stands from "Carl" and "Janelle." They are the running examples throughout the rest of this chapter:

» **Carl's gap:** Carl was a leader in a large digital firm. He had spent years coming through the ranks and truly loved his work and his people. In the latest round of realignments in the organization, Carl ended up in Mark's hierarchy. "Mark" was a proven senior leader who really knew how to put on his game face for top management. However, he was often careless and threatening. To quote Carl, Mark was a "wrecking ball" when it came to dealing with the staff.

Carl knew that Mark's behavior was affecting his team. They weren't motivated and felt hopeless. Several looked like they were interviewing for new jobs outside the company. He didn't want to lose them. Carl first had to take an honest inventory of Mark's feedback on his own leadership. What did he *know* he needed to improve on — separate from what Mark was projecting on him that had nothing to do with him? Additionally, Carl asked himself how he was contributing to the "wrecking ball" energy of the team. This was what he needed to correct so the team could latch onto hope.

» **Janelle's gap:** Janelle worked for the same company as Carl. She was a team leader in another branch of the organization. Her team would sometimes need a little correction, but for the most part everyone was operating within the guidelines of leadership values, even without any formal VBL being initiated. Her manager embraced the role of a level 3 (Elevate) leader (refer to Chapter 5) who cared about the team and the whole. However, upon reflection, Janelle could see that she herself could do a better job. Therefore, her team was drifting a little bit, coloring outside the lines every now and then but not really stepping over the line into questionable engagement with others. There was a low-grade selfishness she could feel but couldn't quite put her finger on.

Janelle was the gap between her up level and the team. Her values stand is different from Carl's in that although VBL wasn't part of the organization, there was a high level of leadership influence around her. She first had to make corrections to her own behaviors, including being more transparent and no longer allowing her staff to risk their reputation or the company's.

Both had to embrace their willingness to change themselves first. Then they could look toward filling the gap that had been devoid of clarity and directives for the team.

REMEMBER Not all values stands are a result of crisis. They can also result from knowing that something needs to be course corrected. Application of the values stand is varied depending on your specific experience.

For entrepreneurs: Considering an alternate point of entry

Entrepreneurs who are participating in this journey should consider this as an alternate point of entry in creating your values positioning. Although the broader, more expansive values statement process offered in Chapter 11 is a great place to start, it may not completely fill your needs when it comes to the daily, operational aspect of business. Perhaps you would just prefer a more tailored, conversational application. You may be the CEO. Depending on your scaling evolution, you could be a team of 1 or a team of 1,000. The same principles being detailed now are applicable for an entrepreneur.

TIP: Feel free to make adjustments to the process as it applies to your venture. If you're a very small organization, jump directly to the next section. You may not need to or be ready to assess your team. But please consider assessing your own mindset in the earlier diagnostic section. Knowing where you stand is as important as knowing where the team stands.

Creating Your Leadership Starlight for the Team

Back in the 1700s, sailors used sextants to guide their way across the ocean. A sextant determined angles so that sailors, early pilots, and surveyors could identify what longitude they were at. Latitude was often determined by the sun, stars, and the moon, but longitude provided the necessary missing factor needed to get from one place to another. The sextant appeared to be a simple device — in fact, it looked like a protractor with a tube attached to the side. However, it was quite a sophisticated device for its time, using mirrors to determine coordinates.

The same could be said for the starlight. It may not be all that fancy or appear sophisticated, yet it's a powerful tool to get where you want to go. In the following sections, you use the simplicity of knowing where you are now and determining where you would like to go in terms of how you and your team will engage in business. Core values plus action equals a desired result. It is your navigation tool. (Check out Chapter 13 for details on career starlights.)

REMEMBER: The starlight is a conversational tool you can use to accomplish the following:

>> **Removing distractions:** Move around potentially negative distractions or influences so they can work more effectively.

>> **Focusing the team:** Operate with values, without lecturing or looking like Moses who came down from the mount with tablets full of rules. You'll be far less dramatic.

>> **Minding the gap:** Get clear on some of your gap management needs.

REMEMBER: A clearly focused leader and team operate effectively and efficiently. Leadership is a commitment to allowing others to shine. Sam Walton summed it up well: "Outstanding leaders go out of their way to boost the self-esteem of their personnel. If people believe in themselves, it's amazing what they can accomplish." Give your team the opportunity to do so.

Unpacking your toolkit: Using what you have to move forward

Much of the information you need to create a leadership starlight is already at your fingertips. Mentors will often tell you that the answers to remedy any situation are usually right in front of you, though you may not see them at first. Change isn't always a comfortable state. It can be confusing when you're trying to get from point A, which you may not be enjoying, to point B, where you want to be. Puzzle pieces are strewn all over the floor. Your job is to assemble them quickly to create a way forward. Easier said than done, correct?

Your toolkit

Several exercises and assessments are the tools you have to identify and create your own statement. Before I move forward, now is the time to gather these items into one place:

- **Values list:** Have your list of desired values from Chapter 11 next to you, along with the actions needed to animate them.

- **Team diagnostic results:** These are based on the earlier assessment of where your team's mindset may be now. Identify the positive mindset shift you'll need to happen to make the change — for example, if they are pessimistic, they need to find optimism.

- **Self-diagnostic results:** Based on the assessment earlier in this chapter, what needs to change within your own mindset?

- **VBL principles:** Which principles, detailed in Chapter 6, have you overlooked or lapsed on? Just pick one or maybe two. This is also part of the self-diagnosis process.

- **You:** Yes, you are a part of this tool kit too, in terms of your commitment to your team, the organization, and yourself. Never underestimate the influencing factor that who you are has on your team.

To begin working on a leadership starlight, you use a modified version of the values statement detailed in Chapter 11. Carl and Janelle continue to be the examples of how to do this. I show you their process in the next sections, using the tools in the preceding list.

TIP Before you fully assemble your starlight, there is one further assessment to consider. Although by now you see what your team needs, or what they're signaling they need, the question remains: What values do you want to integrate? What is truly important to you? If there are any other values you want to include, please make a note of them.

Carl's assessment

Carl used the diagnostic assessment earlier in this chapter. His top two categories were pessimism with a bit of hopelessness and discouragement. Mark's domineering personality had created an environment where the team wouldn't take risks. In the past when they offered new ideas, Mark shot them down time after time. Team members felt demoralized and helpless to move forward on projects. Negativity permeated the ranks. Many felt completely unappreciated by Mark and even, at times, by Carl. Sometimes, they remarked, they didn't feel like Carl had their backs. The team functioned, but unfortunately it was status quo: They kept their heads down, did their work, and became disengaged from the process.

Carl understood that first he had to limit the team's exposure to Mark. This was a big part of minding the gap to ensure the team could operate effectively and with less disruption. The values stand for him became summoning the willingness to make the changes necessary both within himself and outwardly with the team. He could allow this situation to further crumble, or he could step into the gap, be that buffer, and reset his team.

Through Carl's assessment process, the values of collaboration, trust, creativity, and inclusion are identified as the remedy to the current challenges. Figure 12-2 shows the analysis of the team's current mindset and their actions. He reverse-engineers it, starting with what he would like the behaviors to be and matching them to the values associated with those actions. They are his interpretations. Each leader performing this type of assessment may have slightly different definitions of each value and their corresponding behaviors.

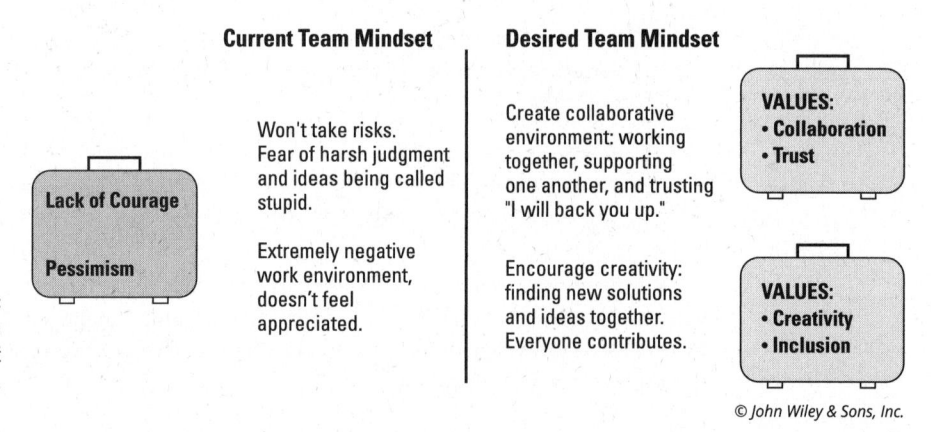

FIGURE 12-2: Carl's team assessment process.

Current Team Mindset

Lack of Courage
Pessimism

Won't take risks. Fear of harsh judgment and ideas being called stupid.

Extremely negative work environment, doesn't feel appreciated.

Desired Team Mindset

Create collaborative environment: working together, supporting one another, and trusting "I will back you up."

VALUES:
- Collaboration
- Trust

Encourage creativity: finding new solutions and ideas together. Everyone contributes.

VALUES:
- Creativity
- Inclusion

© John Wiley & Sons, Inc.

Janelle's assessment

The top two descriptions that Janelle landed on after she assessed the team were lack of trust and hopelessness. That was the problem in a nutshell. The team wasn't falling apart, but there was clearly an issue in the way Janelle was leading.

She realized that her lack of transparency was causing mistrust and insecurity. Additionally, the lack of motivation could be attributed to lack of clarity on goals. However, and almost more importantly, the shortcuts they were engaging in could potentially jeopardize the employees and the company. While the behaviors were very low level, just skirting on the edge of what they could get away with, Janelle knew they could very easily become sloppy.

Janelle adored her team. Her personal goal was to establish values within her team to help resolve the issues and build for a better future. Specifically, she was looking to rebuild trust and deliver clarity to the group. Additionally, she knew she needed to make some adjustments to what she was doing as a leader.

Janelle's values stand is about refinement and growth, whereas Carl's is about repairing a broken workplace and laying the groundwork for a more highly effective team. Figure 12-3 provides a summary of Janelle's assessment.

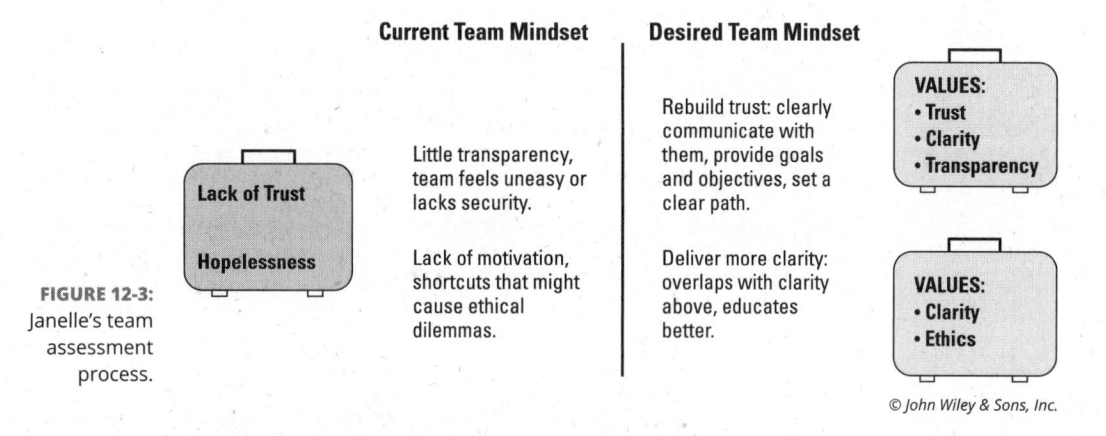

FIGURE 12-3: Janelle's team assessment process.

Current Team Mindset
- Lack of Trust / Hopelessness
- Little transparency, team feels uneasy or lacks security.
- Lack of motivation, shortcuts that might cause ethical dilemmas.

Desired Team Mindset
- Rebuild trust: clearly communicate with them, provide goals and objectives, set a clear path.
- Deliver more clarity: overlaps with clarity above, educates better.

VALUES:
- Trust
- Clarity
- Transparency

VALUES:
- Clarity
- Ethics

© John Wiley & Sons, Inc.

Assembling your starlight

Your starlight is for you and your team. It is meant to serve as the sextant, or guiding principles, for your group. Your starlight establishes a platform from which you can all grow together. And when you're not present, your team will be clear about what you expect of them. Consider your starlight to be an agreement you're making with them and they with you. No contract or signatures on the dotted line — just a way to clearly establish trust, consistency, and expectations.

I provide pointers on assembling your starlight in this section. I continue to use Carl and Janelle as examples.

Assembly guidelines

REMEMBER

The following is the formula you use for starlight assembly. This process is illustrated in the examples later in this chapter.

1. **Provide clarity.**

   Consider the following:

   - **The goal or desired result:** What are you trying to accomplish?
   - **Core values:** What is important to you?
   - **Animation of values (or actions):** How will you ask the team to take action on these values?

2. **Be specific on what you want the team to do.**

   Keep the following mind:

   - Decide whether you have a specific mindset issue that needs to be addressed. If you do, add it in. If not, that's okay.
   - Figure out whether a particular behavior needs to be addressed. If so, you can address it head-on or softly.

3. **Take responsibility.**

   Consider what your part needs to be. Where do you need to raise your game? The attributes of a values-based leader in Chapter 6 come in here.

4. **Make an invitation.**

   Invite the team to be part of the solution.

The starlight values statement is a conversation defining the behavioral expectations you're setting forth. It's not a grandiose statement that feels like an epic event. It is, however, clarity around engagement with one another as employees of the company. This also includes how they will engage with vendors, manufacturers, distributors, and all other external support teams.

REMEMBER

You can formalize your statement using the formats in the following sections to reinforce the expectations. The statement helps to serve as a reminder of the sextant you've put in place for them. It's also the stake you've put in the ground that says *all this other stuff ends here and now*. It's your stand for yourself and your team; you want to improve their working conditions, attitudes, and ability to excel at what they do.

In the following examples, each leader is facing a different challenge. Therefore their approaches are slightly different. Both are valid. Each leader's starlight language will vary based on personality and the specific issues that need to be addressed. No two starlights are the same.

Carl's starlight

Carl chose language that resonated with his own personal style. Here is a summary of how Carl maximized his tools and assembled his statement to the team:

- His opening statement lists his goals for the team.

- He identifies the problem by listing the solution, focusing on where he wants to go rather than lamenting where they've been — in other words, rather than saying they don't trust each other, he details how he wants them to build an environment of trust. This is a combination of both the mindset he wants to achieve and the values he wants to instill in the group.

- He makes his own promise to the group on what he will improve, referencing principles of values-based leadership (see Chapter 6). In this example, that's his commitment to support his team and remove obstacles.

- He asks for buy-in from everyone.

The starlight reads as follows:

> *As a team, we must decide to move forward in a healthier, more productive manner.*
>
> *To create an environment of trust where everyone works together, we need to drop our defensiveness and embrace creatively looking at resolving problems. No matter what your suggestion, there is no stupid idea. Everyone can participate. Everyone has a place on this team and in the processes we undertake. Collaboration is the key to our success. Freshness keeps us engaged and thriving.*
>
> *I am asking each of you to participate as such. And I promise to always have your back if criticism comes. I will do my very best to remove any obstacles that are in your way from doing your job. All I ask you is that you do your very best to work as a unit in this way. Deal?*

Janelle's starlight

Janelle's approach is a bit different from Carl's in the preceding section:

- She also opens with her goals for the team.

- She identifies problems but also shares consequences to help frame the need to resolve them — adhering to compliance as not to compromise the company. That's pretty clear to anyone who works in a compliance-focused profession.

- She also shares education as a core value and the commitment each person is asked to make to stay informed.

» She acknowledges her lapse in transparency and shares in the commitment to do better. People appreciate it when you acknowledge your own shortfalls and admit you need to work on it. Guess what? It makes you human.

» She invites everyone to engage in the starlight.

The starlight reads as follows:

> *We need to become a team who operates with transparency, with clarity around our goals, objectives, and plans. Communication is a key factor in our ability to achieve this. We operate out in the open, we do not hide information, not even the difficult stuff. We are ethical and compliant in everything we do. We never take shortcuts or compromise the client, the team, or the company itself. We are committed to education to achieve sustained excellence.*
>
> *This is our starlight, our way of being, as a team. And it starts with me. I will do my best to become more transparent. This may be causing some of you not to feel 100 percent connected to our goals and objectives, which might cause some uneasiness. I make a commitment to work on these things and ask you to do take this starlight (or mission challenge) to heart.*

Bolstering Your Commitment to Values-Based Leadership with Other Features

There are many ways in which you can share this VBL initiative with the team, as this section discusses. But your example will be the best influencing factor on them. When they see you be transparent, they will be too. When they see you owning your mistakes and taking responsibility, they will too. There are, however, additional components to make use of. If you're an island in the middle of the ocean that is the company you work for, you may feel limited in your ability to effect change in some of the other ways offered throughout this book. You may have resources that can help you, or you may not.

Maintain focus on what you can affect rather than what you may not be able to affect. You may be more inclined to harp on what you don't have or can't achieve at this point. Take heart! You're not being asked to do everything all at once. My suggestion is to decide not only what you can do but what you're willing to do.

Willingness is a decision to move forward. Trying is not. Rolling out many different initiatives all at once will never produce the results you want. Nor will haphazardly working with a dozen or so. Do what you can do now.

TIP: Before you slam the book shut, you have to realize that not everything may be achievable at this moment. Select what you can do. My suggestion is to select only one or two initiatives per year. Consider the delivery of the starlight to your team to be the first initiative. It will take time for everyone to get into step.

Scaling down the four features of values-based leadership

There are four components in the values-based economy model, as described in Chapter 3. These components provide different penetration opportunities. When values in action are the driving force of leadership, determining where and how you will apply them goes beyond your values or starlight statements. Showing that you mean it means following through not just on your stated commitment to them but also on the ancillary actions surrounding VBL.

REMEMBER: Look at where your next opportunity for action could be. I'm keeping this as simple as possible to make it easy to apply. You may feel overwhelmed as you review Chapter 3, which details how to weave the features into your current situation. I can hear you saying, "Maria, I have a team of six people. There's no way I can make a global impact from where I sit. It's not even on my radar." Thank you for your honesty! I've been there myself. As I said, just pick one initiative from the following suggestions, or come up with your own. Continually being in the energy of a values-based form of leadership perpetuates the momentum and the messaging, even without formally stating it.

Here is a look at the four components, chunked into bite-size pieces:

- **How we do business:** The starlight you created earlier in this chapter serves as the guidance system for how the team is to engage with one another, vendors, and clients. The statement may be, in this version, delivered with the immediate team in mind, but it doesn't have to stop there. For example, if creativity and inclusion are part of your starlight, it may be possible to extend that, with measure, to your vendors. They can be involved in problem-solving issues in their area of expertise and encouraged to be creative in how they do so. Creating that partnership rather than dictating your quarterly order to them will reap mutual benefits if you give them a chance. You never know what could be uncovered that will help your business.

- **How we serve/impact the community:** Your company may already be hosting community outreach programs. Consider getting involved yourself — or making it a team effort. If your company doesn't have an initiative, what's stopping you from creating a team volunteer day for a local charity? Consider groups like the United Way, the Leukemia & Lymphoma Society, or the

Make-A-Wish Foundation — or think about smaller, local community agencies. Volunteerism gives back to communities and serves as a team-building opportunity.

» **How we invest in others:** Training is the most direct line to investing in the team at hand. Many companies offer formal trainings, and in those cases, they're tied to performance objectives. Make it fun and encourage them to take some training in something they know nothing about, just to stretch them a bit and gain a different perspective. If formal training isn't an option, encourage learning as a key component to each other's success. Once a quarter, at a minimum, use a team meeting as a training event. If you prefer, you could have someone on the team share their expertise on a specific subject. There's no expenditure, other than the hour reserved for the meeting, which you would have had any way. In Chapter 15 you may find additional ideas on how to incorporate other educational ideas.

» **How we create sustainability:** The ideas offered in Chapter 3 on sustainability may feel daunting in your slice of the world. Distilling them down to something tangible and actionable can focus on creating or reimagining processes. That would be a reasonable starting point. It will take creative problem solving and collaboration — most likely it will involve other teams as well. Pick the one process that needs "tweaking" or a complete overhaul. Engage your team in the discussion so they understand that the objective is to make the process more *sustainable,* which is a far less threatening adjective than *streamlined.* Streamlining is often associated with a potential downsizing of the business.

WARNING: Motion is required. Stagnant intentions fail every time. And your people will lose respect for you.

Leveling with your team

There's a very good chance the team will look at you sideways. "He/she has changed," you may hear whispers at the coffee counter. They will ask what's going on. There may be snickers if you're in Carl's predicament. However, if your team is like Janelle's, they may smile and think, "Well, we work this way already. But maybe I can do better." Either type of team may ask for a lot more clarification of the expectations. You've invited them into the process, so be prepared to continue this conversation with them.

You may hear comments that indicate the team is aware that those around them aren't being asked to work to the same standards. While you can't control how and what other teams do, you do have the ability to influence your own team. Standards vary based on a leader's expectations and accountability.

REMEMBER: Be professional, but level with them. You know there are challenges and you'd like them to focus on their work, what they can control, and how they participate in the workplace. It's certainly their decision. Remind them that the only thing they can control is themselves — how they act and how they react to any situation. That's what is within their grasp.

Make sure you own your part. In both starlight statements from earlier in this chapter, Carl and Janelle own the piece that they must work on. They are vulnerable and approachable enough to ensure that the team knows this isn't a to-do list being given to them. Their leaders are going to follow suit. They've made a commitment to the team to do certain things that are in alignment with the starlight — the mission challenge of the team. That means their feet can also be held to the fire, and they have accountability to the team too.

Holding your team accountable even if others don't

Your organization may not hold your team accountable in the same way you need or want them to be. Organizations are always shifting and changing. People come and go. But if you as a leader are clear and consistent in what you're doing, the team will do the same. Even if you set accountabilities for them that other teams may not have, they will follow suit. There may be a few holdouts, renegades, or natural-born resisters, but ultimately they will honor the accountabilities or find a more suitable leader for their style.

REMEMBER: *Accountability* is the ability to accept responsibility for any outcomes, good or bad, based on your actions. Accountability isn't necessarily something detailed out; it's a given, a general expectation that reflects the respect one has toward others in the workplace and for one's own work. Some of the ways accountability shows up in the workplace can be found in everyday activities, like the following:

- » **Being on time:** Be where you say you'll be at the predetermined time. Lateness indicates lack of respect for others' time.
- » **Honoring your word:** Do what you commit to do. If you fall short, notify any collaborators of any changes you may need.
- » **Showing up for your meetings:** Be present physically and mentally.
- » **Meeting your deadlines:** Remember that you are one person in the relay race to the end goal. Do your best to meet deadlines so everyone has the ability to execute their part to the best of their abilities.
- » **Taking responsibility for your work:** Avoid blame games or deflecting responsibility. Do the best job you can every day.

> » **Attending to detail:** Be mindful of what you're working toward. Those in the next leg of the relay race are depending on you to give them as many details as possible to avoid continual clarifications or requests for more information, which only delays the process.
>
> » **Working with other team members:** Remember that you're one part of a team. Work with others to achieve your goals.

We live in a very fluid time in the evolution of the workplace. Some people work remotely, others telecommute a few days a week, some adjunct team members may be overseas, and so on. Therefore, the common accountability to do your best every day, in everything you do, only works to strengthen the unit as a whole and on an individual level.

An example would be taking responsibility for your own work and working cooperatively with others. Accountability in these areas would mean doing your work thoroughly, complementing each other's skills rather than competing with other team members, and remembering that you're all on the same team. Accountability asks individuals not to play the blame game when things go wrong. Take responsibility and fix it before you point the finger at another person.

Leading when you're gone

Your team will move on from your tutelage eventually. Some will grow into leaders themselves with teams to guide and businesses to run. Others may choose a different route. Regardless, some leaders leave an imprint on others that can last for many years. When standards, principles, and expectations are set that benefit everyone, deep in their minds, they hold onto it.

Often the impact is subconscious. The manifestation is when their mentor's words come out of their mouth automatically. They find themselves setting the same standards that were set for them years prior. On a conscious level, they may adapt some of your assessment techniques, communication strategies, or specific processes.

Establishing values as part of your leadership will be carried through to the next generation, even if it's only one leader you've trained who utilizes it. It will be worth it. When you're long gone from the business world, when you've retired and are building villages in Guatemala for the poor, your legacy will live on. You've brought something useful and good into the world of business: responsible individuals who lead with heart and business acumen. You've done well.

IN THIS CHAPTER

» Crafting your career starlight

» Evaluating job and leader-to-leader fits with your career starlight

» Understanding the effects of your reputation as a values-based leader

Chapter 13
Cementing a Career Starlight for the Long Haul

Every leader wants to be able to look back at their career and say, "I'm proud of what I did and I'm glad to be known for X, Y, and Z." Leaders are often associated with a list of accomplishments, but also with how they impacted others. Every day reputations are built that propel an individual forward and ultimately become their legacy. This can be done in a focused manner, or it may be rolled out as you go. As the world becomes increasingly complex and connected, the effect of one's reputation is more widely known. This reputation builds your capital. Think of it as a way to leverage your success beyond the bottom-line results you achieve. (See Chapter 10 for an introduction to reputational capital, particularly for companies.)

Increasingly, values-based leadership (VBL) is becoming more desirable than the old guard. It's what the workforce is demanding, especially Millennials, who are now moving into leadership positions. Therefore, establishing yourself as a values-based leader becomes a marketing tool to ensure your longevity. Recruiters and companies look beyond a resume and list of accomplishments to what your character may be and how you enlist or engage others. They love tried-and-true, consistent leaders who get results but also seek those who will deploy VBL principles to create a healthy, thriving company culture.

You can purposefully direct your leadership and the legacy you want to leave behind. In this chapter, I show you how to break down your values, leadership qualities, and the actions that will serve as a starlight for your career — a *starlight* is, in this context, the guiding force behind and mission challenge for your leadership legacy (or in more modest terms, the mission challenge for the kind of leader you strive to be).

Building Your Career Starlight from the Ground Up

Have you ever heard the phrase "wherever you go, there you are"? It's one of my favorite ways to express that you can leave a situation, but no matter where you go, you are the constant in the equation. In the context of leadership, if you have a reputation for being a certain way in the workplace, it's rare that you would be different elsewhere. Although stressors may cause behavior to become out of character at times, who you are and how you work are constants — the unauthorized bio file that travels with you throughout your career.

Your reputation follows you wherever you go. You can shift it, change it, and evolve into the next phase of your potential, but as hard as you may try, you can't circumvent a reputation preceding you throughout your career. Rather than resist, embrace it. In fact, own it. Reputation is the intangible capital that either adds to a company or detracts from it. Recruiters know it, as do the leadership and management of any organization.

The following sections help you create clarity and boundaries around the leadership legacy you want to build in your career with the help of a starlight. A starlight describes who you are or how you want to be seen. Having awareness is the first step to creating a more powerful reputation.

Digging into your strengths and weaknesses (with a little help)

In my humble opinion, *be authentic* is an overly used marketing catchphrase. When anyone says that, I cringe a little inside. I'm not sure anyone really can be 100 percent authentically themselves because we spend a lifetime uncovering who we really are. An 8-year-old child could be obnoxious and hurtful. If he becomes an inquisitive and caring adult, it doesn't mean that his innate authenticity has been cultivated. It's a matter of maturity — learning how to convey what we feel inside in a way that makes sense as a fully functioning adult. (Although I do cover authenticity in Chapter 6, there it's from the perspective of doing what you say you'll do.)

Rather than dive into the philosophical side of that discussion, let me offer this for consideration. We really can't be objective about ourselves for the most part. Additionally, we don't always see our own growth and maturity that evolves the expression of character. Though I've spoken about self-awareness, sometimes it's just plain hard to have it. Therefore, the process of creating a starlight will require some self-reflection, but insight from trusted colleagues and/or friends will also be useful. They can fill in the missing pieces that you may not be able to fully see.

TIP

Ask them to provide insights into how they perceive you with the following questions. Strengths, weaknesses, and the things you overlook about yourself are all part of the equation:

- What do they perceive as your greatest strength and weakness?
- What part of you do they perceive that you may not see or know about yourself?
- How do you affect others around you?
- Considering a variety of successes you've achieved, what would they perceive to be the key ingredient in your skill set that made it happen?
- Why do (or don't) people follow you?
- What do they perceive that you truly value in this world?

REMEMBER

Each question is framed around their perception of you and your engagement with others. Perception is subjective, so don't take anything personally. But do ask them to be honest with you. There may be some things you didn't realize you were doing that negatively impact others. There may also be characteristics and values that you unknowingly project into the world that create a positive effect on others.

Breaking down the parts of your career starlight formula

Let's start with the basic formula for a career starlight:

Core Value + Animated Value = Desired Result

HONG KONG INSIGHT

When I was younger and just starting out in my career, I was known for my intensity and hard work. As I stepped into leadership roles, my reputation evolved. One day I was standing in my company's Hong Kong office with the site leader. She said to me, "Maria, you are tough yet fair. I've always told everyone here that you would never be unreasonable, but to understand that you would always push them to perform to their peak potential."

I was stunned: "I'm afraid to ask how you arrived at that conclusion." I really was afraid to hear her answer, because I never wanted to be perceived as mean. In my head, *tough* meant *mean*.

She then explained that my reputation preceded me from prior companies. She also shared that she told the team that my toughness had to do with my being able to see how good they are at what they do. They would have an ardent supporter in me as long as they did their very best and played fair with teammates, vendors, suppliers, and the team in New York. I blushed and agreed with her summation.

I'm fully aware that not *everyone* was a fan. I'm okay with that. I can promise you that you will have haters. It just comes with the territory.

Here in this section, this is all about *you*. For the moment, you can forget about the organization you're currently working in.

Coming up with your core values

What is most important to you in this world? What are those values? What kind of feedback have your colleagues and friends provided that can help you answer those questions? In Chapter 11, you find a chart with more than 60 core values you can work with and select the one that fits best. It's not a complete list, but a starting point.

Another way to think about core values is to ask yourself: When you're done and retired, what is it you want to be known for? That's a view into your legacy. You can create your legacy consciously or unconsciously. The truth is that you are already what your legacy will be. You may not have the awareness yet of what you're creating, but that's okay. Knowing what your special sauce is that distinguishes you from everyone else in the market will help you position yourself better. Having conscious awareness also will help you be more deliberate in your influence on those you lead.

TIP

On a sticky note, scribble the core values that most reflect your convictions. On a second sticky note, write how these values are put into action. Pop them onto this page. I'll come back to them shortly.

REMEMBER

You're working with your *core* values, not other types of values. To recap the explanations in Chapter 11, here are four buckets the value you select may fall into — this should help you make the distinction more easily:

- **Core values:** Fundamental beliefs
- **Aspirational values:** What you aspire to be and achieve
- **Given values:** Implied conduct in the business world
- **Vogue values:** Fads and trends

Taking action to animate your core values

The second part of the equation is the action that backs up your values. The question is: How is your value expressed and/or animated around you? What are you doing, saying, or asking others to do or say to be in alignment with those values?

REMEMBER

Core values (fundamental beliefs) without animation are useless. With all the information provided by your own self-reflection and others (as described earlier in this chapter), look at the pattern that emerges. These are the actions used to implement the values. However, you may see some holes. Plug them now by getting clear on what's missing and what actions need to be put into effect to have the value in play.

Defining your leadership engagement qualities

Knowing your strengths and playing into them (as explained earlier in this chapter) are a great way to maximize what naturally comes to you. There will be enough for you to learn, but natural engagement qualities are dominant in a leader. Although there may be more than the six qualities I offer in the following list, they are a great place to start. Just about every other quality will stem from this grouping. For example, you may want to say you are a creative leader, but innovation would easily cover the most creative leaders:

- Innovative
- Results-driven
- Analytical

- » Interdependent
- » Strategic
- » Collaborative

TIP Consider the last leader you worked with. If you had to summarize their natural qualities, would you say they were innovative or analytical? Perhaps they were results-driven and they went about getting those results with a very strategic methodology.

Can a leader use more than one or two of these engagement qualities? Absolutely. If they do, they're very dynamic indeed. There isn't one "right" combination. Everyone brings something different to the equation. Considering the list, which would you assign to your own personal leadership style? Pick at least two. If you're unsure, go back to the feedback of peers and/or colleagues (covered earlier in this chapter) to help you gain better insight into your natural abilities. Once you've landed on a couple, write them on yet another sticky note and stick it on this page. We're building toward a complete picture.

Putting your career starlight into a cohesive form

Impressionist painting was done with a series of small, thin brush strokes. The nonconformity of the style creates the beautiful, light, airy images hung in major galleries and homes of art collectors. There's always been something about this particular style of art that leaves me standing in front of a painting tilting my head to see what the artist intended me to see. In the end, though the impression of what the artist wanted me to see is there, the interpretation is mine. As the viewer, I place the boundaries around what isn't totally clear and give it a name.

Leadership is like that. It's a collection of small thin strokes that when assembled creates clarity, establishes boundaries, and in the case of the concept as a starlight, establishes a beacon that will always bring you safely back to yourself. Reviewing your sequence of sticky notes will help you assemble your starlight.

I provide the basic formula for your career starlight earlier in this chapter, and now you can add your engagement qualities to fully form it. In the following example, the leader (Sam) has selected *honesty* and *fairness* as his core values and coupled each with his expression of how it will be actioned — the animated value. His two engagement qualities are *innovation* and *results-driven*. Being results-driven, in this statement, is articulated as focused on the bottom line.

Here is Sam's starlight:

> *My leadership will be based on honesty in all my dealings with others. Innovation will always be implemented with the highest level of respect and honesty for intellectual property. I will be accurate, fair, and straightforward, considering the benefits of the whole rather than just a few when working with the bottom line because I want all to benefit.*

TIP: Constructing your starlight and writing it down someplace you can see it daily serves as a reminder of the mission of your leadership. If you feel so inclined, memorizing it will also make it easier to roll off your tongue when a recruiter asks you what type of a leader you are. Obviously, massage it into language that makes sense to you. And use it as you see fit. (Confession: My starlight is folded up into a little square in the change purse section of my wallet. On the days when I need a reminder, I pull it out and read it. It makes me smile and helps me get refocused.)

Translating Your Career Starlight into a Good Fit with a Company

It would be amazing if everyone operated from the standpoint of a VBL model, but they don't. Sometimes they may think they do, but it's simply not true. I say that not to criticize others for their beliefs but to emphasize the fact that if you want a long and prosperous career, you'll need to be mindful of what you want to create. It's so easy to be lured into a situation and later wonder what you were thinking. You may realize the people at that company are not in alignment with who you are and what you believe can be in this world.

On a subconscious level, our limbic system is constantly evaluating the risks, threats, and trustworthiness of everything that comes into your sightline. Unfortunately, it's not always 100 percent correct. Having a starlight for your leadership will help you be able to make a clear-cut comparison between who you are and what kind of company it might be. (*Note:* Being fooled happens. Learn from the mistake and move on.)

The following sections provide some guidance on how to use your career starlight to ensure that your values work well with those of a company you're thinking about joining.

THE TRIPLE DIVISION ALIGNMENT CHALLENGE

A client told me that she was about to be promoted into a position with an enormous amount of responsibility. Her division would merge, tripling in size. But the caveat was that although her current team was highly functioning, the teams she was about to inherit weren't. Still, she was elated. She was open to the challenge.

I asked if she had considered looking at her starlight before moving forward. She laughed and said, "Oh, I already work here, I know this company. I don't think there's a problem." I pressed a bit and asked if she knew if she'd have support to make the necessary changes she had already detailed out. "Of course!" Then she paused. "Oh, I see what you mean." She bit her lip. What she didn't have was a partner who embraced valuing the staff and treating them with dignity and respect. What's more, the partner she was getting wasn't interested in training. He thought they should just know what they're doing or figure it out.

I asked her whether she could work with this person. She hesitated but after listing what they had in common, she felt she could iron out the respect and training wrinkles by addressing them up front — before agreeing to take the new position. It was a difficult conversation to navigate, but ultimately, she had buy-in. There were a lot of speed bumps and a few near-crashes, but she persisted and shifted the team's culture.

The manager that she bumped up against did go along, begrudgingly, but still, he supported her when results rolled in.

Evaluating job offers with your career starlight

A juicy job opportunity has surfaced at a company you've been considering for a long time. For most people, the work itself needs to be challenging, but it also needs to be with a company that resonates with you and your convictions. Ask yourself the following questions before you jump on the deal:

> » Does this company embody the values you hold dear, as described in your career starlight?
>
> » What is the reputation of this organization?
>
> » Are you able to contribute to or enhance the culture positively?
>
> » If their values and your values aren't a perfect match, are you willing to compromise? How much is too much of a compromise?

> » Is there potential here for you to create a positive impact, be a change agent, or take the organization/or department to a new level?

Not every question in the preceding list will be answered with a "Yes, this is a perfect fit and I am running to jump onboard." The truth is, when you're a leader, you're usually not being brought into a perfect situation. They need and want you because you have something they're missing and that they need. This is twofold: You have skills and you have talents. When combined, you have a leadership style they feel will help pivot or move an organization or department forward. Again, rarely is a leader brought into an ideal situation. Leaders are there to lead others to a better place.

So you may well be brought in to be a change agent in some way. They have a problem they're looking at you to fix. Your starlight coupled with the preceding list of questions should help you decide whether you're up to the challenge. Additionally, they should provide you the reality check of understanding what values are nonnegotiable and which ones you know you can imbue into the situation.

Discerning your leader-to-leader fit

Knowing whether you can make an impact in a company will, in part, be determined by the *leader-to-leader fit*. On one level, will the leaders in the organization, the board, stockholders, or other lateral peers work in conjunction with you to make changes? The answer may never be 100 percent yes, but will you have a partner to help you make the necessary shifts and adjustments to the organization?

The second level of the fit has to do with the person you will lead with — a peer or the person above you in the hierarchy. Are you a fit? Many times, I've heard someone say something like, "This is a great job, there's a lot of potential, the company may not be exactly what I want in terms of values, but I know I can make a difference. I can effect change. However, the problem is that Leader X is the one I'd be working with. I just can't see how this would ever work for me, or that person."

WARNING When that happens, it's a red flag. If the leader-to-leader fit isn't workable, the team will feel it. They will see it being played out in front of them. No matter what, leadership needs to be united and cohesive in their messaging to the team — and to the other entities that participate in business dealings.

Again, no match is perfect. But the person you'll be working with most closely shouldn't be an adversary. Nor should they be someone with vastly different value perceptions. For example, perhaps they believe in shortcuts to the end and worry about the compliance issues later, but you're more inclined to consider shortcuts while keeping in mind that compliance is still a necessary part of credibility. This example illustrates different leadership styles, but also a potential ethical dilemma on the horizon.

TIP: Interviews are like dating. Everyone is always on their best behavior when you first meet them. Take the time to ensure that you've had several face-to-face times with the person you will either report to or work in conjunction with to get a better sense of their motives and priorities and what they value.

Pulling back the mask of a narcissist

I would love to believe that those who create career starlights are all in it to create a positive legacy that enriches the lives of others and not just themselves. I wish every leader and manager would read this book, but they won't. So I'll tell you this: Be mindful of the narcissists who walk among us. Actions and deeds speak volumes. Reputation precedes these individuals as well. If you're considering a new job or a new leader to work with, deeply contemplate this single question when viewing potential colleagues and leaders: Is it all about them, or is it about the people they work with and/or serve (the customer)? The answer will speak volumes.

Narcissus was a youth who was legendary for his beauty and his disregard for anyone who loved him. Nemesis, the goddess who punished arrogance, led him to gaze at his reflection in a pool. Narcissus lost the will to do anything other than stare at his own beauty until he died. This myth teaches us that excessive self-absorption and self-adulation can be a person's ruin.

WARNING: Is the company leadership where you're looking at an opportunity, or the leader you'll be working with, more about themselves or are they able to look beyond themselves? That will pretty much sum up whether you'll have a better chance of being on an upward trajectory or going down on a sinking ship. Narcissists don't build organizations that thrive for the long term. They tear down those that don't worship and adore them. Hint: Stay away.

Seeing the Effects of Being Known as a Values-Based Leader

Your resume is one aspect of who you are as a professional. Character is the aspect that cannot be faked, at least not for long. People always reveal themselves eventually.

In the following sections, I briefly describe a few effects of having a reputation as a values-based leader. Although I can't provide a step-by-step process for making recruiters and companies love you, my hope is that in reading this book — by gaining self-awareness and becoming more deliberate in your quest to be a values-based leader — you've come to understand that more companies are inclined to hire strong, talented, and human leaders than not. VBL's character fosters these attributes. It's difficult to fully express this to you, so I offer a story instead in the nearby sidebar "Making a personal impact," where you'll meet one of the most remarkable women I've ever met in my professional experience.

REMEMBER

Every one of us has a different way that we personalize and express our values-based leadership. You will too. Just know that the impact you have on others is what makes you a desirable employee and leader.

MAKING A PERSONAL IMPACT

"Stella" was a vice president running a half billion-dollar division of a major company. She'd had a very long and successful career for several good reasons. Not only was she highly intelligent, competent, and consistent, but she was also someone who impacted a lot of people throughout her working years. Notorious for her attention to detail and high standards, she created a training ground for a number of professionals who went on to greater things. To this day, she is still often thanked by many of her former staffers and associates. Humble and shy, she congratulates them on their success and deflects the thanks back to them for being so dedicated to their own success. This is the outward and obvious impact that she's had on their lives.

What those who have worked with her know about this woman is that she's extremely generous, caring, and loving. She once brought food into the office for an entry-level employee who was struggling to get out of student debt — just so they didn't have to worry about paying for breakfast that day. She intervened when a staffer started showing signs of a serious illness and convinced them to face what was happening and get treatment. Year after year, she volunteered her time to different organizations. She wasn't a person who would allow others to suffer and struggle if she could help it.

The interesting thing is that most people didn't know that she'd taken these actions and more. Yet those who experienced her deep compassion and caring always spoke highly of her, and it rubbed off on those around them. She's still a highly sought-after professional in her industry. Her results, innovation, and analytical mind are without a doubt part of the VBL she's brought to every company she's worked within. The impact she makes on a personal level ripples throughout her reputation — without people even knowing about her highly personal kindnesses. Because that's just who she is.

Companies seeking to establish this type of leadership flock to her. I've watched it happen year after year. Those that don't, in my humble opinion, probably aren't interested in VBL and the human way it balances profits and caring for people in their organization. In short, be nice and care about others, period.

Adding financial value to a company because of your reputation

Reputation is sometimes difficult to quantify on a spreadsheet in the traditional sense — although there are definitely a few line items you'll see change for the better when VBL is put in place. The most glaring item might be retention of staff. Replacing and retraining staff is time consuming and extremely costly to an organization (see Chapter 14 for more on hiring and retention). My observation is that when a new values-based leader is brought into an organization, there may be an initial exodus. People are afraid they won't like the change, and those who know their values are not in alignment with the new leader may flee the scene. It's natural attrition. Later, the retention of the team often increases.

Your starlight helps generate your reputation; it's a reflection of how you lead others. Here are several ways your reputation adds financial value to an organization:

- » Staff will follow you to your new company, bringing consistency and structure and thereby helping fast-track changes.
- » Your established resources, vendors, and providers will want to continue to work with you, thereby opening up new opportunities for the organization because of your relationship with them.
- » Reliability helps curb human resource issues, which means you're less of a financial risk.
- » Retention often increases because employees stay longer, cutting down on hiring and training costs.

Reinforcing what you stand for to add marketability

The principles, values, attributes, and leadership style in your starlight illuminate your pathway forward. During your career, be sure to reinforce to any recruiters you work with what you stand for and why. It is just a part of who you are as a human being and a professional.

A recruiter asked a client of mine a very insightful question: "What would prevent you from staying with us for a long time?" My client smiled and said, "Well, if people aren't given a chance to succeed, then I know I'll fail here, too."

The recruiter said, "Well, that's an interesting perspective." My client answered, "You see, when staff are allowed to grow, try new things, get trained, and so on, then I know we have a winning strategy to grow as an organization. Without those mechanisms, we will all fail."

While my client knew he would have to install many of the mechanisms he considered essential for success, he fully expressed the kind of leader he would be. By the way, his starlight was focused on, in his words, "leveling the playing field for all stakeholders to establish a company culture of education, empowerment, and innovation." That pretty much sums up what he values and his leadership focus.

Being a person with passion and conviction means that your flame won't extinguish so quickly. You're in it for the long haul. That improves your marketability.

Keep these guidelines in mind:

- Wherever you go, *be* a values-based leader.
- Whatever you do, *do* your utmost to live the values-based principles.
- And for goodness' sake, *have* a good time doing it.

These factors make you infectious. Be, do, and have consistently to make yourself viable and marketable in any industry.

4
Supercharging Your Team and the Workplace with Values

IN THIS PART . . .

Position your organization to hire and retain the best talent in the marketplace.

Recognize that employee engagement and job satisfaction are the keys to creating high-performing and effective teams.

Discover how to motivate those around you to exceed your expectations (and why you should do so).

Cultivate new leaders within your organization.

Understand that without innovation, your company will perish on the vine.

Know that not everyone will come along on the journey, so find out how to make peace with their departures and take away lessons from them.

IN THIS CHAPTER

» Understanding why people leave organizations

» Identifying what people want in order to join and stay at a company

» Showing candidates the opportunities you provide to grow

» Ensuring that candidates fit what you've built

Chapter 14
Hiring and Retaining Great Talent

Knowing whom to bring onboard is sometimes difficult. As a values-based leader, it's your job to provide the context for maintaining the company culture and ensuring that all company promises are met. You set the directives and work in conjunction with other leaders and managers to make it a reality. Together, the company brand and reputational capital are assured consistency. (Chapter 10 discusses corporate identity, company culture, and reputation.)

When hiring, initially the question has been "Are they qualified?" But in the new shared values economy (SVE), the question has expanded to "Do they fit into our culture?" Fitting into the team has always been a consideration, but as businesses continue to evolve, the cultural fit becomes a more holistic consideration. The candidates also wonder whether they'll be able to thrive in your company culture, asking themselves, "Why do I want to work for Company X over Company Y?" The dynamics have shifted as the job market continues to open bit by bit. There are more choices for employment; therefore the workforce doesn't feel they need to settle for anything but what they really want. They seek a career they have chosen consciously and not out of desperation. They seek alignment in what they do and what they believe to be important. All of this is subjective.

Companies are facing a battle to identify great talent and then compete to bring them onboard and retain them. According to the Hay Group's report "The War for

Leaders" (see `www.haygroup.com/downloads/uae/Hay_Group_wp_-_The_War_for_Leaders_07_web.pdf`), hiring managers are now finding that it takes about 51 days to fill a vacancy, and one in three will hire someone considered *average* just to fill the position quickly. Needless to say, this creates a revolving door of candidates and can cost a company thousands of dollars.

Assuming you can source the talent you desire, in this chapter I dive into what that talent really wants from you as an employer. Perceptions and desires have changed with each cohort entering the workplace (see Chapter 2 for more about these demographic age groups). Their desires have less to do with the belief that more is better. Instead, they're seeking quality of life, balance within their careers, and unique experiences. This includes those who already work within the organization.

TIP My suggestion is that you read this chapter and Chapter 15 on engagement and job satisfaction in conjunction with one another. They represent two sides of the same coin: growing and maintaining a strong company culture with happy, healthy employees.

Recognizing Why People Leave One Company to Join Another (Like Yours)

Before diving into the components on offer in the rest of this chapter, you can look at why people *don't* stay at an organization. This would also be part of the reason they would want to join your organization — you're the resolution to why they left their last job.

Some say people don't quit jobs or organizations — they quit the leaders. That's only half true. It also explains only half of why an individual would consider a seeking a new opportunity. Overall, the following six categories sum up why they vote to come onboard and/or leave:

- **Pay and/or benefits:** They want better pay and/or better benefits.
- **Potential for growth:** They want different experiences so they can grow.
- **Better manager or management:** They want to be in alignment with their managers and the leadership of the team.
- **Safe company culture:** They want a safe environment in which to work, both physically and psychologically.
- **Job dynamic:** They want to excel at their current job and/or find another job fit opportunity.

> **Life continuity:** They may need to stay in or move to another job due to a life circumstance. They want consistency and stabilization.

Distinguishing Yourself from the Competition

What makes you a viable option for a candidate in the marketplace depends on what you have to offer. Business continues to evolve, as do the needs of the different cohorts introduced in Chapter 2. Your ability to continue to evolve within the values-based leadership (VBL) structure creates your unique proposition in differentiating yourself from the sea of other companies.

There are roughly eight areas to consider that could be customized and tailored to suit your organization, as illustrated in Figure 14-1. Not all may fit your organization nor reflect the priorities of your team, but they serve as a menu to choose from and place into priority categories: *right now*, *soon*, and *perhaps not needed or realistic*. Each is a reflection of the principles, beliefs, and values that create your company brand.

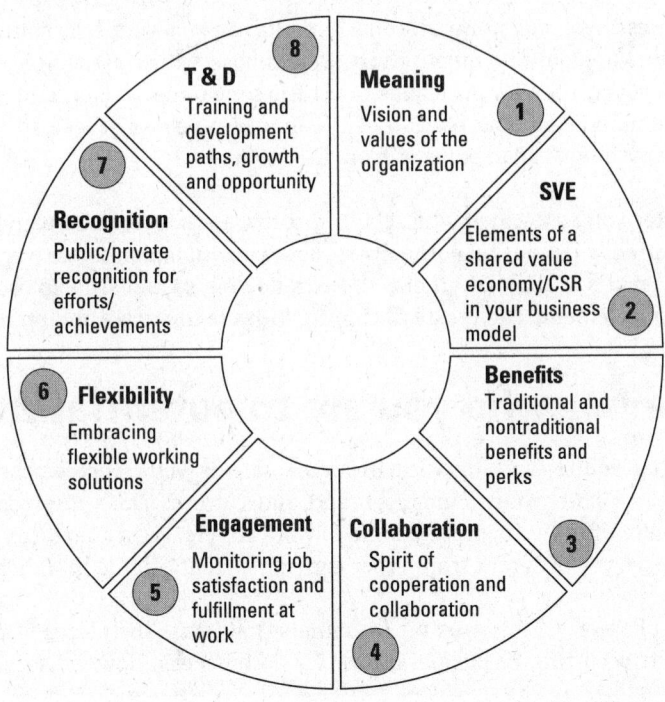

FIGURE 14-1: Creating your unique presence wheel.

8 — T & D: Training and development paths, growth and opportunity

1 — Meaning: Vision and values of the organization

2 — SVE: Elements of a shared value economy/CSR in your business model

3 — Benefits: Traditional and nontraditional benefits and perks

4 — Collaboration: Spirit of cooperation and collaboration

5 — Engagement: Monitoring job satisfaction and fulfillment at work

6 — Flexibility: Embracing flexible working solutions

7 — Recognition: Public/private recognition for efforts/achievements

© John Wiley & Sons, Inc.

Each area provides you the opportunity to customize and develop programs and initiatives or to offer benefits and perks that suit your employees' lives and the company culture. Here's a closer look at the eight areas you can work within:

» **Meaning:** The vision and values of the organization

» **Shared values economy (SVE):** Elements of a shared values economy and corporate social responsibility (CSR; see Chapter 3) as part of your business model

» **Benefits:** Traditional and nontraditional benefits and perks

» **Collaboration:** The spirit of cooperation — basically, teamwork

» **Engagement:** In the context of a value proposition, monitoring job satisfaction and fulfillment

» **Flexibility:** Embracing flexible working solutions and the technology that makes it possible

» **Recognition:** Public and/or private recognition for efforts and achievements

» **Training and development:** Training and development paths, growth, and opportunities

REMEMBER

Each company is different. Flextime may not be a reasonable expectation if your business runs based on a set number of hours where face-to-face interaction is necessary. Some nontraditional benefits can be a very easy concession to the staff without requiring much effort. You choose which areas you want to focus on. However, the VBL principles of creating meaning, vision, and purpose should be the non-negotiable portion of the unique presence wheel. It's your foundation. Everything is an expansion from this point.

After you've decided what you'll incorporate into the company, share the information with your team members, both current and prospective, so they are aware of what's available to them. In the following sections, I explore how using these eight elements can create a winning formula to attract and retain talent.

Selling who you are to potential employees

What you're working with in Figure 14-1 is your *value proposition* (VP), which creates both your company brand and culture. The value proposition is what you're offering to entice people to work for you rather than the competition — it makes you different from other companies that offered them jobs.

In Chapter 3, I discuss four containers that house the pieces of the consciousness shift occurring in business: how we do business, how we serve others, how we invest our resources, and how we become sustainable. All are business concepts, but this section considers them as helping to create a deep human connection between the company and its people. This deep connection is the fertile ground that creates a unique working experience and a strong company culture. What differentiates you from others is that you seek that connection with everyone who works within the organization. It's the reverse-engineering of your ethos that tells others, "This is our commitment to you, dear employee." Establishing yourself as a values-based leader takes more than your values statement (see Chapter 11); it takes action and implementing programs, initiatives, and ways of working that are a reflection of that statement.

REMEMBER

There's no one perfect way to execute this projection of your values, other than to keep in mind that what you choose from Figure 14-1 should reflect those values and enhance the lives of those around you. Your role as a leader is to be of service to others, to be a guardian of the organization and its people, to be generous in finding ways to support others' success, and to be diligent in your pursuits. These are the four Be's of VBL introduced in Chapter 3. Projecting this attitude of leadership in recruiting and retaining talent is powerful. Showing them what this looks like makes it tangible, rather than just words.

How do you execute the wheel for your organization? Try this three-step process:

1. **Identify the pieces of the wheel you want to work within.**

   Try to keep your list down to two to four pieces, even though you may want to work on all eight.

2. **Detail what your initiatives or programs will be to reinforce the proposition.**

   For example, if training and development is one of your choices, what programs will you roll out for the employees to provide training and development for them?

3. **Implement the programs.**

   Consider the breadth of what you're trying to accomplish and create a timeline for the rollout. Be realistic about what is achievable within given periods of time.

An example of one of my clients' VPs is shown in Figure 14-2. The four quadrants — Collaborative Environment (called *Collaboration* in Figure 14-1), Balanced Life (Flexibility), Growth Paths (T&D — training and development), and Recognizing Others (Recognition) — are identified as priorities in what they can implement now. There are plans to move beyond this configuration as they scale. Each concept has bullet points outlining what the execution will be. This serves as a promise to the employees.

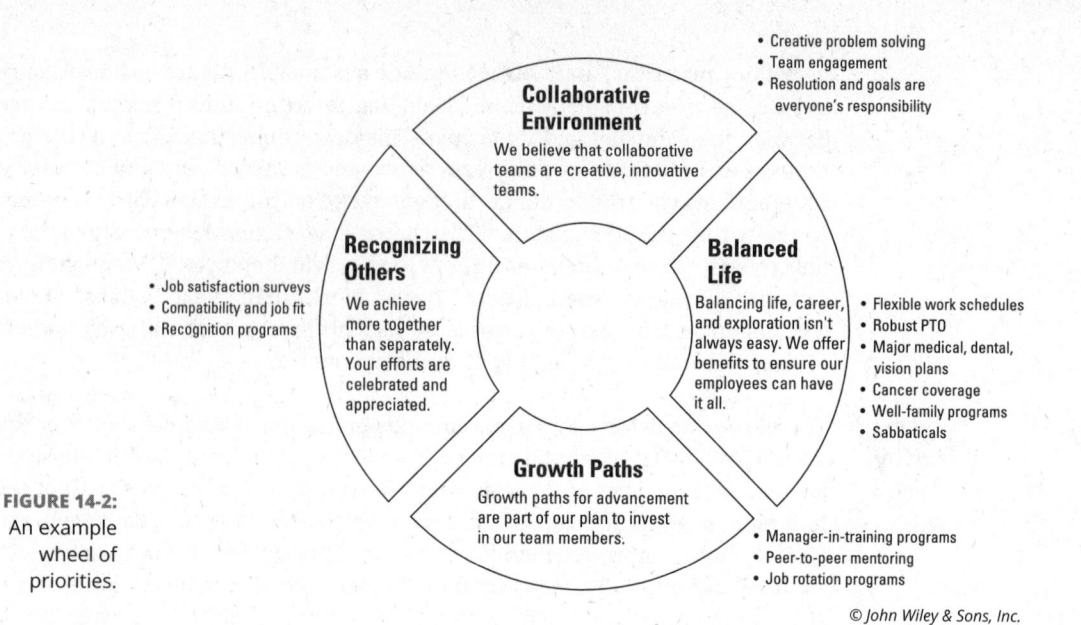

FIGURE 14-2: An example wheel of priorities.

Collaborative Environment
We believe that collaborative teams are creative, innovative teams.
- Creative problem solving
- Team engagement
- Resolution and goals are everyone's responsibility

Balanced Life
Balancing life, career, and exploration isn't always easy. We offer benefits to ensure our employees can have it all.
- Flexible work schedules
- Robust PTO
- Major medical, dental, vision plans
- Cancer coverage
- Well-family programs
- Sabbaticals

Growth Paths
Growth paths for advancement are part of our plan to invest in our team members.
- Manager-in-training programs
- Peer-to-peer mentoring
- Job rotation programs

Recognizing Others
We achieve more together than separately. Your efforts are celebrated and appreciated.
- Job satisfaction surveys
- Compatibility and job fit
- Recognition programs

© John Wiley & Sons, Inc.

TIP Be sure to use language that resonates with you and your company culture. In Figure 14-2, the leader selected the words "balanced life" rather than "flexibility" because that's what makes sense for the company culture. To make the proposition even clearer, the leader provided a brief description for each piece. Never forget that people have different perceptions and assign varying meanings to words. It's best to make your wheel absolutely clear.

TIP When candidates view the wheel, and you've indicated that there are training programs associated with the promise you've made to them, be sure to align these programs into their growth plans.

TIP Be sure to include the bullet points in your wheel so that everyone can understand what exactly you're offering them. For example, for someone whose family has been impacted by cancer, the option for a cancer insurance policy (you find more information on this type of policy later in this chapter) will be very meaningful. Somebody planning to expand their family would want to know whether certain types of wellness programs beyond maternity or paternity leave are available to help them. Not everything can be included in the bullet points, but do your best to create a clear and robust offering. Set your sights on enhancing your execution of each of the current areas and plan for future expansion as you scale.

Uncorking your reputational capital

Reputational capital refers to the values of a company that reflect the character of its leaders and people. It includes their credibility and consciousness in how they operate in the business community with vendors, suppliers, and other staff. It also includes the promises of the company. This is a long-term capital situation that affects all departments in the organization. No one stands alone.

The reputation built is one that creates a competitive advantage in the marketplace. Your company has a brand that it has created with a culture that's a calling card. A great reputation draws people to the organization.

REMEMBER

The two keys in reputation building to keep in mind are these: Who matters to your business, and what matters to them? That, in part, refers to your staff. They are your biggest assets — the steam in your engine and the folks who get it done. Invest wisely in these assets, and they'll continue to be the reason why people want to work for and be led by you.

Reputation is built on how you navigate your relationships. Consider the following list and how you engage with each. Ask whether these relationships add to or detract from the reputation of the organization. Convey your vision and exemplify VBL to everyone in your orbit (see Chapter 10 for an introduction to reputation):

- Clients and customers
- Employees and contractors
- Board members, shareholders, and investors
- Business partners (active and silent)
- Suppliers and vendors
- Competitors, rivals, and industry disruptors
- Home community

REPUTATION ON DISPLAY: THE GLASSDOOR SOCIETY

Technology creates transparency. Glassdoor (www.glassdoor.com/index.htm) is a hub for reviews on benefits, salaries, companies keeping their promises to their employees, and more. It offers surveys to rate companies across the board. In our sharing culture, the company promises and its activities are out there for all the world to read about. More than half of all job seekers read Glassdoor reviews when interviewing with a new company. There's no way to hide who you are and how your employees feel about working at the company. According to the Gallup Inc. survey titled "State of the American Workplace," 36 percent of all job seekers check out the reputation of a company online.

Benefiting Everyone with Nontraditional Perks

Roughly three quarters of all staff will stay with an employer because of their benefits programs. Many will opt to go to a larger company over a smaller one in order to gain access to better benefits. Benefits are no longer just major medical, dental, and vision. There's a world of options out there to consider. The workforce has voted on this issue — Figure 14-3 offers a snapshot of what the more prevalent cohorts (covered in Chapter 2) desire for benefits and perks that support their lives, according to the "State of the American Workplace" report by Gallup Inc. in 2017.

The Desire for Benefits and Perks That Support Their Lives

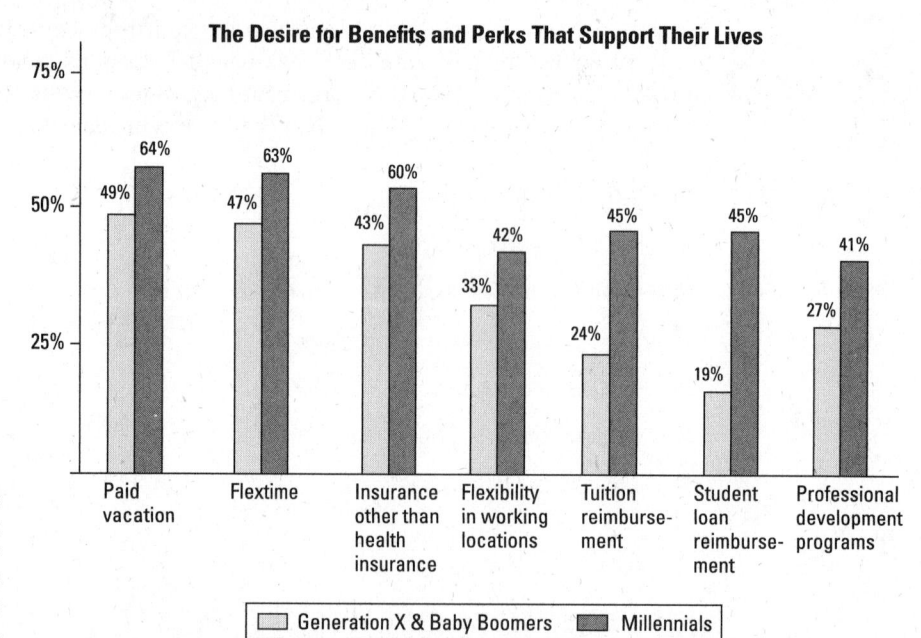

Benefit	Generation X & Baby Boomers	Millennials
Paid vacation	49%	64%
Flextime	47%	63%
Insurance other than health insurance	43%	60%
Flexibility in working locations	33%	42%
Tuition reimbursement	24%	45%
Student loan reimbursement	19%	45%
Professional development programs	27%	41%

FIGURE 14-3: What different generations say they want in terms of benefits and perks.

© John Wiley & Sons, Inc.

You can learn a lot from this research. First, the desire for specific kinds of benefits varies from generation to generation. To see the matchup, refer to Chapter 2, where I provide information about Millennials' deep desire to have a balanced life being of major importance. Figure 14-3 shows exactly what that means to them: paid vacations and flextime. These benefits are also important to Generation X and Boomers but not as important. Overall, these seven areas were of greatest importance to the workforce as it currently stands.

As you can see in Figure 14-3, the workforce is asking for more nontraditional benefits, rounding out the top three priorities. This trend will continue to evolve as workers' lives change shape and priorities reorder. The options are endless and may include such things as counseling programs for new mothers, gym memberships, discounts at museums, sabbaticals, wellness stipends, and/or college tuition assistance programs. More progressive companies are introducing perks such as volunteer time off (VTO) and pet insurance. It's all about making it easier for people to work effectively and efficiently without the stress of worrying about how to pay for what they need in various aspects of their lives.

Inevitably, workplaces will look more like those of Google and Facebook than old-school cubicles and coffee break rooms. Your organization may not have room for a washer and dryer or a daycare center, but you should recognize that the trend of accommodating employees' lives so they can work without distractions will continue to permeate the structures that once were thought of as separate "work" and "private" lives.

REMEMBER

More and more employees are bucking the belief that there is a one-size-fits-all solution; both Baby Boomers and Millennials want to be able to customize their plans. As an employer, that may not be the easiest task to accomplish, but it can be done. Talk to your in-house benefits experts or seek a talented, resourceful broker to help you. There are a myriad of options that could be offered by some very talented benefits experts, providers, and brokers who can help you and your company. I'm fortunate to know a lot of these individuals. I can tell you that they are very creative and live to make your and your employees' lives better. Do yourself a favor: Hire someone to help you. Benefits, traditional and nontraditional, are an important part of how you will entice talent to stick with you over the long haul. Benefits packages are projected to become even more important over the next three to five years.

Instituting time to volunteer

Volunteerism continues to rise. Several companies have instituted VTO for employees to go build a village in Guatemala, bring fresh water to parts of Africa, or participate in buildouts for Habitat for Humanity. For example, Timberland offers its employees 40 hours of VTO per year, which doesn't count against regular paid time off (PTO) or sick days.

WARNING

One word of caution: Any company considering such an expansive version of corporate social responsibility (CSR) needs to keep in mind its profit center. Can you really cover the cost of employees taking advantage of these programs? There is a realistic balance between what you'd like to do and what you can afford to do. Smaller companies tend to have a harder time implementing this type of benefit. A more modest one to three days off to volunteer at a nonprofit of the employee's choice may be a more workable compromise.

REMEMBER: VTO both increases your corporate visibility and helps with recruitment and retention.

Offering voluntary solutions

Voluntary benefits (VB) are on the rise — according to a recent Benefits Pro survey, 62 percent of employees under the age 50 won't consider working without VB. This is more than a trend; it's a movement by the workforce. Employees enjoy the ability to customize their benefits and select the best solutions that fit their lives.

VB providers offer solutions like accident policies, cancer policies, and short-term disability policies, to name a few. Allowing employees to choose what they want beyond their major medical insurance creates a feeling of customization as to how they manage healthcare dollars and reduce their financial exposure. Voluntary benefits are low-cost plans paid for by employees, so they don't cost the company anything. These benefits don't coordinate with major medical insurance, so there isn't a conflict to receive them. Benefits are paid directly to the employee and are completely portable, unlike most other types of insurance.

TIP: Voluntary solutions are a pretty easy offering to make to your employees. If you'd like to find out more about voluntary programs, please go to the resources page on the main website for this book: www.MariaGamb.com.

TECHNICAL STUFF: I'll be transparent on this point. My husband is a cancer survivor. After more than five years of treatment for leukemia and lymphoma, I never leave a company without compelling them to make a cancer policy an optional choice for families. It's just the right thing to do. A 2018 report by the American Cancer Society states that one in three men and women will be diagnosed with cancer in their lifetime.

Providing financial education

One of the largest looming issues for the current workforce is the giant student loan debt incurred by one the most highly educated generations in history — Millennials. Offering a financial services educational resource to help them manage and plan to pay down these debts removes some of their day-to-day pressure.

Additionally, a college tuition assistance program is a good idea because the workforce has already felt the economic impact that their education has caused them. Many want to be able to do whatever they can to offset those expenses for their children.

TIP: Financial awareness isn't just for issues related to college tuition. Employees are seeking more education and counseling on debt reduction, financial planning, budgeting, employee purchase programs, and short-term loans as they seek to overcome their very own financial flu. You can find resources for these types of programs through many of the avenues you may already have engaged; health and life insurance brokers now have access to programs they can offer you. Also, check out your health insurance provider's site. I know it sounds crazy, but I've seen a few providers that have conveniently placed their financial education items near articles on stress reduction.

Demanding balance and flexibility

Flexibility gets its own section because for most mid-to-late range Millennials, flexibility is a non-negotiable part of any employment package. This trend won't change. Talent goes global, and competition will be fierce to acquire and retain the best people in the world — literally. This is one factor contributing to the need for flexibility.

Creating balance can have various meanings; some are tactical and others are philosophical in nature. People want to adjust their work schedules and be able to work remotely without sacrificing the quality of their work. Flextime is an additional perk — an added incentive when the employee feels it is part of the company culture rather than a special dispensation for them.

TECHNICAL STUFF: Offshoring jobs isn't new, and that probably won't change anytime soon. What *is* changing is that your home office and its talent are going to become more global too. Your new human resource director may be in Stockholm. Teams with specific niches may be in Croatia or Finland, or each team itself may be dispersed. The globalization of the workforce is clicking along at a rapid pace. Stay tuned for its next evolution. It's not something that can be ignored.

Another aspect contributing to this deep desire is that GenXers and Millennials watched their parents "live to work." They don't want their own children to grow up without both their parents participating in their lives. These cohorts have a deep desire to experience life in as many ways as they can. As Chapter 2 explains, *experiences* are very important to these generations. They work to live an expansive and adventurous life.

REMEMBER: Flexible schedules, working remotely, and going off on extended adventures or sabbaticals are becoming the norm. This will continue to accelerate. You may find your employees seeking more contracts rather than full-time work to fulfill their demands for balance and flexibility. Or you can build that into your organization. While contractors and consultants may not be eligible for benefits, often their fees are enhanced to cover these costs and beyond. The choice is yours. Pay the premium amount for a contractor or consultant, or build in balance and flexibility as part of your cultural norm.

Craving the Opportunity to Learn

There's no mistaking the drive toward higher levels of skill enhancement in the workplace. Allowing your staff to upgrade, enhance, hone, and even acquire new skills keeps them competitive. It also helps you retain these talented individuals.

GenXers and Millennials are among the most highly educated generations in history. They have a thirst for knowledge. They're open to learning — in fact, they demand it as part of their career development. Baby Boomers will continue to be a relevant part of the workforce as long as they can be trained to keep up with technology and the opportunities that continue to unfold. Learning and development programs (like the ones discussed in the following sections) will continue to be key features your employees will want to see. As a values-based leader, providing the tools for them to succeed must be part of how you operate.

> ## THEY VALUE ME, BUT THERE'S STILL A PROBLEM
>
> Education and training are ranked very high as "must haves" to improve employees' skills, yet only a third of employees give their employer high marks on the combination of training and succession planning. There is still a problem linking value, training, and planning to form one cohesive path for the workforce, as you can see in the following statistics:
>
> - Sixty-three percent of employees feel like their employer invests in their future, according to a study conducted by employee well-being company LifeWorks.
> - Fifty-seven percent of workers ranked opportunities to learn and grow as one of the most important aspects of workplace culture, according to the 2017 Udemy Workplace Stress Study.
> - Seventy-six percent of Millennials think professional development opportunities are one of the most important elements of company culture, according to the 2017 Hiring Outlook guide from Execu|Search.
> - Fifty-nine percent of employees said that access to projects to help keep their skills up-to-date would keep them satisfied at their current company, according to the 2017 Hiring Outlook guide from Execu|Search.
> - One-third of U.S. employees give their companies high marks on career performance, learning management, and succession planning, according to a survey by the ADP Research Institute.
> - Seventy-two percent of employees don't think management cares about their career growth, according to a poll by Monster.

Establishing cross-generational coaching

Millennials are fiercely independent but wise enough to know that they can learn from both GenXers and Baby Boomers. They seek coaching and mentorship from older employees. They're less likely to be ageist. However, there is still a hurdle in getting these groups' cooperation. The older generations still struggle to understand how Millennials integrate technology into their work. Multitasking, networking, collaborating, and being innovative through technology are often misconstrued as goofing off. Millennials' philosophy of "work to live," shown in their desire for balance, seems contradictory to other generations, which may also create tension.

What's the difference between coaching and mentoring? They are slightly different types of relationships with different means to an end:

» **Coaching** is a short-term relationship focused on specific projects, tasks, and outcomes. For example, a more seasoned employee can act as a coach to help onboard a new employee or to guide a new employee through a process they've already had experience with.

» **Mentoring** is a long-term relationship focused on the mentee's personal and professional development and goals. It is less structured than a coaching arrangement. Often, the mentor is acquired through prior association with the mentee, who may have come to admire and respect the mentor for their experiences. For example, perhaps a mentee worked with someone in a prior company who inspired them to want to be the same kind of leader.

A cross-generational coaching opportunity allows everyone to contribute: Experience can show the pitfalls, and the younger generations' innovative, pioneering drive can find the solutions. Both groups have something to contribute to the process. Facilitate this cooperation to ensure that the best wisdom is brought to the table. By doing so, you're also creating another skills-sharing and retraining opportunity for both parties.

The best practice for coaching is to consider your network of new employees and match them up with seasoned employees in order to establish a working relationship. Keep in mind that not everyone wants or needs a coach. However, having the opportunity to offer one is far better than letting a new employee struggle or having the wisdom of a seasoned employee discarded, creating a historical void in what has been done, how it's been done, what's worked, and what hasn't. This is very valuable information to hand over from one set of workforce cohorts to the next. The added bonus is that fresh new employees may have a solution to resolve what has been a challenge in the work life of a more seasoned employee.

Should an employee want a mentor, have them consider who has had the most profound effect on their career thus far. Ask them who they want to emulate or learn from in the industry. If they are very green, then direct them to associations and groups where industry professionals meet. They can find a long-term mentor for their career either through a past association or a professional group. Note that this process takes time and shouldn't be rushed into. Few are fortunate enough to find a mentor in their first few years of work.

Rotating jobs and experiences

The concept of *job rotation* formed in factories decades ago to provide coverage for workers who were out ill or on vacation. One worker on one part of the line could sub in for another who wasn't in that day. Job rotation provided continuity and required less reliance on specific specialties, allowing the employer to have the factory work without interruption.

This concept has moved mainstream as it becomes more realistic to allow employees to cross-train within a business. For a while now, in new employee training programs, an intern has been able to work in various parts of a business in order to determine their area of interest and expertise. Now it's an opportunity to give talent the opportunity to learn more about different aspects of a business — and it may be particularly important to those you seek to raise to a manager or leader position.

Here are some tips for creating a job rotation program:

- **Framework creation:** Determine who is eligible for such a program and make clear distinctions about what jobs are open to rotation.

- **Participation guidelines:** Outline whether the program is mandatory or whether an employee may opt out. Within the participation guidelines, communicate that the initiative is part of a career development strategy and how it would impact employee performance appraisals.

- **Mutual accountability:** Allow both the manager and the employee to participate in the selection of the rotation and note the expectations of each party. Doing so ensures mutual accountability for the success of the program and the growth of the individuals involved.

- **Clear, transferable skills:** To gain buy-in, you'll need to specify the skills the employee would gain in the rotation and how the rotation would benefit them in the long run.

- **Job availability:** Managerial as well as professional jobs should be included in the rotation program.

TIP: Before you jump on this initiative, I suggest that you consult additional resources such as the Society for Human Resource Management (SHRM) at www.shrm.com. There you'll find a lot of valuable information and resources.

TECHNICAL STUFF: I don't think the sentiment that "unless you've done the job how can you manage the process?" will ever fully evaporate. Employees are a tough bunch when their leader has no clue what they do or how they do it. Job rotating helps resolve that issue as well.

Offering skills retraining

A majority of jobs that will be available in 2025 are not the jobs in the market today. This idea is critical to be aware of when you view your team as a whole. Monitoring trends in the skills sets required for your organization to thrive will depend on what your business provides. As needs arise, assess the projected use of the skill and plan to train individuals with a curiosity or aptitude to be trained to meet the new job projected down the road.

Earlier in this chapter, I discuss training and development programs as they relate to growth and development. Skills retraining is another version of this same principle. Here's an example of retraining its simplest form: If your business is a manufacturing plant that has done most of its tasks manually but is now becoming more automated, you have a choice. You can lose a large portion of your workforce or have them retrained on methods and techniques that support the automation of your facility. This retraining has been going on for years as we dive more deeply into technology-driven labor.

Integrate skills retraining into your other training and development programs. Note that not everyone is on the path to management or leadership; allow these individuals to enjoy the opportunity to be better at what they do and how they do it. This retention tool is further strengthened by combining it with job rotation programs, which provide employees with opportunities to learn complementary skills.

TIP: The World Economic Forum report annually provides insight into far-reaching trends that will affect the workplace. See www3.weforum.org/docs/WEF_Future_of_Jobs.pdf.

Working toward Compatibility Triumphs

Compatibility is about how we interact with one another. Personality can be part of it, but even that's too broad to address it effectively. The ways in which a person engages with others — their communication style, conflict-resolution skills, and way of working and supporting others — are all projections of personality that people often can't quite pinpoint. I've had many clients tell me, "We just don't get along. There's just something about him/her that I don't get" — or worse, ". . . that just grates on my last nerve." Often, merely articulating the exact disruption can be challenging.

In the following sections, I address several different aspects of capability, communication, and conflict resolution.

Managing personalities versus maintaining company culture

REMEMBER

To be clear, navigating a personality isn't how compatibility is managed. However, monitoring and enhancing how people interact with one another in a fair and equitable manner is the focus for compatibility on an interpersonal level. Therefore, it's not personal — it's about ensuring that the company culture is established with VBL principles in play every day. When you compare personal feedback like "You're behaving like a prima donna" versus "We all participate in the process and everyone contributes," the difference is clearer.

Walking this fine line takes skill and a lot of practice. My best perspective on this for you is to consider engagements with difficult personalities in the following way. I use the "prima donna" as the example:

1. **Identify the personality issue.**

    What is the personality issue here? Well, the employee wants to be treated differently or special.

2. **Find the nonconfrontational expression of the correction.**

    It's easy to want to want to blurt out what you really think, especially if it's a pressured situation. Rather than doing so, consider the personality issue and reverse-engineer it to express the correction or expected behavior. For example, you say, "We all participate in the process and everyone contributes." There's no blame or finger-pointing, just the pure expression of the expectation.

Overall, my experience is that most employees are cooperative. However, every now and then you may have a personality to deal with. The preceding method is the best way to address the situation without being confrontational and uncomfortable and still maintain the company's values and probably your own too. You wouldn't be tweaked by a personality unless it was an affront to your way of being in the world.

As you can see, the values from Chapters 11 and 12 that you put in place create a thread all the way through to how you communicate with one another. Pretty cool, right?

Ensuring a good job fit based on talents

Another aspect to compatibility is knowing whether your candidates are going to thrive in their position. Each of us possesses what I call *apparent talents* (AT) and *cloaked talents* (CT):

- **Apparent talents** are those that the world sees. You clearly excel at these tasks, challenges, and opportunities.
- **Cloaked talents** are those at which you also excel but perhaps have never had the opportunity to explore or learn more about, so you don't tap into them. Or you may have a talent but it's not valued and so remains dormant.

I don't believe there's a single person on this earth who doesn't have both kinds of talents. What's key here is the ability to assess your candidates or current employees in terms of their talents for the job you're placing or have placed them into. Someone you may be hiring to be an accountant would need to have a very linear way of thinking and approaching their work. Someone with a very different way of thinking would likely be incompatible for the job.

Another reason to consider talents involves the growth potential for the individual. I'll stick with the accountant as an example. What if you discovered that this person also possessed an analytical capability combined with an element of creativity that would make them a good computer programmer? Wouldn't you like to know that this desire may appear later during their tenure with the company? Wouldn't it be great to know that this could be a skills retraining opportunity — that this person could potentially be placed in a development program to fill that position in the company?

REMEMBER: You want to retain talent and avoid restaffing costs and draining the wisdom pool. These considerations are a way to gain insight into the investment you're making within the team. (Find out more about job fit and manager fit for your current staff in Chapter 15.)

You can use several different assessment and surveys to ascertain compatibility, including Myers-Briggs and the DISC assessment. However, I find that using a tool that integrates all aspects of compatibility along with an interactive component makes the process seamless.

Working with teams as a starting point, when assessing an individual I look for markers of how they are communicating, how they react to stress, and how they problem solve. Those are the first touch points, beyond the content of their resume. Second, I consider whether they value the same things the company values. For example, is *order* and creativity, though conflicting at times, their priority? Or do they prefer *chaos* and creativity? There's a big difference — especially if the manager is the former way but the candidate is the latter! There will be a conflict unless the manager can be flexible with the chaos portion of the process until the work can be put into order. These are all key factors in considering a candidate.

I use a formal assessment to find their AT and CT factors. I find this information useful for growth planning. If someone comes into the organization in a creative role but shows a cloaked talent for analytics, that's someone I would shift into a role that requires both creativity and analytical abilities, rather than someone with the makeup of creativity and deep convictions. It's like having a looking glass into who they really are and being able to gently guide them into work they may not even realize they'll excel at.

TIP

This type of assessment is highly customized based on the individuals involved. For more information, go to the "Communications and Compatibility" tab on www.MariaGamb.com.

THE FISHBOWL TEST

Your company culture is like a perfect fishbowl. The container is a beautiful, clear glass tank filled with pristine, well-balanced water, decorated with blue pebbles on the bottom and a small fish village of golden towers and treasure chests, all for the enhancement of your fishies! And oh, what beautiful fish they are! Brightly colored red, orange-red, golden, yellow, black, shades of blue — some are even calico. It's a diverse, happy bunch. You feed the fish quality food and clean the tank regularly.

What would happen if the environment were disrupted with a drop of blue food coloring? Well, the vessel would become clouded. After two or three drops the water would get murky, and the fish might become confused. This is what can happen when you bring a new person into the mix. If they are a fit, the environment isn't disrupted. Everyone continues to swim around undisturbed. However, if they aren't a good fit, they can cause a disruption to the team and/or company culture, creating confusion.

Be sure you're confident that your new candidates will pass the fishbowl test before the offer letter goes out. Though you can never be 100 percent sure, do your level best to ensure the best possible integration and enhancement to the group.

Showing respect and value to candidates

Beyond the formal assessments mentioned in the preceding section, the ability to read another person is a necessary skill. I've spent years teaching people how to interview potential candidates for two reasons (besides the obvious importance of finding the best person):

>> First, you need to know how someone engages with another person. People may be nervous during an interview, but you should still be able to glimpse something about who they are. That's the skill to learn: to see and read.

>> Second, the automation of job searching, in my opinion, has killed personalization and individuality in the process. I'm all for technology, but there's still a need for soft skills in the workplace. Trending now is the deep desire for each candidate to feel like they're unique, individual, and valued even before they show up, because it's so challenging to get that interview in the first place. Project respect, and you'll get respect. Show value, and you'll be given value.

Your first impression to a candidate is an important one. They never forget their first dealing with you and the organization. These become legacy stories that are handing down throughout their career. It's your best advertisement testimonial — or, if you flub it, completely the opposite.

I've seen organizations hold interviews like cattle calls, where 25 candidates all show up at the same time and are interviewed en masse. Others may call in three candidates and rotate individual interviews in timed intervals. Then there's the old-school, one-on-one interview. Which do you think create respect and value for the company? The last two, for sure. They project that the leaders care about who comes into the organization. Some HR professionals may disagree with me, but I think cattle-call interviews are demeaning and show a lack of regard for candidates' time and qualifications.

You may not want to display your version of Figure 14-2 in the lobby as the company culture model then host a cattle-call interview scenario. Actions speak louder than words — or diagrams. Besides, I can pretty much guarantee that your reputational capital would be smeared all over Glassdoor within days.

> ## SIMPLE WAYS TO SHOW RESPECT FOR CANDIDATES
>
> Over the years I've worked with a number of recruiters, retained search consultants, and human resource professionals. There are some I will never forget because of their level of professionalism, caring, and attention to detail. One in particular serves as my example of how to make those she interviews feels valued and respected:
>
> - Every incoming candidate is greeted warmly and professionally by email within a short time of their application arriving.
> - Appointments are set quickly.
> - When she interviews someone, they are greeted with her warm smile and welcoming handshake.
> - She makes the time to ask candidates about themselves both personally and professionally to get a better idea of who they are, not just their qualifications.
> - She's quick to follow up with a note of thanks or feedback on the process.
> - She does a great job of making sure the fit is right for the candidate, the team, and the manager.
> - Even if there isn't a fit at the moment for the candidate, she's adept at building her network, often later tapping candidates for jobs they may never have seen in a job posting.
>
> This recruiter regularly checks in with people in her sphere of influence and is always willing to offer help, insight, and guidance to others. She's a prime example of treating people with respect and valuing each person for who they are; by doing so, she has created an amazing amount of reputational capital in her industry.

Answering the question of why someone should work for your company

Fulfilling a person's needs and desires for a position in a company that cares, contributes to the community, and invests in those within the organization is one part of the equation. Next is the company culture that those elements create: positive or negative. These are the big enchilada issues.

What about the manager the candidate will be working for? Two talented and motivated people may click — or they may repel one another. Such a matchup can be similar to a blind date. Everyone always shows, or tries to show, their best side — at first. It's only later when you realize that magnificent, heart-centered person is in fact rude and doesn't value the people around them. We've all been there, right? That can happen when recruiting and retaining staff.

At the beginning of this chapter, I mention several reasons why people leave organizations. The last I want to discuss is fit with the manager. Self-reflection and self-awareness are a vital part of this equation. Skills and experience aside, the manager needs to assess their fit with the candidate. Values-based leadership is the subject of this book. VBL also means an organization that requires its managers to embrace the principles and live by them. That's when people will want to work for you — and stay working for you.

In every job I've ever had, I created a chart for interviews. Yes, each interview chart definitely had the candidate's skill set list on it; that was easy to ask about during an interview. I also had the candidate's capacity to fit into the team. This section was equally important. My teams were always made up of individuals who were all very unique but shared similar (or similar enough) values. For example, the willingness to work hard and with others was important to the team and me. I never asked anyone to be a workaholic; all I asked was that they give their best and work with each other without drama.

TIP
So the next time you're interviewing, consider listing the values and some of the attributes you'd like someone on your team to have. Ask questions or simply make observations about what they're saying to determine whether they suit your values and team. For example, one of the questions I always ask people is this: What do you like to do outside of work? Simple enough, right? Usually the answer will give me a good idea of whether they are a team player — do they play sports, do they volunteer, are they working on some special project with friends? What they do and how they do it shows me whether they can work together with others in a group setting.

You can set up this same line of questioning to coincide with any value you want to ensure is part of the members of your team. However, not every person will 100 percent fit the list you have. Allow candidates to bring something new to the mix. Focus only on the one to three values you identify in your work in Chapters 11 and 12 to be the "must haves." This helps ensure manager and candidate fits. It's the basic foundation you can build on.

REMEMBER
Why *should* anyone work for you? Because you're not threatened by their talent. You encourage creativity, you seek their input, you're committed to their growth, and you do what you say. Because they know you're as committed to their success as you are to your own. Because they know you'll help them grow — you're not intimidated by them. The list goes on. Create, engage in, and live a values-based culture, and people will want to work for you.

IN THIS CHAPTER

» Understanding why engagement and job satisfaction are crucial

» Keeping employees engaged, active, and happy

» Linking job satisfaction to more than productivity

Chapter **15**

Maintaining Engagement and Job Satisfaction

You've assembled a great team. You've created value propositions for these employees with growth paths and desirable benefits and perks to support their lives. Some people will see you as innovative due to your creativity in projecting your company brand out into the world, making you a company others want to work for. This is all fantastic news — it enhances your competitive edge, and you've done it using fair play rather than undermining others.

This is not all you need to do, however. Retaining people is a giant umbrella that encompasses engagement and job satisfaction. Lack of either creates a void in the organization. Both reflect continuity of the company culture and the ability to exercise your emotional intelligence (to see what's really happening) in relationships with others.

Grasping the Importance of Engagement and Job Satisfaction

Human resource professionals consider *engagement* to be one of the top issues to resolve moving forward. It reaches beyond productivity. As the workforce shifts, priorities and needs also shift. A Gallup survey on engagement shows a rapid decline in employee engagement, ranging from a low-level atrophy, where employees are more like bystanders rather than advocates, all the way to departures of key employees causing a wisdom drain in the organization. The effects of this issue are layered, ultimately costing U.S. employers roughly $550 billion annually.

Successful leadership depends on partnering with HR and all managers to find ways to get employees to come to work, be actively engaged, become challenged, take initiative, and claim ownership of processes and results. The sad truth is that a disengaged workforce is a reflection on the company leadership, but the good news is that you can shift disengagement.

The other piece of your success results from assessing and auditing job satisfaction in your organization. The different generations working today (introduced in Chapter 2) are receptive to regular review and feedback of what they're doing, how they're doing it, and with whom. That can be viewed negatively, but the goals of regularly auditing and assessing satisfaction are to continue to adjust and ratchet up growth paths, to create points of structured recognition, and to have any issues dealt with as immediately as possible.

With that said, it's not just employee job satisfaction being audited — it's also their managers' satisfaction. Again, this can be perceived negatively, so frame it as monitoring the ability of managers to learn more about what they're doing well and where they may need coaching or training. The entire process can be wrapped up in a bow by helping the team understand that this is a way for everyone to grow. It's not punitive — it's growth oriented and provides the ability to better customize and individualize plans.

These processes also bring to mind the importance of compatibility, a topic I introduce in Chapter 14. Does the job fit the individual? Do the manager and the team member fit? Can they work together? Ensuring compatibility is the way to create an understanding of one another and work together harmoniously and effectively. If one or more components get out of sync, you'll have a less-than-ideal productivity situation. Understanding compatibilities also provides insight into where and how each person can grow in the organization. I find this to be the most refreshing and optimistic way of approaching growth, based on a level playing field.

Staying Active and Happy: Engagement

The impact of disengaged employees on a company is tremendous. Consider Gallup's 2017 "State of the American Workplace" report findings (see `http://news.gallup.com/reports/199961/7.aspx` for details):

> » Thirty-three percent of American workers are engaged, versus 70 percent of the best worldwide organizations.

> » Disengaged employees cost U.S. organizations between $483 billion and $605 billion annually.

> » Thirty-seven percent of engaged employees are looking for jobs or watching for opportunities. Also, 56 percent of somewhat disengaged employees and 73 percent of actively disengaged employees are job hunting.

> » Engaged employees show up for work. Engaged business units realize a 41 percent reduction in absenteeism and a 17 percent increase in productivity.

> » Highly engaged business units experience 54 percent less turnover than less engaged units.

Pulling out any one of the preceding statistics is sobering. Together, they're very sobering. There *is* an engagement problem. The truth is that people avoid going to work when they're unhappy and disengaged, and they're probably interviewing to resolve both of those issues.

The following sections explain the costs of disengagement to your company and provide tips on how to improve engagement among your staff.

REMEMBER: People typically leave their employment for a few reasons: They don't like or agree with their manager, they don't like the company culture, the job doesn't suit them, or they seek better pay and/or benefits.

Understanding that revolving doors cost a pretty penny

Retaining great talent isn't just a nice thing to achieve — it's a cost-effective and responsible achievement that preserves the bottom line. Often it's the up-front costs of hiring that are considered: How much the ad will cost, the recruiter's fee, and so on. The up-front costs are definitely important. But there are other costs to replacing people often.

A survey from the Center for American Progress (www.americanprogress.org/wp-content/uploads/2012/11/CostofTurnover.pdf) states that it would cost 20 percent of a mid-level position's annual salary to replace them — for example, for a $40,000 manager, the replacement cost would be about $8,000. For a highly educated position, the replacement cost could be as high as 200 percent or more of the annual salary. The numbers are staggering. Training these individuals compounds these numbers. Additionally, the impact of the learning curve for new employees can drag on the productivity of the team overall, as other staff cover shortfalls until the new colleague, manager, or leader gets up to speed. These aren't always fixed costs and can sometimes vary based on the individual.

The retention and management of employees is one of the biggest hurdles facing employers today, being both economic and social in nature. At its core, values-based leadership (VBL) resolves many of the compounding factors by creating a work environment and company ethos of inclusion, fairness, equality, and safety. But there are more details to uncover. Feeling good about the company is one piece of the puzzle — treating others well is another piece.

Creating an environment of engagement from day one

The methods for engagement are dispersed throughout this book. I cover everything from shared values, philosophies, vision, and open communication. I also consider reducing social distancing in various ways, at all layers and levels within the organization. The responsibility of engagement is also in the hands of the employee as they agree to participate in that which you model for them.

Two additional areas increase engagement: job satisfaction (addressed later in this chapter) and setting the standard of engagement from day one. Engaging your team members from day one is the secret for setting the right intention and energy while they work at the company. You want them to know that you care deeply about the work done at the company and that you value what they bring to this important work.

Chapter 14 goes into more detail on hiring and retaining new talent. Here, I provide some pointers related specifically to creating an environment for engagement from the get-go:

» **Bypass 100 pounds of paperwork.** Set your onboarding to include as little paper as possible. Make it easy for employees to access all their consent and benefit information online. That includes the employee handbook.

» **Break it down, mission critical.** Managers should break down the mission and values of the company to a digestible size (see Chapter 16 for details). Be sure to tell the new employee how what they're doing contributes to that end. That builds confidence and underscores the importance of what they're doing.

» **Anticipate greatness.** Have someone welcome the new hire. They shouldn't be left in the waiting area for more than a few minutes. Make them feel like you've been waiting for them because you're so excited they're joining the team.

- **Make the rounds.** Give them a tour and introduce them to everyone. For the immediate team, a coffee meet and greet helps them clearly identify and connect to those members they'll be collaborating with.

- **Give them what they need.** That means clean workstations with the tools necessary to do their job. Again, you're projecting that you value them enough to give them the best you can so they can contribute.

- **Set expectations.** Tell them more about what they'll be doing. Get them started on their first project.

- **Check in on them.** For the first few months, you'll need to check in on your new hire to make sure everything is going well. Direct them to resources they can utilize in the organization — "Talk to Brad in production," for example.

Nearly one-third of all new hires will leave a new job within the first 90 days if they don't feel engaged or satisfied. Start off on the right foot!

Avoiding the disengagement of current staff

There is a belief that if you just leave people alone, they'll do their jobs. And that can sometimes be true, especially as the workforce evolves to more remote working conditions. However, being *too* far removed from the organization can create a gap in engagement. Engagement, remember, is the emotional connection to the commitment, passion, involvement, and enthusiasm of one's work and workplace. The connection between what they do and where they do it creates the powerful *why* to keep doing it. When engagement lags, the employee no longer feels passionate or connected to the mission, its tasks, or the resulting fulfillment of purpose.

Chapter 16 is all about motivation — knowing what another person wants, what makes them hum and purr with focus and resolution to move toward a goal — and this is also a part of the engagement equation. Once you've read Chapter 16, come back to this section. The words here will take on a deeper meaning for you.

Here are a few ways to keep current employees engaged:

- **Do** keep reminding them that their contribution helps achieve the group goals. Use the Olympic relay race as a metaphor: Each member of the team, by doing their piece of the process, hands the baton over to the next team member. Ultimately the process is completed and the entire group wins, not just the last person over the finish line.

» **Do** continue to make sure they have everything needed to do their job. If they need access to specific resources or specialized tools to do their job, make sure they have them. Sometimes it's as simple as having a comfortable chair or as specialized as having access to confidential reports or controlled purchasing areas online.

» **Do** find opportunities for the team to gather and participate together. I'm not a big believer in forced fun — most staff would rather eat nails than be forced into fun and games. However, impromptu gatherings to discuss the project together as a whole can help create an open door and collaborative feeling.

» **Do** continue to give them work that challenges them. (I talk about ideas like job rotations, job satisfaction surveys, and growth paths later in this chapter.)

» **Do** celebrate steps on the way to milestone achievements. They've got to know you see them and appreciate the work they're doing. *Don't* assume they know. A high five for a job well done, an impromptu team huddle to announce the birth of a child, or decorating a weekend warrior's workstation after they successfully run a marathon are easy ways to joyfully celebrate milestones and achievements.

RESIDENT ROTISSERIE CHICKENS

"Elaina" is a super-talented business woman and respected leader in her organization. She can quickly dissect problems, find solutions, and masterfully utilize all the tools the organization has to move her clients and team through a compliance-ridden process. Senior leadership doesn't worry about Elaina. They say she's a *rotisserie chicken — you just set it and forget it.* In other words, she doesn't need supervision or help. She just does her job.

The epithet was never intended to be anything but a compliment to Elaina's effectiveness. However, the compliment of being self-sufficient falls short when it comes to keeping Elaina engaged in the organization. Although many managers would love to have the kind of autonomy Elaina has, engagement and inclusion with the other managers are critical to her job satisfaction. When you know what another person needs, it's a simple thing to give it to them. In Chapter 16 on motivation, I share that there are only three things that motivate others: power, achievement, and affiliation. In Elaina's case, the fact that she values her relationships is an indicator that what motivates her is the affiliation with others.

Even the most accomplished and independent team members need to have a lifeline back into the organization. Most human beings desire a sense of connection and inclusion. Don't let them go out too far or they'll ultimately disconnect. Even "rotisserie chickens" want to be included, supported, and connected to other like-minded people.

Keeping the Wisdom Pool Full: Job Satisfaction

Job satisfaction goes beyond the actual jobs your employees are doing. Move past annual reviews and see what's really happening with your team. Are they challenged? Is there room for advancement? Do you have a path for everyone to grow? Are there chances to upgrade their skills? Are they committed enough to the organization for you to care?

Every one of those points is valid. But here's the truth: When you invest in others, the reward comes back to you. It may be the reward of loyalty from a staff member who grows with the organization, which retains wisdom and key talent. Or it may simply be the ability to give someone the chance to excel where no one else may have seen their potential. Both situations can make the leader feel satisfied in their own job too.

Retaining people is how you avoid draining the wisdom pool. As you find out in this section, there are several ways you can assess the level of job satisfaction that will keep your wisdom centers of influence from dispersing to other companies. Remember, this workforce seeks engagement. They like and want feedback. And they want to feel like you think they're worth the time, effort, and investment to make them a better employee.

Rethinking the annual performance review

The annual review was once the gold standard for setting goals and directing growth plans. Today, these old methods require updating to meet the needs of the workforce. HR professionals may send me scathing emails on this topic. However, I believe it's unrealistic to put staff and their managers through this lengthy exercise annually, giving formal feedback only once a year, and think the growth plan will be followed for 12 months. The impact of such performance reviews lasts, on average, three or four months at the most. From my own personal experience, everyone is just glad when they're over and they can move to more important things — like doing their job and making money for the company.

Be honest. When was the last time you heard someone say, "I can't wait for my annual review! I've been tingling with anticipation for 364 days!" Yeah, no. Or several months after a review, have you ever heard a staffer say, "Let me refer to my performance review. Yes, here it is. I still need to take five courses before my next review to fulfill last year's requirements. Wow, I can't wait!" Yeah, no. That rarely happens.

STARTLING TURNOVER STATISTICS

Depending on the size of your organization, you may or may not realize the rate of turnover. One day someone is in the cube across the room from you, and in a few weeks they may be gone. They seemed happy. But, oh well, it's just one person. However, statistics (like the following) show that employees appear to be looking for new jobs at a high rate, which makes retention your HR department's top challenge:

- Sixty-eight percent of Millennials say they would stay at a job they like for at least three years (www.accel.com/interests/QualtricsAccelSeries).

- Half of employees say they're planning to stay at their current company for two years or less (www.execu-search.com/~/media/Resources/pdf/2017_Hiring_Outlook_eBook).

- Forty-two percent of employees earning $75,000 or more intend to quit in the next six months (www.mequilibrium.com/2017/06/26/high-education-and-income-do-not-guarantee-a-resilient-employee/).

- Forty-one percent of Millennials expect to be in their current job for two years or less, compared to 17 percent of GenXers and 10 percent of Boomers (http://jobapplicationcenter.com/perceptions-employment-opportunities/).

- Forty-six percent of HR pros list retention as their top challenge (www.globoforce.com/resources/research-reports/shrmgloboforce-recognition-experience-business/).

- Twenty percent of employers have replaced nearly half of their staff in the last 12 months (www.spherion.com/workforce-insights/survey-findings/survey-findings-2017/).

- Thirty-six percent of businesses see engagement as a top challenge (www.globoforce.com/resources/research-reports/shrmgloboforce-recognition-experience-business/).

Here's why: We're living in a society of Instagram, Facebook, Twitter, and all kinds of other social connectivity. We want our information fast, on time, fresh, and in the moment. The staff members want to know what works and doesn't — *now*, not 364 days from now. They also want to know they're appreciated. That appreciation needs some formality to it, although certainly "thank you" and "great job" are also part of the equation.

My suggestion is to create a more fluid feedback plan for each staff member that has both vision and a few bite-sized feedback points. Simplify it — less starch, more heart and practical application. Consider the following guidelines to improve employee satisfaction on this front:

- **Create an annual master plan** for each staff member that lays out a growth path and describes how they'll get there. Simplify it as much as you can from what you've done before.
- **Set discussion touch points** quarterly, or every other month, to review how everything is going, check milestones, and investigate training opportunities. You can do this with an employee job-satisfaction survey first, and then a sit-down chat.
- **Assess** whether the initial growth plan is valid or whether they want to shift to another track. Often people start with an idealized goal. Once they start working toward it, they may find something more interesting to them.
- **Recognize their good work often and provide feedback** — beyond the formal sit-downs.
- **Cheer them on.**

Assessing job satisfaction with a customizable survey

Even the best managers can miss that an employee is completely dissatisfied with their job. Great talent will seek higher ground; it's inevitable. When people aren't challenged or are stuck in repetitive work, they become bored and restless. For some it means they desire to learn a new skill; others may need to find deeper meaning in their work or reduce the stress in their environment. A relationship with a manager can also affect job satisfaction.

There are two ways to consider assessing satisfaction:

- Ask them whether they're challenged, connected, and engaged in their work.
- Ask them whether their supervisor is helping them get where they want to go. It's a two-way street. If there's an issue with a supervisor effectively coaching the team, that's an opportunity for improvement and the reinforcement of values-based principles.

Here are some of the kinds of questions you may want to include to better understand your employees. Take notice that each example is prefaced with the word "how" or "what" to create an open-ended question:

- How do you identify meaning in your work?
- What challenges you in your work?
- On average, how often do you feel stressed at work every week?
- How well are you compensated for the work you do?
- How much do your opinions about projects or processes matter to your coworkers? Managers?
- What tasks that have been assigned to you by your supervisor help you grow professionally?
- What is the career path to get promoted where you work? How is that being executed?
- How likely are you to look for another job outside the company this year? In the next three years? In the next five years?

TIP: There's a very accessible tool you can use to audit job satisfaction across the board. Survey Monkey does a great job of providing a variety of templates that you can customize to suit your needs. There's one on job satisfaction and another on management performance — check out www.surveymonkey.com/mp/job-satisfaction-survey/. I believe tools should be accessible to anyone who wants to use them. If you're a big multinational company, I'm sure there are far more sophisticated ways to deliver an assessment. But for the everyday leader, this is a great starting point. Customize as needed. Offer job satisfaction survey initiatives annually or biannually. They should be discussed in whatever format you choose to regularly check in with your team members on their performance and progress.

In an employee satisfaction survey, the information will be specific to the individual. It's important to know who took the survey so any needs can be addressed — be sure to have them include their name in the survey. Set up time to discuss any concerns and celebrate what they've accomplished. Never forget to continually tie what they do back to how the end goal is achieved. Additionally, watch the meaning and purpose area of the survey. This is an important trend in the Quad workforce (introduced in Chapter 2).

TIP

There is a place, of course, for anonymous surveys. Whenever administering assessments about others, such as a management performance survey, it's best to keep the identities of participants anonymous. Remember that one manager can affect the entire group. Although each person is individual, and their experience may be unique, in general a group survey can provide a compact summary of how everyone is either feeling engaged, supported, or not. There are many variations of questions that can be asked. I suggest that the following three always be included — they'll let you know whether the manager needs coaching and training on leading:

» Manager communicates expectations clearly.

» Manager communicates the value of working in this organization.

» Manager actively engages and lives the company values and promises.

Compatibility: Piecing together employees, skills, and managers

Often a departure or disengagement is caused by the relationship between the employee and the manager, coupled with job fit. In Chapter 14, I talk about compatibility between a candidate and the potential manager, but here I'm talking about a long-standing employee and their manager.

Keep in mind that in creating a values-based organization, you're always seeking to harness the brilliant talent of your managers and team members. As discussed in the previous section, an assessment process can provide the manager important employee feedback about how it's going. This is a very valid tool, but to implement such a tool without first ensuring a proper compatibility fit on both levels would be unfair to both parties.

Four factors contribute to the *animation* of an individual. Certain factors act as stimuli that mobilize them. When factors closely match between a manager and team members, it's almost as if they are speaking the same language in terms of how they operate in the workplace:

» **Motivational factors:** What makes your motor hum at work?

» **Communication factors:** Are you straightforward or tactical?

» **Conviction factors:** What do you believe is important about the work you do?

» **Belief factors:** What do you believe is non-negotiable in terms of your values?

Knowing who you are and who the individuals you work with are will determine whether you have a workable relationship. It also works as an equalizer. When an employee realizes a manager's or leader's behavior isn't personal — it's simply the way they're wired — that can shift not only job satisfaction but also the relationship individually and on a group level.

Sometimes there are misfires due to unclear communications or not providing clear enough communication to employees who may need a little more dialogue. There are those who will always ask more questions and require further clarification even when you think you've done your best to be clear and concise. This is simply their communication style: They require a lot of detail that, consciously or subconsciously, helps them feel more in control of executing the expectation better. When you have a person like this on your team, you need to acknowledge that this is their style and make time to further communicate with them. If you are hardly even in the office, then an individual with this need may not be a fit for your team.

Breaking factors down into four categories should help you identify what you can and can't work with, how much you can compromise, and your ability to give people the things they need such as recognition, acknowledgment, deeper communications, resonance in their mission, and boundaries around values within reasonable measure.

> **REMEMBER:** In our world, one of the most heartbreaking issues I see is people reacting to others without thinking, rather than pausing to consider where the other person is coming from. Giving another person what they need costs you very little — especially when you know what it is. In Chapter 6, I share that one of the positive attributes of a values-based leader is grace. This section is another version of grace in action.

Voting on job satisfaction five ways

Job satisfaction or dissatisfaction can be registered in different ways. There is no one signal that your team is dissatisfied with their work. As I mention throughout this book, all situations are subject to polarity — that is, in every situation there's potentially a positive aspect and a negative aspect. Employees vote on their job satisfaction accordingly. They may not realize what they're signaling in their vote to you, but having awareness of the ways job satisfaction manifests will help you circumvent a negative impact on your organization. It also provides insight into who will partner with you and who won't. The success of your leadership is contingent upon how well you can reduce departures, retain the best people, and help them find hope in what may be a disappointing situation.

COMPATIBILITY AND AWARENESS

One of my Canadian clients combed through, as a team, the four factors discussed earlier (motivation, communication, conviction, and belief). They considered that although they had a great working relationship, it could always be better. We workshopped the concept of compatibility together as a group so everyone could learn from each other. After a series of questions, I was able to show them that although the leader of the team was balanced in her approach, her need for structure wasn't because she didn't trust them. A sense of order provided safety in her mind. She wanted to make sure everyone was clear and moving in the right direction. Reporting was her means to that end. When the team realized she wasn't trying to micromanage them — it was just her communication and conviction style — there was a collective sigh in the room.

Next were the two rabble-rousers, as rabble-rousing as accountants can be! They attested to that perception with great laughter. They could always be counted on to bring humor and happiness to the team. For straitlaced members of the team, though, they were perceived as flaky — even though both individuals were always reliable. Their quirkiness was simply their method of encouraging others. Encouraging others was their motivational factor.

The team discovered that they had people who were motivated by everything from encouraging others, to the need to make the choices for the team, to the desire for order and detail and the need to be helpful and train others. The simplicity of this may seem trivial, but it's really not. Once you know *why* people behave in a certain way or believe what they do, instead of just assuming you know, finding compatibility is much easier.

To date, this is still one my most sought-after workshops and consulting opportunities. I can tell you that it's remarkable work. It's also a lot of fun.

To help you pinpoint how your team may be feeling about their jobs, check out the following list. Every day, a team member votes on their level of satisfaction by how they engage with you and those around them. The first type of vote (departures) is a pretty clear action. However, the others offer a little more refinement to your perceptions of team members' behaviors:

>> **Departures:** Employees may leave, they may be looking for a new opportunity, or they may have resigned themselves to moving on. Just about every departure signals some level of dissatisfaction in their current work, whether they're seeking more challenge, money, flexibility, or autonomy — or some combination of those. The way a departure is initiated by the employee can clue you in to which side of the polarity it resides on.

Connection to the leader (that's you!): Pessimistic/Neutral.

- **The atrophied and the complacent:** Passive complacency atrophies these individuals. They may be doing their job, but they don't engage in any way to improve the situation. They're disconnected from their work, meaning, or purpose. They just don't care, and don't care to care.

  Connection to the leader: Passive aggressive/Often unsupportive

- **Eternal optimists:** Individuals in this category voice their ideas and suggestions to constructively try to resolve the situation. They seek resolution often for themselves and others. They are the somewhat quieter supports of the leader, but even when they're smiling on the outside, you can see they're having a hard time putting their heart into their commitment.

  Connection to the leader: Optimistic/Hopeful/Supportive

- **Holdouts:** They may have segued from eternal optimist to holdout. Often silenced in frustration, they wait for the solution to be found so everyone can move forward. They do their best to remain optimistic, but just doing their job and placing one foot in front of the other to make it through is often tough for them. They won't put their hands up to take on extra responsibility or projects. They compartmentalize their work and just get it done. They shrink into the woodwork.

  Connection to the leader: Cautiously optimistic/Could go either way/Trusting the leader to make it right

- **Super fans:** These are the never-say-never die-hard advocates, cheerleaders, and rebels. They're not disengaged but struggle to keep everyone else in this list to stay engaged. At their extreme, they become exhausted givers to the leader, team members, and the organization. Super fans can crash, though, and suddenly depart. But it will take a lot to push them to that point.

  Connection to the leader: Die-hard advocates/Loyal

Overall, there are more bystanders in the organization than active participants. There are more individuals disconnected from the entire team and organization winning than those who are connected. Unfortunately, you probably have fewer super fans and advocates than you need to move everyone to the goalpost. Bystanders are a result of apathy. This situation simply won't get you where you want to go. That's why job satisfaction is a critical topic for today's organizations.

TIP Consider your current team. Scribble the names of the individuals you feel fit into each category on five sticky notes and stick them in this section — one sticky note per vote (one sticky for departures, one for holdouts, and so on). When you're done, keep reading.

Correlating job satisfaction with morale, learning, and growth

There has been some interesting research done on job satisfaction. Researchers have found that people who are more satisfied perform better, but higher performance doesn't *cause* better job satisfaction. Also, happiness is subjective. What makes you happy may not make another person happy. Scientists chalk this up to genetic makeup. People experience well-being differently. For example, someone with arthritis who starts their day pain free may feel a deeper sense of well-being as opposed to someone who took an aspirin for a headache. And some people are more positive than others. All you have to do is look around a room to see this is true.

Consider the sticky notes from the preceding section. Ask yourself why certain people may be casting an unhappiness vote. You may recall Chapter 14, which details the following possibilities: They're seeking better pay and/or benefits, they're seeking growth opportunities, they're not jibing with their manager or leader, they don't feel supported by the company culture, they don't like their job, or they need a different working situation to create stability in their lives. Any or all may be possible.

Another way to consider disengagement goes beyond these factors. Trust, confidence from their manager, and respect also factor into the equation. Of course, we all want to be treated fairly and given an opportunity to excel at what we do.

Happiness brings other benefits. Here are some benefits of employees who feel happier:

- » They're healthier and more likely to rebound quickly from an illness.
- » They're more engaged and productive.
- » They attract others who want to be more effective parts of the team.
- » They make the work environment more joyful, lighter, and fun — insert laughter into a group of talented people and it's a home run.
- » They're more creative and more consistently work toward resolving challenges.
- » They give better customer service, both externally and interdepartmentally.
- » They're more willing to learn new skills and expand their talent set.

REMEMBER Although you can't make everyone happy all the time, you do have a responsibility to ensure compatibility and engagement in the terms detailed in this chapter. Rome wasn't built in a day, but when you deploy the right leaders and managers, ones who are in alignment with your values-based leadership, you're at least starting off on the right footing. Sharing the ethos of creating a company culture that ensures fit, satisfaction, and engagement helps reduce the departure of employees. Yes, employees will come and go, but your responsibility is to do whatever you can to make them want to stay. And if they do choose to leave, your proactive efforts may create the opportunity to have them return at a later time. Because your competitive edge is different than other companies' — it's better, right? They just don't realize it yet.

TIP Go back to those sticky notes from the preceding section and ask yourself what is leading to job dissatisfaction. Are they in the right jobs? Are they with the right managers? Do they need more flexibility? Be very honest with yourself on these issues. No shame. No guilt. This is your opportunity to consider what you can do better and formulate a plan to do so.

> **IN THIS CHAPTER**
> » Uncovering the triggers that motivate others
> » Establishing a platform for personal meaning and purpose
> » Selecting the tools that work best for you and your team

Chapter **16**

Motivating the Masses

Welcome to Motivation Central! As you've traversed this book, you may have picked up the sprinkling of different factors and techniques that would perpetuate a motivated state for your company and individuals. Who you are as a leader makes a profound difference to the state of your employees because you're the individual who sets the tone for the company. On-the-ground leaders also set the tone for your team.

This chapter provides you with a few different ways of considering motivation. The first is the basic human motivational theory, derived from needs-based principles discussed in Chapter 9. Everyone has needs on a variety of levels, of course. Here I consider the needs most commonly seen in the workplace. When you know what these needs are and why people behave the way they do, it's much easier to take their cues. Knowing what someone desires on a deep level helps you motivate them. In essence, it's a reverse-engineering process.

The topics of purpose, meaning, and mission also interplay throughout this chapter. Your company has an overall direction, and robust social initiatives may be in place, but people still like personalization. One of the most compassionate things you can do for another human being is to take the time to really try to understand them. After all, there's a real reason — beyond a paycheck — that most people end up doing the jobs they do and sticking to a career niche. Subconsciously, they're addressing a deep need within themselves.

I also consider how to motivate not just an individual but teams as a whole. There are a few ways to do this. One of the most powerful is to create an environment where team members motivate each other and teach each other in a supportive manner. There's no one size fits all, so choose what you feel you can accomplish first and start there. My goal is to provide you with options, insights, and statistics. Which path to take is your choice.

REMEMBER As a values-based leader, you're self-aware, emotionally intelligent, and empathetic — not a soft and squishy plush toy, but a fierce leader who puts connection and engagement as priorities in your business. Taking the time to understand others is a demonstration of these attributes.

Peeking into the Human Motivation Theory

I devote an entire chapter (Chapter 9) to trust because it's the foundation from which all relationships form. Trust creates a stable environment and eliminates doubt that basic needs will be fulfilled, promoting feelings of safety. When trust isn't in place, doubt overtakes a group — and doubt is the killer of motivation. If the members of an organization don't feel that their leaders have their best interests at heart or are trustworthy, the general refrain becomes "Why should I bother?" When you have enough people saying that, it's safe to assume they aren't motivated. Often, their level of engagement is so low that you're not sure they're really working at all. They're just dialing it in for the day's pay. (Figure 16-1 shows the connection between trust and doubt.)

TRUST eliminates doubt

DOUBT sabotages motivation

THRIVING ENVIRONMENT
Trust creates a safe place to work
+
Meaning and purpose
= Motivated employees

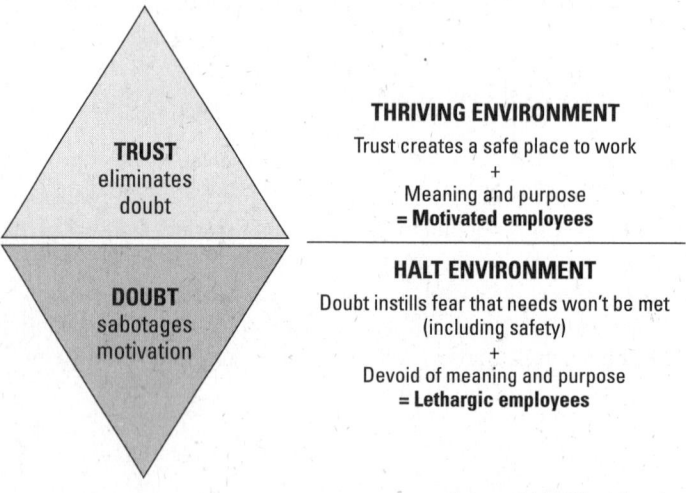

HALT ENVIRONMENT
Doubt instills fear that needs won't be met (including safety)
+
Devoid of meaning and purpose
= Lethargic employees

FIGURE 16-1: Trust's impact on motivation.

© John Wiley & Sons, Inc.

Human motivation most often stems from the needs system discussed in Chapter 9. There are three categories:

- **Deficiency needs:** The bare basics of life, including food, water, health, shelter, sex, safety, and employment
- **Growth needs:** Accomplishment, achievement, self-esteem, connection, and meaning
- **Self-achieving needs:** Self-awareness, giving back, and helping others

When deficiency and growth needs are met, they increase the possibility that an individual can meet a self-achieving need. Having these needs met builds trust and esteem to accomplish whatever the individual wants to achieve. With that said, assume that deficiency needs are met and your employees are seeking to fulfill their growth and self-achieving needs. In the following sections, you can find out how to identify and understand the components that will motivate them.

Looking, listening, and categorizing

One of the attributes of being a values-based leader is the ability to listen and really hear other people by pausing long enough to get a sense of who they are. This chapter is about using that ability to learn how to identify what motivates them. Active listening is great, but getting at the intent behind someone's words is a sign of an empathetic leader. Everyone communicates in a way that reflects their deepest desires and motives. This section starts with basic classifications to help provide some framework for exactly what you're looking and listening for.

Noting the three things that motivate people

In 1961, Dr. David McClelland looked deeper into needs and classified motivational principles into three more categories: power, affiliation, and achievement. According to this theory, everyone possesses one or more of these motivational triggers. One trigger is dominant, and the others vary in intensity:

- **Power:** Those who are motivated by power like to plan and use that word a lot. Creating *the plan* is a way to ensure that they've secured power, authority, and/or control over a situation. Power-focused individuals fear a loss of power or the perception of lack of authority more than anything else. They'll keep a lid on anything that deviates from the plan. The lighter, brighter side of power is the thought process that a plan ensures others' safety. Safety, to power-focused individuals, means making sure that everyone is clear and moving in the same direction. They take ownership of this duty.

» **Affiliation:** Here we have social butterflies, group leaders, and those who love being on the inside track. They're group-centric, want to be liked, and are often deemed social directors or ringleaders. Affiliation-focused individuals fear rejection. To be rejected would mean they've been excluded. Everybody wants to belong, to some extent, but those motivated by affiliation seek it as a means to exert their own form of power.

» **Achievement:** Achievers are always focused on the next goal, sometimes even before the present goal has been achieved. They're always looking at what's next. They're motivated by the achievement of goals. Failure is their kryptonite. Their mantra is "Failure is not an option." It's important to know that these individuals often move from one goal to another without much of a pause. Another way to view this trigger is that these individuals like a challenge and thrive on having another mountain to climb or land to conquer.

Depending on their use, the triggers can be profoundly positive or destructive; there are always positive and negative aspects to everything. Someone with power needs may well be a mobilizing and unifying force behind a plan. And a control enthusiast may squelch the energy of a whole team with their need to be in complete control. Positive and negative possibilities exist within each of us.

Assessing yourself

Did you immediately recognize yourself as you read the categories in the preceding section? Most people do. If you've read other chapters, you've probably realized that I'm fond of sticky notes. Consider writing your perceived motivations on one of those and keep it in this chapter. But before you do, consider the questions in this section to further refine your assessment.

Working within the three categories in the preceding section, what would you consider to be your dominant motivational trigger? Ask yourself these questions:

» What motivates you to come to work?

» What's the reward you're really seeking?

» Why this job and/or this company?

Forget preconceived notions, like the idea that wanting power is necessary to be a leader. Leaders come in many different forms, with different strengths. Some are more socially driven, relying on their connections and group influence to create success. A drive to achieve promotes the idea that they're highly focused. Whatever motivates you, knowing *yourself* can provide insights into your own behaviors, both known and previously unknown. Additionally, assessing yourself first creates a platform for understanding and compassion for yourself — and ultimately for others. Knowing why you react in a certain way in any situation will help you understand the same about members of your team (see the next section for details).

It's honesty time. No one else is looking at the notes you've made in this section. Regardless of which trigger motivates you the most, you can discern more about who you are and how you operate, and when you're feeling down or demotivated, you can usually find the answer in your dominant motivating factor not being fulfilled.

If affiliation is your dominant motivation, for example, having an inclusive, team-spirited, or community-centric form of expression in your leadership motivates you. However, exclusion in any form demotivates you. With this awareness, consider the importance of affiliation for you in your life. What does it bring you? Some answers can be acceptance, influence, and/or using that influence to gain something for either yourself or someone else. That can include simple things like networking through your circle of influence to help someone else find a job.

Assessing your team

After you assess yourself, consider your team and ask the same questions from the preceding section. Jot down those answers on a piece of paper or a sticky note. Put a star next to the one or two you think rank highest for your team and stick the note here in this chapter for now.

Keep in mind that motivation sometimes looks as if one stimulus moves a person forward, but if you look more closely, it turns out to be something completely different, or at least the context of it may become different. This is an important distinction to be made and one that will help you speak directly to those triggers. When you know the root cause, it's much easier to see through the weeds.

Consider the last staffer you engaged who seemed not to be "feeling it" any longer. They used to be engaged and motivated. What changed? What were they getting that's missing now? If you know the person well enough, you may be able now to look through the motivational trigger material in this chapter to figure out which one reflects who they are. Or you may need to have a conversation to learn more. Listen to what they say and how they say it. Notice what their body language cues are expressing. Then remotivate the individual by tapping into what they truly want. This is the reverse-engineering I mention earlier. Here is one example of how to do this.

"Lila" was once a motivated, energetic part of the team, but recently she has been quiet and a bit withdrawn. You ask her how things are going. Her body language is a bit slumped, and she looks at her shoes a lot while you're chatting. After a little coaxing, she reveals that she just feels unhappy but she can't quite pinpoint why. Her work is still good and it's challenging, but it's just not . . . fun.

Lila's manager realizes that for the past 18 months, Lila was involved in a large-scale initiative bringing people from various offices together to problem solve a part of the business. Now Lila engages with only her manager daily. It becomes apparent that Lila misses the ability to set and reach goals in her work. The prior setting had her in a very structured type of work, and she loved it. Her manager realizes that Lila has really excelled every time she has been in that type of structure. Realizing that Lila needs that achievement in her work in order to feel fully engaged, her manager moves her work around to include others and asks her to lead structuring benchmarks and checkpoints for an upcoming project. Within weeks Lila perks up and is back to normal energetic self.

You find other means to reverse-engineer motivation in the nearby sidebar "Motivating Denise." Additionally, check out the example of Sam and his toy cars in the next section, which uses a slightly different tactic.

REMEMBER

Each process follows the same basic formula:

- **Be observant.** Take the time to notice changes in your employee's connection to their work.
- **Identify patterns.** Consider patterns of when the employee worked happily or excelled in certain situations.
- **Identify the motivation.** Based on the pattern, is the motivating factor power, affiliation, or achievement?
- **Reverse-engineer the motivating factor.** Give them what works for them — for example, if they like to achieve goal after goal, give them another goal to strive for. Otherwise you'll lose that person.
- **Take action.** Redirect the employee's work into the form that works as a motivating tool: Power people want to plan and be the authority, affiliation people prefer a community-driven environment, and achievement folks want to check off goal completions.

REMEMBER

When assessing others, consider the dominant behavior, but also be aware that there may be secondary motivational factors. People are multifaceted, not one-dimensional. So you'll probably be working with a dominant trigger and a secondary trigger. Look, listen, and watch the engagements of your team to see what really motivates them, and dispense your motivational remedies accordingly.

TIP

The great news is that once you know these triggers and how to recognize them, you'll be able to utilize them in many facets of your life. In fact, I encourage you to do so. As always, I suggest you practice this concept on your friends, partners, and, yes, even your family. I guarantee that your next holiday dinner together will be infinitely more interesting when you view everyone at the table through this filter. No, you're not being manipulative. You're honing your ability to understand others.

MOTIVATING DENISE

"Denise" is a big team player and an exceptional employee. She's always been viewed as an introvert, except when it comes to team activities. During those times, she shines and can mobilize the group. The organization promotes her to work with many work groups. But now Denise isn't part of one team that she feels is her own.

Her trigger is affiliation. She loves being *part of* a group. The new role may have seemed ideal for a social butterfly, but it disconnects her from that group/team environment of inclusion that makes her so happy. So, Denise begins to lag and doesn't seem to be motivated anymore. She does her work, but she isn't happy. Her manager realizes the disconnect for her, reassigns her to a lateral position within a work group environment, and voilà — she begins to excel again. Motivational issue resolved.

For another person motivated by affiliation, the social butterfly aspect of the role offered to Denise might have been perfect. Always consider that there could be several applications within each trigger. Customize to the individual.

Understanding that fear motivates more than anything else

Unfortunately, people are even more motivated by what they fear than by what they want. If you set a goal to do something — it doesn't matter if it's losing weight, saving up for a new car, or finding the perfect job — beware your internal saboteur. The severity of the sabotage depends on your perception of self. In some people, self-sabotage is more prevalent than in others, but no one goes completely unscathed.

Fear can manifest as defiance, procrastination, or self-doubt that you can do, be, or have something. Some may feel resigned to staying where they are now as the only way forward. People are likely to stop themselves from getting what they want without a cause/effect that's framed as losing something vitally important — the motivational trigger. I'm not talking about threats, although fear-mongering has certainly been used as a menacing way of manipulating others.

Do you remember when one of your parents would tell your sibling something like, "Please clean up your toys, Sam"? (Of course they never had to tell you — I'm talking about your brother.) Sam would ignore the request. So they tried another tactic: "Sam, you love it when your room is clean. Don't you want to see all those fancy, fast racecars lined up on your shelf?" Sam's position on the matter didn't change. He loved his cars, but he still wasn't motivated to act. So, the third attempt: "Sam, please clean up — otherwise, there won't be time to go to Nancy's birthday party later. If you do it now, we can make it. But if you don't, then you won't have time to go because you'll be cleaning your room." If what he feared he would lose was important to him, he would finally clean his room. (If it wasn't, even that trigger wouldn't motivate him.) It turned out that Sam's trigger was affiliation. Your parents knew Sam loved playing with other kids and liked being part of a group, so nothing would stop him from going to that party.

The same is true for each of us, even in the workplace. For example, if someone is motivated by power, the thought of not being able to lead, participate in an authority role, or be heard as an expert would be tough to entertain. To motivate someone fitting this profile, you could offer a cause/effect such as this: "Feeling powerless and frustrated by this situation will only make it worse. However, if you decide to participate in X change process, you'll be using your expertise to help everyone."

WARNING: This is a big warning. This kind of motivation should never, ever be framed as a threat or delivered in a threatening tone.

TIP: You can learn a lot from watching children's behaviors. The next time you see a child having a temper tantrum, ask yourself when and how *you* do that as an adult. Now, I highly doubt that you throw yourself on the office floor and demand that someone get you a hazelnut coffee. However, everyone has an adult version of a tantrum, right? The next time it happens to you, ask yourself what you fear you're losing: Is it power, affiliation, or achievement?

Deciphering the money motivation myth

When leaders and managers are asked what they believe motivates their teams, the most common response is, of course, *money*. You may be wondering whether that's true about yourself and those around you. But is it really about money? Or is there something deeper going on?

Consider the meaning of money to those in the workforce, keeping in mind that philosophies about money vary from generation to generation. Offering money as motivation isn't *always* effective. Considering that a majority of your workforce is made up of GenXers and Millennials, knowing what money means to *them* will help you determine their priorities (see Chapter 2 for more about these generations):

» **Baby Boomers:** Money is a status symbol.

» **Generation X:** Money is a means to an end.

» **Millennials:** Money is today's payoff.

>> **Silent:** Money is livelihood.

>> **Homelanders:** Too early to tell, but maybe money is livelihood as well.

As you can see, money doesn't mean the same thing to everyone. That said, not everyone in a generation thinks exactly alike, either. But being aware of general attitudes about money can give you insight into the different thought processes. Unfolding McClelland's motivational triggers (see the earlier section "Looking, listening, and categorizing") will also help you understand what money may mean to different people.

Clearly, there's been a generational shift in mindset regarding the meaning of money. The current workforce of Millennials seeks financial means over career advancement. This jibes with their desire for a more experiential life over one spent acquiring stuff. They generate income to create a life and experiences they want, but they aren't necessarily interested in climbing the corporate ladder as Boomers were. In general, U.S. customer spending on live experiences and events has increased, indicating that it may not be just Millennials feeling the need to live life differently. Priorities have shifted. Living an experiential life is a motivator that can fall under any of the three motivational triggers in the same way money once did.

For example, a Millennial's deep desire for power may have more to do with the ability to control a situation and bring about a positive result at work, then have the flexibility to book their next trip to Vietnam, backpack to Machu Picchu, or swim with sharks around the Galapagos Islands. Millennials' translation of power is making a difference but also working to fund their adventures. Boomers may have the same desire to make a difference, but trends show that material possessions are more of their focus — a new house, a new car, or another item that projects the persona of success and power. The motivation may be the same (power), but the context of money, its use, how much is needed, and the projection of power are very different. So while power may be a Millennial's dominant motivator, money is secondary in creating their lives.

This shift from acquiring stuff to having experiences will continue to change the trends in workplace incentives. Consumer reports will indicate how deeply these desires grow within the culture. Stay tuned — and stay informed. What people spend their money on will tell you what their motivation may be. Think of it this way: Ask what a person wants to do with the money they make. Their answer will tell you whether they are motivated by power, affiliation, or achievement.

Helping People Find Their Meaning and Purpose Again

The concepts of meaning, impact, and purpose have been peppered throughout this book. Feeling the need to be *useful* in this world is a major motivating factor for all generations:

>> An Intelligence Group survey found that 64 percent of Millennials would rather make $40,000 per year at a job they love than $100,000 a year at a job they think is boring. *Boring* to Millennials is a place where they're either unchallenged or disconnected from any meaning or purpose in the work they're doing.

>> A Clark University study found that 82 percent of Millennials said it was important for them to have a career that does some good in the world.

>> A Brookings University study said 63 percent of Millennials like their employers to contribute to social or ethical causes.

Considering that this group is already the largest generation in the population and soon will be taking leadership positions, meaning and purpose will be a more prominent focus than ever before. Meaning and purpose are increasingly key motivating and retention factors. Both GenXers and Millennials are deeply connected to a desire for meaningful work in the world. Cogent corporate social responsibility (CSR) initiatives that are organized and integrated will be increasingly key for motivation, as will the creation of shared values economy (SVE) structures that address human and social needs. The workforce wants to help resolve problems both in the world and locally by embodying the battle cry of "If not us, then who?" (Flip to Chapter 4 for more about CSR and the shared values economy.)

REMEMBER

Helping people find their meaning and purpose is a motivational tool. Tap into their emotion in order to connect their hearts to the work they're doing.

Chunking it down: Bite-sizing purpose and meaning

You may be wondering how you would apply all this meaning and purpose stuff in your company. Theory can be fascinating, but practical application is the name of the game here. Not all readers may be leading massive corporations (yet — I believe you can!). What can you do about motivation, meaning, and purpose?

I want you to know that no matter where you are in your current organization, you can be a leader steeped in values and you can set a positive example for those all around you. (In Chapter 12, I discuss how to set yourself up as a values-based leader even when your senior leaders aren't interested in it.) Being motivated in your own work will help you motivate others. This is your opportunity to help your staff see what you see in the work you're all doing together.

Pull out a scrap piece of paper and follow along with Table 16-1. Break down what *your* business does. Whatever goods, services, or opportunities your company provides, list them out as I've done for a few examples in the table. Remember, *every* product and service fills a need — if it doesn't, it won't be around for long. Consider the needs that your company addresses and add them to your breakdown. Making it personal, as in the third column, makes it really stick in your heart and your mind. Thinking about what your company does in this way creates an attachment or hook that in turn creates emotion around the meaning and purpose.

TABLE 16-1 Bite-Size Purpose and Meaning Amplifications

Product or Service	What It Does	How It Fulfills Personal Needs
Directional app for use in the United States (for example, Waze or Google Maps)	Keeps user from getting lost and finds the quickest routes around traffic. Helps locate gas stations, places to eat, points of interest, and other fun places on their routes.	Helps people get to work and attend important events in their lives. Takes stress out of journeys. Makes traveling easier, richer, more fun, and more interesting.
Food business (Whole Foods, Fairway, Blue Apron, Hello Fresh)	Provides high-quality food and meals to the community.	Fuels and nourishes families so they can mobilize their dreams (including education, work, contribution to community, and engagement with others).
Clothing business (J. Crew, Madewell, Lululemon, Gucci)	Provides clothing and fashion for men, women, and/or children.	Makes people feel good about showing up in the world and experiencing the events of their lives. Enables a person to impress important people and be successful, such as on job interviews, and helps people feel confident in expressing themselves.

Emotion is the fuel. Passionate people are emotional people — they have energy, express their points with gusto, and fight fiercely for what they believe in. But sensitive people are emotional people, too. Their sensitivity often binds them to a specific cause, purpose, or meaning. There are many forms of emotion that form that bond. People may express it differently.

REMEMBER

Find your emotion. If you don't experience something emotional when you read the statements you develop in the third column, go back and try again. It needs to mean enough to inspire action or stay the course. This is your *why*.

> ## PURPOSE AND MEANING CONFESSIONAL
>
> Meaning is highly personal. Consider the following statements:
>
> - **Abraham, architect:** "I create homes that hold memories."
> - **Sarandi, advertising executive:** "I show people how to get their needs met."
> - **Sampson, financial professional:** "I give people peace of mind to know their loved ones will be taken care of even after they've gone."
> - **Bryn, career coach:** "I help people realize their potential and get the job of their dreams."
>
> Abraham, the architect, was raised in a small, modest home by a single mother. "We didn't have much growing up," he says, "but we sure had a lot of great laughs. I have so many wonderful memories. That's why I do what I do. I want to help other people to have a home where meaningful memories are created."
>
> His is just one story revealing a meaningful and purposeful motivation. Sarandi, Sampson, and Bryn all have equally moving stories behind their statements. Every person has one.

TECHNICAL STUFF: In the many years I worked in the apparel industry, during tough times what motivated me to stay the course was this: I knew that although some might have considered what I was doing to be fluff, I didn't. I knew that the clothing we produced helped people go to interviews and get jobs. Even as I type those words, emotion wells in the base of my throat. That meant something very special to me. And it still does.

Helping a team find its footing

The process described in the preceding section can be executed for a team within an organization or a small work group. In any case, it needs to be a collective process. Not everyone may agree, and some may be too shy to admit that they care enough to participate at all. That's a façade. Never forget that. Likewise, a defensive posture is usually a smoke screen to cover real emotion. Don't be fooled, and don't let such things stop you.

TIP: Ask team members why they're doing the job they do. Be prepared for several to say they need the money! That's fine. Ask them what they'll do with the money. This is a clue to why they are in their position. Remember, it's not the money but what they'll do with the money that is the underlying motivating factor.

Digging deeper will permit you to see why the work they do matters to them. Sometimes it's a connection to the CSR or SVE initiatives in place at the company — which is great! But they also want a job they find meaning in, whether they currently have that or not. Be inquisitive. Ask them questions about the work they're doing together as a team. Mold that into a motivating statement that unifies them. This isn't a slogan. What you're crafting is a *unifying statement.*

Keep it informal. I've had teams come back with simple statements like "We make [stuff] happen" (you may imagine the more colorful word the team used!). That particular team is all about marketing research for Millennial companies, so that *would* be one way of saying they mobilize industries and companies, for sure. It was a completely authentic statement. Other teams have come up with variations such as "We take care of people as if they were our own family." Coming from a small team of healthcare professionals, this statement brought tears to the members' eyes as they nodded in agreement. It means something to them. And it motivates them to do their jobs every day.

REMEMBER

Unifying statements can really help those who may not be clear on the *why* of the work they do. Not every person can articulate it, but those around them share their experiences. People learn and gain clarity from others' experience.

Practicing and Reinforcing Motivation

The jury is still out on the best reward perks package. The space is constantly evolving and refining its approach, carefully balancing the desire of employees and the affordability of incentive programs for the company. I believe this area will continue to be a moving target for the next few years. Millennials are redefining the workplace, so we'll have to wait and see what happens. In the meantime, you may gain a little insight into nontraditional benefits that are on the rise to recruit and retain employees in Chapter 14.

However, there is something you can do in the here and now, and it costs nothing. Throughout this chapter, I try to impress upon you that empathy is essential to connecting with a team. Think back to the basis of what human beings want: They want to be seen, heard, and recognized. Often, we see what another person needs: a kind word, a little recognition, or maybe a reminder of what they really are motivated by.

Sometimes leaders and managers hold back such simple expressions of recognition and validation from an employee, considering them too "needy" or time-consuming. And without healthy boundaries, they'd be correct. Becoming the team's therapist *would* become a major time suck. That's not the intention here.

The tools and insights provided thus far are a means to gain a glimpse into other people and help move them forward. I'm not talking about participation trophies and gold stars being handed out to every team member. What I'm suggesting in this chapter is a way to validate team members and inspire and motivate them.

Creating an environment where people can fail but learn from it

First, you can shine a light on a glaring issue that can cause a team to feel disempowered, fearful, and like a failure. That's when they're caught not knowing something they should know or they make a mistake. It's demotivating, even demoralizing for your dedicated employees. When I talk about the workplace being a safe place to be, I'm talking about more than just being healthy physically and mentally. There's an emotional component of safety that can be folded beautifully into the motivation of others.

Many years ago, I heard Sarah Blakely, founder of SPANX, speak at a conference. She shared a story about sitting at the dinner table as a child every night. Her father would ask her what was her win and what was her loss for the day? (I'm paraphrasing.) After she told her dad about her loss, he would ask, "What did you learn from that?" This anecdote left such a profound imprint on me that I adopted a similar practice with my team at the time. (For details, see the next section and the later sidebar "Shifting the orchestra of discontent.")

REMEMBER

A mistake or misstep is only a failure if a lesson isn't learned from it. I'm not dismissing negligent behavior; I'm saying that when an honest error is highlighted in a constructive manner, it's less likely to occur again. Moreover, others can learn from these mistakes too. How do you wrap all this up into a tidy little delivery system? Keep reading.

Playing with pickup sticks: You can always find a solution

A mentor told me years ago that everything you need is right in front of you. Clearly, when you're lost in turmoil — or if you're trying to motivate your team — that's not what you want to hear. But it's the truth. Playing pickup sticks is about working with what is scattered before you — your situation. Each stick represents a team member. Each stick has a certain amount of strength, but placing it together with other sticks creates something far stronger. Together we're better. Apart we're scattered.

Having team members teach and motivate one another creates a deep bond among them. It's never *only* the leader's role to motivate the team. They also need to do it for themselves and be willing to support others around them. You just need to show them how to do so.

Here's an exercise I've used with great success. This isn't something you may need to do every week — perhaps only during times when people are feeling a little scattered or the team feels defeated. Set it up in an informal, relaxed spot in the office. Explain that you know they're working hard and you understand they may not always feel like they're getting very far. So it's time to play the high/low game:

- » Ground rules: No judgment, no retribution.
- » Ask team members to keep track of their highs and lows for the week. That should also include something from outside the office; it can be as simple as going to the gym three days this week or a major life event that may have happened.
- » Gather them together the following week. Ask someone to share one high for the week. Celebrate the high with congratulations.

  But also ask for a low: a disappointment, mistake, misstep, or error. This one is usually met with caution. If they resist, ask them for an experience where they learned something new this week or a challenge they're stuck on.
- » Circle back around to a few of the highs. Ask what those lessons may have been: "What did you learn from this experience?" or "What did you learn about your abilities?"

Continue the conversation, encourage everyone as you go, and make it light. Do this exercise a few weeks in a row to help motivate them to see their contributions and where they can support their teammates. Thereafter, perhaps run the game once a quarter or as needed. Just don't wait to conduct this exercise until the situation is dire.

Pulling it all together

As you watch your team members engage in the exercise illustrated in the preceding section, you will notice patterns. Who loves the group interactions? Those people are motivated by affiliation. Who likes to be in control of the situation or becomes a bit bossy or defensive about not knowing something? Those are your power people. Who are the individuals who lock up with frustration over not winning or have a deep desire to just move forward? Those people are motivated by achievement.

SHIFTING THE ORCHESTRA OF DISCONTENT

Motivation, as I've said, isn't just the leader's job. The team plays a big part in creating a positive environment where others thrive. The leader can set up the environment for each person to win, but ultimately it's each person's decision whether to participate. Motivation occurs not just because a leader recognizes the team or taps into triggers — peers play a big part in the process as well.

As one particular team sat in a room together, I asked them to take out some paper and write down three highs, or wins, they had in the past week. It didn't matter how big or small it was — if it was an accomplishment, they should write it down. They went to work. Next I had them write down a couple of disappointments, missteps, or blind spots they'd experienced this week. Well, that went over like a ton of bricks. I heard things like "Are you trying to get us in trouble?" and "Really? Is this an inquisition?" But after some reassurance, everyone went to work on their short lists.

Wins, of course, are joyful and full of laughter. But the group, without being cued, started taking notes on their wins and asking questions about how someone did what they did. Some team members said things like, "Now I know how to do this — thanks, dude." As we moved into the disappointments, missteps, and blind spots portion, they tensed up a bit. Finally one brave soul, "Meghan," stepped up. She was the newest team member. She shared that she'd made a mistake on an email she sent to a vendor. When I inquired about it, she said, "Well, yeah, it was a mistake, and I'm not proud of it, but here's what I did to resolve the problem." I will tell you that the resolution she described took a lot of investigation. It was impressive. And I wasn't the only one who thought so. Everyone around her spoke words of support to her: "Wow, I would have never known that was the solution or where to get that! How did you figure this out?" Meghan exploded with pride as she explained her process.

Next up was the team skeptic, "Tina." "Okay, I'll play," she said. She admitted a misstep she had made that week. She wriggled in her chair and looked uncomfortable. Her manager jumped in and said, "Tina, no one thinks you're perfect. Mistakes happen. Do you want help fixing this issue?" She agreed after a bit of protesting. The group rallied and helped her. Tina's demeanor changed to become more open and less defensive.

After a few weeks of engaging with each other in this manner, team morale and motivation increased tremendously. They encouraged each other more. They became more open to being part of finding a resolution rather than allowing another team member to struggle.

"Stu" came to see me a couple of months later: "Um, okay, I see what you did here." I smiled at him as I peered over my glasses. Oh? "Yup, you got us to teach and encourage each other without making it uncomfortable — well, it was uncomfortable in the beginning." And now how do you feel? With a big smile he said, "Well, it doesn't suck." Coming from Stu, that was a high compliment. I'll take it! Today Stu uses his own version of this exercise with the teams he leads.

Remember: People want to be seen, heard, and recognized. In this variation of motivating your team, you would be doing just that without getting into too many complexities. Not everyone may enjoy participating in the exercise, but they will learn a lot from observing the process.

REMEMBER

There is brilliance in all of this. Come back around to the three categories shared earlier in this chapter: power, affiliation, and achievement. When you're really paying attention to your team (or spouse, family member, friend, and so on), you will know what motivates them — what it is they really crave in their lives. (Side note: Knowing this information has also saved many of my clients' personal relationships. I tell clients all the time: Practice everything I'm teaching you about motivation on your family and see what happens.) It's not as hard as you think. When you know what someone really wants, it's not hard to give it to them:

» **Those motivated by power:** Give them the chance to shine and to provide their point of view. They also like to keep people safe, so allow them to provide input on "efficiencies" — a code word for safety in a variety of ways.

» **Those motivated by affiliation:** Give them the opportunity to work with others in groups and as in-house coaches. Recognize that they are social, so many of them can be very communicative. Job functions that allow them to use that skill make them so happy.

» **Those motivated by achievement:** Give them a clear line to achieve their goals. When they've reached a goal, you must give them another one to strive for or you will lose their attention.

IN THIS CHAPTER

» Developing shared responsibility for leadership

» Identifying the successors in the bunch

Chapter **17**

Slicing the Pie: Creating a Culture of Leadership

It would be impossible for one single leader to do everything necessary to run an organization. Control enthusiasts (also known as control freaks) may think they can do everything, but ultimately that doesn't work. They burn out, and resentment sets in. The pie needs to be sliced so that everybody gets their share. Effective leadership spreads the work of leading to all leaders in an organization — indeed, to everyone.

This chapter offers an overview of selecting, developing, and training new leaders. It's not enough to carefully put in values as the cornerstone for the organization — you have to ensure that they're carried out by the on-the-ground field leadership. That's how you build a tall structure on your strong foundation. That structure is made of leadership that can and will advance the company's mission and create new opportunities for everyone around them.

Recognizing That Leadership Is a Job for All Staff Members

All employees have the ability to participate and be guardians of the organization. That guardianship — the preservation of the brand and its values — is part and parcel of maintaining a company culture reflective of the values-based principles laid out in Chapters 6 and 7. Employees act as their own leaders as they engage in their everyday work inside and outside the confines of the office. Every person in the organization has the capacity to make an impact by leading with the common principles, such as high standards, inclusion, and being part of a culture that helps cultivate future leaders. These principles help the organization's culture remain rock solid and consistent from year to year, team to team, or division to division. The cultivation of leaders being developed is each manager's responsibility, not solely that of the HR or training department.

Setting high expectations

Empowerment is a liberating and mobilizing component to building an environment where everyone shares responsibility and takes ownership of the tasks at hand.

Here's one of those moments in my own life that left a profound impression on me: I'm sitting across from a leader named "Bob," and several of us are discussing staff capabilities. One manager asks, "Are you sure Alice can do this job?" Bob looks up, smiles, and says, "I never hire people I don't believe will exceed my expectations. Of course she can do this." Later I asked him about this philosophy. He told me that unless he's all in with the team, then he can't expect them to be all in with him and the company direction.

There was another meeting with Bob where I presented an issue I was struggling to resolve. He gently asked me, "What do you think I would do here?" I answered. He smiled, nodded, and said, "You know what to do. Go do it. I have complete confidence in your ability." Bob's philosophy of accepting others and trusting them to do a good job is a philosophy I've adopted for leading my own teams.

Bob was masterful at allowing others to lead, even when they didn't have a title that would indicate leadership. He established a culture of expecting those around him to amaze him. He made sure that each team member understood that they represented not only him but also the brand itself. Believing and conveying to the staff that they were all leaders and were all able to make many decisions on their own was powerful to everyone around him.

Overcoming elitism with input and inclusion

When it comes to allowing everyone to be a leader, there's a central principle to consider in how you engage with the team. I've talked about *social distance* a few times in this book (especially in Chapters 6 and 9). Social distance is the gap created between a leader and others; it's a direct reaction to power. One form of social distance to be mindful of is the elitist aspect of problem solving. I'm not sure people actually sit around a table and say, "We're better than they are, so they don't need to be part of this solution." Perhaps Hollywood would paint that picture. I do believe, though, that some leaders feel a need for control and self-preservation, and therefore utilize exclusion to manage those needs. Decision-making is often restricted to a very small group of individuals.

REMEMBER

Values-based leaders not only allow everyone to lead, but they're also wise enough to know that they're not always the best person to create solutions anyway. Thinking you're the best at everything and only you can see the right path is an elitist attitude. The right attitude is more like this: I can help put the pavers on the pathway. Allowing key decision-makers and/or influencers to participate in problem solving and planning creates the binding for the shared responsibility of various groups within the organization. Bubbling up their input to create the plan enables their insight to become the pavers on the pathway to achieving the end goal.

That doesn't mean everyone will agree. Ultimately, you do need to make the best decisions possible to execute the plan. That's your job. Being self-reflective and considering the best routes will get you there.

Developing a culture of leadership for sustained impact

Values-based leaders are secure in themselves. They understand that sharing their leadership may result in a team member rising beyond them someday. Establishing a culture of leadership encourages advancement and mobility, both laterally and upward. It's a strategy that creates seamless continuity. Perpetuating a culture where leaders grow cements the ethos that you're all in it together and the team is motivated to work harder. Exceptional results occur as a result.

Being able to create this culture doesn't happen overnight, and it's not a quick five-step process. It is the unfolding of your values and the demonstration of trust and the things that build trust (see Chapter 9). That trust folds into motivating others to do the best they can (see Chapter 16). Adding the advancement of others as part of your hiring strategy (see Chapter 14) reinforces the value you place on each employee. Planning to develop talent creates a pool of successors you can pull from for upcoming opportunities.

Correctly managing this pool of talent allows for consistency of action. It also lets you tap into the history of past wins (and not-so-great results) to build toward a better future. Additionally, retaining talent keeps down the expenses associated with hiring from outside the company.

The added benefit is that the staff sees the company keeping its commitment to hire from within. When this promise is fulfilled, they're motivated to stay the course, knowing that advancement is truly an option in the organization. There is a path for them to get there too. (I talk more about promoting from within later in this chapter.)

Following leadership demographic trends

Who are emerging leaders in the workplace? Keep your eye on three key things: the rate of retiring leaders, the expansive population boom in developing nations, and the globalization of the workforce. All of these are leading to a more integrated, more diverse workforce.

TECHNICAL STUFF

The aspect that will likely have the most impact at this point in time has to do with Boomers moving aside to make way for fresh new leadership. Here are a few examples of what this looks like (see www.haygroup.com/downloads/uae/Hay_Group_wp_-_The_War_for_Leaders_07_web.pdf for more information):

» The Corporate Leadership Council (CLC) reports that 97 percent of all organizations report a leadership gap. Forty percent say those gaps — the voids left by retiring leaders — are "acute," given that the Baby Boomers and some older talent are leaving many positions open and hard to fill based on the lapse in experience.

» The American Medical Association (AMA) is concerned that 60 percent of all CEOs in healthcare will retire in the next five years.

» Half to three-quarters of all senior management are now eligible for retirement.

Another interesting stat to consider comes from the Millennial Leadership Survey, which indicates that 91 percent of Millennials aspire to become leaders, and more than half of those are women (https://workplacetrends.com/the-millennial-leadership-survey/). The workforce wants to lead, and women will be even more of a driving force in leadership.

Clearly, the desire and opportunities for leadership are there. Training and education are therefore important tools for values-based leaders. However, managers need to be able to help identify future leader candidates and encourage them to take the initiative to get the training offered. Leaders need to identify and encourage managers to get onto a leadership path if it's a potential fit. Take the creation of future leadership seriously and be patient — cultivating a leader takes approximately ten years. It will take many steps in the process to get your candidate there. We are on the precipice of the Millennial generation absorbing the vacancies discussed earlier.

> ### A MANAGING DIRECTOR'S PATH
>
> When "David" started at a Fortune 500 company, he was fresh out of school, doe-eyed, and excited about the possibilities in his future. When I met him, he told me he was going to run this organization someday. I absolutely knew he would. Over an 11-year period, David learned and trained with many different coaches in that organization as well as outside mentors. Last year his profile popped up on my LinkedIn account. He'd been promoted to executive vice president and managing director of the company's China operation. The commitment to learn, on his part, got him there. And commitment from the company to grow someone like David made it possible. Everyone wins. I still believe that someday he will run that entire organization.

TIP Here are four ways to educate and prepare your emerging leaders (you can find additional information on these points in Chapter 14):

- Establish a peer-to-peer coaching system along with skip-level feedback and coaching from the manager above your manager.
- Train the aspiring leaders *before* they are in those positions — otherwise, it's too late.
- Rotate job assignments to provide maximum exposure to varying skills, processes, and experiences.
- Offer MBA opportunities (online or real-world) to your middle management so they're trained up, and do it earlier rather than later.

Identifying the Leaders in the Field Who Can Help Your Organization

One common blind spot among leaders is the ability to foster new talent. Where are all the amazing future leaders? You may wonder whether it's better to hire from within or recruit externally. Both have validity, but home-grown individuals from your *farm team* will provide longevity and consistency. Here are two good reasons to grow your own talent:

- **It shows commitment to your people.** When you invest long-term in your team and promote them to leadership, they tend to stay on longer. Gallup's poll on employee engagement found that 82 percent of all employees are disengaged from their work. This costs the economy billions of dollars, in more ways than the bottom line. Lethargic, uninspired staff members seek jobs elsewhere. Why wouldn't they? This in turn costs organizations a good deal of money to recruit and onboard new employees (Chapter 14 has more on hiring).

» **It preserves institutional memory.** People who already work there know not only the ins and outs of the organization but also its history. That history includes the good, the bad, and the ugly. When we don't know our history, we tend to repeat mistakes that were made before. There's no one to say, "No, we tried that five years ago, and it didn't go so well." Repeating mistakes is very costly. Promoting from within is a safeguard against it.

Developing leaders and managers from within the company encourages others to reach higher. It also creates a sense that the company values its employees. Look within first, with the help of the following sections. Set a strategy in place to train, educate, and develop leaders from within the ranks.

If you can't find the leaders in your ranks, you'll have to venture outside. There are benefits to that too. An external candidate can bring a fresh perspective to the situation.

There are some pitfalls of external candidates worth noting: It can be a risky proposition because external candidates aren't always in alignment with the company culture. They may be slow to adapt and integrate with the group. Although an external candidate may sometimes be your best option, if you've set up a support system to cultivate existing talent, you won't usually need to go beyond your own four walls to find the perfect person.

Breaking down three tiers of leaders

Identifying the right people for leadership is a process. Have a look at the framework in Figure 17-1, which shows different growth tiers, capacities, and readiness levels. I believe in keeping it very simple. Complicating this or any other strategy can lead to feeling overwhelmed and paralyzed.

Tier 3 is perceived as the place to tap talent — often, as the only place to tap talent. However, there's a wellspring of talent in each tier.

Consider who you spend most of your time with. Is it with those who are eager, engaged, and excited? Perhaps you spend time with a group of highly successful, continually mobile individuals, or maybe you're with friends who are happy to just have a job and collect their paychecks. Whoever it is, on some level it's a reflection of where you are. People tend to gravitate toward those who are similar. If you hang out with people who have a victim mentality that everyone has wronged them, very likely there is an element of that in you. Otherwise, you wouldn't be able to tolerate it.

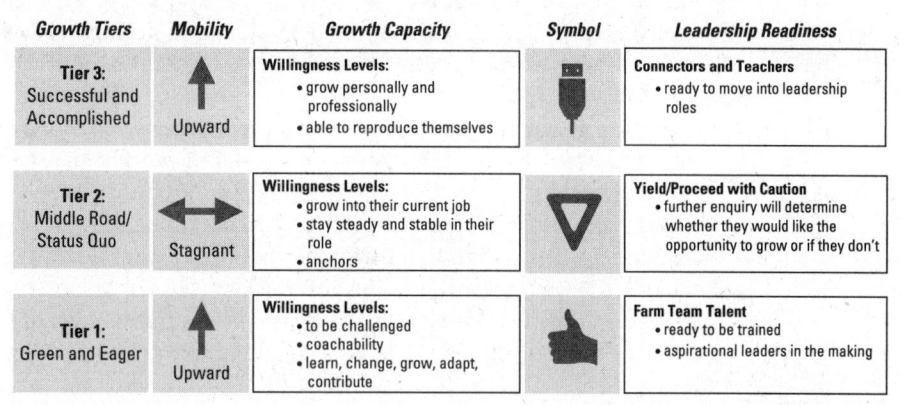

Growth Tiers	Mobility	Growth Capacity	Symbol	Leadership Readiness
Tier 3: Successful and Accomplished	Upward	**Willingness Levels:** • grow personally and professionally • able to reproduce themselves		**Connectors and Teachers** • ready to move into leadership roles
Tier 2: Middle Road/ Status Quo	Stagnant	**Willingness Levels:** • grow into their current job • stay steady and stable in their role • anchors		**Yield/Proceed with Caution** • further enquiry will determine whether they would like the opportunity to grow or if they don't
Tier 1: Green and Eager	Upward	**Willingness Levels:** • to be challenged • coachability • learn, change, grow, adapt, contribute		**Farm Team Talent** • ready to be trained • aspirational leaders in the making

FIGURE 17-1: Growth and mobility tiers for leadership.

© John Wiley & Sons, Inc.

Look at your team and your current leadership, and think about which tiers from Figure 17-1 they may fall within. Are they excited, hopeful, and ready to roll? Are they ready to help others grow into new roles? Consider looking at the momentum within each tier.

Tier 1: Green and eager

The individuals in Tier 1 are excited, engaged, and eager to learn. The sponges of the organization, they have their minds wide open to exciting possibilities. They could be new hires, entry-level employees, or career changers. They could be any age. *Green* refers only to their ripeness — they're not jaded or tainted. They're just new, fresh sprouts of genius, potential, and enthusiasm.

They're the farm team, to use a baseball analogy — the future of the organization. Invest in them, and they will be the leaders of the future. Training them also helps teach *them* how to teach, and lead, others. It's a cycle: Let me show you how, then you do it, then teach others to do the same. Being in the process provides experiences that will help them lead others. Train them and train them well! It will be worth your investment.

TIP

Career changers or those entering the workplace later in their work life can also exhibit the same green and eager attitudes as someone fresh out of school entering their first position. Be mindful of what may be your own internal bias on these matters.

Tier 2: Middle of the road/status quo

Tier 2 is inhabited by a few different types of individuals. There are those who aspire to do their job well but don't necessarily seek advancement. They like what they do and see no reason to move beyond what they're currently doing. Others are set in their ways and refuse to change, adapt, and grow, even as the organization does just that. They're not really interested in leading. That's okay! If everyone wanted to be a leader, nothing would get done. That's the truth!

The third group in this tier is made up of individuals who for one reason or another desire to stay in their current positions — for now. Some may be the primary caregiver for a child or an aging parent. Some may be battling cancer or another illness. Due to their circumstances or priorities, maintaining the status quo is the normalizing factor that helps them manage their challenges. I call these individuals on hold in the *waiting room*. It's in your best interest as a values-based leader to keep an eye on this tier. Eventually, when the time is right, many of them will be ready to leave the waiting room. They should definitely not be penalized for pausing.

Stable, steady anchors are within this tier. Value them. Those in the tier who whine, complain, or are always unhappy? You can leave them to sort themselves out.

Tier 3: Successful and accomplished

Tier 3 may seem to be the obvious place for finding leaders, but keep in mind that not everyone who is accomplished and successful is a leader. The defining factors within this tier are a desire to develop other leaders and the willingness to teach. These are your connectors and teachers who will propel the organization forward. They've been on the ground and know how things happen. Their insight is invaluable. This is your pool to consider tapping into both internally and, if necessary, externally.

But not all successful people become leaders. They may be great salespeople, riveting innovators, or coveted programmers. Their talents may not always translate to the next level. It's okay. Don't force the situation.

Here are three examples of devotion to leadership development from top companies (see `www.haygroup.com/downloads/uae/Hay_Group_wp_-_The_War_for_Leaders_07_web.pdf` for more information):

>> Former CEO AG Lafley of Proctor & Gamble spent half to one-third of his time on leadership development.

>> Former CEO Wayne Colloway of PepsiCo spent two-thirds of his time on identifying leadership talent for the future.

>> Sam Palmissano of IBM dedicates two weeks a year to doing nothing but reviewing high-potential leaders.

Tapping into a winning formula

Those who lead and desire to build other leaders spend most of their time with people from Tiers 1 and 3, with only certain Tier 2 folks. (See the earlier section "Breaking down three tiers of leaders" to understand who they are.) Here's why: You want to surround yourself with excited people who can see the possibilities for the future and those who are eager enough to want to be part of that motion. Status quo people often complain and spend too much time telling you why something won't work rather than considering what will. Find those who seek to be part of the solution rather than part of the problem.

Some may materialize as big voices with a passion to make things better for everyone. There's an important distinction to be made here: Big voices that are "me-focused" won't be well received in a values-based environment. However, big voices who have the team in mind are individuals whose energy and passion are worth harnessing.

For someone in Tier 3 to be around Tier 1 enthusiasm can be a refreshing boost. Tier 1 learns from Tier 3's experience, and that makes them move past FOMO (fear of missing out) — almost like getting a heads-up and a shortcut to success. I discuss coaching and mentorship in Chapter 14 — linking these two groups in a meaningful way of getting things done. It's also an essential component to developing talents and new leaders. This is the winning formula.

In case you're wondering how the Tier 2 folks fit into this formula: Well, those who are happy doing their jobs and plan on staying in their position are an integral part of the organization, but they are probably not interested in a leadership position. What about those who have paused their career due to extenuating circumstances? When they are ready to take themselves out of the waiting room, you'll have the opportunity to see where they fit: Tier 1 or Tier 3.

Empowering potential leaders to assess their own values

Values-based leadership (VBL) becomes the thread that runs through in everything in the organization, including who each person is and how they engage with everyone around them. Whenever you raise someone to the rank of formal leadership in the company, whether internally or as an external hire, be mindful to carefully assess who they are and what they value. Use the four attributes in Chapter 6 as a quick checklist. You've worked hard to create this beautiful company culture. The key to preserving it is to maintain what you've built. Those who create high performance and energized cultures outperform status quo or negative work environments every time.

REMEMBER Self-assessment is a key feature of VBL, as I've emphasized from the beginning. Ask yourself how you're doing. Ask other trusted colleagues how you're doing in order to gain some perspective. This should be a regular activity. We can be blind to our own faults as well as our strengths.

Have your potential new leader be self-reflective too. Ask questions that aim to get to who they are and what they value. Even those who were raised up in your values-based organization are entitled to their own desires and motivations. We are, after all, individuals. Here are some self-reflective questions to pose:

» What is your greatest value?

» How do you action that value?

» What happens when it isn't applied?

Such questions often provide an interesting portal into how they move in the world and workplace. Then dive a little deeper. Ask the question most people won't ask them: What would prevent you from staying with us for the long haul? The answer to this question will tell you exactly what they want during their time with the organization. It will provide insight into what they deem important and non-negotiable.

So how do you know if someone is truly ready to be a leader in the organization? Everyone brings something different to the table. Consider the following checklist to evaluate your potential candidates:

» **Skills, talents and successes:** These are easy to gauge based on the individual's track record, or in terms of the tiers described earlier in this chapter.

» **Matching the values of the company:** The questions asked earlier in this section skim the surface of the exercise on values given in Chapter 11. Someone may have success in your organization or show enormous potential, but will they uphold the values of the company? This is a make-or-break moment for your culture.

» **Transferable skills:** This point is critical: Are they able to transfer their skills and talents to those in the organization? A leader is always a teacher, so here's the way to consider this: Where have they taught others great disciplines, methods, techniques, and skills? Where have they imparted other knowledge to team members and colleagues?

» **Character:** I devote entire chapters on the principles and attributes of a values-based leader (see Chapters 6 and 7). Decide which of these principles and attributes are most important to you. Assess whether your leader candidates embody your most important ones. If they don't, your culture will be in jeopardy.

TIP In Chapters 6 and 7, pay particular attention to the willingness to be teachable. Whatever may be missing in a leader candidate, or needs a bit of polish or needs to be nurtured, can be addressed through training, coaching, and mentoring. However, those who are arrogant will never submit themselves to such refinement. In those cases, I suggest you consider another candidate.

IN THIS CHAPTER

» Understanding the complementary intellects that are required for innovation

» Establishing ground rules and other pointers for fostering new ideas

Chapter 18
Fostering an Environment of Innovation

Place two people in a locked white room with a white table and chairs with little stimulation. How innovative do you think they'll be? There's a pretty good chance they'll lose their minds with boredom after a while. Yes, that's what the workplace feels like to many people.

I've spent a good amount of time talking about engagement on various levels (especially in Chapter 15). One of the paramount reasons is that if you don't have engagement with the team, they're not motivated or encouraged to invest in finding solutions. Everything about values-based leadership (VBL) and the principles to support it within the organization creates an environment where innovation and creativity are not only permitted but encouraged. In this chapter, I discuss the fundamentals of introducing and keeping innovation in your workplace.

REMEMBER Here's a summary of the components that perpetuate an innovative environment:

» Development of the staff on an individual level with skills, training, and growth opportunities

- » Development of the team as a whole, which creates ownership, a sense of fair play, and appropriate job fit
- » Development across the organization, creating a healthy workplace that supports the staff and its resources

TIP Throughout this book, I share several different ingredients for creating an environment that allows an organization and its people to flourish. They are also the concepts that set the stage for innovation, using the principles of VBL to connect to employees' basic needs and the bottom line. Here's a brief recap:

- » Chapter 3 discusses moving beyond your own ego to consider the whole rather than just yourself.
- » Chapter 4 introduces the concept of a shared values economy, which also sets the stage for innovation across a number of employees, resources, and supports.
- » Chapter 6 establishes the level of development and opportunities to grow into a well-rounded leader.
- » Chapter 7 lays out the principles to embody as a values-based leader, permitting employees to feel safe enough to be innovative.
- » Chapter 8 provides tools to identify the stumbling blocks your team may be having and to give you the opportunity to move them into a state of hope for the future. Without hope, there's no innovation, my friend.
- » Chapters 14 and 15 lay the foundation for creating trust, motivation, and retention. All three concepts are interwoven.

Beginning with a Few Basics on Innovation

As I say throughout this book, the workforce is poised to re-create business as we know it. Millennials are about to move into leadership positions. They watched the stock market crash of 2008 that left their parents in financial peril and in some cases jobless. They recognize the shaming effects on these generations, which have become a catalyst for the way they are reimagining just about everything in the world. They are the generation that never wants to see a government-run bailout with taxpayer money again. They recognize that the only way to avoid that is to pave their own way and in their minds "fix" business and reinvent leadership.

That means giving form and dimension to creating innovative new businesses, solutions, products, and services. Just give them the opportunity to soar.

Simple truths about innovation include the following:

REMEMBER

- Innovation stems from dissatisfaction with the status quo.
- Innovation is a result of a disruption, crisis, or need.
- Innovation can't occur in a locked-down, metrics-ridden environment.
- Innovation requires a different thought process at first, prior to the implementation and analytical processes.

The following sections explore a few fundamentals of innovation in the workplace.

Revealing unconscious and conscious intellects

The principles of VBL create an environment where creativity and innovation flourish. Everything stems from a leader who creates a place where people can, in a word, play. *Play* has been a dirty word in business for a very long time. But play creates an opportunity for the mind to disengage from the linear, deadline-driven box. Play takes on a few different forms that feed into specific types of intellect.

Here are the two forms of intellect to consider:

- **Unconscious intellect:** This refers to your intuitive, meditative, and often slower intellect. *Slow* not in a negative sense, but slow in that this part of your mind ponders, walks to think, or finds another activity to distract (play) the conscious, rational side of the brain while the subconscious quietly sorts things out.
- **Conscious intellect:** This is the more analytical, calculating, measured part that moves faster and sometimes operates like a high-speed computer. It's language-dependent, meaning that if you switch languages from your native tongue to another language, it's harder for the conscious intellect to run its analytics.

They both have their parts to play. Both can reside within one person, but some people favor one or the other. Sometimes this is called *left and right brain thinking*. I prefer *conscious and unconscious intellect* because both are valid in the creative and innovative processes. Neither is a judgment — it's merely a reference to the different thought processes that help you reach a desired goal during different parts of the overall process.

The only way both types of intellect can work within an organization is when the playing field is level and the principles of VBL are in place. That creates an atmosphere where those who innovate and those who calculate can both reside harmoniously.

Comparing traditional and innovative business mindsets

There are two different business mindsets (summarized in Table 18-1). One represents a traditional thought process with regard to how businesses are developed. The other is the innovative mindset in which growth occurs as a result of tiny shifts or micro moves to processes, procedures, or manufacturing opportunities. There are also macro moves, which create a large repositioning of a brand, product, or company. Both types of innovative moves are valid, but the mindset that perpetuates either comes from crossing over from a traditional mindset. An innovative mindset creates the opportunity for the unconscious intellect to operate within the framework of the organization.

TABLE 18-1   Mindset Summation

Traditional Mindset	Innovative Mindset
Knowledge is held at the top.	Knowledge is decentralized.
Top leadership and managers hold fast to knowledge and wisdom.	Knowledge is shared and dispersed so the team can make better choices.
Command and control instruction (see Chapter 3).	Bottom-up participation.
All marching orders come from the top, limited to top direction and goal-planning activities.	Ideas and solutions are generated from all levels throughout the organization. Restrictions are limited.
Results-driven priority.	Questioning period.
While results are imperative, it limits the scope of the process.	The focus is on questioning before arriving at a solution that provides the desired result.
Perfection the first time around.	Error, correction, testing.
Expectation that it will be right the first time.	Proofing solutions and tweaking as needed.
Strategy and business models.	Emerging options.
Mapped and determined ahead of innovation.	Uncovering emerging strategies, trends, and solutions before finalizing.
	Re-creating and reconstructing business models.
Ensuring profitability.	Establishing innovation, balanced with the known, to drive profits.
Bottom-line focus without flexibility to make changes or shifts.	Profitability balanced with exploration of how best to get there.

WARNING: Make no mistake, profitability is necessary to maintain any company. The innovative process can't become a free-for-all because the paychecks of your employees and vendors depend on maturity and a sense of responsibility to be profitable. However, you need give your team some space so that the innovation process can work.

Deploying "shades of gray" thinking

In Western society, people have a tendency to swing the pendulum left to right in very extreme ways. Everything is either black or white. Up or down. In or out. Not only does that tendency continue to perpetuate extremes, but it also creates breakdowns when whatever solution brought before a group is narrowed down to an either-or situation.

I've watched this phenomenon in business and in society repeat itself over and over again only to create impasses and, in worst cases, complete breakdowns. It creates a thought process of "It's my way or the highway." Did your skin just crawl a little bit? Mine did! In business, we see strategies such as high quality–low cost, complexity–simplicity, and opportunity–simplicity as strategies for products and services. There, too, we see the either-or principle — one or the other but not both. So the pendulum swings back and forth as one day the strategy works and the next it doesn't. Is it any wonder why consumers are often agitated and corporate dwellers sometimes feel like they've got PTSD?

What if there were more than one choice? What if, rather than black or white, there were some shades of gray in between? The new group in town, the Millennials, is embracing this concept of more choice. We see evidence of this everywhere — Millennials often combine two common, known quantities and create something new out of them.

Additionally, Millennials are seeking to dispel satisfaction in the marketplace. They're accelerating everything from how our workplace looks, feels, and operates to the products and services that are created. However, as what I term *new-generation traditionalists,* they understand the value of keeping what is familiar and known. Subconsciously, I believe they've experienced enough of the boom-and-bust cycle of the past few decades to know that this is a wise and important strategy. This innovative pioneering comes from the ability to utilize the unconscious intellect they possess and mobilize and analyze it with their conscious intellect.

Every business is different, and I can't give you a specific strategy other than to tell you that between the two polar choices in this world, there is a variety of lovely shades of gray where you will find solutions, creativity, innovation, and collective achievement. Rather than locking down your people into cubes and spreadsheets all day, allow them to use their unconscious intellect. If they're walking and talking, usually to themselves, it doesn't mean they're goofing off — they're working out a solution or figuring out how to express what's bubbling below the surface. (See the nearby sidebar for an example of the power of walking and talking.)

Just so you know, people who spreadsheet all day also have an unconscious intellect if you give them a chance. They'll just express it differently.

REMEMBER

Innovative solutions can be found when you allow your unconscious intellect to slow the pace down enough so you can hear it. Then your conscious intellect can analyze it, spreadsheet it, and put it into action.

WALKING AND TALKING TO AN END

Over the years I've worked with executives who have at times experienced deadlock in their units or organizations. It happens. We just get stuck in a rut and nothing is working. One day, a client of mine in New York City asked if I would take a walk with her. We left the big office, went over to Bryant Park, and walked through the grass lawn behind the New York Public Library. As we walked, she talked and I stayed silent. We made our way onto the lovely pathways littered with French bistro tables and chairs. She kept talking. I just nodded. Finally, after a half hour we settled on a bench. She looked at me and said, "Oh my goodness, I think I've got the solution. Thanks for helping me work this out." I laughed and reminded her that I hadn't said a word during the time we walked and talked.

To this day, this executive does a walk and talk in whatever patch of nature she can find to connect to her unconscious intellect. And nearly every time, she finds her solution. The best part of this story is that recently, as it snowed here in NYC, I saw her walking in Bryant Park with two other executives, hands waving, intently chatting, super focused. I rang her later in the day and mentioned I'd seen her and the crew. She said that's how they have meetings now when there's a deadlock — it's a walk and talk. Unless it's horrible weather, they hit the park and walk until they find solutions. Sometimes it takes a few rounds over a few days.

Exercising your unconscious intellect

TIP Walking and talking — in which you take a leisurely walk and talk about an issue you're having and see whether you come up with a solution — is one strategy for exercising your unconscious intellect. Personally, interaction with the outdoors really helps me slow down what's going on enough to be able to think more clearly and interrupt tension or frustration. Some people love it. Others recoil from it.

However, there is also something to activities with rhythmic patterns that becomes very meditative and defuses *brain lock* — you know, when you just can't think your way out of a problem. Often you see an individual starting at you, blinking as the super computer that is their brain is completely locked and unable to find a solution. Here are a few other ideas for you to overcome these blocks. Please feel free to add to this list:

- **Go to a local museum.** If you work with creative people and they're blocked, take the walk and talk concept to a local museum. Something in their consciousness needs to be unclogged. New shapes, colors, mediums, and executions can act like Drano for their creativity.

- **Meet at the beach.** When I worked in Australia, I used to take my team to St. Kilda Beach and have our weekly meeting in the sunshine. The meetings took a bit longer, but it was far more impactful, creative, and light.

- **Try the botanical gardens.** This is one of my favorites. On a weekend, I'll head out to Coe Hall in Oyster Bay to walk through the greenhouses on the estate. It's beautiful. I'm sure there is either a local garden or park nearby that will do the trick for you.

- **Get a Ping-Pong and/or pool table.** For those who aren't Millennials or wired like Millennials, this one may be harder to embrace. Playing games such as these lets you depart from a routine and relax your mind. Obviously, a two-week tournament wouldn't be a great idea, but having this playfulness in spurts works.

- **Chop, cook, knit.** Activities outside of the workplace that create a repetitive rhythm are another way to engage your creativity. The repetition satisfies the conscious side of your brain — you're doing something useful, so it won't freak out. It also allows your unconscious side to bubble up and sort things out.

- **Row, run, kayak.** Basically, this invokes the same principle as the preceding point. Repetitive rhythmic activities are immensely useful.

Notice that the preceding activities are all opportunities to be taken outside of the normal confines you're working within. Outside stimulation shakes the cobwebs, impasses, or roadblocks free.

There are many other ways to tap into this side of your brain. Go forth, experiment, and don't apologize for wanting this for yourself and others. As long as everyone is on the same page and committed to their part, you'll be fine. You still have a deadline to hit and expectations to meet to satisfy the corporate gods and your goals.

Dovetailing the basics into an HR strategy

Who are your people? And what are they actually good at? Not what they tell you they're good at, but what is inherent in them that possibly has gone untapped? A strong human resource team that understands human capital is the most valuable tool in the company will take the time to understand who their people are. In an organization that spans several states or countries, this is a tall order. However, the skill of segmenting HR professionals to work with specific teams in the organization is commonplace. How well do they know what these assets are capable of?

My personal preference when working with clients on this issue is to use a system called Worktraits (www.worktraits.com) to determine job fit and hidden skill sets. After all, just because someone comes into the workplace to do a specific job doesn't mean that's all they're capable of. Uncovering their latent skills and natural aptitudes, creative or not, will help you build a more proactive organization in a very organic manner. It will also provide insight into where and how to move people through the organization. Organic growth is far less expensive than externally recruiting. Feel free to reach out if you're interested in this work for your organization: info@mariagamb.com.

Millennials and most of the workforce today crave new challenges and experiences in their work — they like to change their positions faster than an organization may stipulate. Often an employer requires an employee to be in their position for 18 months before moving into a new role. Awareness of this cohort's desire to move is great, but it may not always be realistic to fulfill in their desired time frame. However, you can prepare for it by identifying those who are natural innovators, creators, and adventure seekers/risk takers through evaluations mentioned earlier. These folks should be scattered throughout the organization to stimulate innovation across the board.

Igniting Innovation with a Few Principles and Pointers

To further clarify how the VBL model helps create an environment where change, innovation, and creativity thrive, consider the principles and pointers in the following sections.

Setting ground rules with five agreements to foster innovation

REMEMBER

Setting ground rules, even in a VBL organization, is always important for clarity, even when you think you've been clear already. Implied rules can be misunderstood or even twisted to the benefit of those who may have less than pure motives. The following five agreements can be transposed onto many processes throughout the organization. The ideal is to be a resilient organization focused on keeping pace and exceeding expectations:

» **Transparency:** Change, creativity, and innovation require transparency of facts, findings, and truths. All the information can't be held at the top — it needs to be shared so that innovation can follow an informed thought process. Briefs and directives must include all facts you have on hand, which may influence or even deter your innovators and creatives.

» **Refinement:** The process will require refinement, which may or may not include opinions and ideas from others. Top leadership needs to consider that the solution may not be 100 percent right the first time around. Tweaks and refinements will always be part of the process. Once a solution has been created, consider testing it across a sample group of managers and the hands-on employees who would be engaging with the solution. The insights and suggestions from those who are end users will help the solution's creator peek into its feasibility. Other options are customer surveys, focus groups, and user assessments.

» **Servitude:** No matter what, the group will return to the concept of servitude. We, the group, create, innovate, and offer change ideas to serve the people of this company and our customers. (See the later section "Challenging your team members to look beyond themselves" for more information on this concept.) At times those who offer solutions may have a conscious or unconscious attachment to their particular solutions. They may need to be right, seen as in charge or as the authority. Remind them that it's about serving the end customer. I've found that once you do so, they will right themselves.

» **Cocktails:** A variety of resources, support functions, and vendors are required to create the perfect cocktail for getting something done. I'm willing to be open to newness in these areas as part of the process. Create a think tank of trusted resources and knowledgeable partners, both internal and external, to find solutions or the pathway to innovation. Just be mindful not to cast your net too widely early on. Too many opinions can dilute the process. Be sure to circle back around to the refinement point earlier in this list.

» **Consciousness:** The group will consider the effect on the communities we serve where our products are produced and the organization's teams are housed (remote offices) by utilizing a singular question: Are we violating the rights of these individuals with our choices? That means, at a minimum, considering environmental and social effects on others. Today, a hot button for corporations is to consider where they produce their products: Are we polluting the water, causing chemical waste that endangers the people who live around the production site? Or are the workers being paid a fair wage? This may sound like common sense, but finding the balance between profits and the impact you have on others must be considered in the same moment.

TIP There are a number of resources supporting the five agreements listed. Consider jumping to Chapter 4 to reacquaint yourself with the shared value economy concept, which illustrates how companies cooperate and find solutions that benefit all parties involved in the process. Of particular interest would be how the organization partners with vendors to create solutions. The model, in my humble opinion, is truly one of inclusive cooperation that leads to innovative solutions. Also, in Chapter 16 you find a section on "pickup sticks" that also supports learning from mistakes to find solutions.

Reducing control, increasing trust

Trying to control the team and the innovative process is very much like squeezing a tube of toothpaste: Treat it gently, and the tube will yield enough toothpaste for weeks to come. Handle it roughly or try to cram it into a small compartment of your bathroom drawer, and it will burst all over the place. With that said, consider the following guidelines for your team:

» **Do** establish parameters with a project timeline and deadlines.

» **Do** set benchmarks and check-in points along the way.

» **Do** create *think tank* or *collaborative* opportunities for the person, team, or group to exchange ideas as the process unfolds.

» **Do** use the "what if" line of questioning to stimulate the group's thought process. For example: *What if this feature could XYZ?* This triggers deeper thought about how or what can be done.

» **Don't** micromanage the process.

Handling the process gently is key, but you need to establish some structure to corral the geniuses, thought leaders, and innovators in your company.

REMEMBER: Give people enough space to think, dream, ponder, and operate, sometimes even when there isn't a particular goal in mind. This is an exercise in trust. The more staff members feel like they're trusted, the more likely they'll be to take risks (calculated ones, of course) and try new things to find solutions.

Keeping it fresh by rotating contributors

Have you ever listened to a conversation in a meeting and thought to yourself, *The answer is so darn easy. They're just complicating it.* People who are detached from a process or who have no ownership of an idea are far more objective than those who are close to it.

TIP: Rotate people from various skill sets within the company into areas where they may not normally be considered for a stint of a week, a month, or more. The guy from accounting may have an unusual take on current projects or processes that could improve the group's effectiveness. Flip to Chapter 14 for more on job rotation.

Challenging your team members to look beyond themselves

I briefly touch on this point in the earlier section "Setting ground rules with five agreements to foster innovation." However, it's a concept worth reinforcing a bit more. Considering what a team needs to remedy in terms of processes and procedures to make things flow more easily is one part. The second part is always about serving customers better. I'm not necessarily talking solely about client relationships. I'm suggesting that you consider how to improve the quality of the life of your customers through the product(s) or service(s) offered. Often a team has a myopic point of view that limits their effectiveness.

WARNING: Refrain from offering either-or options during the process of improving customer service. As mentioned earlier, either-or thinking limits the choices, possibilities, and potential evolution while you're in this process.

What serves the *customer* rather than the group's own attachment to the product or service? This is a point of self-reflection for the unit as well as an opportunity to teach them this skill to prepare them to think, be, and do in a different manner than they may do in other companies. It's not always easy to bypass attachment — even with its good intention. Attachments can be debilitating and limit the expansion of the offering because the end intention is more about the individual offering it rather than the goal of finding a solution. Now that's just out of whack.

Recognizing that people won't necessarily embrace change or growth

Innovation brings change, and change is necessary for a company to grow, expand, and keep pace. Bifurcation is the fork in the road. Choose to up level, change, grow, and adapt, and the company moves toward continued commerce. Take the other road, and risk extinction. (Flip to Chapter 1 where I illustrate the concept of bifurcation.) Creating change is, after all, in part why we are all here in this book. Table 18-2 summarizes the pros and cons of innovation in business.

TABLE 18-2 **Pros and Cons of Innovation**

Arguments for Innovation	Arguments against Innovation
Serve and keep pace with the marketplace.	Stick with what we know.
Ideally create a unique selling proposition by being a market leader.	Newness creates risk.
Use proactive measures.	Shifting focus from the core of our business takes our eye off the bread and butter that pays the bills.
Avoid extinction caused by refusing to innovate.	Too much change too fast can't be accomplished.
Reduce stagnation and boredom.	The future is to be feared.
Break free of routine.	Progress should be rejected.

The beauty of individuality is that you need a point of difference in thinking to create balance. I can assure you that not everyone will be onboard with innovation. There will be a naysayer in the corner looking at you with contempt, or those who grumble over their steaming coffee and kombucha tea. Guess what? You need them. Yes, that's right. You actually need them to be the voice of reason when or if the pendulum swings too far in one direction. I know; they can be so annoying. However, some of their points may indeed be valid.

People will self-select their level of commitment to VBL and the initiatives the organization has set out. Some will leave. That's okay. Refer to Chapter 19 for more on this point.

> **IN THIS CHAPTER**
> » Auditing and assessing each departure to make repairs
> » Establishing the factors to create and maintain a resilient organization

Chapter 19
Being Willing to Let People Go

You've done your best to set a leadership style that creates an environment in which everyone can participate fairly. You've involved your downline managers and set a course for action within the organization. Still, you may find a group of people standing in front of you with their arms folded in resistance, saying, "This isn't for me." You may not be able to change their minds, and if you can't, unfortunately they will leave your company. But life is funny. They may boomerang back to you at another time. Either they need perspective by taking another job, or they simply may not be a fit for the culture of the company.

For most of my working career, I've understood that people don't quit jobs, they quit leadership. Either they respect you and will follow you to the goalpost, or they view you with contempt and lack of respect — and sometimes they just plain don't like you. The liking part is often beyond your control — it's personal, period. The rest is a matter of perceptions: Will their needs be met, will you invest in them, will you back them up, and do they believe in your collective vision?

The other buckets for leaving come from a family or relocation need. The rest would still fall under the categories of fulfillment of their needs, expectations, and having an opportunity for growth.

There may be things you can do to change their minds, but sometimes you have to let them go. In this chapter, I provide pointers on the assessment you should undertake when people leave and discuss how to maintain the values of your organization.

Asking Questions and Showing Acceptance When People Leave

Values-based leadership (VBL) is a mission to unify and create safe workplaces without regard to race, gender, sexual orientation, or economic standing. It aims to hit the reset button and remind all leaders that there's a way to be balanced, powerful, and an instrument for good in this world — while still being profitable. Within this framework, everyone can find elements to customize their impact.

Leadership is a practice of love and selflessness. VBL is pioneering work that creates innovation. It's heart-centered work that creates meaning. Best of all, it comes in one package. Thank you for having the willingness to take on the role to make this shift. Thank you for your commitment to change what has been the norm in business. By doing so, you're changing the world around you.

With this shift, the dynamic of the company will change. It's impossible for it *not* to undergo change. People will leave, and that's okay — you can assess what happened with the help of this section. It's about assessing your own self-doubt or concern: Did you do the right thing?

Playing the "what if" game of possibilities

Here is a game I often play with staff and clients: "What if" this or that happened? The point of the game is to open up your mind to possibilities new and old or even those buried deep in your mind. The following are some examples of "what if" questions to ask when someone decides to leave the organization:

» What if I hadn't shifted the organization — what would have happened? If I had left it alone, would this person be leaving?

» What if there are people with even more exceptional skills to replace them?

» What if I could let go and allow them their journey?

» What if I could let go of my own personal hurt or disappointment — how would that change things?

» What if this was the right catalyst for all of our lives?

Each question is open ended to allow you the opportunity to consider the alternatives. You may come across a few answers that will provide insight into adjustments you may want to make to your current structure. That's fine. While you may be happy to see some people go, others will make you wonder about what you could have done better. Follow the line of questions to see what that could possibly be.

REMEMBER

We may seek to control every aspect of life and want to do so for those in the organization. Free will is a powerful thing. Each of us has the ability to make the choices we think are best for our lives. Respecting each individual's path is a sign of being willing to let go.

Conducting a more detailed kind of exit auditing

This section moves on to the more clinical process. There will always be a number of talented people leaving any organization. Attrition is normal. Regular exit interviews and/or surveys will provide insight into why. However, if there's a mass exodus from a particular team or area, or if a pattern of leaving is emerging across the organization, then it's time to take a deeper look.

Whatever the catalyst has been to bring them to the point of wanting to leave, you have to go back to the beginning. Ask yourself these questions:

» Is it them?

» Is it us? *Us* meaning the leadership and management teams.

» Where did we fall short?

A formal survey is also suggested. Exit interviews or surveys are a standard part of most businesses' human resource toolkit. Over the years I have filled out more than one. They are not always about complaints; you can find useful information to refine certain aspects of your approach, management, succession planning, and so on. Human resource professionals have told me that they've seen exit interviews where an employee nearly bursts into tears because they may not want to leave but their spouse is being relocated. Or sometimes a key individual loves the company, their manager, the mission, and the context of their work, but they are leaving to either take care of a family issue or just take a year off to explore the world.

In these examples, you see what's *good*. But they are also clues: Flexibility is a common thread in these examples. Employees tell you this without actually saying the words. It may be time to consider whether some positions can be executed remotely, which would make some resignations due to relocation unnecessary. Perhaps a more robust family leave or sabbatical policy can retain those who seek such options.

So is it *us* or is it *them*? I'll reframe that: What can *we* do better? Listen to your exit interviews and surveys as the guide to answer that question.

If the mechanisms aren't in place to retain employees, then head to Chapter 1, where the basic principles of setting out to create a values-based culture are detailed. What's missing? Could it be trust? If so, check out Chapter 9. Perhaps you've not invested in education and training; head to Chapter 14 for some options on those topics. There are any number of possible issues. Asking, or auditing, is always a good idea.

TIP: For examples of exit interview options, head to the Society for Human Resource Management's website: www.shrm.org. It's an invaluable resource for many human resource–related topics.

Practicing forgiveness and acceptance

No matter what the cause of the departure, it's critical to forgive errors that you or your deputies or managers caused. It's important that those in leadership positions understand that mistakes, missteps, and miscommunication are part of being human. Leaders and managers shouldn't be tormented, exiled, or ostracized for making mistakes as long as they're making moves to correct the issues.

Forgiveness, acceptance, and correction keep everything moving forward. Learning from a mistake, even a person's departure, helps you course correct to build a better environment.

REMEMBER: Forgiveness and acceptance should be extended to you forgiving yourself as well. If you're having sleepless nights, tossing and turning as you mull over the mistake you made the other day, it's time to consider accepting that you're human; make your apologies for the error or misstep, and take actions to correct the situation. Then let go of the self-judgment. It's easier said than done for some. Consider activities such as meditation or something more physical such as kickboxing or running to help you let go.

TIP: I can't finish this section without mentioning the words of one of my long-ago coaches: "Would you rather be right or happy?" The first time he said those words to me, I was distressed over something. The question is about the willingness to accept what is and move forward or to continue to thrash about and make yourself miserable. You can translate this question in many ways: Do you need to be right — so much so that you'll go to whatever lengths to prove that you're right and that everyone knows you're right? Additionally, is it important to make another person *pay* for their mistakes or perceived violations because, after all, you're right? These questions are just a little something to consider.

Staying True to Your Values

Not all people want to play the values-based game. It's not aggressive enough for them, or it threatens them in some way. I honestly can't explain why it would threaten them, except that yes, it's different. Sometimes that's enough. People don't like their apple cart overturned. In this section, I explain what to do so that your organization stays true to its values.

REMEMBER

People will come and people will go. Some may leave on poor terms. Others will hug you goodbye and shed a tear. No matter how it transpires, if you allow them the dignity of their departure and know that at another time your paths may cross, you'll be remembered for your grace. And when they come back into your orbit years later, you may be looking at the exact answer to your prayers! That person who annoyed everyone may have matured, and the one who fought you the hardest on deploying values in the workplace may admit to having been wrong. In any case, accept their decision and move forward. You never know — you may be walking through an airport on your way to a family vacation and be stopped by an old employee who says, "I'm sorry I was such a pain in the butt." Or even: "Thank you for everything you've done knowingly and unknowingly. I wouldn't be where I am today without your leadership and powerful example. You probably don't even remember me! But I'll never forget you." Pass the tissues! Know that you've changed people's lives.

Rebalancing your efforts

The basic principles and applications of VBL are timeless. Kindness, compassion, fairness, and the ability to engage and impact communities will never be passé — unless ego takes over. *Snowflake* is a term we hear nowadays, referring to the opposite of prior generations' aggressiveness. I ask you to embrace these VBL concepts as an equalizer to both extremes.

REMEMBER

Business models, even the shared values economy, will continue to evolve. I'm counting on the Millennial generation to show us some new stuff. Regardless, continue making your tweaks. Add more here, and take a little bit from there, until you find the correct balance for you and your organization. You may be the one who creates the next dynamic business model that further improves our interconnected, shared responsibility to one another. In the meantime, hold fast to what you can action right here and now. Each of the following represents commitment to creating and maintaining a resilient organization:

- Utilizing your values in every facet of the organization to create a strong corporate culture and operational presence
- Ensuring a healthy workplace for everyone
- Practicing economic corporate social responsibility, both locally and globally (see Chapter 4)
- Using your reputation as a values-based organization to recruit and retain the best talent (see Chapter 14)
- Continuing to invest in a culture of learning (see Chapter 15)
- Creating values partnerships with vendors and resources (see Chapters 4 and 21)
- Reinventing and pioneering new processes and business models (see Chapters 4 and 18)

Locating your fellow travelers

It won't always be easy. It may comfort you to reflect that countless others are on the same journey. You'll find one another — leaders just like you. Like attracts like. In fact, I'll bet you already have many colleagues on the same quest. It's always interesting to me to notice that I tend to sit with those who are like-minded at a conference or networking event. Those who hold similar values seem to find each other in a crowd. I can't quite explain how this organic process happens, but it does. If you're less likely to want to leave it to chance, explore groups, associations, and institutions that are as passionate about leadership and meaning in business.

VBL is a conduit for returning commerce to a way of being both a noble good and a way of working that will bring profits. They're complementary — they're *not* mutually exclusive. It takes a special group of individuals to persist.

When you and I see one another at events, airports, and social media sites, please stop, say hello, and extend a handshake — or even a hug. We're all in this together. I applaud you and support your commitment. You're not alone. And you most certainly don't need to be perfect.

CREATING THE CIRCLE OF CONTINUITY

I've been telling a story for years about the circle of continuity. It was a valuable lesson provided to me by a sweet woman I worked with in Hong Kong for several years. In my circle, she's a bit of a celebrity. To this day I still have so much love and respect for her because she raised me in this business for years and taught me to be a more mature leader — one with compassion and tolerance.

For weeks, we had been negotiating over a particular product. I became frustrated because we weren't getting anywhere. As we pored over the details, I finally said to her, "I give up. Tell the vendor this is the price. Take it or leave it. I don't care." Ah, the exuberance of youth, inexperience, and misplaced confidence that I knew what I was doing!

She put her hand on my arm and softly said, "Maria, the world is round." Smiling, she sat back in her chair. I had no idea what she was talking about, so I asked her — what goes around comes around, maybe? She smiled. "No, the world is round. You will work with this vendor again or you will work with someone here again — perhaps in this organization or in another. You must always be the best you can: Cooperate, bend when necessary, and give when asked. This is the road to cooperation." I blushed at my own stupidity. She continued, "So, where will you bend? Forget what you've done before on this project. Where will you bend to allow them to save face?"

It was a lesson beyond negotiation and fairness. It was a *life* lesson — to understand that we will always be in the same orbit. That it's not always necessary to be right, or to be the strongest, or smartest, or most clever. What is important is to allow people their dignity, and when they give you the best they can, be gracious.

ём # The Part of Tens

IN THIS PART . . .

Find your own self-reflection practice, through meditation and other techniques, to stay on track as a values-based leader.

Find ways to ensure that you connect with your team with ease, grace, and personalization.

Recognize the massive impact that the new Millennial-driven workforce will have on commerce and many other aspects of society.

Unmask common myths in the workplace about women, flexibility, and other often overlooked blind spots.

IN THIS CHAPTER

» Boosting your self-awareness and clarity

» Establishing a support network

Chapter **20**

Ten Practices to Stay on Track as a Values-Based Leader

Leadership is not for the faint-hearted. There's a delicate balance between having confidence and being insecure. Leaning to one side or another can cause an imbalance in your approach: Excessive confidence can lead to being perceived as arrogant, and showing insecurity can make you seem wishy-washy. As always, of course, you're human. Meaning you're imperfect. Everything that comes before you on your journey in values-based leadership (VBL) can help refine you as a human and a leader.

People will tell you that it's hard work. At times, it will be. However, the best way to combat this perception is to build in practices that will help you lay a strong foundation and traverse the times when bumps can't be avoided. It takes honesty and a willingness to check in on yourself regularly. That can be done in a variety of ways, as this chapter explains. Self-reflection and awareness, as I say throughout this book, are important aspects of VBL. For times when you can't do that for yourself, I also offer you some outside assistance in this chapter.

Setting a Daily Audit Practice

People often lose sight of what they're doing because they're just too close to what's going on. Taking a moment to pause, focus, and become aware takes only a few minutes each day. (I can tell you want to skip this one. Hold on! Don't go yet.)

Take a few minutes each morning to ask yourself the following questions and set an intention for your day:

- What do I need to accomplish today?
- How can I best serve the organization and my team today?
- If there were one thing I could impart to others today that would make a difference, what would that be?

At the end of the day ask similar questions:

- What did I accomplish today?
- How did I serve the organization and the team today?
- Where and how could I have been a better leader?

REMEMBER: The point is not to flog yourself or create a litany of to-do lists, but to realize that you *lead* people — which means they'll follow you. It's a matter of checking in to remind yourself of that authority and to use it with care. Everyone knows a leader they could refer to as a *wrecking ball.* Make sure you are not among those leaders. Constant self-reflection and self-awareness are important ingredients in VBL.

Embracing Meditation

Clearing the goop out of your head is a useful thing, yes? Yes! As a values-based leader, your goals, as prescribed in this book, are to have a clear vision, foster an atmosphere of innovation, guide others to success, and encourage teamwork. That's the short list. Meditation quiets your mind, clearing the path to accomplish these objectives with clarity, focus, clearer communication, improved relationships, and increased productivity.

TIP *Harvard Business Review* offers a wonderfully concise overview of the benefits of meditation by CEOs at `https://hbr.org/2015/12/how-meditation-benefits-ceos`. Here are a few other resources you may want to check out — choose what works best for you:

- Pick up a copy of *Meditation For Dummies* by Stephan Bodian (published by Wiley).
- Deepak Chopra, a renowned alternative medicine advocate, provides online and in-person resources: `https://chopra.com/meditation`. (By the way, he and Oprah Winfrey regularly run a 21-day mediation series. Feel free to join in with millions of others meditating.)
- The Center for Transcendental Meditation offers classes in many cities. Visit `www.tm.org`.
- Check what's available locally in your area; online resources are plentiful.

TIP Depending on the breadth of your influence as a leader, you can keep this technique for yourself or roll it out to your staff as an option for them too. It's completely up to you. However, if mindfulness is improving the performance of top leaders, you'd have to wonder what it could do for all who would like to participate in your organization.

Finding Your Own Spiritual Practice

You're a spiritual being having a human experience each and every day of your life. No matter what your beliefs may be, I encourage you to connect to them deeply as a way of centering yourself and staying in touch with the good inside of you. Handling people and balancing business's bottom-line requirements aren't always the easiest thing. People with spiritual practices, I've noticed, seem to be more connected to the bigger reason they are sitting in their role. But, as I said, this is my observation — VBL isn't about faith, spirituality, or religion. But if you've got some of that in your personal life, it may help sustain you through the good times and the bad times.

TIP At the very least, find a piece of literature that you enjoy and read a bit of it each day. If you pray, pray. If you meditate, meditate. If you like to go to church or on retreats, do so. Any practice can be helpful.

Disengaging Your Ego

I've set self-reflection points throughout this book. Some are calls to action. Self-reflection and managing one's ego are keys to a long shelf life as a values-based leader. There are times when any one of us can feel anger and want to lash out. Sometimes people have a knee-jerk reaction to a particular situation that may or may not be associated with anger. It could be a matter of self-protection and survival.

No matter how focused or well intended, you and I are mere mortals who are driven by sometimes conscious but often unconscious triggers. Classify it as a combination of ego and our primal limbic systems:

>> The part of the ego I'm pointing to is the one that places you above everyone else. Call it selfishness or narcissism as part of our psychological makeup.

>> The limbic system is the part of your brain that's been programmed to ensure that you survive — fight or flight. When triggered, it will always make the choice for your survival.

In either case, you have the power to hit the pause button in order to evaluate a situation and make a better, more neutral choice. Ask yourself the following:

>> Is this reaction about me or them? Go with your initial reaction.

>> Will this reaction serve and/or advance everyone? What about at least a majority?

>> Am I violating the rights of others with my choice and/or reaction?

REMEMBER In any given situation, these points of self-reflection can be deployed to assess and disengage your ego from the process. When you know it's about you and your gain solely, you may have a moment of shame or embarrassment internally. It's better that it happens internally, rather than publicly being pointed out. How's that for a motivating factor to deploy this type of reflection? So just do it. Make it a practice, and it will become part of how you operate every day.

Forgiving Your Shortfalls

Telling someone to forgive themselves is often met with a grimace. They may think they don't deserve to be forgiven. Embarrassment and shame seep in, and the normal course after that is to want to hide. But if you can accept your shortcomings and diligently work toward not making the same mistakes again — without self-flagellation — you'll be more likely to succeed.

WARNING: Mistakes are learning tools. If you can embrace this simple truth in your own life, then you can impress it upon others in your organization. This is the critical factor in forgiveness. When you don't forgive yourself or others, you create an energetic jail where no amount of penance or recompense is enough. And that's demoralizing and counterproductive, so avoid it, okay?

Every shortfall or mistake is an opportunity to learn something and then make the necessary adjustments. Consistent movement in this direction will make you a better person as well as a better values-based leader. Folks who don't operate with this in mind may be perceived as lazy, careless, or, well, a wrecking ball. I think we all could name several high-level leaders in the public eye who fit into that category. Be better by learning from your mistakes.

Eliminating the Things That Cause Brain Fog

Full disclosure. I'm not a supermodel, nor am I a nutritionist. But I am a high-performing human being who's very aware of what happens to my brain and body when I don't eat well (with *well* being a subjective term — everyone is different). Several things will cause brain fog, crankiness, and moodiness — high amounts of simple carbohydrates, sugar, soda, and saturated fats, for starters. Human beings aren't really built to consume those items.

Think about the last time you ate pasta. Did you wake up feeling almost hungover? Or as if you hadn't gotten a good night's sleep? If so, it was most likely the pasta. You want to start your day with clarity and focus, right? Some individuals suffer from mood swings if they consume too much sugar. For example, I can eat two squares of really good dark chocolate, but any more sugar than that and I'm annoyed with everyone around me.

Your job as a values-based leader is to be *on* almost 100 percent of the time. That means you can't afford to be routinely foggy, tired, or moody. Do your best to eliminate whatever doesn't serve you. Some people can drink espresso without having any caffeine side effects — I'm that person. However, a friend who is in a high-level leadership position at a major international bank can't even look at any kind of coffee after 3 p.m. He wouldn't sleep because he'd be bouncing off the walls. Know yourself and what causes you not to function at the level you need to. Then remove it. Seek the support of a trained nutritionist to help you balance yourself out.

Raising Endorphins to Gain Clarity and Reduce Stress

Running, kickboxing, Zumba, cycling, or most classes at your local Y will all work to raise your endorphins. Releasing endorphins reduces stress and pain, acting similarly to codeine and morphine. Removing or lowering stress in your body won't just help your attitude —they'll help you think more clearly too, which is always important for a values-based leader. Extra benefits include boosting your sex drive, modulating appetite, and increasing feelings of euphoria. Now that's not bad!

TIP If you're like me, running isn't ever going to happen, so resort to a small amount of super dark chocolate — 80 percent cacao or higher — which also helps release small amounts of endorphins. Beware chocolate with lower levels of cacao, because they're loaded with sugar. (Sorry to say, but milk chocolate is the enemy, my friend.)

Couple any of the preceding items with laughter to ensure a healthy blast of endorphins daily. Yes, laughter also releases these powerful brain feel-good chemicals. To find out more about how laughter impacts human beings positively, check out the Harvard Maloney Neuroscience Institute Letter article titled "Humor, Laughter, and Those Aha Moments" (https://hms.harvard.edu/sites/default/files/HMS_OTB_Spring10_Vol16_No2.pdf).

Using Technology to Prompt Excellence

If you're a Millennial, me telling you which apps and technology tools to use would be laughable. By the time this book is printed, they'd be out of date anyway. My point here is that you should make use of the technology available to create a culture of excellence. What that means is keeping people organized, on time, and on schedule with the appropriate tools. In particular, that means you. People follow your disciplines and behaviors when you're a values-based leader. Show them the best practices by using the tools yourself.

Establishing a Trusted Feedback Group

Peer groups are essential to your continued success as a values-based leader; they can point out what's not obvious to you or what you may be kidding yourself about. Every person needs a small group of people who will be honest with them about not only behavior and decision-making processes but also the effect they have on those around them. For example: "Jim, do you realize what a jerk you were to that person?" Or: "Barbara, that decision you made had short-term value, but in the long term this is going to become a big problem for you." Your peer group also won't be afraid to call you on it: "So, how are you going to fix this?"

Peers will be the most honest with you. Sometimes they're within your own organization — those you work side by side with or previously worked on the same team with. Choose those who won't placate you or tear you down. Peers who are willing to be honest, even if it's not what you want to hear, can help you become a better leader by providing an outside, more objective yet informed view for you.

Alternately, the group may be a combination of friends and colleagues who are happy to be your sounding board. However, choose those who have experience in what you do. Otherwise their feedback is only advice unfounded in practical application or experience. They love you, so you may not always get the best direction from them. It's not their fault.

WARNING The purpose of this circle is to be honest with each other. It shouldn't become a group where egos are stroked and backs are slapped. When it turns into a coffee klatch, to put it politely, it may be fun but it will be useless for gaining feedback.

Engaging a Mentor

You can't be all things to all people. Myths of superwomen and supermen have led to exhaustion and self-loathing when we find we can't do it all. So don't do it alone.

Engage a mentor who can help guide you through some of the more difficult decisions and hurdles you'll face. This can be someone in the organization, but more than likely it's someone you either worked with at a previous company or know through personal or professional networks. Mentors are based on long-term relationships and insights into both your personal and professional growth. (Refer to Chapter 14 where I make the distinction between having a mentor or coach just so you're clear on the difference.)

To this day my most important mentor is a person I worked with about a dozen years ago. She knows me well on many levels and can often tell me when I'm off base or not considering different angles to create a resolution. Thank goodness she's very gentle, but she's also honest enough to tell me whether I've gone rogue on something or to point out when I'm missing a critical piece of an equation. That's the kind of relationship, in my opinion, you should seek.

Keep in mind that having a mentor doesn't necessarily mean you have weekly check-ins. The engagement between both parties is based on the need of the mentee and the availability of the mentor. Additionally, fees aren't usually paid to a mentor. A mentorship is usually an exchange of building goodwill in the world to create stronger professionals. In my experience, it's also often an unspoken agreement that the mentee will pay the same in kind someday to another person who may need their guidance.

Another option is to hire a coach. Coaches serve a short-term purpose to resolve a specific issue you seek to resolve, which is great. If you're having trouble, for example, motivating or retaining your people, a coach can help. However, in my opinion, it's also good to work with a mentor — someone who knows you and will be direct. It saves ramp-up time. I know my mentor would look at me and ask me a direct question about the kinds of work habits I have and my prior track record, which may be creating the situation I'm trying to resolve.

> **IN THIS CHAPTER**
> » Boosting your ability to engage with the team
> » Providing clarity and kindness
> » Establishing and following best practices

Chapter **21**

Ten Tips for Staying Connected with Your Team

There are companies that when you walk through the door, you immediately know who they are. You get the personality and the vibe of the people and their attitude toward the work they do. Others, not so much. Rather, they can feel sterile.

I can recall walking into the downtown office of a large national nonprofit and I immediately got it. It wasn't about decoration or music. It was about the people there. How the receptionist greeted me when I walked through the door even before she knew my name. How long it took my contact to retrieve me from the lobby. What the environment felt like as I walked through the maze of cubicles to the fishbowl meeting room overlooking the skyline.

We can lose sight of the fact that we, the leaders, create this environment. We set the tone, the pace, and the sense of connection to the work. Anyone with some sense of awareness can pick up on these aspects of the culture. The connection between leaders and their teams is what makes or breaks an organization, as you find out in this chapter. Consistency and modeling become the action points for all who are participating in the growth of the organization. It starts with you.

Making Time to Get to Know Everyone

The truth is that not everyone will want to be your friend. If you try too hard with an employee, for example, they will suspect that something is either wrong with you or wrong with them. As in, they're wondering whether they're in trouble for something or whether you're stopping by to see if they're working.

TIP As you walk around the office, stop by and say hello. I find walking around with a favorite caffeinated beverage first thing in the morning can be an instant conversation icebreaker. "What's that giant frappé-latte-mocha-thing you're drinking?" "I don't know; I just picked it up off the counter at the local Starbucks. What do you have there?" I don't know why it is that we seem to bond over hot beverages — maybe because beer isn't acceptable to carry around the office at 9 a.m. Coffee can replace the adult beverage as a social icebreaker.

REMEMBER My point is to just be you. Walk around and talk to your team — and not necessarily about metrics, results, or the latest project. Talk about anything else *but* work. Topics like local restaurants, TV shows, music, movies, and sports can be fruitful. Each office has certain staffers who create a mystique around them — for example, "coffee guy," "travel girl," or "football fan." These people make it super easy to find a direct conversation point with them and those who share their passions. Always look for the obvious clues.

Acknowledging Life Accomplishments

The people who work at your organization are human beings. They have home lives, go on adventures, and have all kinds of experiences outside the office. They have families. They have passion for many causes. Some may be on the road to an MBA or competing in a local merengue competition. Others may be celebrating a bat mitzvah or wedding. Life goes on outside the walls of the organization. It isn't necessary to have a cake for everything, but it is always nice to acknowledge others' life accomplishments, milestones, and steps on their journeys. As a values-based company, you'll be considering the best approach to a work-life balance to support the inhabitants of your company culture. It's also nice to celebrate more than the work part of that equation.

REMEMBER People in your organization also want to know that *you* have a life outside of work too. It makes you human, just like them. When you keep that from them, they'll never believe you're authentically interested in who they are as human beings. Obviously, use your best judgment as to what and how much you do share.

Keeping an Open Dialogue

Leadership can lose sight of where the people in their organization are. Things may seem rosy, but maybe the team is struggling for one reason or another. Your values may seem to be in place and rolled out into every nook and cranny of the organization. However, training may have fallen off or completely evaporated over the last few quarters. Managers may be starting to stray from the path you've set. Processes may no longer be working. Regular surveys are a great way to determine whether the ship is still on course.

Some of the following opportunities are formal surveys, while others are assessments that will serve as an opportunity to gain deeper insights:

- Diagnosing what ails your team (Chapter 8)
- Reputation surveys (Chapter 10)
- Going it alone and resetting your team environment (Chapter 12)
- Job fit surveys (Chapter 15)
- Job satisfaction surveys (Chapter 15)
- Management satisfaction (Chapter 15)
- Exit interviews (Chapter 19)

As always, make formal surveys anonymous or optionally anonymous. Anonymous surveys allow employees to be more honest and direct in their responses without fearing any type of consequences.

Equally important is to know what's going well. What *is* working? What matters to them? As business plans change, so can their effects. Surveys help identify how to get ahead of the curve, do more of what's great, and fix what needs fixing. This is a reminder to celebrate what you and the organization are doing well.

Communicating Expectations with Clarity

REMEMBER

"If I know what the expectation is, then I can handle it. Guessing? I'm not good at guessing," said just about every employee on the planet. Never forget that it's your job to make the objectives and plans as clear as day to the leadership team, managers, and ultimately the staff. Make sure steps are clearly defined for getting it done, and communicate it down the line so the plans are executed. Be clear. Be concise. And communicate often. Don't complicate things.

Throughout this book, I discuss making your values statement clear to the team. You can jump to Chapter 11 for details on the construction and delivery of that statement. Here, I am suggesting that in your everyday plans you articulate your expectations on deadlines, project time lines, needs, goals, and just about everything else you ask of your team. For example, if your business is set up based on quarterly goals, create a master calendar with benchmark delivery dates and assignment to pieces of the process. How you accomplish this in your company depends on how you work: project to project, quarterly goals or metrics, account-specific goals, and so on. Your leaders and managers should be in the loop so they can distill the direction down to the hands-on people in the organization.

Saying "Thank You" Often

Thank you should be administered liberally — always. It's a sign of respect for others' time and effort and shows that you're paying attention to the good work they do. If the message to employees is always "Hey, you're not doing enough!" wouldn't it stand to reason that after a while they become discouraged or develop bad attitudes?

> **WARNING:** Guess what spreads faster than the flu in an elementary school? Discontent. What do you think people notice when they walk across your company floor? People who are laughing and smiling or focused and intent. But those who look ticked off all the time are also easy to spot. They have a dark cloud over their head with an invisible sign that says *Keep away*.

Maintaining Promises, Inside and Out

As the leader, it's your responsibility to maintain the company promises and adhere to the values you've established for the organization. If you have an outreach corporate social responsibility (CSR) program, make sure it's in action. If you've invested in your vendors and are moving toward a shared values economic system, make that a priority. On the base level of the organization, keep the promises you've made to the internal team with regard to how they're all to work together and how the organization will sustain them through training, benefits, a safe work environment, and whatever else you've decided to deploy. (See Chapter 4 for more about CSR and the shared values economy.)

When a leader keeps promises and takes actions in alignment with them, others are more apt to follow suit. Baby chicks imprint on the first moving object they see upon leaving their shells. Your staff certainly isn't a brood of baby chicks, and you most certainly aren't the first thing they ever saw, but you *are* the moving object in front of them day to day. They will engage in their own version of imprinting.

REMEMBER: Keeping your promises is a building block to the reputational capital of the organization and, well, you as a leader. You can find more on this concept in Chapter 10.

Keeping Your Door Open

There's nothing more off-putting to the people in your workplace than always having your door closed. Is it sometimes necessary? Absolutely. No question about it. But generally, an open-door policy fosters an atmosphere of cooperation.

In a values-based organization, people operate with an open-door policy. Collaboration is king. If you're aware that your door is closed more often than you like, set up management forums or standing meetings where everyone has the opportunity to talk to the leadership about, well, whatever needs to be dealt with. Establishing such a practice allows you to get your own job tasks done but maintain communication with the team. It provides a necessary boundary and some structure around exchanges.

WARNING: If your door is always closed, people will create stories around what's going on in your office. Humans need to fill in blanks. They don't like voids, and you never know what they'll fill that void with. Get me?

Surveying the Vendor and Resource Base Often

Business needs are always changing, growing, and evolving. That will never change. When you're a values-based leader, keeping your vendors and partners informed and in the loop will help you understand how your relationship is working; new initiatives and consistent work can always be evaluated. Additionally, helping determine where they can extend a growth opportunity is one benefit of communication. If a vendor has a way to do something better, faster, or more economically while still being responsible, you should know about it. Sometimes cutting out the middleman in communications helps get new ideas and opportunities to bubble up to the top more quickly. Finding new solutions helps everyone win. As a values-based leader, these people are your partners that extend beyond your own staff.

TIP: Try not to send the standard, impersonal email: "Click here to take our survey." Sorry to disappoint you, but chances are they're too busy to fill out your survey. In-person forums allow everyone to relax, mingle, and form better relationships. One of the most successful engagements I've seen between a company and its vendors was a yearly gathering in the home office. The successes of the vendors' contributions were celebrated, and projections for future partnership projects were discussed in working groups. The vendors felt included, often commenting that they appreciated the opportunity to participate more intimately with the organizational leaders, managers, and teams. To this day, this company continues this process. It's no wonder that the vendors feel like partners rather than just providers.

REMEMBER: Never forget that without your resources, vendors, production, and service channels, you'll be lost. Treat them like part of the internal team.

Showing Transparency

The younger generations are skeptical and even a bit suspicious. They like to validate facts, figures, and perceptions. Sometimes I think Generation X and Millennials are the ultimate fact checkers, trained by scrutinizing the media all their lives. They're pretty savvy!

Stand and deliver is a technique used in sales organizations. Each team leader stands in a room of peers and makes a commitment to numbers and/or projects completed. It's a way to hold one another accountable for the total organizational goal. Check-ins are done quarterly — at which point it becomes clear who's struggling and who's blowing it out of the water. Can that be embarrassing? Sure, but if the culture is a supportive one, others will offer help to the struggling leader. Because we're all in it together, right? Yes!

Additionally, at the ground level, teams are provided sales results in Monday morning meetings. They celebrate winning teams, cheer on those who are breaking out, and — again, if it's a supportive team — will help those that are fighting an uphill battle.

On both levels, it's a matter of transparency in action. Everyone makes a commitment and everyone participates in the lead-up to the final result. Each organization has different types of markers, stand and delivers, and sales results. Customize it to your group and allow everyone to be part of the win, rather than only part of the shortfall (which, unfortunately, has been the norm in many organizations).

If and when things aren't going so well, everyone will be able to see why. Sometimes you're just going through a growth and/or reset period. It helps people understand why things are tight. They're more apt to cooperate, be supportive, and stretch themselves to help make things better when transparency is the rule of the road.

Modeling Best Practices

The best workplaces are maintained by everyone modeling best practices and engagement principles. Simply put, if you give respect, you'll get respect. When you operate with transparency, others around you will be less likely to hide stuff when things go wrong. Why? Because the atmosphere of cooperation has been cemented — staff can watch leaders and other staff members stumble or get a bit tripped up but still lead with integrity and grace and learn from their experiences.

One of the most powerful active opportunities can be holding week-ending shoebox meetings (sometimes done less often). Shoebox meetings include all the bits and pieces from the week. They're recaps hosted by a leader for the team or teams. I encourage a practice that goes something like the following.

One of the younger associates may have had a meeting with a prospect, vendor, or other adjunct entity to the process. I ask them to tell everyone about the meeting — good, bad, or indifferent. As they describe the highs, lows, and things they weren't quite sure about, people in the room can relate to the situation. When appropriate, they also offer insights, ideas, and tips to the person. But it's not a free-for-all. It's done respectfully.

The last question I always ask is this: What did you learn from this meeting? Usually they can recount what they could do better, list what they didn't know, and describe what they now have a better understanding of. The group will nod in agreement. Participants and observers often take notes.

Best of all, occasionally the leader and top managers will have me do the same thing with them, in front of everyone. It's so important that leaders model the behaviors they expect of others. And it's pretty sobering to have a senior leader say, "Man, if I had only asked this question, rather than that question, it would have been a much quicker process." Or, "I could kick myself for that mistake, but I learned X, Y, or Z."

Healthy values-based organizations share and support one another. Cross-coaching organizations model transparency, dignity, and collaboration and encourage their people to always do their very best.

> **IN THIS CHAPTER**
>
> » Understanding the new group of Millennial leaders
>
> » Discerning the reasons behind what Millennials do and crave
>
> » Digesting how much Millennials will affect every aspect of culture

Chapter **22**

Ten Facts about the Millennial Market, Its Values, and Its Influence

The Millennial generation is set to take over the world. Unfortunately, this group has gotten a very bad — and inaccurate — reputation for being narcissistic and uncaring. It's simply not true. They will prove it, as they are set to move into more leadership positions around 2020 and will continue for decades to come.

The Baby Boomers will begin to retire as soon as they recover from the 2008 financial crisis. They may be hanging around a little longer than anyone expected. But with their longevity comes the passing on of wisdom, knowledge, and history to the 75 million Millennials seeking leadership positions in the coming years. Millennials will represent 2.5 billion people in the global workforce. Millennials will consume the workplace — what they want and need will become non-negotiable in the coming years because they will be writing all the new rules.

The theme of this new breed of leaders is making business more human and full of heart, and values-based leadership (VBL) is a big part of this movement. Knowing more about Millennials and their influence can only help you prepare your organization for the future. (Flip to Chapter 2 for an introduction to all the generations currently in the workforce.)

Millennials Are Powering Different Aspects of the Economy

According to the Pew Research Center, by 2050 there will be 79.2 million Millennials, surpassing the Baby Boomers as the largest generation in history. At this moment, it's as if we're living through the gold rush again. Everyone is running toward this group, who will represent the newest, most powerful economic sector in our history. They will create new businesses and ways of doing business, and will redefine leisure time with their thirst for downtime and off-the-beaten-path travel experiences while balancing family, friends, and work. The sky's the limit in terms of their economic influence.

This new generation of pioneers is also migrating to major cities in droves and staying indefinitely. Statistically, cities are experiencing a greater percentage of growth since the 1920s. Therefore, Millennials will also influence transportation, housing, and the creation of a greater sharing economy. That in turn will influence where and how companies will do business.

Emerging Leaders Have Heart

Women will continue to emerge as leaders, shattering the glass ceiling. A generation that came of age with diversity simply embraces that we are all pretty much the same. In in a time of multicultural saturation and the #MeToo movement, women may experience less discrimination. The future is still to unfold.

According to "The Millennial Leadership Survey" released by Virtuali and WorkplaceTrends.com, 91 percent of Millennials seek to have a leadership position, and 52 percent of those are women. We may finally see the first female president of the United States.

REMEMBER The leadership desire within this cohort is one of wanting to help others succeed, which is counter to the belief that Millennials are selfish and narcissistic. When Millennials are surveyed, money and power only rank in the single percentage digits. They are here to create leadership with, dare I say, *heart.* They will make the workplace one where human beings can be humans without being turned into robots. They are so far beyond the assembly line mentality of the worker that it almost never comes into play when they conceive the new workplace.

Coaching Takes Center Stage

Millennials may be considered the most educated generation in history, and they've established a habit and desire for sustained learning. There are no boundaries for them, as they don't see any difference learning from a late-generation Baby Boomer or an early-stage GenXer. They crave wisdom and insight and are wise enough to want to fast-track their work progress by having a coach from within the organization.

TIP
Access to coaches will need to become a cornerstone of many company packages. There are a variety of ways to set up such programs. One way is purely peer-to-peer to help a new employee get up and running faster. Skip-level coaching fosters accelerated growth and advancement — sometimes, but not always, this would fall into a cross-generational coaching format. Additionally, more and more late-generation staffers are thrilled to be paired with a tech-savvy Millennial. After all, they too are willing to learn how to communicate more effectively with this powerhouse generation. (See Chapter 14 for more about seeking out coaches and long-term mentors.)

Work Cultures Are Collaborative and Connected

Hands down, one of the biggest shifts within the walls of corporations is that this new Millennial workforce overwhelmingly prefers a collaborative work culture over a competitive one. They also want the technology to make competitive work culture a reality. For them, there are no boundaries, so they seek to have technology in order to maintain their assertion, and they expect the organization to supply it.

Collaboration also means building a dynamic network of peers, colleagues, leaders, and resources. They're linked through common mission, purpose, and ambition within each silo. The ability to move in the world with a network that supports them is paramount to their pathway to creating success. Millennials are interconnected through various forms of social media and technology, which they utilize at a dizzying pace. They are always connected. Period.

Flexibility Takes on Heightened Importance

The number one initiative for internal recruiters and human resource professionals is to increase retention. Although great comp packages are part of the equation, the workforce is demanding a high-touch approach. We're living in the age of customization. Millennials aren't interested in the big-box, one-size-fits-all approach. While automation makes their life easier, the high-touch approach is a form of intimacy they seek in the workplace.

Millennials want their leaders to invest time in knowing who they are as individuals, and they want to be challenged and learn. They want a collaborative, dynamic relationship experience, bonded by purpose and inspired by the mission. Above all else, they want to be unleashed to lead initiatives and find new pathways or solutions by using their natural entrepreneurial skills. This means flexibility to explore, create, and innovate. That's quite a tall bill for any organization.

Making a Difference Matters

Millennials crave making a difference in the world around them. They prefer the satisfaction of helping to create social change over professional recognition. This is why integrating meaning, social awareness, and community service are essential to all companies who seek to recruit and retain Millennial talent. More than 80 percent say that making a positive difference in the world is more important than professional recognition.

REMEMBER: Stay on your toes, because you're about to join the roller coaster over the next few decades as Millennials redefine making a difference in the world around them.

Old-School Values Make a Comeback

Often called, the "value-driven generation," Millennials are focused on community and family. As a nation, we've not had a generation so committed to kicking it old-school since the 1950s, although they have no illusions about having a perfect family or perfect children. They do seek to reestablish roots to ground themselves. There's an interconnectedness they seek in order to create a sense of consistency, normalcy, and reliability that they're embedding with a sense of community. But that doesn't mean they'll be stagnant.

Baby Boomers vacationed in Florida, camped out, and drove across the United States, taking in the sights. Their children, the Millennials, will take their tribe (partner and children) to Bali and hike in Nepal or Afghanistan. But they always return to home base, to the community they've created and supported.

Buyers Vote at the Checkout Counter

Millennials are skeptical buyers. They're socially driven and seek companies that fulfill their desire to do good in the world. Nearly 90 percent will purchase from socially driven companies. They seek to be part of something they truly believe in. When job hunting, they'll research a prospective employer's corporate social responsibility policies (see Chapter 4 for details on CSR) and check out their promises with search engines. They're savvy enough to research where they spend their dollars and their talents. If your company can satisfy both their purchase and employment needs, you'll have a very loyal individual before you.

Millennials Resist Mass Media Traps

Millennials are market disruptors in a big way. Media, for example, will be completely overhauled in the coming decades. It's already been turned upside down with the continued penetration of technology. They can get the information they want anywhere, at any time, and in any language they choose. Being interconnected through technology with a plethora of options makes them one of the most informed generations ever. Mass media — traditional TV and cable — are being bypassed as sources because they can't keep up the pace.

Online, almost three quarters of all users deploy an ad blocker. Additionally, advertisers are finding that banner ads and pop-ups are not producing the engagement or sales they used to. Branded content, lifestyle products, and ease of access are the pathways to a Millennial's heart, mind, and wallet. I'm sharing this with you here because it will ultimately be overlaid in the workplace too. Look for your recruitment platforms to evolve considerably in the coming few years too.

A Career Should Have Multiple Experiences

Millennials are more loyal than they are made out to be. They like a bit more consistency in their careers — more than the GenXers, who tend to job hop. Millennials seek some level of consistency and commitment to what they're doing. However, more than half believe they will have anywhere from two to five employers in their lifetime, with an estimation of each stint lasting three to five years. Their priorities are flexibility and new experiences to keep them interested. They want to continually expand their horizons by having multiple experiences within the workplace they've chosen — ideally within 6–12 months of each other.

This desire pairs with the need for career path options as an important piece of your value proposition discussed in Chapter 14. Skills retraining and job rotations help provide the variety of experiences Millennials want to help craft their career path. However, you need to recognize that this group will want to move from one position in the company to another to solidify that desire. If your company policy requires an employee to stay in the same position for at least 18 months (the current norm) before moving into a new position, you may want to either relook at that policy or be sure that the new employee understands this stipulation in the onboarding process.

REMEMBER: The easiest way to make Millennials leave a position or prospective career is to tell them that there is no growth or movement and that their work hours will be a standard nine to five with two weeks of vacation. The way to retain them? Challenge them.

IN THIS CHAPTER

» Uncovering the misleading statistics that skew perceptions

» Discerning where myths derail the needs of an organization

» Identifying opportunities for training

Chapter **23**

Ten Workplace Myths

Misperceptions lead to incorrect conclusions. Ultimately, they can rock your tidy values-based organization by upsetting the talent pool. This chapter debunks ten myths found in the workplace today. Consider them carefully. There just may be a few clues as to what new or different types of training or benefits you may need to support your teams better.

Women Primarily Leave Their Jobs to Have Families

This one had to be placed at the top of the list because it's one of the most common myths in the workplace. So let's set the record straight. Millennial women were surveyed by the London School of Business in 2015, and the survey found the following disparity between the real reasons Millennial women choose to leave their job five to ten years after they've graduated college, as opposed to what most companies perceive to be the reason. Both are listed in order of impact. (Visit www.london.edu/faculty-and-research/lbsr/be-the-company-millennial-women-love#.WkfnWminHct for full details.)

Millennial women say they leave their jobs for these reasons:

» I've found a better paying job elsewhere.

» Growth and learning opportunities are limited in my current organization.

» I'm seeking bigger challenges in my career that also have meaning.

Organizations typically believe women leave for the following reasons:

» I'm seeking more flexibility to create a healthier work-life balance.

» I'm planning on starting a family.

» Growth and learning opportunities are limited within my current organization.

While flexibility is currently a big topic in the workplace — as discussed in Chapter 14 — it's not just about starting a family.

REMEMBER: The remedy is just about everything covered in this book. Smart leaders pay attention to the facts. Make the necessary shifts to retain women in your organization; they will factor into being more than half of those seeking leadership positions in the coming decades. The truth will set you free — it will also help you keep great talent.

Men Aren't as Interested in Work-Life Balance

Fathers, like mothers, are finding it difficult to balance work and raising a family. Nearly an equal amount of men and women would prefer to be home raising their children but can't for financial reasons. More and more, fathers who can are choosing to stay home to be the primary caregiver. The belief that only women can hold such a role is a myth.

According to Pew research (see www.pewresearch.org/fact-tank/2017/06/15/fathers-day-facts/), 52 percent of working fathers find it challenging to balance work and family, and 60 percent of working mothers feel the same stress. But it's nearly a 50/50 split percentage wise for both men and women desiring to continue working anyway. Keep in mind that balance and the desire for flexibility is, yes, in part about family. It's also about wanting to be part of life and not just work all the time.

These statistics continue make clear that work-life balance isn't one sided — it's for men as well. Organizations need to meet employees where they are, as discussed in Chapter 14.

Flexibility Means Shorter Hours

Not necessarily so! Flexibility is the ability to work on a schedule that makes sense for the employee's life while still being able to engage in their work and still make deadlines.

If you're someone who can't get started until 10 a.m., your body clock may not cooperate with meetings earlier than that, so make sure you don't open a slot on your calendar until then. If you need to drop the kids off at school at 8 a.m., don't have your workday start until after 9 a.m. There are other variables, too. Single parents or caretakers may need to be off the grid from 4–7 p.m. but can work on either side of that 3-hour block. Flexibility doesn't mean a shorter work day with less hours. It just means that work time is being distributed differently than the prevailing norms.

Customize your workplace to the industry you work in and the times engagement between teams and customers may be necessary.

Everyone Knows How to Advance Their Careers

Some people are blessed with negotiating skills. Others aren't. Even the most assertive person I've ever known, who was amazing at the bargaining table, couldn't advocate and campaign for their own advancement. Overall, in our society we're raised to be polite. Negotiating, which is what a career path can become, is a much-needed skill set to be developed by all employees.

I once shared that perspective with a set of team leaders. They were stunned, and the immediate response, almost in a knee-jerk manner, was to say, "Well, we don't want to train people to ask for more!" However, when I reframed it around the cost of losing great talent and the cost associated with replacing these individuals, it made more sense. I'm not talking about bargaining down the price of bananas at the farmers market. I mean negotiating to get the training and clear path to one's goals.

In Chapter 15, I discuss options for review where the individual's goals and path are evaluated. However, your leaders and managers need to be trained or coached on how to develop a plan for each person with their input. My suggestion is to review Chapter 16 on motivation to help you read your employees better and therefore be able to help guide the employee to the paths that may be a fit.

Decision-Makers Know the Key Talent

There is a list with names on it identifying candidates with potential. Some at the table know these individuals and may have advocated for them to be on the list, which is great. But does the ultimate decision-maker, the person who holds their fates in their hands, know them at all? Chances are, depending on the size of your organization, they don't.

REMEMBER: People are not their resume or accomplishments. People are *people*, with the drive, personality, and skills to mobilize teams to cross the finish line. Make the time for all peak potential candidates to spend time with the ultimate decision-maker about their career. Sometimes those who may not look as good on paper as others can make better leaders than those at the top of the achievement lists. Make the time to know who everyone is. (Flip to Chapters 14 and 15 for more on hiring and retaining talent and on keeping your team engaged and satisfied.)

Conflict-Resolution Training Is Passé

Hmm, well. This is certainly false. Put four people at a dinner table, and they all will have a slightly different take on a given situation. Given their various positions on anything from sports, the environment, immigration, to how to complete the project at hand, you'll need conflict-resolution skills. There are roughly a dozen or so tactics that you can deploy to come to a resolution. I'm not saying we're all equipped to know all of them. Even if we do, it takes time, tact, and practice to hone this particular skill set.

Conflict resolution improves relationships, cooperation, and effectiveness of the leader and teams using it. It's one thing to say, "Be kind to one another." But without the tools to communicate effectively and carefully, things may turn out to be a bit of a mess.

The basic framework for conflict resolution is as follows:

- **Establish expectations of behaviors.** I cover the basics of setting the standards of a workplace that treats employees with dignity and respect throughout this book. This is the basis of values-based leadership (VBL). So you should have a pretty good idea of how to do this.

- **Address the situation immediately.** There are two parts to this step. First, do your best to always communicate openly in order to avoid conflicts that arise through misunderstandings or mistakes. Everyone deserves the benefit of the doubt, as I share in Chapter 7. Secondly, should conflict occur, find a way for each person to state their issue and agree to a solution. In particularly emotional conflicts, it's a good idea to have someone act as a mediator to ensure clarity and resolution.

- **Recognize others goals.** Both parties are usually headed toward a specific goal. Keep in mind that the people in conflict are both trying to get there. As part of VBL it's imperative that everyone work toward each person being able to do so, as discussed in Chapters 6 and 7.

- **Prioritize your battles.** Not every battle needs to be fought. Pick what's important and avoid becoming embroiled in needless conflict that will serve only to distract you from what you're currently working on or toward.

TIP: Make conflict-resolution training part of your self-selective learning. You may just improve your own personal relationships as well as defuse some sensitive situations in the workplace. If your company doesn't offer conflict-resolution training, consider consulting outside resources. I recommend the Society for Human Resource Management (www.shrm.org). It has a lot of information and resources you can access easily.

Technology Takes Care of Communication

Technology can be a lifesaver in so many ways, but it will never truly replace human connection and conversation. Over the past few years, more and more executives lament the fact that team members lack the skills and finesse to effectively communicate with one another and with leadership. Moreover, leadership, depending on age and experience, may also find it challenging to connect with technology-driven staffers.

REMEMBER: No matter how much technology is in place, nothing will fully replace interfacing with each other on a personal level. One of the areas to consider expanding is training on effective communication skills; everything from the basics to advanced communications skills will continue to be important for generations to come. Chapter 7 discusses communication skills in more detail.

You Have to Build a Fortress to Stake Your Claim

Do you know someone who has staked a claim to a cubicle? Perhaps they've decked it out with photos, inspirational quotes, stuffed toys, or memorabilia reflecting their greatest passion. Creating a *home* within the office environment is great. But sometimes doing that can create a barrier between the inhabitant and the rest of the crew: "This is my space — scram."

Some companies have created a *nomad culture,* where desks are randomly assigned on a rotating basis. Nomad *station desks* are situated in the middle of the main workspace where employee traffic passes through. When I saw an example of this, at first I thought, *Oh my goodness, this is terrible.* But the more I thought about it, the more I realized it really does break down the invisible fortress that some employees may build to either keep others out or establish a kind of members-only clubhouse mentality. I know it sounds ridiculous, but consider your current workplace. How many people have built a moat around their little castles? Yeah, you know them.

Nomading allows more opportunity for different teams to interact with one another because, well, they're right in the main traffic pattern through the office! It also makes creating different turfs hard. I'm not saying it's for everyone, but if you need to break down a walled-in culture, this would do it. Me personally, I will admit to having built my own fortress and moat at times.

Managers Don't Need to Coach Their Teams

One of the key skills to impart to managers and other field-level leadership is the ability to coach teams to success. *Coaching* doesn't mean providing marching orders and walking away. It's the ability to encourage, help refine, and offer guidance when needed — without the whistle.

Some inexperienced leaders and managers I've observed will assume that all the players know what they're supposed to do and where to find the resources and information they may need to do their job. As we continue to explore allowing this new workforce to have multiple experiences within the same organization, coaching becomes a constant. You may have fresh, green staffers at all times, or you may need to coach someone who's been in your organization for a while to upgrade their skill set. (Check out Chapter 14 for more on coaching.)

WARNING

Coaches are also cheerleaders. A big mistake I see people who lead teams make is that they get lazy. They forget to be that cheerleader. Everyone needs encouragement. Just be mindful not to become annoying to the team.

Understanding Motives Isn't Necessary

You may have skimmed over sections where I discuss motives, thinking maybe I'm talking about *good* or *bad* motives. There may be those around too, but what I'm imploring you to be aware of is what motivates, or propels, others to do what they do. Understanding another person's motivations will key you in to why they communicate a certain way and what becomes a hot spot for them. Then you can recognize how to properly resolve conflict with them. Sometimes it may seem as if people are speaking in different languages. Often that's because they have different motivations. Chapter 16 gives you the scoop on motivation.

Become motivational-lingual. Be aware. Meet them where they are. Don't expect people to be different than they are. Otherwise, you risk being annoyed all the time.

Index

A

Aburdene, Patricia (author)
  Megatrends 2010: The Rise of Conscious Capitalism, 11
acceptance, 102, 153, 310–311
accountability, 103, 113, 194, 208, 209–210, 240
achievement, as motivation, 268, 273, 281
acquiring stuff, shift from, 273
active listening, 114
ad blockers, 337
ADP Research Institute survey, 238
affiliation, as motivation, 268, 273, 281
agile leader, 91
agility, 78, 79, 91–94, 99
American Cancer Society report, 236
American Medical Association (AMA), 286
Angelou, Maya (author), 110
animation of a value (AV), 183, 185, 186, 190, 215
animation of an individual, 259
annual master plan, 256
annual performance review, 255–257
apparent talents (AT), 243, 244
Apple
  investment in Microsoft, 128
  slogan, 156
aspirational values, 177, 215
assessment
  to ascertain compatibility, 243
  of current level of leadership, 72–74
  empowering potential leaders to assess their own values, 291–292
  of ethical decisions, 86
  of fairness decisions, 85
  of job satisfaction, 256–259
  of motivational trigger, 268–269
  of where you stand, 163
atrophied/complacent, as vote choice in job satisfaction survey, 262
attachment, 121, 123–126
attitudes, evolving, thriving ones as result of grounding principles of VBL, 104
audiences, having insight into, 21–22
authenticity, 82–83, 114
autumn (reveal period), 132–133
AV (animation of a value), 183, 185, 186, 190, 215
awareness, rise of, 11

B

Babin, Leif (Navy SEAL), 139
Baby Boomers
  in current workforce, 22, 23
  influences on/description of, 24–25, 30, 31, 33, 110, 234, 235, 238, 256, 272, 333, 337
  years of, 23
backstabbing, replacing of with kindness, temperance, patience, and acceptance, 19
balance. *See also* work-life balance
  demands for, 237
  indicators for, 31
  as power, 149
Balanced Life (Flexibility), on example of wheel of priorities, 231, 232
Be a guardian, as one of four Be's of VBL, 37, 39, 137
Be diligent, as one of four Be's of VBL, 37, 40
Be generous, as one of four Be's of VBL, 37, 40
Be of service, as one of four Be's of VBL, 37, 39
Be the Solution: How Entrepreneurs and Conscious Capitalists Can Solve All the World's Problems (Mackey and Strong), 11
belief factors, in animation of individual, 259
benefit of the doubt (BOD), giving of, 111
benefits, 229, 230, 234–237
Benefits Pro survey, 236
Best Buy, 170
best practices, modeling of, 331

betterment of individuals, as category for grounding principles of VBL, 102
bifurcation, 13
bifurcation decision point, 14
big picture, fitting VBL into, 42–45
Bill & Melinda Gates Foundation, 68
Blakely, Sarah (SPANX founder), 278
blind spots, 63, 64, 66, 67, 68, 69, 287
BOD baby, 111
Bodian, Stephan (author)
 Meditation For Dummies, 319
body language, 89, 122, 146, 155, 269
bonus materials, 4
brain fog, eliminating things that cause, 321
brain lock, 301
breathing, importance of controlling, 93
Brookings University, study of Millennials, 274
Buddhism, on kindness, 41
bumper generations, 22, 23, 27–28
Bureau of Labor Statistics, Consumer Price Index–All Urban Customer (CPI-U), 53
burnout, 32
business
 answering why someone should work for your company, 246–247
 capacity of small businesses, 52
 distinguishing yourself from the competition, 229–233
 ego-focused businesses, 70
 government-affiliated business, 52–54
 identifying leaders who can help yours, 287–293
 reframing your perception of, 49–57
 understanding how others view yours, 159–168
 unraveling bad reputation of, 50–54
business practice, creating opportunity, 54–55
buyers, Millennials as skeptical buyers, 337
bystander effect, 87

C

California Milk Processors Board slogan, 156
Campbell, Joseph (author), 35, 77
candidates
 answering why someone should work for your company, 246–247
 myth of decision-makers as knowing key talents, 342
 showing respect and value to, 245–246
career starlight, building yours, 212–220
careers
 of Millennials as having multiple experiences, 338
 myth of everyone knowing how to advance theirs, 341
 putting yours into cohesive form, 216–217
caring, as investment and commitment to excellence, 168–169
Catalyzing Conscious Capitalism Conference, 11
catchphrases, 156
cause and effect, use of to shift organization, 102–103
celebration, importance of, 40, 134, 149, 254, 258, 279, 326, 327, 330
cell phone voyeurism, 87
Center for American Progress, 29, 251
 Cost of Turnover, 251
 The State of Diversity in Today's Workforce, 29–30
Center for Transcendental Meditation, 319
central business initiative, 51
CEO Summit, 11
change
 factors to consider when making, 138
 knowing when it is needed, 13–16
 rating your willingness to, 74–75
 recognizing that people won't necessarily embrace it, 306
 seasons of in evolution of thriving, values-based organization, 105, 130–136
change-management model, 104
character, 17, 18–19, 78
charisma, overstating importance of in leader, 69–71
Cheat Sheet, 4
Chopra, Deepak (alternative medicine advocate), 319

Christianity, on kindness, 41
circle of continuity, 313
Cisco, social media policy, 170
clarity
   communicating expectations with clarity, 327–328
   creation of across the board, 185–188
   importance of in communication, 113–114
   importance of in creating hope, 136
   raising endorphins to gain, 322
Clark University, study of Millennials, 274
CLC (Corporate Leadership Council), 286
cloaked talents (CT), 243, 244
coaching, 239, 286, 335, 344–345
Coca Cola, social medial policy, 170
cocktails, as one of five agreements to foster innovation, 303
collaboration, 229, 230, 304, 335
Collaborative Environment, on example of wheel of priorities, 231, 232
college tuition assistance program, 236
Colloway, Wayne (PepsiCo former CEO), 290
command and control temperament, 45–47
common belief, 156
communication
   communicating expectations with clarity, 327–328
   myth of technology as taking care of, 343
   providing effective communication, 112–115, 118
communication factors, in animation of individual, 259
community groups, surveying of, 163–164
community service, 44, 207–208
company
   answering why someone should work for your company, 246–247
   distinguishing yourself from the competition, 229–233
   identifying leaders who can help yours, 287–293
   thinking of as living thing, 42–43
   unraveling bad reputation of, 50–54
company culture
   creating proactive one as category for grounding principles of VBL, 101
   evolution of, 10–11
   as like perfect fishbowl, 244
   managing personalities versus maintaining of, 242
Comparably survey, 113
compassion, as characteristic of values-based organization, 102
compatibility
   answering why someone should work for your company, 246–247
   author's work with clients on, 261
   as contributor to job satisfaction, 259–260
   defined, 241
   ensuring good fit based on talents, 243–244
   managing personalities versus maintaining of, 242
   showing respect and value to candidates for employment, 245–246
   working toward, 241–247
competition
   assessment of competitive nature in your organization, 128
   as component of FARCE Syndrome, 121
   curtailing negative competition, 128
   distinguishing yourself from, 229–233
   unhealthy competition, 127–128
conciseness, importance of in communication, 113
conflict resolution, basic framework for, 342–343
conflict-resolution training, myth of it being passé, 342–343
Conscious Capitalism, 10, 11
Conscious Capitalism Alliance, 11
"Conscious Capitalism: Creating a New Paradigm for Business," 11
Conscious Capitalism, Inc., 11
Conscious Capitalism Institute, 11
Conscious Capitalism: Liberating the Heroic Spirit of Business (Mackey and Sisodia), 11
conscious intellect, 297, 299
consciousness
   as one of five agreements to foster innovation, 304
   shifting of beyond self, 35–49
consensus, moving forward even without, 176

consistency, providing predictable consistency, 110–112
constructive feedback, 111. *See also* feedback
Consumer Price Index–All Urban Customer (CPI-U), 53
content, paying attention to in communication, 113
control, reduction of, increasing trust, 304–305
control enthusiasts, 46, 123, 124, 125, 268, 283
conviction factors, in animation of individual, 259
cooperation, as not always meaning reaching a consensus, 176
core values (CV), 177, 178, 180–181, 182, 183, 185, 186, 190, 214–215
corporate identity, 160
Corporate Leadership Council (CLC), 286
corporate social responsibility (CSR)
  consideration of expansive version of, 235
  defined, 55, 162
  evolution of, 55–56
  as motivation, 274
  of Starbucks, 52
  as way of serving community, 44
courage
  as category of mindset, 196
  defined, 197
  four traits of values-based leader as needing, 79
  as not for faint-hearted, 78
  self-reflection as requiring, 92
  as singular trait all leaders require, 18
  transitioning model in creation of, 134
  VBL principles as fostering environment of, 104, 132, 134
courageous individuals, as one of four phases of thriving team, 106
course correction, 104, 107, 130, 137, 197, 198
cross-generational coaching, 239–240, 335
CT (cloaked talents), 243, 244
cultural entropy, 148
culture
  company culture, 10–11, 101, 242, 244
  corporate culture, 161
  creating culture of leadership, 283–293
  developing culture of leadership for sustained impact, 285–286
  as eating strategy for lunch, 16–19
  nomad culture, 344
  work cultures of Millennials as collaborative, 335
CV (core values), 177, 178, 180–181, 182, 183, 185, 186, 190, 214–215
CVS Health, values statement of, 182
cycle disruptions, handling of, 137

D

daily audit practice, 318
Dalai Lama (spiritual leader), 41
deadlock, 300
defiant workplaces
  becoming part of solution or exiting, 138–140
  evolving mindsets of people and organizations, 131–137
  facing effects of FARCE Syndrome, 120–131
deficiency needs, 267
DeLevie, Rena (chief compassion officer), 111
Dell, social media policy, 170
departures, as vote choice in job satisfaction survey, 261
direction
  creation of across the board, 185–188
  setting of as category for grounding principles of VBL, 101
DISC assessment, 243
discontent, shifting orchestra of, 280–281
disengagement, 250–251, 253–254, 259, 263
diversity, conversion of into inclusion, 29–30
do no harm, 96–97
doubt, relation of with trust, 266
Drucker, Peter (management expert), 16

E

Edelman Trust Barometer report (2017), 144, 145
education. *See also* learning and exploration
  as essential to shifting, changing, and growing, 92

ranking of as "must have" for employees, 238
   as retention tool, 71
ego, disengaging yours, 320
ego-focused businesses, 70
Elevate, as level of leadership, 63, 65, 67–68, 72
elitism, overcoming of with input and inclusion, 284–285
EM (evolution of mindset and environment), 117
embezzling, 171
emotion, as fuel, 275
Emotional Intelligence (EQ), 47
emotional reactions, cautions with, 93
Employee Benefit News, 154
employees
   being willing to let people go, 307–313
   giving staff choice, 138
   making everyone trustee of company, 168–171
   making time to get to know everyone, 326
   meeting of where they are, 115–116
   selling who you are to potential ones, 230–231
   showing respect and value to candidates for employment, 245–246
   turnover of as sign that change is needed in leadership approach, 14
   what they want from bosses, 113
employees engaged, as one of five sectors of VBL, 12, 13
empowerment, 85, 223, 284
encouragement, of others as sign of trust, 154
endorphins, raising of to gain clarity and reduce stress, 322
engagement
   as area of unique presence wheel, 229, 230
   creating environment of, 252–253
   importance of, 249–250
   maintaining of, 249–264
   staying active and happy, 250–254
Enrich, as level of leadership, 63, 65, 68–69, 72
Enron, 36
entitlement, 121, 129–130
entrepreneurs, alternate points of entry for, 199–200
EQ (Emotional Intelligence), 47

equality, environment of, 89
equalizing triggers, 30
eternal optimists, as vote choice in job satisfaction survey, 262
ethical behavior, 145, 171
ethical dilemmas, 84, 86–87, 219
example
   being powerful one, 96
   setting standard for others by being, 151–154
excellence, caring as investment and commitment to, 168–169
exceptions, avoiding of, 152–153
excessive competition, as sign that change is needed in leadership approach, 14
excessive gossip and rumors, as sign that change is needed in leadership approach, 14. *See also* gossip
exclusions and exceptions, as sign that change is needed in leadership approach, 14
Execu|Search
   Hiring Outlook guide (2017), 238
exit auditing, 309–310
exiting, becoming part of solution or exiting, 138–140
expectations, 284, 327–328
experiences, importance of to GenXers and Millennials, 237, 273, 338
exploitation, avoiding of, 111
extended adventures, 237
extinction, avoiding flatline to, 13–16
extreme ownership, 139

F

Facebook
   as influencing Millennials, 26
   living in society of, 256
   organizations as having account on, 183
   social media policies about, 169
   use of in candidate prescreening, 167
   workplace of, 235
   Zuckerberg, Mark (Facebook founder), 65–66
failure, utilization of as teaching moment as component of agility, 92

fairness decisions, 84, 85
FARCE Syndrome, 120–131
farm team, 287, 289
favored, 18
fear
  assessment of fear mechanism in your organization, 122
  as component of FARCE Syndrome, 121, 122–123
  as motivation, 271–272
  use of to manipulate values, 123
feedback
  current workforce as liking and wanting, 255
  establishing trusted feedback group, 322–323
  every failure as providing, 92
  fluid plans for, 257
  as part of give-and-take of an exchange, 112
  requesting of, 115
  role of constructive feedback, 111
  skip-level feedback, 287
  soliciting of from community groups, 163
  360 Review, 93
financial education, as nontraditional perk, 236–237
financial value, adding financial value to company because of your reputation as values-based leader, 222
"fireman carry" attitude, 155
FiRMS, personalizing your reputation plan with, 165–168
Firms of Endearment (Sisodia and Wolfe), 11
fiscal responsiveness, 161, 163, 166
flexibility
  as area of unique presence wheel, 229, 230
  avoiding exceptions yet remaining flexible, 152–153
  demands for, 237
  myth of flexibility as meaning shorter hours, 341
  as taking on heightened importance with Millennials, 336
flexible work hours, 32
FLOW, 11
focus, commitment to as component of agility, 92
forgiveness, practicing of, 310–311

The Fourth Turning (Strauss and Howe), 28
Freeman, R. Edward (author)
  Strategic Management: A Stakeholder Approach, 11
freewill, 137, 138
Fun Theory, 184

G
Gallup
  State of the American Workplace survey, 233, 250–251
  Strength Finder, 93
  survey on engagement, 249–250, 287–288
  survey on why people considering taking a job with particular company, 165
Gamb, Maria (author), website, 4, 244
Gandhi, Mahatma (Indian activist), 100
Gates, Bill (Microsoft founder), 68, 128
General Electric, slogan, 156
general public/promises, assessment of, 162, 163
Generation Edge, 27
Generation X (GenXers)
  in current workforce, 22, 23
  influences on/description of, 25–26, 30, 31, 33, 45, 109, 234, 237, 238, 256, 272, 274, 330
  years of, 23
Generation Z, 27
generational cohorts, 22
generational demographics, 23
Genovese, Kitty (murdered woman), 87
Genovese syndrome, 87
given values, 171, 177, 215
glass ceiling, 334
Glassdoor survey, 112, 233, 245
global financial crisis (2008), impact of, 23
Global Leadership Theory (GTL), 47–48
Goleman, Daniel (author), 47
good, creation of, 96–97
Google, workplace of, 235
gossip
  as potential sign that change is needed, 14
  as potential way of being, 80

replacing of with kindness, temperance, patience, and acceptance, 19
sidestepping rumor mills and gossip hounds, 153–154
government-affiliated business, 52–54
grace, as one of four traits of values-based leader, 78, 79, 88–91, 99
Grameen Bank, 66, 67
gratitude, 78, 154
great talent, hiring and retaining of, 227–247
green and eager, as tier 1 of growth and mobility tiers for leadership, 289
grounding principles
 assembling framework for deployment of, 115–118
 introduction to, 100–109
growth
 correlation of job satisfaction with, 263–264
 recognizing that people won't necessarily embrace it, 306
growth needs, 267
Growth Paths (T&D), on example of wheel of priorities, 231, 232
GTL (Global Leadership Theory), 47–48

H

hair-trigger temper, cautions with, 111
Halt environment/Halt organization, 126, 130–131, 148
happiness
 benefits of, 263
 as compared to meaning, 33
Harvard Business Review, article on benefits of meditation, 319
Harvard Maloney Neuroscience Institute Letter, 322
Hay Group report, 227–228
heart, emerging leaders as having, 334
Herfurth, Carolyn (The BizTruth owner), 189–190
hero's journey, 77
Hewlett-Packard, social media policy, 170
high/low game, 279
hiring
 answering question of why someone should work for your company, 246–247
 benefiting everyone with nontraditional perks, 234–237
 craving opportunity to learn, 238–241
 demanding balance and flexibility, 237
 distinguishing yourself from competition, 229–233
 ensuring a good job fit based on talents, 243–244
 establishing cross-generational coaching, 239–240
 instituting time to volunteer, 235–236
 managing personalities versus maintaining company culture, 242
 offering skills retraining, 240–241
 offering voluntary solutions, 236
 providing financial education, 236–237
 recognizing why people leave one company to join another, 228–229
 rotating jobs and experiences, 240–241
 selling who you are to potential employees, 230–232
 showing respect and value to candidates, 245–246
 uncorking your reputational capital, 232–233
 working toward compatibility triumphs, 241–247
Hiring Outlook guide (2017), 238
Hitler, Adolf (political leader), 69
Hofstede, Geert (social psychologist), 47
holdouts, as vote choice in job satisfaction survey, 262
Home Depot, values statement, 181
Homeland generation
 coining of term, 27
 diversity/inclusion awareness in, 29
 as emerging generation, 22, 23
 influences on/description of, 273
 years of, 23
honesty, as cornerstone attribute, 80–82
hope
 as category of mindset, 196
 transitioning model in creation of, 133
 VBL principles as fostering environment of, 104, 132
hopeful individuals, as one of four phases of thriving team, 106

Index 353

how we create sustainability, as one of four components of VBL, 44, 208
how we do business, as one of four components of VBL, 44, 207
how we invest in others, as one of four components of VBL, 44, 208
how we serve/impact community, as one of four components of VBL, 44, 207–208
Howe, Neil (sociologist), 22, 28
humility, 78, 88–89, 99, 115
"Humor, Laughter, and Those Aha Moments," 322
humor, value of, 135

I

icons, explained, 4
identity, corporate identity, 160
inclusion, conversation of diversity into, 29–30
individuals, betterment of as category for grounding principles of VBL, 102
influence, responsible. *See* responsible influence, as one of four traits of values-based leader
innovation
  basics on, 296–302
  challenging team members to look beyond themselves, 305
  comparing traditional and innovative business mindsets, 298–299
  deploying "shades of gray" thinking, 299–300
  dovetailing basics of into HR strategy, 302
  exercising your unconscious intellect, 301–302
  fostering environment of, 295–302
  igniting of with few principles and pointers, 302–306
  keeping it fresh by rotating contributors, 305
  pros and cons of, 306
  recognizing that people won't necessarily embrace change or growth, 306
  reducing control, increasing trust, 304–305
  revealing unconscious and conscious intellects, 297
  setting ground rules with five agreements to foster, 303–304
innovative mindset, 298
innuendo, as potential way of being, 80
Inspire, as level of leadership, 63, 65, 66–67, 72
Instagram
  living in society of, 256
  Millennials use of, 30
  organizations as having account on, 183
  use of in candidate prescreening, 167
institutional memory, 288
integrity, 84, 93, 150, 162, 194, 331
intellect, forms of, 297
Intelligence Group, survey of Millennials, 274
Internet Explorer, 128
interviews, with candidates, 245, 247
Islam, on kindness, 41

J

job offers, evaluating of with your career starlight, 218–219
job rotation, 240–241
job satisfaction
  assessment of with customizable survey, 256–259
  compatibility as contributor to, 259–260
  correlation of with morale, learning, and growth, 263–264
  importance of, 249–250
  as increasing engagement, 252
  keeping wisdom pool full, 255–264
  maintaining of, 249–264
  rethinking annual performance review, 255–257
  voting on in five ways, 260–262
Judaism, on kindness (*chesed*), 41

K

kindness, 39–41, 102
King, Martin Luther, Jr. (civil rights leader), 188, 189
Kramer, Mark R. (academic), 56, 57

L

Lafley, AG (Proctor & Gamble former CEO), 290
latchkey kids, 25
leaders. *See also* values-based leader
  empowering potential ones to assess their own values, 291–292
  tiers of, 288–291
leadership
  as ascension process, 71
  assessment of current level of, 72–74
  character of as one of five sectors of VBL, 12
  courageously making your own values stand, 197–198
  creating culture of, 283–293
  creating your leadership starlight for team, 200–206
  C-suite individuals as not the only leaders, 192
  curtailing mutiny and getting everyone back on track, 194–195
  defining your leadership engagement qualities, 215–216
  demographic trends in, 286–287
  determining where you are on journey of, 71–75
  developing culture of for sustained impact, 285–286
  diagnosing team's hurdles, 195–197
  examples of companies' devotion to development of, 290
  facing truth about who you are, 159–171
  following path cut by influencers of, 47–49
  getting others to trust in yours, 149–151
  giving yourself permission to take reins, 194
  growth and mobility tiers for, 289
  guiding your crew when you're not the captain, 193–200
  as job for all staff members, 283–284
  leading when you're gone, 210
  levels of, 63
  locating fellow travelers, 312
  minding gape between you and team, 198–199
  as not for faint-hearted, 317
  overstating importance of charisma in, 69–71
  planning your adventure into different levels of, 62–75
  as practice of love and selflessness, 308
  rebalancing your efforts, 311–312
  unpacking your toolkit, 201–203
  women as increasing force in, 286, 334
leadership gap, 286
leadership impact trajectory, 63
leader-to-leader fit, discerning yours, 219–220
learning and exploration. *See also* education
  commitment to as component of agility, 91
  correlation of job satisfaction with, 263–264
  cross-generational coaching, 239–240
  employees as craving opportunity for, 238–241
  example of commitment to, 287
  job rotation, 240–241
leaving company
  asking questions and showing acceptance when people leave, 308–311
  being willing to let people go, 307–313
  recognizing why people leave, 228–229
left-brain thinkers, 136, 297
letting people go
  being willing to, 307–313
  conducting more detailed kind of exit auditing, 309–310
  playing "what if" game of possibilities, 308–309
  practicing forgiveness and acceptance, 310–311
  staying true to values, 311–312
life accomplishments, acknowledging of, 326
LifeWorks, study of employees, 238
Lincoln, Abraham (former US president), 68
listening
  active listening, 114
  importance of ability of, 267
living thing, thinking of company as, 42–43
local engagement, assessment of, 162, 163
London School of Business, survey of Millennial women, 339
loyalty, 83, 147, 150, 255

M

Mackey, John (Whole Foods CEO)
  Be the Solution: How Entrepreneurs and Conscious Capitalists Can Solve All the World's Problems, 11
  Conscious Capitalism: Liberating the Heroic Spirit of Business, 11
  as spearheading Conscious Capitalism, 10
Mad Men (TV show), 10
making a difference, desire for, 24, 30, 33, 133, 273, 318, 336
management confidence, assessment of, 162, 163
management performance, template on Survey Monkey for assessment of, 258
management skills, working on, 167
manager, fit with, 247
market disruptors, Millennials as, 337
marketability, reinforcing what you stand for to add marketability, 222–223
Marriott, values statement, 181
Maslow, Abraham (psychologist), 143, 146
mass media traps, Millennials as resisting, 337
MasterCard, slogan, 156
maximum capacity, performing at as one of five sectors of VBL, 12, 13
McClelland, David (psychologist), 267–268, 273
McCobin, Alexander (Conscious Capitalism, Inc., co-CEO), 11
meaning
  as area of unique presence wheel, 229, 230
  bite-sizing of, 274–276
  creation of, 32–33
  as equalizing trigger, 30
  examples of, 276
  happiness as compared to, 33
  helping people find again, 274–277
means value, 183
meditation, 318–319
Meditation For Dummies (Bodian), 319
meetings
  reduction in number of, 32
  shoebox meetings, 331

mega-corporations, de-villainizing of, 51–52
Megatrends 2010: The Rise of Conscious Capitalism (Aburdene), 11
men, myth of men as not as interested in work-life balance, 340
mentoring, 239, 323–324
#MeToo movement, 334
Microsoft
  Gates, Bill (Microsoft founder), 68, 128
  investment in Apple, 128
  Microsoft Office, 128
middle road/status quo, as tier 2 of growth and mobility tiers for leadership, 289, 290
Millennial Leadership Survey, 286, 334
Millennials
  in current workforce, 22, 23
  diversity/inclusion awareness in, 29
  influence of, 10, 15–16
  influences on/description of, 26–27, 30, 31, 33, 45, 69–70, 109, 234, 235, 236, 237, 238, 239, 256, 272, 273, 274, 286, 296, 299, 302, 330, 333–338
  women's reasons for leaving jobs, 340
  years of, 23
mindset
  categories of, 196
  comparing traditional and innovative business mindsets, 298–299
  evolution of, 131–137
  evolving one of thriving organization, 105
  examples of, 101, 105, 106
  summarizing of one of thriving team, 106
missteps, handling of, 171, 278, 310
mistakes, handling of, 93, 94, 278, 310, 321
momentum, creation of, 116–117
momentum equation, 116
money, as no longer main motivation, 32
money motivation myth, 272–273
Monster, poll of employees, 238
morale, correlation of job satisfaction with, 263–264

motivation
  assessing your team, 269–271
  assessing yourself, 268–269
  creating environment where people can fail but learn from it, 278
  deciphering money motivation myth, 272–273
  decline of as sign that change is needed in leadership approach, 14
  defined, 253
  fear as, 271–272
  helping people find their meaning and purpose again, 274–277
  helping team find its footing, 276–277
  human motivation theory, 266–273
  impact of trust on, 266
  looking, listening, and categorizing, 267
  myth of understanding motives as not necessary, 345
  pickup sticks metaphor for finding solutions, 278
  practicing and reinforcing of, 277–281
  pulling it all together, 279–280
  shifting orchestra of discontent, 280–281
  three things that motivate people, 267–268
motivation factors, in animation of individual, 259
motivational triggers, 267, 273
Myers-Briggs, 243

N

Napster, as influencing Millennials, 26
narcissist, pulling back mask of, 220
near-mean, 18
needs, hierarchy of, 147
needs system, 267. *See also* needs, hierarchy of
Nestlé, reinventing new profit center to meet human needs, 57
new-generation traditionalists, 299
nomad culture, 344
nontraditional perks, 234–237

O

offshoring jobs, 237
old-school values, as making comeback, 336–337

online guidelines, establishment of, 169–171
online reputation, 164–165
open dialogue, keeping of, 327
open door, 329
opportunity
  creation of as business practice, 54–55
  expansion of business opportunities as category for grounding principles of VBL, 102
Opportunity Ripple Illustration, 54
optimism, 91, 104, 132, 135, 196
optimistic individuals, as one of four phases of thriving team, 106
organization
  answering why someone should work for your company, 246–247
  building winning organizations, 16–19
  distinguishing yourself from the competition, 229–233
  evolution of, 104–105
  identifying leaders who can help yours, 287–293
  unraveling bad reputation of, 50–54
Organization for Economic Co-operation and Development (OECD), 24, 31
ownership, lack of as sign that change is needed in leadership approach, 15

P

paid time off (PTO), 235
Palmissano, Sam (IBM executive), 290
passive-aggressive personalities, circumventing of, 156–158
peer-to-peer coaching system, 286
people power, harnessing of, 155–158
perception
  of others of your business, 159–168
  reframing of for your business, 49–57
performance review, 255–257
personal time off (PTO), 32
personalities
  managing of versus maintaining company culture, 242
  types of, 184–185
personality, infusing of into values statement, 183–185

Index 357

Pew Research Center
  Fathers' Day Facts, 340
  Millennials statistics, 23, 334
philanthropy, as essential to society, 56
play, benefits of, 297
polarity, 63, 64, 69, 78, 260, 261
Porter, Michael E. (academic), 56, 57
posture, 89
power, as motivation, 267, 273, 281
PricewaterhouseCoopers CEO 2016 Survey, 162
principle plan, creation of, 117–118
Proctor, Bob (author), 173
promises, keeping of, 110–111, 328–329
Prudential, corporate identity, 160
PTO (paid time off), 235
PTO (personal time off), 32
public values statement, using self-reflective method for, 174–182
purpose
  bite-sizing of, 274–276
  conveying of, 181
  examples of, 276
  helping people find again, 274–277

Q

Quad workforce. *See also* Baby Boomers; bumper generations; Generation X (GenXers); Millennials
  defined, 22
  leading of with insight and understanding, 29–34
  pinpointing of, 22
  as reflection of society, 34
  trends in, 258
  wondering whether it cares about your leadership, 33–34
questioning
  importance of, 109
  as sometimes perceived as resistance, 108
quiet confidence, 88
quiet time, 88–89

R

recognition, as area of unique presence wheel, 229, 230
Recognizing Others, on example of wheel of priorities, 231, 232
refinement, as one of five agreements to foster innovation, 303
reinforcement strategies, in principle plan, 117–118
relationships and affiliations, 162, 163, 167
remedies, 137
reputation
  assessment of your company's reputation, 161–162
  building of, 233
  corporate reputation, 161
  on display, 233
  personalizing your reputation plan with FiRMS, 165–168
  recognizing that online reputation is big influencer, 164–165
  unraveling bad one of business, 50–54
reputational capital, 17–18, 232–233
resilient organization, creating and maintaining of, 63, 64, 303, 312
resistance
  assessment of resistant environment in your organization, 126–127
  as component of FARCE Syndrome, 121, 126–127
  defined, 108
  example of, 137
  as part of life and evolution, 108–109
resource base, importance of surveying often, 329–330
resource connectivity, assessment of, 162, 163
respect, simple ways to show respect for candidates, 246
responsible influence, as one of four traits of values-based leader, 78, 79, 95–97, 99
retaliation, 121, 126–127
retention
  burnout as biggest sabotage to, 32
  coaching as tool for, 324

as cost-effective and responsible, 251, 285
education as tool for, 71
as encompassing engagement and job satisfaction, 249
as how you avoid draining wisdom pool, 255
as HR department's top challenge, 256
impact of recognition and appreciation on, 154
impact on of adding financial to company because of reputation, 222
meaning and purpose as key factors of, 274
as number one initiative for internal recruiters and HR professionals, 336
pointers for creating engagement from get-go, 252
skills training as tool for, 241
VTO as helping with, 236

retirement
rise in late retirement, 25
statistics on, 286
U.K. as abolishing default age for, 24

retraining, 241, 243, 338
revolving door, costs of, 251–252
reward perks package, 277
right-brain thinkers, 136, 297
Rohn, Jim (entrepreneur and author), 78
Roosevelt, Eleanor (former First Lady), 47
rotisserie chicken, metaphor of, 254
rules of engagement, 44, 182, 186, 189
rumors, 14, 153–154

S

sabbaticals, 235, 237
saeculum, 28
scalability, 52, 53
Schweitzer, Albert (Nobel Prize winner), 96
seasons of change, in evolution of thriving, values-based organization, 132–136
self-achieving needs, 267
self-assessment, 133, 292
self-awareness, 147, 151–152, 213, 220, 247, 267, 318
self-denial, 81

self-leadership, 189–190
selflessness, 16, 37, 39, 40, 42, 68, 139, 308
self-rationalization, 81
self-reflection
exercises on, 80, 89–90, 94, 96, 97, 104, 108, 175, 185, 292, 320
as key component to uncovering values, 175
as one of four traits of values-based leader, 78, 79–87, 99
role of, 92
use of, 16
using self-reflective method for public values statement, 174–182

self-reflective method (SRM), 174
self-sabotage, 271
servitude, as one of five agreements to foster innovation, 303
sets direction, as category for grounding principles of VBL, 101
seven capitol vices, 78
"shades of gray" thinking, 299–300
Shared Value Initiative, 57
shared values economy (SVE)
as area of unique presence wheel, 229, 230
defined, 55
evolving corporate social responsibility initiatives, 55–56
as motivation, 274
as one of two main parts of reframing your perception of business, 50
reinventing new profit centers to meet human needs, 56–57

sharing, as caring, 168–169
shoebox meetings, 331
shortfalls, forgiving yours, 320–321
sick days, 235
Silent generation
as almost completely retired, 22
Homeland generation as possibly mirroring of, 28
influences on/description of, 109–110, 273
recognition of, 27
years of, 23

sins, seven deadly sins, 78
Sisodia, Raj (author)
   Conscious Capitalism: Liberating the Heroic Spirit of Business, 11
   Firms of Endearment, 11
skills retraining, 241, 243, 338
slogans, 156
Snapchat, as influencing Millennials, 26
snowflake, 311
social awareness, 162, 163, 167–168
social connectivity, 256
social distance, 88, 89, 150–151, 284–285
social distancing, 91, 252
social imprint, 162
social media policies, 169–170
socially conscious capitalist enterprise, 11
Society for Human Resource Management
   examples of exit interview options, 310
   as resource on conflict-resolution training, 343
Society for Human Resource Management survey
   survey of employees, 136
solopreneurs, 189–190
solution, becoming part of or exiting, 138–140
Spark, as level of leadership, 63, 65, 72
special treatment, 129
spiritual practice, 319
spring (adapt period), 134–135
SRM (self-reflective method), 174
stagnation, as sign that change is needed in leadership approach, 15
staking your claim, myth of having to build fortress for, 343–344
stand and deliver, 330
Starbucks
   corporate identity, 160
   as mega-corporation, 51–52
starlight, 200, 203–206. *See also* career starlight
station desks, 344
Strategic Management: A Stakeholder Approach (Freeman), 11
strategy, conveying of, 181
Strauss, William (sociologist), 22, 28
Strength Finder (Gallup), 93

strengths
   digging into your with a little help, 212–213
   unpacking yours, 92–93
stress, raising endorphins to reduce, 322
Strong, Michael (author)
   Be the Solution: How Entrepreneurs and Conscious Capitalists Can Solve All the World's Problems, 11
success, commitment to as component of agility, 91
successful and accomplished, as tier 3 of growth and mobility tiers for leadership, 289, 290
summer (expand period), 135–136
super fans, as vote choice in job satisfaction survey, 262
Survey Gizmo, 93
Survey Monkey, 258
surveying, use of to see whether correction is necessary, 163–164
sustainability, 42, 44, 55, 144, 208
sustainable momentum, 118
sustained impact, developing culture of leadership for, 285–286
SVE (shared values economy). *See* shared values economy (SVE)

T

Takata Corporation, airbag recall, 34
talents
   apparent talents (AT), 243, 244
   cloaked talents (CT), 243, 244
   ensuring good fit based on, 243–244
   hiring and retaining of great talent, 227–247
   myth of decision-makers as knowing key talents, 342
Tao Te Ching, 68
teaching moment, utilization of failure as, 77, 92, 93
team
   assessment of motivational triggers for, 269–271
   creating your leadership starlight for, 200–206
   diagnosing hurdles of, 195–197
   engaging principles for, 155
   helping team find its footing, 276–277

holding team accountable even if others don't, 209–210
leveling with, 208–209
loving yours too much, 125
making it easy for your team to buy into you as leader, 109–115
minding gap between you and, 198–199
myth of managers as not needing to coach their teams, 344–345
tips for staying connected with, 325–331
team failure, as sign that change is needed in leadership approach, 14
technology
  myth of it taking care of communication, 343
  use of to prompt excellence, 322
temperament, maintaining even temperament, 111
ten-plus hour days, 32
Tesco, slogan, 156
thank you, 112, 154, 328
think tank opportunities, 304
360 Review, 93
Tiffany and Co., corporate identity, 160
Tinder, as influencing Millennials, 26
toolkit, 201–203
Tracy, Brian (motivational speaker), 150
traditional mindset, 298
training and development (T&D), as area of unique presence wheel, 229, 230
transferable skills, 240, 292
transparency
  importance of showing, 330–331
  as one of five agreements to foster innovation, 303
  use of term in defining trust, 145
trust
  assessment of, 146
  building environment of as one of five sectors of VBL, 12–13
  as category of mindset, 196
  decline of as sign that change is needed in leadership approach, 14
  defined, 144, 145–148
  encouragement of others as sign of, 154
  four traits of values-based leader as building, 79
  getting others to trust in your leadership, 149–151
  harnessing people power, 155–158
  impact of on motivation, 266
  increasing of by reducing control, 304–305
  as key factor in leader's ability to influence group, 143, 144
  lighting pathway to establishment of, 143–158
  relation of doubt with, 266
  role of, 19
  setting standards for others by example, 151–154
  shifting from Halt to happiness, 148–149
  surveying ideas for building of in business, 144–145
  transitioning model in creation of, 136
  using Maslow's hierarchy of needs to determine baseline trust, 147–148
  VBL principles as fostering environment of, 104, 132
trustee, 168–171
trusting individuals, as one of four phases of thriving team, 106
truth, facing truth about who you are, 159–171
turnover, 14, 251, 256
Tway, Duane C., Jr. (academic), 145–146
Twitter
  corporate identity, 160
  as influencing Millennials, 26
  living in society of, 256
  organizations as having account on, 183
  social media policies about, 169

U

Udemy Workplace Stress Study (2017), 238
unaligned actions, 171
unconscious intellect, 297, 298, 299, 300, 301–302
unifying statement, 277
unique presence wheel, 229, 230
United States Postal Services (USPS), challenges of, 52–53
us versus them, as sign that change is needed in leadership approach, 14

V

value equation, changing of, 103–104
value proposition (VP), 103, 230, 338
value-driven generation, 336
values
   animation of (AV), 183, 185, 186, 190
   aspirational values, 177, 215
   choosing ones that speak to you, 178–181
   core values (CV), 177, 178, 180–181, 182, 183, 185, 186, 190, 214–215
   defined, 17
   emulating of, 96
   given values, 171, 177, 215
   identification of, 173–190
   old-school values as making comeback, 336–337
   staying true to, 311–312
   terminology regarding, 17–18
   types of, 176–182
   understand and selecting of, 176–182
   as vital component of building winning organization, 17–18
   vogue values, 177, 215
values stand, 107, 126, 137, 195, 197–198, 199
values statement
   creation of, 173–190
   deciding whether to involve anyone else in creation of, 175–176
   formulating and assembling of, 181–182
   importance of in defining how you do business, 44
   importance of making it clear to team, 328
   infusing of personality into, 183–185
   rolling out to your company, 182–190
values-based leader
   adding financial value to company because of your reputation as, 222
   as allowing everyone to lead, 285
   defined, 17
   practices to stay on track as, 317–324
   as recognizing they're not always best person to create solutions, 285
   as secure in self, 285
   seeing effects of being known as, 220–223

values-based leadership (VBL)
   accepting that top brass isn't interested in, 192–193
   bolstering your commitment to, 206–210
   as business proposition, 43
   correlation of to leadership levels and impact, 72
   escalator effect of, 11–12
   as expanding on Conscious Capitalism, 12
   fitting of into big picture, 42–45
   four Be's of, 36–41, 231
   grounding principles of, 99–118
   as marketing tool, 211
   model of, 101
   nurturing four attributes of, 77–97
   as pathway to creating meaning for everyone, 33
   as pioneering work, 308
   scalability as important to, 53
   scaling down four features of, 207–208
   self-assessment as key feature, 292
   as shift of consciousness beyond ourselves, 35
values-based organizations, defined, 17–18
values-based principles, as one of five sectors of VBL, 12
vendor base, importance of surveying often, 329–330
Virtuali, The Millennial Leadership Survey, 334
virtues, examples of, 78
vogue values, 177, 215
Volkswagen, company culture of, 184
voluntary benefits (VB), 236
volunteer time off (VTO), 32, 235–236
volunteerism, 32, 52, 57, 162, 179, 208, 235

W

waiting room, 290
walking and talking
   as strategy for exercising unconscious intellect, 301
   as way to shift out of deadlock, 300

Walton, Sam (Walmart founder), 200
"The War for Leaders," 227–228
weaknesses
   digging into yours with a little help, 212–213
   unpacking yours, 92, 93
WeWorks, as co-working company, 184
"what if" game, 308–309
wheel of priorities, example of, 232
Whole Foods
   Mackey, John (Whole Foods CEO), 10
   personality of, 183
Willink, Jocko (Navy SEAL), 139
Winfrey, Oprah (media proprietor), 319
winter (evaluate period), 133–134
wisdom, sharing of in constructive and timely manner, 111
wisdom pool, 243, 255–264
Wolfe, David (author)
   Firms of Endearment, 11
women
   as increasing force in leadership, 286, 334
   Millennial women's reasons for leaving jobs, 340
   myth of women primarily leaving their jobs to have families, 339–340
work, creating meaning and reason to go to, 32–33
work cultures, of Millennials as collaborative and connected, 335
work ethic, pivoting of into work ethos, 30–31
work ethos, pivoting of work ethic into, 30–31
workforce. *See also* Quad workforce
   composition of current workforce, 22
   evolution of, 23
working remotely, 210, 237, 309–310
work-life balance
   Generation X (GenXers) fierce commitment to, 25
   indicators of, 32
   myth of men as not as interested in work-life balance, 340
   as one of two main triggers that propel work ethos, 30
   recalibrating concept of, 31–32
   values-based companies as considering best approach to, 326
workplace myths, 339–345
workplace needs, conversion of Maslow's hierarchy of needs to, 148
WorkplaceTrends.com, The Millennial Leadership Survey, 334
Worktraits, 302
World Economic Forum
   study of company's market value, 165
   on trends that will affect workplace, 241

Y

Yunus, Muhammad (economist), 11, 66, 67

Z

Zuckerberg, Mark (Facebook founder), 65–66, 67

About the Author

Maria Gamb is founder and CEO of the coaching and training company NMS Communications, focusing on creating powerful leadership and happy, healthy organizations that thrive.

As a former executive, she spent more than 20 years in corporate America directing and managing successful businesses valued in excess of $100 million. Her global experiences led her to write the Amazon bestselling book *Healing the Corporate World* (NMS Communications, 2010), which made her one of the few women to rank in the top ten of Amazon's Leadership category.

Direct, to the point, and with a healthy dose of humor, Maria is a sought-after speaker, consultant, trainer, and retreat leader on the topics of values-based leadership and gender and team communication dynamics. She's worked with executives and groups from Capital One, Oppenheimer Funds, the Jamaican government, Raymond James, Astra Zeneca, Mid-Atlantic Permanente, Kronos Incorporated, Women's Health Business Association, and Women's MBA International. Additionally, she has partnered with Colonial Voluntary Benefits, bringing much-needed critical illness benefits to corporations.

Maria has been a contributor to *Forbes* magazine, writing about leadership. She's been featured in *Inc.* magazine, *Time* magazine, and the Wall Street Radio Network. She is a member of the Women's MBA International (WMBAI) association and the United Nations Association of New York (UNA NY).

Nicknamed "Gypsy" by her family, she's spent most of her adult life traveling, seeking adventure, and working in numerous countries across the planet. Her favorite adventure: swimming with sharks and seals in the Galapagos Islands. Failed adventures: learning to surf and skydive in Australia. But it was worth the try.

Maria lives in Brooklyn, New York, with her charming husband and their rambunctious cats.

Dedication

This book is dedicated to my husband, who has lovingly supported me on this journey and through the process of writing this book. You're the most amazing man I've ever met. I love you more than I can ever express.

And to my wonderful mother, who has brought lightness, laughter, encouragement, and unconditional love to me throughout my life — I could not have done this without you. Thank you for being a powerful advocate for achieving my dreams.

Author's Acknowledgments

This book was written based on my cumulative experience and working knowledge of business that I've gained through leading my own teams, mentors, friends, leaders, colleagues, and clients. Each of you has shared a lesson that I've taken with me on my journey through life. For this, I am eternally grateful. You've provided me with so much great material!

Without the support of my sweet husband, this book would have been impossible to execute. Thank you for taking care of literally everything as I wrote, paced, edited, and worked until early in the morning. You've been the best partner, support system, and champion I could ever have asked for. Your book widow days are over. Balance, adventure, and exploration are back on the horizon for us.

To my parents, thank you for teaching me what a well-oiled, cohesive unit looks like and the importance of teamwork. It has shaped who I am in this world. To my sibs, Deb, Joe, and Anthony, you are my heart and soul. I love you all and am honored to be part of your families.

Life is a journey. Those who come along with us color the experience. I am so incredibly blessed to be surrounded by a delightful, intelligent, successful, quirky gaggle of friends. You've made this part of the journey fun. Bonnie, thanks for your undying, humorous insights into some of this material. Bryn, my lifelong sister, thank you for the loving support over the hurdles and speed bumps. My texting thumbs have been run ragged! Oge, energy moves, energy shifts and morphs into what we choose it to be. Thank you for always reminding me to choose wisely. Liz, our work together has shaped where I am today. Who knew this publisher would seek me out to write this particular book? Well, you did, ten years ago. Each one of you has blessed my life and made me a better person and professional.

I especially want to thank my dear friend and most influential mentor, Donna. I could never have found a more amazing woman to be led by or to call friend. You . . . are . . . amazing!

I can't thank the team at Wiley enough for their help and guidance on this journey. Tracy Boggier, my acquisitions editor, thank you for convincing me this would be a good thing for me to do. Michelle Hacker, my project manager, your undying patience as I stumbled through formatting and endless questions about TOCs will be rewarded in heaven, for sure! Georgette Beatty, my development editor, I will forever see red notes signed "Thanks, gb" to the end of time! Thank you for making me sound brilliant. Corbin Collins, my copy editor, thank you for keeping my opinions but always circling me back to facts. Everyone else who has contributed to this book, from the graphics, marketing, and editing departments and beyond, thank you for bringing this important and timely message into the world with a sense of humor and grace. You have all been a joy to work with.

And to all the readers of this book, I'd like to acknowledge and thank you for your courage to consider leadership and the workplace differently. I'm counting on you to change the world for the better. The tagline of my business is "change the norm, change the world" — together we can do this!

Publisher's Acknowledgments

Senior Acquisitions Editor: Tracy Boggier
Project Manager: Michelle Hacker
Development Editor: Georgette Beatty
Copy Editor: Corbin Collins
Technical Editor: AndreAnna McLean
Production Editor: Magesh Elangovan
Cover Photo: © vkstudio/Alamy Stock Photo

Take dummies with you everywhere you go!

Whether you are excited about e-books, want more from the web, must have your mobile apps, or are swept up in social media, dummies makes everything easier.

Find us online!

dummies.com

dummies
A Wiley Brand

Leverage the power

Dummies is the global leader in the reference category and one of the most trusted and highly regarded brands in the world. No longer just focused on books, customers now have access to the dummies content they need in the format they want. Together we'll craft a solution that engages your customers, stands out from the competition, and helps you meet your goals.

Advertising & Sponsorships

Connect with an engaged audience on a powerful multimedia site, and position your message alongside expert how-to content. Dummies.com is a one-stop shop for free, online information and know-how curated by a team of experts.

- Targeted ads
- Video
- Email Marketing
- Microsites
- Sweepstakes sponsorship

20 MILLION PAGE VIEWS EVERY SINGLE MONTH

15 MILLION UNIQUE VISITORS PER MONTH

43% OF ALL VISITORS ACCESS THE SITE VIA THEIR MOBILE DEVICES

700,000 NEWSLETTER SUBSCRIPTIONS TO THE INBOXES OF **300,000** UNIQUE INDIVIDUALS EVERY WEEK

# of dummies

Custom Publishing

Reach a global audience in any language by creating a solution that will differentiate you from competitors, amplify your message, and encourage customers to make a buying decision.

- Apps
- Books
- eBooks
- Video
- Audio
- Webinars

Brand Licensing & Content

Leverage the strength of the world's most popular reference brand to reach new audiences and channels of distribution.

For more information, visit dummies.com/biz

dummies
A Wiley Brand

PERSONAL ENRICHMENT

Staying Sharp	Facebook	Guitar	Investing	Beekeeping	Digital Photography
9781119187790	9781119179030	9781119293354	9781119293347	9781119310068	9781119235606
USA $26.00	USA $21.99	USA $24.99	USA $22.99	USA $22.99	USA $24.99
CAN $31.99	CAN $25.99	CAN $29.99	CAN $27.99	CAN $27.99	CAN $29.99
UK £19.99	UK £16.99	UK £17.99	UK £16.99	UK £16.99	UK £17.99

Meditation	Pregnancy	Samsung Galaxy S7	iPhone	Crocheting	Nutrition
9781119251163	9781119235491	9781119279952	9781119283133	9781119287117	9781119130246
USA $24.99	USA $26.99	USA $24.99	USA $24.99	USA $24.99	USA $22.99
CAN $29.99	CAN $31.99	CAN $29.99	CAN $29.99	CAN $29.99	CAN $27.99
UK £17.99	UK £19.99	UK £17.99	UK £17.99	UK £16.99	UK £16.99

PROFESSIONAL DEVELOPMENT

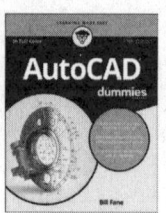

Windows 10	AutoCAD	Excel 2016	QuickBooks 2017	macOS Sierra	LinkedIn	Windows 10 All-in-One
9781119311041	9781119255796	9781119293439	9781119281467	9781119280651	9781119251132	9781119310563
USA $24.99	USA $39.99	USA $26.99	USA $26.99	USA $29.99	USA $24.99	USA $34.00
CAN $29.99	CAN $47.99	CAN $31.99	CAN $31.99	CAN $35.99	CAN $29.99	CAN $41.99
UK £17.99	UK £27.99	UK £19.99	UK £19.99	UK £21.99	UK £17.99	UK £24.99

SharePoint 2016	Fundamental Analysis	Networking	Office 2016	Office 365	Salesforce.com	Coding
9781119181705	9781119263593	9781119257769	9781119293477	9781119265313	9781119239314	9781119293323
USA $29.99	USA $26.99	USA $29.99	USA $26.99	USA $24.99	USA $29.99	USA $29.99
CAN $35.99	CAN $31.99	CAN $35.99	CAN $31.99	CAN $29.99	CAN $35.99	CAN $35.99
UK £21.99	UK £19.99	UK £21.99	UK £19.99	UK £17.99	UK £21.99	UK £21.99

dummies.com

dummies
A Wiley Brand